Land of Sunshine

History of the Urban Environment

Martin V. Melosi and Joel A. Tarr, *Editors*

Land of Sunshine

AN ENVIRONMENTAL HISTORY OF METROPOLITAN LOS ANGELES

Edited by

William Deverell and Greg Hise

University of Pittsburgh Press

Published by the University of Pittsburgh Press, Pittsburgh, PA 15260
Copyright © 2005, University of Pittsburgh Press
All rights reserved
Manufactured in the United States of America
Printed on acid-free paper
First paperback edition, 2006
ISBN 0-8229-5939-9

10 9 8 7 6 5 4 3 2 1

Contents

Acknowledgments

The idea for this book came from members of an advisory group at the University of Pittsburgh Press; we appreciate the press's commitment to publishing environmental history and the Senate Committee of the University Press's assessment that we ought to edit a volume on Southern California. Niels Aaboe, then editorial director, brought us on board and shepherded the project through its first iteration. Director Cynthia Miller ably oversaw the latter stages of editing, design, and production. Reports from two anonymous reviews helped us rethink the book's structure; their suggestions made a good book better. Both the press and we as editors thank the authors for their contributions and for their patience. By any measure, the value readers find in this volume is a testament to the quality of their scholarship and to the larger whole created through bringing individual studies together for a collective analysis of the region. We thank as well those authors who provided photographs and original art. Carolyn Cole (Los Angeles Public Library), Jim McPartlan (University of Southern California), Lisa Padilla (Zimmer Gunsul Frasca Partnership), Dace Taube (University of Southern California), and Jennifer Watts (Huntington Library) helped us secure artwork and permissions and format illustrations for publication. We think Frank Romero's "Cityscape" evokes the region's cultural landscape and are pleased he agreed to our request to reproduce it. Our thanks go to Patricia Correia and to Dean Dan Mazmanian (School of Policy, Planning and Development) for their assistance in securing the image and its use. John McPhee graciously allowed us to publish an excerpted version of "Los Angeles Against the Mountains." Victoria Fox of Farrar, Straus and Giroux assisted us with permission and reprint rights. Ann Walston and Deborah Meade (University of Pittsburgh Press) and copy editor Trish Weisman did much of the work of turning a manuscript into a book.

A grant from the John Randolph Haynes and Dora Haynes Foundation allowed us to offer contributors a modest honorarium and to offset some costs for reproduction and permissions. As helpful, most likely more so, was the foundation's support for "A Sustainable Future? Environmental Patterns and the Los Angeles Past," a symposium held at the California Institute of Technology in September 2003. Each of us benefited from time away from our usual duties and the ideas generated through a community of scholars. Bill Deverell acknowledges the Center for Advanced Study in the Behavioral Sciences. Greg Hise thanks the Rutgers Center for Historical Analysis, conveners Susan Schrepfer and Phil Scranton, and participants in the center's "Industrial Environments" workshop (2001–2).

Land of Sunshine

Introduction

The Metropolitan Nature of Los Angeles

GREG HISE AND WILLIAM DEVERELL

Whatever man has done subsequently to the climate and
environment of Southern California, it remains one of the ecological
wonders of the habitable world.

Reyner Banham, *Los Angeles: The Architecture of Four Ecologies*

As we send this book to press, questions over the environmental sustainability of greater Los Angeles figure prominently in public and policy
debates. In everyday conversation, talk about sustainability is shorthand
for natural capital, environmental carrying capacities, and our ability to ensure
that the needs of the present are met without compromising future generations. With this understanding, it is obvious that any assessment of sustainability must include temporal perspectives. In other words, history matters. It
matters a great deal. Looking back, timelines of environmental stability and
change must be carefully constructed and scrutinized to fashion appropriately
sophisticated practices and policies supportive of sustainability. Looking ahead,
the concept's moral and ethical principles also assert that what we do today
matters for those who follow.

In an attempt to contribute to discussions of sustainability, *Land of Sunshine* explores the environmental history of greater Los Angeles. Rather than
sketching out a past and tracing a chronological route to the present, the
authors instead range widely across time and theme, speaking in sum across a
large set of regional environmental factors, environmental perspectives, and
environmental challenges. Accordingly, we have broken the book into three

largely thematic sections: analysis of place, land use and governance, and nature and culture.

Several threads run throughout. One concerns the regional particularities and problems of a utilitarian ethos regarding the environment, the continuing belief that nature works for us when we work nature. Another is the related idea, now several centuries old, that Southern California is a "paradisiacal garden," to quote a nineteenth-century newspaper, the *Los Angeles Star*, awaiting only the shaping hands of human action and labor. In their respective investigations, several authors take up aridity and the control and use of water: interrelated processes of nature and culture that characterize (even caricature) much about the environmental history of the region. A few take up discrete environmental topics—pollution, oil, the vegetative landscape, and planning, for example—while others work at larger scales of environmental change through imagery, text, or both. Some have produced deep histories of the region (the archeologist Mark Raab's analysis of the consequences of environmental change in precontact periods and ecologist Paula Schiffman's reconstruction of the Los Angeles prairie, for example). Each chapter stands alone as an investigation of altered landscapes and altered perceptions of environment over time in Los Angeles, and each contributes to a larger whole that concerns time, nature, and culture.

The concerted regional effort to harness nature in service of an earthly Eden in Southern California has required enterprise and given rise to technological innovation. Enterprise and innovation have in turn attracted capital and generated wealth. Contrary to most accounts, greater Los Angeles has been on the map of global trade for two centuries. Capitalism and international trade link ecosystems once discrete. Growth created and continues to create dynamics of environmental change: migrating people have brought plants and animals with them, and these organisms have transformed local ecologies and, as Unna Lassiter and Jennifer Wolch note in their chapter on the metropolitan presence of farm animals, local neighborhoods.

Other chapters examine regional governance, mostly in historical perspective. There has been a marked and relatively consistent growth in jurisdictions over time. In the face of challenges over property and land use, water and aridity, growth and open space, jurisdictional complexity and political shortsightedness have created a policy of brief and narrow utility.

Brief and narrow are not, however, synonymous with failure. Los Angeles is widely perceived as a museum of failed urbanism, the great what-not-to-do of twentieth-century city building and civic enterprise. Study of the region's environmental history suggests otherwise. We are living with the consequences of regional "success" defined simply as the cumulative realization of discrete policy and planning objectives, advanced from the turn of the twentieth century forward, intended to recast American cities as metropolitan regions. Despite stereotypical notions to the contrary, planning—whether defined as physical, environmental, or social planning—has been and remains ubiquitous throughout greater Los Angeles. This is a surprising or at least unexpected finding from studies of a metropolis most people equate with smog, sprawl, and endless variants of "sixty suburbs in search of a city." But again, noting the ubiquity of planning is not the same as suggesting that the story of planning and land use policy in the region is a history of ideal tools used in ideal ways. Rather, it is to suggest that the failure many contemporary critics call to our attention cannot be defined simply as a failure to plan. There is much more to the story than that false assumption. The environmental consequences of planning—the environmental history of urbanism—is one place we can turn for insight, if not lessons.

As William Cronon, Ted Steinberg, Donald Worster, John Richards, and others have brilliantly demonstrated, natural systems are dynamic.[1] Changes in these systems, whether "natural" or the product of human actions, affect us all. Causality works both ways, and it has become a truism of historical observation to note that most of our actions have environmental consequences. A history of first nature, first patterns, and environmental transformation in Los Angeles ought to provide us a record of the beliefs, practices, policies, and the like of native Californians and Spanish, Mexican, and American visitors and settlers. Conceivably we can then correlate these ideas with a record of processes, practices, and outcomes to better understand how the past has led to the present and what the consequences and ramifications of that temporal journey are. For the former, we survey primary sources to fix a baseline for measuring the degree, magnitude, and pace of subsequent change. The latter is a history of cases, a compilation of past decisions and actions, of successes and failures. We analyze and interpret representative or unusual events, legal decisions, and acts of nature in a search for the relevant lessons history might suggest to the present. Whether it is history as scene setting or an instrumental history of cases, our primary interest is insight to help us understand, address, and work toward resolution of current problems.

As we hope this book suggests, urban environmental history offers critical scholarly perspective on questions and challenges of sustainability. Three points of view in the general environmental history literature tend to align with themes from contemporary debates on sustainability. One set of authors casts cities as parasites. City dwellers suck the life out of nature in the form of resource extraction and the conversion of natural goods into commodities that are then introduced or reintroduced into urban systems and eventually depleted or exhausted. From this point of view, cities and nature are in opposition, figuratively and literally, and the transformation of land into property, for example, comes at the expense of wilderness or open space. Nature is the loser in this competition, and urbanites are left with remnants and fragments: the overlooked or abandoned parcels found along a river basin, a shoreline, or a hillside too steep or too friable to develop, the rare unspoiled niche ecology of a park or preserve. In this literature, debate, analysis, and interpretation falls easily into unhelpful opposites: land developers and builders versus farmers, nurserymen, and dairies (often with scant attention to how agriculture and cattle transform nature); economic development versus quality of life; jobs and housing versus preservation of open space; smokestacks versus geraniums.[2]

Other scholars view cities as sites where different groups engage in a zero-sum contest over resources and their distribution. Here we find communities and neighborhoods, racial or ethnic groups, and differing classes, institutions, and special interests, all with competing claims and variable access to clean air and water, adequate and health-enhancing services (sewerage and waste treatment), and other environmental goods. These groups struggle as well for protection from environmental hazards such as harmful wastes and the pollutants, carcinogens, and other deleterious by-products of manufacturing, energy production, and chemical storage.[3]

There has been increasing attention to and growing interest in yet another vantage—one that characterizes the overall thrust of this book—what we might call metropolitan nature, the study of how people transform nature in particular sites and of how what is created in particular locales is generative for local and broader culture. These studies consider geomorphology, climate, and local biological ecologies in concert with property regimes, the state and its regulations, social and market economies. They assess first nature as a fundamental factor for city building while analyzing how city builders and city dwellers transform local ecosystems and in the process create a new environment with different plant and animal species, an altered landscape, and a modified climate. William Cronon's *Nature's Metropolis*, Ari Kelman's *A River and Its City*, Karl Haglund's *Inventing the Charles River*, Mathew Gandy's *Concrete and Clay*, Matthew Klingle's *Urban by Nature*, and similar projects reveal the complexity of what Cronon has termed second nature through the study of urban systems (for water, power, waste removal), land use, design, engineering, construction, the conservation of local ecologies, and the provision of open space, parks, and community gardens.[4]

As noted in chapters by John McPhee, Blake Gumprecht, and Jared Orsi, in particular, regional aridity and the struggles to control water (either too much or too little of it at inopportune moments) offer an apt angle of scholarly insight into Southern California's first-to-second-nature transitions and ideas. Certainly no environmental history of the region would be complete without close attention to water. Nineteenth-century Los Angeles sources speak as unceasingly about rainfall (when it first arrives, whether it is absent or excessive) as they do about water (sources, need for, uses of, quality, and abuses or pollution). The Los Angeles surveyor and engineer William Moore kept a diary of his practice and enterprises. Rain was a blessed event. On the twenty-fourth of January, 1870, he reported: "No rain yet is the cry. It will be too late to sow grain on high ground if it should rain." Three weeks later (February 13): "The rain still continues. We think the ground is wet enough to flow. This rain will save us all. There is no estimating its value." In 1874, Moore celebrated "god the younger's birthday," and noted "Rain, Rain, heavy rain. Just in time—ground needs it." On New Year's Eve, he looked back on "a good year for crops plenty of rain and plenty of everything."[5]

When the temperamental features of regional precipitation proved incapable of satisfying the region's agricultural and demographic ambitions, the divinity of irrigation replaced rainfall in regional hearts and hopes. Bureau of Reclamation commissioner Elwood Mead led an investigation of irrigation in California for the U.S. Department of Agriculture and in a 1901 essay, "The Agricultural Situation in California," encouraged readers to visit Southern California to see what "irrigation has accomplished." Here water previously running "unused to the ocean" has been "diverted and used by irrigators" who have settled tracts where a small farmer and his family "would starve to death if compelled to cultivate [a parcel] in its natural state." Land worth less than five dollars an acre dry had been whetted into orchards planted in orange trees "valued at $1,700 per acre." Despite his apparent respect for and the praise he lavished on settlers and their families striving to harness an errant resource, Mead considered crop raising and rising land values secondary benefits of irrigation. The highest and best use of water, the source for a "far larger gain," Mead tells us, "has come from the beautiful landscapes created . . . by oases of fruit and foliage. . . . Limited trains or the transcontinental railways would not be crowded if Pasadena looked now as it did when first viewed by the mission fathers. . . . The cities of Los Angeles, Redlands, and San Diego are just as much creations of irrigation as [are] the orange groves which surround them."[6]

But water alone, its presence or absence, whether rain or irrigation, was but a portion of an environmental equation. As Moore, Mead, and other observers noted, water, whether falling or distributed, had utility, and hence value, wherever it wetted land. Arable land is a principal element for understanding what nature and sustainability have meant in Los Angeles: land as first nature, land as property and capital, land transformed through labor and through the mind's eye. Like water, the land is preeminent in the sources; it is what captured the attention and in many cases the imagination of travelers from the end of the eighteenth century forward: it set the parameters of what was possible and thus the bounds of opportunity and constraint. Such is the cultural and economic backdrop to the chapter exploring the mid-nineteenth-century transitions in landholding and land law by Karen Clay and Werner Troesken.

The geomorphology of Southern California, its climate, and its local biological ecologies were the subject for a constant outpouring of surveys, pamphlets, treatises, and reports as well as travelers' accounts and the personal recordings of diarists and memoirists. These visitors, members of a mobile population in search of opportunity and wealth, included thrill seekers, émigrés and settlers, romantics, geologists and surveyors, and those simply curious about the Far West and the wonders of an American Mediterranean. Their accounts spawned a popular genre rich in descriptive detail, telling anecdotes, and prescient observations. It is a literature rife with essentialisms: about a landscape of antiquity awaiting reclamation, about a superabundant paradise "naturally richer than India" awaiting the guiding hand of an "enterprising nation," and about nature's service in the rise of a great city.

Frank Meline, an investor in Los Angeles real estate, believed nature created the terrain here to house a great city. In 1929, he looked out upon a cityscape of "vast industrial districts spread out in many directions, all easily accessible, with splendid transportation facilities, ample room for expansion, and yet segregated from residential areas." For Meline and many of his contemporaries, nature appeared to have parsed the region into districts or zones, zones that served as the natural sites for specific land uses and activities.[7]

Of course, nature had not zoned the region, people had, and any number of cases might be offered to reveal changing land use patterns and the legacy of regional planning in Los Angeles. When we consider land use and sustainability, as Douglas Sackman, Christopher Boone, and Daniel Johnson do in their chapters, what demands our attention are the liabilities and constraints of past policy and practice—an expanding urban footprint, increasingly hazy distinctions between what is urban and what is not, the profligate use of natural resources, functional and social segregation.

Often scholars, elected officials, and pundits seize on the putative lessons such cases provide to move, if not immediately then quickly, to a search for correctives that might mitigate past failure. In the process we forget that at the beginning of the past century, functional segregation, for example, which we now decry, was seen by sanitarians, social workers, progressives, and advocates for urban redevelopment as a cure-all for urban ills. This vision was so successful that current guides to planning define practice as the "arrange[ing] of people and activities in a rational, efficient manner."[8] What was once hoped for is now commonplace. The same is true for distinctions between what is urban and not. Blurring this boundary was a primary objective, that is, a goal, for designers of urban park systems from Frederick Law Olmsted forward. The urban parkway epitomized this, and planners who strove to make nature a part of urban life staked their efforts on the automobile as a critical tool, as they saw it, for city dwellers who might experience nature as they drove through it.

In some cases, the success of prior planning is ubiquitous; even as we work to do different or better we reinforce established norms. For example, while we decry the social, economic, political, and moral costs of a long history of social segregation, from covenants to exclusionary zoning to neighborhoods proclaiming "not in my backyard," it appears increasingly likely that so-called smart growth and growth management—a corrective intended to mitigate detrimental aspects of past success—may maintain rather than redress patterns of social segregation.

We can appreciate the hold prior intentions, practices, and structures exert on current planning if we trace the changing use, meaning, and definitions (both quantitative and qualitative) of keywords in land use planning, such as density, over the course of the twentieth century. In the late nineteenth century, density was an evil and reformers struggled mightily to prune the so-called congested districts and to move immigrants and the working poor out to areas where, as Los Angeles cleric and progressive Dana Bartlett claimed, "better housing, better sanitation, fresh air, freedom from temptation, flowers and parks and bright work rooms [make] life seem worth the living."[9] We now call the success of that vision sprawl. And we now use density as a barometer for public life and civic health as we struggle just as mightily to bring middle-class and well-to-do whites back into the core areas of American cities.

Why have certain plans been adopted while others languish? In a world of competing interests, with near universal suspicion of big plans, how might we do good in the midst of "failure"? Are there lessons of best or better practice? We may not yet know nearly enough to answer such questions, precisely because we have been such poor students of the environmental history of Southern California. Historical perspective on environmental change in Los Angeles is neither well developed nor comprehensive enough to suggest patterns in the long term. We know more of the punctuated moments of planning during times of crises and less of a regional planning ethos or culture. There have been and continue to be economic crises (how best to generate or sustain regional economic development, how best to accommodate growth or manage decline), historic and ongoing competition among cities and municipalities for economic development (municipalities within Los Angeles County, for example, with varying ability and willingness to reallocate land use to meet the requirements of business, the military, or the State Department of Corrections), and environmental crises associated with place promotion, growth, or decline. Often Angelenos have responded to such crises by bringing in outside consultants. In one case, in the later half of the 1920s, the planning firms of Olmsted Brothers and Harland Bartholomew and Associates together assessed environmental patterns and projected future development. Their findings spell out how nature as amenity, the climatological and topographical advantages of the region (the "goose that lays the golden egg," to use their phrase), was threatened by further construction along the coast and across the slopes and hillsides.[10]

Their plan, a bold vision for an area of more than fifteen hundred square miles, was in many respects doomed to fail. It was so big, so ambitious, so comprehensive, so politically savvy that efforts to delimit its purchase seem, in hindsight, nearly inevitable. Because Olmsted and Bartholomew had proposed such sweeping environmental recommendations and, more to the point, equally sweeping reconfigurations of local governance to make it all happen, the Los Angeles Chamber of Commerce killed off the report it had commissioned and financed in the first place. A print run of under two hundred copies ensured that the report would be more keepsake than blueprint; the people of Los Angeles never had the chance to push for it, never even had the chance to hear much of it. While there is little need here to rehearse its demise and subsequent rediscovery in the very recent past, we refer to the report to underscore the extent to which design professionals in the Olmsted and Bartholomew offices peered into our collective future.[11]

Planning is a historically weak tool for shaping economic development at the scale of a region or state, yet local regulations such as zoning and city and county land use policy have been the tools boosters, institutions, elected officials, business leaders, and voters have used to shape city building in Los Angeles and Southern California. Although popular wisdom pits public sector planning in an inevitable and ongoing struggle with private sector development, historical records reveal a putatively private sector working closely with, and at times almost interchangeably with, public agencies engaged in planning. In many cases, private interests have taken the lead in land use planning. Los Angeles has been the site for a number of significant innovations, as both Daniel Johnson and Christopher Boone point out in their contributions. In response to the noise, filth, and hazards associated with noxious industries, the Los Angeles City Council approved an ordinance restricting certain industrial uses in a primarily residential district in 1904. Subsequent statutes, passed in 1908 and 1909, parsed the city into two industrial and seven residential districts. Then in 1910, voters passed an ordinance declaring all city land outside the industrial districts residential. Those Los Angeles regulations intended to protect single-family housing and to enhance the value of residential property had an unintended consequence that industrialists were quick to capitalize on, the creation of entire districts where their interests held sway. Asked in 1922 whether the Chamber of Commerce endorsed zoning, the director replied, "It is a child of the Chamber . . . we invented it." During the interwar years, when the city shot from twenty-eighth to ninth to fifth in industrial output, manufacturers created new industrial districts in Vernon, in Torrance, in what is now Commerce, and at the harbor, as well as in discrete segments of Burbank, Glendale, and Pasadena, a pattern of land use and development with production for export and for local markets assigned to discrete districts.[12]

In addition to seeking pragmatic regulation, Angelenos have long valued the symbolic power of big plans. The Los Angeles Municipal Art Commission, automobile club, Chamber of Commerce, Haynes Foundation, and others have brought in outside experts with national, even international, reputations to advance Los Angeles' status in the rank of the nation's cities, a legacy extending from Charles Mulford Robinson's City Beautiful proposal of 1909 to the Downtown Strategic Plan of 1992. There is a legacy as well of regional plans whose impetus has been both local and exogenous, such as the Colorado River aqueduct; projects from the 1930s forward to contain the Arroyo Seco, the Los Angeles River, and other regional watercourses; and the post–World War II freeway system. Implementing such plans has shaped land use and regional ecologies considerably.[13]

Given the depth and breadth of regional planning in Southern California, it is appropriate to ask why success has taken the form it has. (Here we are defining success as a consensus of a moment that leads to partial implementation and effects change.) There are related questions concerning priorities and preferences, how these change over time, and what has spurred such change. Policies, especially those offering fiscal incentives—through tax relief and subsidies or through mortgage insurance, for example—have been powerful drivers of preference. An obvious case in point is the detached single-family house: a dwelling of choice, perhaps, but a house type that would not have become a realistic aspiration without a federal restructuring of the mortgage industry and national banking policy in the 1930s. In a similar vein, we would want to assess the ways municipal, county, and state codes, and the enforcement or lack of enforcement of these regulations, have shaped land use materially as well as shaping what people imagine is within the realm of possibility.

There has been less attention paid to the creation and maintenance of a planning discourse, a rhetoric of text and image that shapes what people imagine is possible. A discourse defines norms and standards; it conveys what the profession approves and disapproves and what it asserts is good, healthful, or right. Pamphlets and broadsides denounce the evils of blight. Overcrowding, rotting slums, and delinquency are paired with glistening apartments, outfitted with modern appliances, flooded with natural light, surrounded by common greens for leisure and supervised recreation. This is a discourse articulated by government officials, academics, design professionals, pundits, investors, business leaders, and home buyers; it is a vision disseminated at conferences, in journals and pamphlets, through exhibits, in Sunday real estate sections, in children's books.

Consider land use plans, basic, ubiquitous documents, diagrams of sanctioned activities, agreed-upon blueprints of current planning. They can be, and have served to great effect as, a means for maintaining a prevailing paradigm. However, these diagrams and plans, generally read as a map of the present, offer all who view them an image of the future. Plans and diagrams can serve as a call to action, a tool for advancing an alternative vision. Acknowledging and analyzing this dynamic is crucial for assessing current conditions and for strategic intervention. We can gauge just how crucial this is simply by reference to the New Urbanists, who have built little but have so skillfully presented themselves as paradigm shifters that much of the debate over sustainability in the design professions begins and ends with transit-oriented development.[14]

In Los Angeles, we begin the twenty-first century struggling with the consequences of success, both hoped for and unintended. Entrepreneurship and technological innovation, demographic dynamism, and a utilitarian ethos stimulate development and the continual recasting of zones where land use, infrastructure, and improvements were dictated by the requirements and vision of a prior moment. In the so-called first-ring suburbs and in the districts surrounding the central business district we find adaptive reuse (commercial to residential, manufacturing to assembly) and in many cases increasing population density and more diverse use, whether through formal rezoning (such as the recent designation of transit nodes along boulevards) or informal conversions (for example, recent immigrants, individual workers and families, living in garages or renting a bed for part of a day in Huntington Park). In this sense, Los Angeles is different from cities such as Philadelphia, St. Louis, and Detroit. There population decline, disinvestment, and abandonment are seemingly endemic, and contraction rather than expansion is the nature of urban crisis.

What might history reveal of challenges then and now? Case studies demonstrate unequivocally that the structures and scale of governance have been and remain a critical variable. Planning for a sustainable future, for regional economic development, for an adequate and appropriate provision of

infrastructure and services and the like are so complex and so complexly inter-
linked and interconnected that they practically defy adequate analytic description, much less the generation of adequately comprehensive solutions. At the
same time, in the material world where engineers, planners, and design professionals work every day, the environment (air quality, aridity, floods), economic forces and factors, and other structural drivers elide the tidy jurisdictional
boundaries of the nation, state, county, and municipality we use for governance. Elected and appointed officials, agencies of the state and private businesses, property owners, and citizen planners are all engaged in a contest over
land and its uses. Whether the scale of a case is national environmental policy,
state transportation policy, or the actions of a county planning commission,
municipal zoning board, or neighborhood council, decisions are made whose
effects extend beyond the nominal purview of the agency involved. It is a nest-
ed system, as we all know, but it bears repeating that it is a system with weak
mechanisms and procedures for bridging scales, where efforts at one level are
often undertaken without benefit of a framework for adjacent levels up or
down the hierarchy. We should not be surprised then to find neighborhood
councils banishing service facilities to adjacent districts or the City of Los
Angeles pushing solid-waste disposal and treatment on to county land at Sunshine Canyon.[15]

Consortia of governments and government agencies are one mechanism to
redress these jurisdictional disputes. The Southern California Association of
Governments is representative but limited by design to an advisory capacity.
The Alameda Corridor Task Force and Alameda Corridor Transportation
Authority, intermunicipal agencies formed to coordinate planning, oversee
construction, and manage operations for the express freight rail line connect-
ing the San Pedro Bay ports and the central business district, might serve as a
model of governance calibrated to the scale of an enterprise or endeavor. Can
we imagine like consortia charged with conservation, remediation, or landscape restoration?

Recent efforts to enhance the quality and the long-term viability of metropolitan nature (that is, urban sustainability) and struggles to ensure equitable
access to recreation and leisure sites in the city have enlarged and continue to
enlarge the ranks of citizen planners. Just as critical, elected officials, professional planners, and citizens have begun framing these debates in a broader
geographic context. While continuing to work at the scale of neighborhood
recreation and locally accessible open space, advocates for urban parks and
urban nature increasingly have been eager to embed discrete projects in a larger framework, a metropolitan system of interrelated parks and preserves.
Thinking comprehensively and planning at multiple scales has led many to

rethink long-held distinctions between an urban core and urbanizing margin, or edge.[16]

In Los Angeles, urban nature had been preserved in remnant, often lower-utility, lower-value land on the then urban fringe. On a map the city's parks are arrayed like a tree's annual growth rings—Elysian, Eastlake, Westlake, Griffith, Sycamore Grove, Exposition, continuing out to beaches and national forest—dating epochs of development and moments when the city, philanthropists, or both seized an opportunity to set land aside as open space for public use. To continue the analogy, we are returning now to the built-over districts and seeding a second-growth forest of parks at the Cornfield site and Taylor Yard and atop the Baldwin Hills.

Projects and programs once viewed as fanciful, quixotic, or utopian have come to be seen as prescient, prudent, and necessary. Activists such as Lewis MacAdams and Friends of the Los Angeles River or Andy Lipkis and TreePeople share the stage with mayoral and council candidates striving to outdo their rivals in a commitment to and expansion of parks, conservation, and restoration. Street trees, green neighborhoods, watercourses supporting a riparian habitat—nature has become natural and seemingly intrinsic for everyday life in Los Angeles. As history shows, there is nothing natural—inevitable—about this turn of events. Rather, it is a significant achievement, the product of commitment and hard work, organizing and political engagement at all levels of governance and government. The great hope, the shining promise, is that recent accomplishments might be a foundation for additional achievements. In our role as citizen planners, we might begin to link existing parks, parks now in the design phase, and restoration along the Los Angeles, San Gabriel, and Santa Ana rivers to regional watersheds, water supply, and water use. We could tie park bond monies and the current enthusiasm for developing parks to air quality and public health and to food supply and even food security. In other words, we could plan comprehensively and integrate open space and land use with social equity and a civic, collective good.

Some may view this as optimistic, even naive. Perhaps, but these issues are fundamental for rethinking Los Angeles and for recasting the region as a sustainable metropolis. Part of that recasting—a critical part, in our estimation—demands very close attention to regional history and the ways in which metropolitan nature has been constructed and construed for well over a century in greater Los Angeles. History matters, and we turn to it in the ideas and images that make up *Land of Sunshine*.

PART ONE

Analysis of Place

As we begin this volume, we reach deeply back into the ancient past of the Southern California region. What we find there, thanks to chapters by Mark Raab and Paula Schiffman, may be surprising. Raab, an archeologist, posits disturbing correlations and theories about environmental limits, especially those prompted by drought and rising social violence within the resident native populations of the coastal regions of what is now Southern California. Raab also reminds us that any concerted effort to understand environmental change must be at least cognizant of, if not beholden to, timescales of duration not usually used by historians. If, as Raab suggests, droughts have provoked deep fissures within the human populations of the region, it behooves environmental scholars to pay close attention to long-range understandings of drought and other environmental patterns. The primary historical data for all such investigations and interpretations must include nonhuman sources: tree ring and archeological data among them. Only then can assumptions about environmental change be placed in contexts appropriate to both earth science and the study of human change. The ecologist Paula Schiffman concurs. She reminds us, in writing about the vegetative change in the Los Angeles basin (and her discovery of the Los Angeles prairie), of both the fleeting nature of human societies and, ironically, of the transformative power of such societies in changing that very nature. As she notes, the once vibrant Los Angeles prairie, an ancient ecosystem of the basin's flatlands, disappeared not long after European contact in the late eighteenth century.

Karen Clay and Werner Troesken take us to a more recent Los Angeles landscape, one just beyond the reach of memory. By the late 1840s, Manifest Destiny, that complex nineteenth-century amalgam of national zeal, xenophobia, religious assurance, and Jeffersonian obsession with land, had yanked California into the United States as a fait accompli. The question of the day was not whether California would come into the Union but whether it would do so by tilting the balance toward slavery or abolition. Gold of course helped accelerate the process, but James Marshall's 1848 discovery of that famed northern California nugget merely put an exclamation point to a journey already well under way.

Americans knew California well before gold convinced them they could become rich by going there. After all, a number of Anglos or Yankees had already become rich by being there. In Southern California, a pioneer generation of traders, land speculators, vintners, and merchants—a number of whom exchanged their New England habits for hybridized lives at the intersection of Californio (Spanish/Mexican frontier) and Yankee cultures—marked out terrain and influence well before the beginning of the American war against Mexico in 1846. A number of these individuals, along with a rising generation of postwar arrivistes, found themselves in the right place at the right time when regime change and environmental challenges conspired to render Californio landholdings unstable. Economists Clay and Troesken investigate the critical years of the mid-nineteenth century when a Spanish-Mexican system of land tenure based on usufruct gave way to an Anglo-American system of land as property and concomitant changes in patterns of land use. This was by no means a simple process, and scholars have been right to depict the decline of a Spanish-Mexican ethos of property and the actual loss of an ethnic Mexican land base as critical political and economic by-products of Anglo-American conquest. But as these authors illustrate, this process was more complex than the solely one-sided exercise of racial power that it has often been understood to be.

Mid-nineteenth-century visitors to greater Los Angeles often expressed surprise at what they found. Perhaps conditioned by recent events to see Southern California as environmentally deficient when compared to the gold-rich regions to the north, many 1850s migrants, arriving by ship or overland route in the so-called cow town of Los Angeles, seemed barely able to contain their excitement, even astonishment, at the fecundity of the landscape. By century's end, excitement had become full-blown regional ambition, and Angelenos set about altering the very landscape that had stunned them in the first place. This section opens with a view of that turn-of-the-century moment, offered by William McClung in the shape of an illustrated consideration. Chronologically, his exploration of landscape perception in the Los Angeles of 1900 is an apt counterpoint to Raab and Schiffman's re-creation of an ancient, foundational Los Angeles environment.

Folio One: Southern California, 1900

WILLIAM A. McCLUNG

In 1900 the California Photogravure Company published a boxed set of twelve soft-bound fascicles entitled *Art Work on Southern California.*[1] The text, which promotes investment in real estate, is brief; it is the plates that are charged with the mission of presenting Southern California as attractive to prospective purchasers and develop-

Plaza, Los Angeles, and Central Park, Los Angeles.

ers. They do this by displaying Los Angeles and its environs as an achieved balance between nature and the arts of design.

The celebration of a stable order of phenomena as a commodity available for exploitation and development lies contradictorily at the heart of the mythology of the region. To this replete Arcadian landscape, improvements, in the form of landscaping, public works projects, and commercial and residential architecture, have been carefully accommodated. Framing all subjects similarly, the photographer erases distinctions between public and private spaces and functions. Architecture and construction are consistently subordinated to terrain and plantings, roads are presented as objects of admiration in and of themselves, and discontinuities between the images imply an infinite extension over the landscape.

Presented in *Art Work* as a pair, these photographs muffle the expected contrast between the historical heart of the pueblo and what is now Pershing Square. The two public spaces are equated. The planting and layout of the walkways are in the foreground, and architecture is either peripheral or, in the case of the bandstand, merely a detail of the park itself.

The Plaza Church, soon to be revived as an icon of Old Los Angeles, is invisible, and other structures associated with the mid-nineteenth century have disappeared under the same envelope of lush vegetation that gives each park the look of a botanical garden in a resort town: provincial, but urbane, and unrevealing of the cultural tensions that had caused Central Park to be set aside at the edge of town in 1870 as a kind of Anglo alternative to the Plaza, its Mexican prototype.

No principle distinguishes the landscaping of public from private space; St. James Park, for example, was not a park at all, but a residential enclave. Although some

St. James Park, Los Angeles.

actual parks, such as Central or East Side parks, appear in *Art Work* with mature planting and amenities, others, such as Echo and Elysian, look recently created and still
somewhat raw. Still others, despite designation as a park, seem barely distinguishable
from open fields.

Street Scene in Alhambra.

View on Adams Street, Los Angeles.

Parks are virtually indistinguishable from residential streets. The majority of urban images in the portfolio place streets and roads in the foreground, ranging from *Street Scene in Alhambra*, which is only a stage beyond open country, to the refinements of the fashionable Adams Street district of Los Angeles.

On Magnolia Avenue, Riverside.

Cactus Beds, Riverside.

The normative photographic take throughout the fascicles privileges planting over architecture, as in the case of Riverside's most famous boulevard. Plates like this recur throughout, framed and shot to emphasize the importance of the road that marks both the way through, and the boundaries of, zones of planting that are themselves, in various degrees, artfully improved.

Roads typically appear to lead from nowhere to nowhere and to service nothing; they are self-sufficient entities framed and defined by trees and other plantings. "Cactus Beds, Riverside" literally marginalizes the houses, allowing the road and a screen of vegetation to dictate the composition, which consists of a twisting road-way with its manicured and engineered curbing, a screen of elaborate and even fantastic planting, and finally a conventional, virtually irrelevant house.

The ambiguity of what constitutes a place of residence or recreation or public infrastructure is compounded by images such as this, a utility that looks more park-like than many of the images of actual public parks.

In the work's conceptual sequence, shots of wilderness are interspersed with those of agriculture, as in the representation of mechanisms such as flumes and of farming at scales ranging from an isolated orchard to the environment of a town. The synopsis embraces not only the region's landscape but its history—with the caveat that the history presented is a mythology of that landscape's progress from wilderness

Reservoir at Smiley Heights, Redlands.

Scene on Little Rock Creek Showing Waste Gate in Irrigating Flume, South Antelope Valley.

Scene in Santa Ana.

through countryside to parks and communities, lavishly watered and supplemented, though not supplanted, by constructions.

Small towns such as Santa Ana, one of several examples, appear either parklike or as extensions of, or backdrops to, parks; their streets perpetuate the morphology of vegetation and corridor that dominates or displaces architecture.

In the metropolis itself, the business district, an apparent exception to the privileging of planting over architecture, materializes in a single detached composition of neat, impressive new buildings on an orderly, nearly empty street. How proximate this and satellite downtowns might be to the lush residential areas is not clarified; there is, for example, no map or balloon view of the city or the region. It is impossible to construe a relationship between the commercial and residential districts, just as it is impossible to situate the parks and residential districts within a controlling urban or regional scheme. Public buildings important enough to rate a photograph appear throughout the fascicles only as isolated objects. Downtown Los Angeles, as the camera captures it, is an area zoned for productivity. It is one of a series of the autonomous zones that constitute the Southern California imagined by the producers of *Art Work*.

Scene on Spring Street, Los Angeles.

1

Political Ecology of Prehistoric Los Angeles

L. MARK RAAB

REHISTORY may seem an unlikely influence on a place such as contemporary Los Angeles. Massive physical and socioeconomic transformations have overtaken the region since the nineteenth century, with a pervasive sense of newness in infrastructure and lifestyles particularly apparent since the Second World War. The result often seems to be a civic ethos so present oriented as to exclude all but the sketchiest historical consciousness. Spanish place names and a scattering of buildings with pre–World War II architectural themes lend a vague sense of historical roots deeper than living memory, but unlike urban centers of Latin America, Europe, or Asia, Los Angeles has none of the ancient palaces, pyramids, or other obvious monuments that many take as hallmarks of a notable antiquity.

Yet, the effect of Los Angeles' prehistory is greater than we might suspect. Before the first Europeans arrived with Juan Rodriguez Cabrillo in 1542, the Los Angeles region was occupied for at least twelve millennia by hunter-gatherers. While the peoples left behind few obvious clues of their presence, the idea of an ancient hunter-gatherer Los Angeles underpins a good deal of theorizing about the area's environmental history. Hunter-gatherer Los Angeles offers a foil to social, political, and environmental theories of urban-industrial society.

For centuries, the tendency of social and environmental theorists to employ hunters and gatherers in a kind of natural experiment has proven all but irresistible. This experiment derives from the fundamental assumption that cultures are more or less natural. Since peoples who obtain their survival from hunting and collecting are imagined by many to be closer to nature than members of industrial society, hunter-gatherers can be viewed as models of how people might coexist with nature apart from the unnatural influences of civilization. To many, the study of hunter-gatherers allows us to peer into times and places uncorrupted by industrial civilization. This outlook has allowed our own society to ascribe a variety of values and behaviors to California hunter-gatherers. To the extent that this process involves projecting the values and goals of modern interest groups into the cultural and environmental past, the resulting patterns of thought might be described as political ecologies.

In a physical sense, the Los Angeles region could be defined as roughly the area encompassed by Los Angeles County. Unfortunately, urban-industrial growth during the nineteenth and twentieth centuries obliterated a great deal of the archaeological record of this area before it was examined by researchers. Even when the area did come under archaeological scrutiny, the results often fell short of contemporary research standards. When work began in the latter half of the nineteenth century, most archaeological practitioners could be described as inspired amateurs. The emphasis during this era was collecting museum-grade artifacts, with little concern for scientific problem orientation.

At the turn of the century, California archaeology turned professional with the creation of the first academic programs, notably the Department of Anthropology at the University of California, Berkeley. There, Alfred L. Kroeber and others exerted an immense influence on the subsequent development of California ethnography and archaeology. Archaeological research on Los Angeles prehistory was under way between the world wars at institutions such as the Southwest Museum and the Los Angeles County Museum of Natural History. After the Second World War, archaeological field programs shifted largely to universities, including the University of California, Los Angeles; the University of Southern California; and several campuses of the California State University. In the 1960s and 1970s, state and federal environmental protection laws were enacted, extending protection to archaeological resources threatened by development projects. Since the 1970s, the bulk of archaeological research in the United States has been conducted under the auspices of legal mandates rather than academic institutions.

Archaeological research necessarily builds up broad patterns across time and space. While archaeological studies have produced a substantial body of information about Los Angeles regional prehistory, this information draws on studies from across Southern California. Using this information, archaeologists working in the Los Angeles region reconstruct successive cultural stages extending back in time to the Ice Age, a period spanning perhaps thirteen thousand years. Questions of when California was first settled and by what kinds of cultures remain a matter of debate. A number of claims of extreme antiquity (thirty to one hundred thousand or more years) have been made for Southern California archaeological sites over the years, but these have failed to win support from most archaeologists. The oldest securely dated archaeological sites in the area have produced radiocarbon ages of between about eight and ten thousand years. Many authorities believe that the earliest occupations were derived from Paleo-Indian cultures, composed of foragers who specialized in hunting large Ice Age animals such as mammoths. Evidence for such connections is scanty, however, with no currently confirmed kill sites showing that Paleo-Indian hunters occupied the Los Angeles basin. Alternatively, some researchers point to early coastal occupations, noting California Channel Islands archaeological sites with radiocarbon dates of around eight to ten thousand years.

Between about nine thousand and two thousand years ago, a variety of Archaic stage cultures occupied much of California. Archaeologists use the term Archaic to refer to cultural adaptations oriented toward a broad range of plant and animal species that appeared in Southern California after the Ice Age. Living in small, egalitarian groups, Archaic peoples appear to have occupied a series of temporary camps during a seasonal round of hunting and plant collecting. The Topanga Culture, named after several archaeological sites investigated in the Topanga Canyon area of western Los Angeles County, illustrates this type of cultural adaptation. This era frequently is called the Millingstone Horizon by archaeologists because archaeological deposits from this period tend to contain large numbers of stone slabs (metates) and hand millstones (manos) that were used to process seeds.

Beginning about two thousand years ago, new cultural patterns began to emerge in Southern California, particularly along the coast. Fishing combined with terrestrial hunting and gathering to support comparatively large and permanent coastal communities. Many archaeologists believe that by about AD 700 to 1000, large coastal populations were evolving rapidly into chiefdoms; i.e., socially stratified communities presided over by hereditary chiefs and other sociopolitical elites. The Chumash Indians, whose territory is thought to have extended from portions of western Los Angeles County to near the city of San Luis Obispo to the north, are the premier example of this trend. The Chumash are one of the most extensively researched groups in California and often are cited as exemplars of Native American culture in California.

The bulk of Los Angeles County, however, is reconstructed as the territory of the Gabrielino Indians. In 1771, the Mission San Gabriel was established on the Los Angeles Plain. Aiming to convert the Indians to Christianity and train them in the European traditions of agriculture and commerce, this mission also lent the name Gabrielino to the native peoples of the Los Angeles basin. Linguistic information, combined with historical and ethnographic data, shows that the Gabrielino occupied much of present-day Los Angeles County, portions of northern Orange County, and the southern Channel Islands, including Santa Catalina and San Clemente. Unfortunately, few historic and ethnographic accounts exist concerning the culture of the Gabrielino prior to contact with Europeans.[1] Long before scholarly studies of this culture could be initiated, the Gabrielino culture was largely obliterated by disease and oppression.

The Gabrielino population at the time of European contact occupied perhaps one hundred *rancherias* containing fifty to one hundred inhabitants each. The Gabrielino were supported by a hunting and gathering economy broadly similar to that of their Chumash neighbors. In his summary of Gabrielino Indian history and culture, *The First Angelenos*, William McCawley argues that they also possessed a tribal organization similar to the Chumash.[2]

Traditional archaeological reconstructions have thus featured a sequence in which the prehistoric inhabitants of the Los Angeles region gradually evolved more elaborate and economically productive cultural arrangements, culminating in the complex social formations of the Chumash and Gabrielino. These climax cultures frequently are featured in theories of romantic primitivism, including reconstructions of the pre-European natural environment.

During the twentieth century, two major academic paradigms characterized the effects of the natural environment on California Indian cultures. Remarkably, these paradigms envision almost diametrically opposite consequences. The first of these traditions was heavily influenced by Alfred L. Kroeber, an extraordinarily energetic scholar of California archaeology and anthropology and one of the most influential American anthropologists of the century. Kroeber suggested that most California Indian groups were essentially immune from serious privation, owing to the state's natural abundance: "The food resources of California were bountiful in their variety rather than in their overwhelming abundance along special lines. If one supply failed, there were a hundred others to fall back upon."[3]

Kroeber later offered this judgment about the cultural effects of this abundance: "In most of California, the climate was easy, food reasonably abundant, and the human population relatively dense for a nonfarming one. If cultural progress was quiet, it was not because of nature's adversity but rather because, in Toynbeean concept, challenge was feeble and response mild."[4]

This view was pervasive, as illustrated by comments by Edwin Walker, an active field worker in Los Angeles County archaeology and a contemporary of Kroeber. Although Walker's comments appear in an undated leaflet intended for visitors of the Southwest Museum, it appears likely that this publication was prepared during the 1950s. Walker characterizes the Gabrielino Indians of the Los Angeles area: "Many of these Indians belonged to the great Shoshonean family, who had penetrated the country unknown centuries ago, doubtless as conquerors; but once having secured a foothold, they seem to have settled down to enjoy in peace the climate and abundant food supply. At the time of discovery they probably were as inoffensive, contented, and happy as any Indians in America."[5]

This account is similar to the glowing description of the Gabrielino's neighbors, the Chumash Indians, in Kroeber's classic volume, *Handbook of the Indians of California*: "Marine life along the Chumash shores is exceptionally rich, the climate far famed, and every condition favored the unusual concentration of population among a people living directly upon nature."[6]

The unmistakable image that emerges from these descriptions is one of Indians constrained to comparatively simple, passive, and contented cultural reactions to existence in a natural hunter-gatherer paradise. Today, the Indian cultural traits described in these accounts appear naive and patronizing, if not racist. It must be remembered, however, that Kroeber's age was ruled by conceptions of history and culture that prized the economic and technological advancements of Euro-American civilization as benchmarks of social progress. The weight of such judgment had long been severe, as seen from the perceptions of settlers, fur trappers, sea captains, and others who had occasion to observe California Indians during the nineteenth century: "The image of California that emerges from the accounts of such men as William Shaler, Jedediah Smith, and Richard Henry Dana is that of a land of abundant wildlife, fertile soils, great harbors, and an unsurpassed climate. The Indians of California, while not occupying a prominent position in these accounts, appear almost universally as an inoffensive and extremely primitive people. Their primitiveness was a matter of some curiosity, and visitors responded with a mixture of pity and disgust."[7]

For centuries Europeans routinely perceived California Indians as primitives and attributed this condition to a benign natural environment that demanded only minimal cultural responses. That this perception continued to plague public perceptions of California Indians well into the twentieth century is suggested by the attitudes described by Walker in his museum leaflet: "Nature had not favored most of these Indians with very attractive features or figures—their faces were wide and their bodies squatty—and the mild climate did not necessitate the building of very large houses nor the wearing of much in the way of clothing. And so to the pioneers they were nothing but naked savages—'diggers.'"[8]

Walker went on to condemn the "digger Indian" stereotype in the same discussion, defending California Indians by pointing out their unrivaled artistic and technical skill in certain crafts, such as basket making. Still, to current observers, this seems a tepid defense. Comments by authorities such as Kroeber regarding mild cultural responses to the natural environment make it clear that many professional anthropologists endorsed a minimalist conception of California Indian culture, and this stance made it difficult for them to mount a truly effective attack on anti-Indian cultural prejudices.

Even a passing familiarity with the portrayal of California Indian cultures in contemporary public and academic contexts will reveal that an astonishing transition has occurred between the Kroeberian era and today. The minimalist image of California Indian culture has been dramatically rehabilitated since the 1950s as a result of important developments in American academia and popular culture.

During the 1950s, ecology and ecosystems emerged as new fields of investigation in biology. Anthropologists immediately found these concepts useful because they offered a framework for examining patterns of cultural behavior in relation to ecological conditions. By the 1960s, cultural ecology was a well-established program within American archaeology and anthropology, and this program was also driving a revitalization of anthropological research on hunter-gatherers. Ethnographers moved in with foragers around the globe, where they could make detailed, firsthand observations of how these groups interacted with the natural environment. The results of this work quickly and radically reshaped anthropological thinking about the nature of hunter-gatherer cultures. In the landmark volume *Man the Hunter*, foragers were portrayed as affluent, in the sense that clever, highly effective adaptations to the ecosystem typically yielded a living with less work than that required of citizens of industrial societies. As Robert L. Kelly notes, this characterization has since been transformed into a stereotype in which foragers are imbued with adaptive tendencies that almost unerringly select for an optimal balance between population size, modes of economic production, and compatibility with the natural environment.[9] In any case, anthropological thinking moved quickly away from any lingering tendencies to regard hunter-gatherer cultures as functionally simple or primitive. This shift in thinking simultaneously presented a powerful new paradigm for judging cultural success. Where Kroeber and his contemporaries were forced to defend California Indians in an intellectual climate stacked against them by Victorian concepts of cultural progress, cultural ecology moved the question to an entirely new and scientifically respectable arena, emphasizing the adaptive success of ecological foragers.

This new model proved far too powerful to be contained by its academic handlers. During the 1950s and 1960s, the middle classes of the United States and Europe experienced increasing anxiety about the effects of industry on the natural environment, leading to a popular ecology movement and potent environmentalist political agendas. As Robert L. Bettinger points out, hunter-gatherer ecologists became fashionable instantly with audiences experiencing "a pervasive disillusionment with technology, the politics of industry and industrial states, and the callous treatment of the natural environment."[10]

The possibilities of the culture-ecology model were quickly exploited in California, as they were in virtually every corner of American anthropology. The influential volume *Native Californians: A Theoretical Perspective*, edited by Lowell Bean and Thomas Blackburn, is a good example of the expanding influence of cultural-ecological thinking:

> The abundance of plant and animal resources and the development of storage techniques and other truly skilled applications of human ingenuity allowed these people to develop beyond the normal parameters of hunting and gathering, particularly in the sociological, philosophical, and religious realms. The social structures of native communities, autonomous corporate groups called tribelets by Kroeber, were characterized by extra tribal alliances and political confederations sometimes achieving the level of nationhood. Within communities, populations were administered by powerful hereditary chiefs and a bureaucratic elite whose principal function appear to have been control and management of production and redistribution.[11]

Remarkably, where earlier theorists had cast a rich natural environment as a brake on cultural elaboration, Bean and Harry Lawton and subsequent theorists transformed this very condition into a launching pad for degrees of social complexity that anthropologists had once reserved for Neolithic or early state-level societies.[12] The docile, culturally complacent Indians of Kroeber and Walker completely vanished in this account. In the meantime, the notion of natural abundance as an engine of social complexity achieved orthodoxy, as indicated in this description of the Chumash found in a widely used textbook on North American prehistory: "The Chumash achieved a level of social complexity that represents about the limit of such complexity possible without adopting agriculture. Like more complex hunter-gatherer societies elsewhere in North America . . . they were able to achieve this elaboration because of unusually favorable environmental circumstances."[13]

McCawley, in his *First Angelenos* volume, reconstructs a similar dynamic for the Gabrielino, explicitly assuming that the Chumash and Gabrielino shared functionally similar social and economic adaptations, as reconstructed by cultural-ecological theorists.[14]

If it can be said that nature shaped aboriginal culture in California, many anthropologists have argued that the opposite holds as well. Nearly all commentators have envisioned the same natural environment: a California teaming with all manner of plants and animals prior to European contact. This orthodoxy suggests that the Americas as a whole, but particularly California, supported a profusion of plant and animal life that existed unchanged for thousands of years, until it was despoiled by Euro-American land use. But what, exactly, was the aboriginal role in this pre-European paradise? To this question, the Kroeberians and the cultural ecologists advanced two quite different answers.

Kroeber and his colleagues envisioned paradise by default. Implicit in this view was the assumption that prehistoric Indian populations were too small and their technology generally too primitive to have any significant effects on nature. Burning of the landscape to improve hunting and gathering conditions was seen as a possible exception to this pattern. Even so, Native Americans were generally seen as fundamentally passive and technologically inferior. This outlook seems to reflect the same mind-set that habitually characterized California Indians as inoffensive and mild.

More recent theorists envision paradise by design. The passive Indians of the Kroeberian era have been replaced by active agents of environmental control—activists both in ideology and deeds. As Brian D. Haley and Larry R. Wilcoxon note, some anthropologists and much of the public perceive California Indians, indeed all Native American groups, as instinctive preservationists, with the roots of their preservation ethic extending into the prehistoric past: "The Chumash of today are prominent spokespeople for many environmental issues facing the people of California and the rest of the world. They have lived in balance with their surroundings for thousands of years, and they realize that this balance must be maintained if cultures are to survive and prosper. In this way, they continue their spiritual and cultural relationship with their ancient homeland while embracing the issues that affect their life as twentieth-century Americans."[15]

Some of the most ambitious claims about native conservation practices in California are advanced in the 1993 volume *Before the Wilderness* by Thomas Blackburn and Kat Anderson. The thesis of this volume is provocative: regions of California that many today see as natural, or wilderness, are in fact landscapes that have fallen into ruin after the removal of the Native Americans who once maintained these domains in more biologically diverse and productive ways than did Euro-Americans. The chapters in the *Wilderness* volume detail the various techniques that California Indians are believed to have used to manage whole landscapes, including selective burning, pruning and protection of valuable species such as oak trees (for acorns), and selective propagation of useful plants.[16]

Claims of this kind go far beyond the undisputed notion that foraging peoples possess sophisticated knowledge of the natural environments in which they live. For instance, in a report commissioned by the Santa Monica Mountains National Recreation Area, a large portion of which is located in metropolitan Los Angeles, Chester King, a contributor to *Before the Wilderness* and a leading cultural-ecological theorist, presents a bold model of aboriginal landscape management. This model refers to various mountain settings as fields and the plants that were collected there as crops.[17] Nor is this characterization unique. It has become fairly common to attribute a high degree of positive environmental manipulation and quasi-agricultural food production to groups such as the Chumash and the Gabrielino, particularly in publications aimed general audiences.

The broader social and historical contexts of the Kroeberian and cultural-ecological paradigms explain their rise as popular political ecologies. In the earlier Kroeberian model, Indians who could be viewed as passive and undistinguished wards of nature presented a useful justification for policies that marginalized native peoples in pursuit of economic growth.

After World War II, as the environmental consequences of economic growth in the United States provoked fear and resentment, cultural-ecological images of Indians as aggressive and accomplished managers of nature provided a powerful critique of urban-industrial society. The model advanced by works such as *Before the Wilderness* finds highly receptive audiences in groups who are dissatisfied with current environmental conditions or policies. This pattern is not unlike that documented by Roy Harvey Pearce, who noted that during periods in which the American public holds optimistic views of social and economic change, Indians tend to be disparaged as primitives, while periods of societal anxiety evoke images of Indians in the tradition of Rousseau's noble savages.[18]

Were prehistoric California cultures relatively static and complacent in their response to environmental stimuli or did ancient Californians aggressively carve out a near paradise through successful manipulation of the natural environment? Recent research suggests that both of these political ecologies fail to reflect the real dynamism and complexity that characterize California prehistory. While prehistoric cultural and environmental conditions in California remain far from completely understood, a substantial body of data collected during the past two decades casts serious doubt on the principal assumptions and conclusions of political-ecological models.

At first glance, political-ecological theorizing appears to enjoy the support of uniformitarian principles, an impeccable scientific methodology. The doctrine of uniformitarianism, employed by fields as diverse as geology, archaeology, and astrophysics, holds that the forces of cause and effect that operate today are the same as those that shaped the past. More often than not, however, political-ecological models rely on misapplications of this concept. We cannot, for example, assume that Indian cultural patterns and environmental conditions observed at present, or even during initial contact with Europeans, reflect the prehistoric past. Only in the past two decades have archaeologists been able to assemble reasonably large and detailed collections of information on the actual living conditions of ancient California populations from a combination of archaeological and paleoenvironmental studies. Recent research advances reveal two previously unrecognized forces at work in prehistoric California that have direct implications for political-ecological reconstructions.

The first of these forces is a long-term loss of foraging efficiency. Detailed analyses of food bones excavated from archaeological sites around California have recently demonstrated that comparatively large or productive species of mammals, fish, and shellfish became increasingly scarce in the prehistoric diet.[19] Typically, as the dietary contribution of these species declined, they were replaced with a broad array of smaller, less productive animals and an increasing array of plant foods. This is a robust pattern that has been demonstrated for many areas of prehistoric California, including the San Francisco Bay area, the Sacramento Valley, the Sierras, and the Southern California coast. A particularly dramatic illustration of this phenomenon can be seen in the San Francisco Bay area, where deer and elk, fairly numerous in the oldest archaeological deposits (ca. twenty-six hundred years), virtually disappeared from food refuse by about one thousand years ago. Instances of this kind are representative of a phenomenon frequently referred to by archaeologists as resource intensification.[20] Resource intensification, documented in many regions of the world, represents a shift toward use of food resources that are more expensive in time and labor to collect and process for consumption than are larger animal species. The effect of this process was to require an increasing amount of labor to sustain a given level of food production.

An excellent illustration of this dynamic is the use of acorns as food in prehistoric California. In a provocative paper, Mark E. Basgall argues that the widespread use of acorns in California reflects intensification dynamics.[21] This analysis questions a long-cherished assumption that hunter-gatherer affluence of quasi-agricultural proportions was anchored in California by acorn consumption. Basgall's analysis reveals that intensive use of acorns arose in various parts of the state between about four thousand and one thousand years ago. This time frame is crucial: if acorns are such a rich source of food, why did it take so long for people to exploit them, given that humans and acorns were in California more than twice this length of time?

If this question troubled early researchers, it was brushed aside with explanations based on changing food tastes, settling in to the environment, dietary experiments, and other inscrutable factors. Another answer may be obtained from examining the costs and consequences associated with acorn consumption. Basgall makes a convincing case that when the cost-benefit characteristics, chronology, and health correlates of intensive acorn use are all considered, this food source is much less productive than researchers have traditionally assumed. Eric Wohlgemuth found at least partial support for Basgall's model in an analysis of floral remains and ground stone artifacts from archaeological sites in central California. Recent archaeological research at the Camp Pendleton Marine Corps base in northern San Diego County shows that acorn use in that region appeared only after about AD 1000.[22]

Fundamentally, resource intensification is driven by stresses resulting from an imbalance of population size and food supply. This is a condition that can be caused by a variety of forces, including increases in population size, changes in the natural environment, and overexploitation of the species that are most energetically efficient to hunt or collect.[23] Resource intensification casts an interesting light on discussions of native peoples living in balance with nature, where these discussions imply that this balance is a stable condition involving a fixed set of food resources. Research on foraging efficiency in California shows that equilibrium between prehistoric human populations and their food supplies was temporary and that the resources people relied on for survival changed significantly over time. Moreover, it appears that at least some of these changes were prompted by overexploitation of top-ranked prey species, if overexploitation means that the availability of these species was depressed to the point that populations were forced to shift to less productive food types.

Some authorities, such as Charles E. Kay, argue that prehistoric hunters in various parts of North America depressed populations of large ungulates such as elk and deer to levels that would make them eligible under today's legal guidelines for listing as threatened species. Recent archaeological findings on the depression of large mammal populations in California and elsewhere stand in stark contrast with early historical accounts of California, in which bird, fish, and mammal populations were repeatedly described as so large as almost to defy belief. It is these descriptions, of course, that many have cited as evidence of a rich, pristine pre-European world.[24]

Before reflexively equating game superabundance with a prehistoric paradise, it would be well to examine the arguments of those scholars who present strong evidence in favor of a rebound of animal populations in California in the wake of European-induced diseases and massive Indian mortality.[25] William Preston and Jack M. Broughton would probably agree that California landscapes were drastically affected by removal of their indigenous inhabitants, but hardly in the fashion envisioned by Blackburn and Anderson. Clearly, recent findings contradict the assumptions of both the Kroeberian (little or no native impact on nature) and the cultural-ecology (preservation-minded environmental management) paradigms.

To date, scholars have not conducted archaeological dietary studies in the Los Angeles area. This task is not easy, since many of the region's most promising archaeological sites have been destroyed by urban-industrial expansion. However, one of the most serious blows to the image of Indians living in paradise is testimony from the dead. Current discussions of Southern California archaeology rarely incorporate the large body of information that has been published in the last decade on prehistoric health trends in the Chumash area.[26] This research, involving evidence from thousands of human skeletons spanning a period from about eight thousand years ago to Spanish contact, shows that health conditions fluctuated during this interval but generally declined. The frequency of disease-induced bone lesions and trauma resulting from interpersonal violence and estimates of stature support this conclusion. Patricia M. Lambert points out that the body size of people who lived in the Santa Barbara region (Kroeber's "far famed" land of abundance) literally shrank across an eight-thousand-year span of occupation: "The total loss in average femur length is 2.8 centimeters (2.6 for males, 3.0 for females). Since femur [thigh bone] length accounts for approximately 27 percent of a person's total height . . . this roughly translates into an average reduction in stature overall of about 10 cm between the earliest and latest populations."[27]

The osteological data are telling for three reasons. First, the bone data are relatively sensitive and direct evidence of the overall life conditions of people who lived during various periods of prehistory, compared with the much more indirect reconstructions featured in political-ecological discussions. Second, these data are derived from the Chumash area, perhaps the premier area where California Indians are said by political ecologists to have worked out highly adaptive cultural arrangements; these reconstructions are frequently used to model the prehistory of the Gabrielino and other native Californian groups. Third, if prehistoric populations of this area were able to exert the sorts of environmental control envisioned by political ecologists, particularly productive manipulation of their food supply, it seems logical to expect health conditions to at least remain stable, if not improve over time. The human osteological data are more consistent with a gradual loss of foraging efficiency than with the rise of utopian environmental control.

A second force that should be taken into account in evaluating the images of the past promoted by political ecologies is paleoenvironmental flux; that is, changes in the physical environment such as climatic variation. This is an area of potential stress on ancient California cultures that will take some by surprise, since reconstructions of California prehistory, regardless of theoretical orientation, have often stressed the "far famed" climate of the region. Recent studies show, however, that prehistoric climatic variation in California was much more pronounced, and sometimes far more punishing, than was recognized previously. Prolonged, severe droughts in particular have emerged from recent studies. Jonathon T. Overpeck, for example, summarizes "warm climate surprises" revealed by recent studies of post–Ice Age (Holocene era) climatic variation:

> Changes in moisture availability were . . . large in North America. Large areas of the Great Plains were mobilized in the form of eolian dunes during multiple intervals of the Holocene, most likely coincident with changes in ground-water and lake levels in regions now heavily farmed. There is little doubt that these episodes of drought were more severe and persistent than any recorded since Europeans came to North America (including the "dust bowl" droughts of the mid-twentieth century) and that other parts of the continent experienced drought and flood events significantly more extreme than any recorded in the instrumental period. . . . *Decades- to centuries-long droughts were apparently more common in California before this century but are not well understood.* (emphasis added)[28]

Terry L. Jones and others and Raab and Daniel O. Larson summarize the data that point to "epic" California droughts of the medieval period, from about AD 900 to 1300, and the impact of these events on the ancient cultures. Abrupt changes in native cultural patterns across California occurred during this period, including collapse of trade networks, shifts in diet, altered settlement patterns, declining health, greatly intensified warfare, and emergent social complexity among groups such as the Chumash.[29]

Findings of this kind will no doubt continue to be debated by specialists for some time to come, with the inevitable charges of environmental determinism leveled at studies linking cultural and environmental change in California. Anthropologists have long, and correctly, condemned explanations of culture change that invoke simple, mechanistic connections between climate and cultural behavior. Here it should be noted that Jones and colleagues are careful to qualify the linkage between climate flux and culture change in late-Holocene California. They argue that prehistoric California groups probably experienced episodes of climatic stress a number of times since the end of the Ice Age, without necessarily experiencing dramatic cultural changes. On the other hand, during the medieval era, some of the most severe and persistent droughts of the past three to four thousand years coincided with high population levels and relatively low levels of foraging efficiency. Unlike in earlier periods, late-Holocene groups appear to have been at particularly high risk for trouble in the event of serious climate flux. Human osteological research reveals that some of the most severe problems with health and violence of the whole prehistoric era came about during this medieval-era climatic deterioration.[30]

This model can hardly be described as subscribing to a simple, mechanistic connection between climate and culture. The same cannot be said, however, about recent political-ecological models that attribute California Indian cultural complexity to unusually favorable environmental conditions. Oddly, while anthropologists are vigilant in criticizing environmental explanations that posit negative cultural outcomes, the benign determinism of environmental richness seems to strike many as reasonable, despite the fact that this position is no more defensible on logical or empirical grounds than any other kind of environmental determinism.

There is no question that political ecologies, particularly the more recent, idealized versions, are widely applauded. After all, these ecologies draw attention to problems that deserve solutions. The fact of environmental degradation in Los Angeles is clearly a serious problem, and some might credit the positive environmental symbolism of political ecologies with just the kind of consciousness raising required for effective action on this problem. At the same time, the legacy of California Indians has been marred for centuries by ugly cultural prejudices, a condition that has been ameliorated to a substantial degree in recent decades by images of the ecological Indian.

Pointing to the flaws in political-ecological thinking will likely strike many as threatening these benefits; worse, the critics of political-ecological thinking may be dismissed as shills of the environment-wrecking establishment or anti-Indian or both. Unfortunately, utopian political ecologies are so popular that critics of these models are almost automatically cast as the Grinches that would steal paradise. It will be unfortunate if debate about the proper foundations of environmental history is framed in such a simple, ad hominem way, because a number of significant issues need thoughtful consideration.

One of these issues, of course, is how California Indians are likely to be perceived by the larger society, and by themselves, as a result of research on environmental history. Here, I only suggest that we consider how we have been encouraged to choose between two extreme Indian cultural stereotypes: passive, childlike residents of a vast nature park or unerringly successful ecoengineers. Both of these are heavy burdens to impose on the indigenous peoples of California or anywhere else. The first image portrays Indians as hapless, with only Euro-Americans able to effect real change on the environment. The second image sets up Indians as environmental saints, denying them the complex and sometimes less than adaptive motives and behaviors that characterize all cultures. But recent research points to a third alternative. California prehistory reflects an extraordinary saga of change and readaptation to far more challenging and complex social and natural environments than was previously recognized. Native Americans, along with the rest of us, have a powerful interest in information about this prehistory that is as complete and accurate as possible. On that account, the story of prehistoric cultural and environmental change in the Los Angeles region is increasingly revealed as much more informative and interesting than the stereotypes promoted by political ecologies.

2

The Los Angeles Prairie

PAULA M. SCHIFFMAN

I call our world Flatland, not because we call it so, but to make its
nature clearer to you.

Edwin Abbott Abbott, *Flatland: A Romance of Many
Dimensions*, 1884

FLATNESS once defined the ecological essence of much of the Los Angeles region. The areas of flat topography—the Los Angeles Plain and the
adjacent valleys—were ecologically unique. These were the segments of
the precontact landscape most rapidly and profoundly altered by European settlers through agriculture and urban development. The natural structure and
species composition of the original prairie ecosystem on these flatlands differed
considerably from the ecosystems on the slopes of the surrounding mountains.
In addition, the region's steep hillsides were relatively inaccessible and were
therefore much less vulnerable to historical human activities. While the chaparral and coastal sage scrub on those hillsides have become more and more susceptible to suburban development and the effects of fragmentation with each
passing year, significant tracts of these ecosystems persist today, and conditions
still resemble those that existed at the time of European contact. Moreover,
these hillside ecosystems and their constituent species have been the focus of
scientific attention and conservation efforts for the past few decades.[1]

The same cannot be said about the prairie ecosystem that once carpeted
Southern California's vast flatlands. It disappeared soon after European settlement, before the intricacies of its ecology could be studied or even the most

basic aspects of its natural history could be described. Nonetheless, ecologically meaningful clues remain, and these can be synthesized into a coherent descriptive reconstruction of the presettlement and early postsettlement ecologies of what was once a very large and important ecosystem. Any such reconstruction requires attention to the complex set of historical circumstances and ecological processes that caused the rapid disappearance of the Los Angeles prairie.

Ecographic Context

Southern California's human and natural histories are inextricably linked to its characteristic Mediterranean-type climate. In addition to attracting millions of people to Los Angeles, the hot, dry summers and cool winters with annually varying rainfall are the primary determinants of the region's native vegetation composition. Climate is also the main force behind natural patterns and ecological processes. The great importance of the Mediterranean climate in shaping Southern California is all the more interesting when one realizes that it is of relatively recent origin and is found in only a few small and widely scattered places on Earth. Developing over just the past 3 million years during warm interglacial periods, Mediterranean-type climates occur only in California, central Chile, south and western Australia, the Cape region of South Africa, and lands surrounding the Mediterranean Sea itself—places where the effects of latitude, proximity to cold ocean currents, and terrain combine in just the right way. Because of convergent evolutionary forces driven by this unique climatic regime, the floristically disparate vegetations of California and the other Mediterranean-type climate regions bear remarkably strong resemblance to one another.[2]

It is likely that similarity between the California environment and the landscapes of Spain was a major reason why Spanish settlers in California were so successful at establishing self-sustaining settlements. Southern California provided a familiar environment with resources that were amenable to exploitation via established agricultural techniques and land use practices. In addition, preadaptation to California's climate was responsible, in part, for the ease with which invasive Mediterranean weeds were able to spread and naturalize following European contact.[3]

Though similar in physiology, growth form, and other attributes, most of the native plants of the California Floristic Province that the Spanish encountered when they arrived were unique and not closely related to the European plants with which they were already acquainted. The Pacific Ocean to the south and west and mountain ranges to the north and east acted in concert as geographic barriers to isolate coastal California from the rest of the world. Like an island, the California environment hosted the evolution of unique species and ecosystems. The region's climate, its isolation, and its terrain supported considerable native-species diversity and became the sole habitat for a very large number of endemic organisms. In what is now the Los Angeles region, three natural ecosystems dominated the landscape at the time of European contact: chaparral, coastal sage scrub, and prairie.[4]

Each of these ecosystems had a characteristic vegetation structure and species composition. Most steep hillsides were covered by impenetrably dense evergreen chaparral shrubs such as California lilac (*Ceanothus* spp.), chamise (*Adenostoma fasciculatum*), scrub oak (*Quercus berberidifolia*), and manzanita (*Arctostaphylos* spp.) or sparsely shrubby and drought deciduous coastal sage scrub vegetation that included buckwheat (*Eriogonum fasciculatum*), sages (*Salvia* spp.), and sagebrush (*Artemisia californica*). In contrast to the shrubby hills and mountain slopes, the dense, clayey soils of the flat valleys and plains supported a diverse prairie vegetation of colorful ephemeral wildflowers mixed with grasses and other plants of low stature. In addition, woodlands of walnut (*Juglans californica*) and oak (*Quercus agrifolia* and *Q. lobata*) were found in canyons and on some hillsides, and broad corridors of willow (*Salix* spp.), alder (*Alnus rhombifolia*), sycamore (*Platanus racemosa*), and mulefat (*Baccharis salicifolia*) lined the river floodplains and feeder creeks that dissected the landscape.[5]

The high levels of native biodiversity and endemism of these uniquely Californian ecosystems, along with the fact that human activities have caused the loss of more than 70 percent of the region's primary vegetation, have led to the ranking of the California Floristic Province among the earth's top twenty-five biodiversity hot spots for which greater conservation should be a priority.[6] The Los Angeles region, with its tremendous human population, constitutes a significant proportion of this hot-spot area. Designation as a biodiversity hot spot serves to highlight the importance of linkages between human and natural processes at both local and global levels. In the case of Southern California, this connection between humans and nature has a significant historical component.

A Lost Prairie Ecosystem

The first human inhabitants of the Los Angeles region, the Tongva people, had a traditional oral system of information transfer and did not keep written records describing their environment. Because their culture was decimated when the Spanish mission era began, only a sparse history of the environment as they experienced it survives today. It is known, however, that at the time of European contact, numerous Tongva communities were established throughout Southern California, particularly on the flat terrain. William McCawley has mapped the historical presence of twenty-four distinct communities on the Los Angeles Plain, ten in the San Fernando Valley, nine in the San Gabriel Valley, and eight in the San Bernardino Valley. Although the actual numbers of people living in these communities are uncertain, there is evidence indicating that the San Gabriel Valley and the Palos Verdes Peninsula were considerably more densely populated than were the San Fernando and San Bernardino valleys. It is certain that the flat sections of Southern California's wildlands supported a significant human population many centuries before the Spanish established their first settlements.[7] The people in these communities relied on a diversity of local natural resources for food, shelter, and cultural purposes and, therefore, manipulated and otherwise affected the ecology of the wildlands they occupied. Nevertheless, if evaluated according to current criteria, this landscape would be considered wild.[8]

Spanish explorers recorded the earliest written depictions of California's flatland environments. The priests and soldiers who explored and settled the region kept diaries describing their observations and experiences. Although these writers did not know the exact identities of plant and animal species, their accounts offer a vision, if somewhat less focused than we would hope for, of the natural landscape that they encountered. Among the most ecologically informative of these initial natural history accounts of the Los Angeles region are those recorded in 1769 by Pedro Fages, a soldier in the first Spanish expedition from San Diego to Monterey, and in 1775 by Pedro Font, a priest who participated in Juan Bautista de Anza's second expedition across California. Fages's descriptions are unusual because his diary is filled with detailed listings of organisms, particularly animals, encountered in various places during his journey. Font's journal entries also contains many vivid descriptions of scenery and organisms. Because every animal has a specific set of habitat requirements, the mere mention of a certain habitat indicator species in the context of a particular locale can be used to make good inferences about what the historical terrain and vegetation were like. For example, Fages's description of the San Fernando Valley includes mention of antelope, as does his characterization of the Los Angeles region as a whole.[9]

These specific references to antelope are important because they are strongly suggestive of an entire ecological landscape. The pronghorn antelope (*Antilocapra americana*) is North America's fastest-running mammal. The presence of this species, which is adapted to wide-open, treeless country and is associated with Southern California's enormous tracts of flat terrain, was indicative of a prairie ecosystem. This vision was corroborated by Font, who, after traveling through the Conejo Valley area, wrote, "We saw in the plain a very large drove of antelopes which, as soon as they saw us, fled like the wind, looking like a cloud skimming along the earth."[10]

Rabbits (*Sylvilagus audubonii*), hares (*Lepus californicus*), and rodents were the animals most often noticed by early chroniclers of the California landscape. They were mentioned because of their value as hunted game and because they occurred in tremendous numbers on the flatlands where people established settlements. Rodents were also probably of particular concern because of their potential importance as pests of agricultural products and as vectors of disease. California ground squirrels (*Spermophilus beecheyi*) and valley pocket gophers (*Thomomys bottae*) were especially numerous, and nearly every commentator noted their presence and the fact that their burrows riddled the landscape with disturbed soil and holes that were hazardous to horses and other livestock. Fages included "squirrels of three kinds" in the list of fauna that he observed as he trekked from San Diego to El Toro.[11]

In 1832, when Los Angeles resident Hugo Reid traveled across the plain, he noticed "squirrels, rabbits and gophers continually scurrying down into their holes, out of harm's way. Indeed, these tiny animals had so honeycombed the surface of the ground as to make it dangerous to ride anywhere off the roadway faster than a walk." Similarly, in 1853 when Harris Newmark settled in Los Angeles, he observed that "soon after leaving San Pedro, we passed thousands of ground squirrels." Four years later, in 1857, he wrote about this subject again, stating that "there were millions of ground squirrels all over this country that shared with other animals the ups and downs of the season. When there was plenty of rain, these squirrels fattened and multiplied." Also in 1857, zoologist Janos Xántus wrote that on the plains near Fort Tejon, northwest of Los Angeles, there were "ground Squirrel[s] really in countless numbers, they dwell in holes & you can kill tausan [sic] in a day." In like fashion in 1860, William H. Brewer, a botanist and member of the Whitney geological survey expedition, described the San Gabriel Mission as being the "abode for myriads of ground squirrels." It is clear from these many accounts that small native mammals and the soil disturbances that they created constituted an important ecological feature of the Los Angeles prairie.[12]

The region was also the habitat of another native animal that was renowned for the soil disturbances it produced, the grizzly bear (*Ursus arctos*). Grizzlies used their enormous claws to excavate large tracts of soil in search of buried foods such as rodents, roots, bulbs, fungi, and insect grubs. Like antelope, rabbits, hares, ground squirrels, and gophers, the grizzly bears of California occurred in greatest density in broad valley landscapes. The openness of a grizzly's habitat was different from that of the smaller and generally less aggressive black bear (*Ursus americanus*), a montane forest and woodland dweller. The Los Angeles region's expanses of flat terrain and its enormous resident populations of rodents and other prairie foods meant that the region was perfect grizzly bear country. A skull collected in 1875 from a bear killed at the San Fernando Mission and now housed as a museum specimen at the Smithsonian Institution serves as a modest voucher of this fact.[13]

Early travelers and settlers frequently saw grizzlies on the Los Angeles Plain and in the valleys, and the apprehensive tone of their writings reflected a clear understanding of the bear's great speed and strength. For example, Brewer's recounting of his visit to the Los Angeles region included repeated mention of his concern about the nearby presence of grizzly bears. In 1861, after enjoying a panoramic view of the San Fernando Valley from a vantage point in the Santa Susana Mountains, he wrote, "The real soon roused me from my reveries—I must get back. I was alone, far from camp—grizzlies might come out as the moon came up, for the weather was warm." Just three and a half years earlier, in 1857, Xántus stated, "we have here grizlys [sic] in great abundance, they are really a nuisance, you cannot walk out half a mile without meeting some of them, and as they just now have their cubs, they are extremely ferocious."[14]

The effect of this single species on the ecology of Southern California prairies should not be underestimated. Mammalogists Tracy I. Storer and Lloyd P. Tevis Jr. state that "only the badger could vie with the bear in digging rodents out of the soil." They quote Xántus, who observed a bear amusing himself digging like a pig in 1860, "sometimes during moon-light night he will dig up many acres of lands [so] that not one [blade of] grass is to be found on it." The tremendous volume of churned soil that these animals continually produced would have significantly influenced the native vegetation. Short-lived ruderal plant species with adaptations that enabled them to tolerate or escape the effects of such disturbances would have been particularly common in the Los Angeles prairie landscape.[15]

The grizzly bear's multifaceted interactions with its environment (as a generalist carnivore, herbivore, and soil disturber) meant that it was a keystone species. Bears played a pivotal role in determining and regulating the species composition, structure, and function of the entire regional ecosystem until they were driven to extinction during America's predator-suppression movement in the early twentieth century.[16] The extinction of an animal of such extraordinary ecological importance means that we will never truly understand the nuances of historical ecosystem dynamics in the Los Angeles region. It also means that genuine restoration of relict Southern California prairie fragments to a pre–European settlement condition is no longer possible. Despite these problems, hundreds of species native to the historical Los Angeles prairie environment persist in today's wildlands, and much can still be conserved and restored.

Antelope, rabbits, rodents, and grizzly bears were only a few of the animals that would have been found on the flatlands. Because their collective historical presence strongly attests to the existence of a prairie ecosystem, we can confidently assume that a broad diversity of other native prairie animals would also have been common in this landscape (see table 2.1). A few such species include the badger (*Taxidea taxus*), long-tailed weasel (*Mustela frenata*), western meadowlark (*Sturnella neglecta*), horned lark (*Eremophila alpestris*), and ferruginous hawk (*Buteo regalis*). Early observers mentioned additional prairie animal species. For example, Fages noted coyotes (*Canis latrans*), buzzards (probably both the turkey vulture, *Cathartes aura*, and California condor, *Gymnogyps californicus*), tarantulas (*Aphonopelma eutelynum*), and vipers (western rattlesnake, *Crotalis viridis*). Font recorded observations of "many geese, ducks, cranes and other fowl" in the Santa Clara River, and Brewer made a brief mention that somewhere near the San Fernando Valley his expedition colleague, Chester Averill, "shot an eagle with his revolver. It measured fifty inches from tip to tip." This was probably a juvenile golden eagle (*Aquila chrysaetos*), an important prairie predator.[17] These were just a few of the many prairie animal sightings mentioned by early Southern California settlers and travelers.

Establishing the identities of Los Angeles prairie plants is a much more difficult task. Early descriptions of vegetation were generally vague, with few or

TABLE 2.1

Uncommon or extirpated native bird and mammal species that were once abundant on the flatlands of the Los Angeles prairie

BIRDS	MAMMALS
California condor (*Gymnogyps californianus*)	Grizzly bear (*Ursus arctos*)
Golden eagle (*Aquila chrysaetos*)	Broad-footed mole (*Scapanus latimanus*)
White-tailed kite (*Elanus leucurus*)	Longtail weasel (*Mustela frenata*)
Northern harrier (*Circus cyaneus*)	Badger (*Taxidea taxus*)
Ferruginous hawk (*Buteo regalis*)	Bobcat (*Lynx rufus*)
Rough-legged hawk (*Buteo lagopus*)	California ground squirrel (*Spermophilus beecheyi*)
American kestrel (*Falco sparverius*)	Valley pocket gopher (*Thomomys bottae*)
Prairie falcon (*Falco mexicanus*)	Little pocket mouse (*Perognathus longimembris*)
Greater roadrunner (*Geococcyx californianus*)	Western harvest mouse (*Reithrodontomys megalotis*)
Short-eared owl (*Asio flammeus*)	Deer mouse (*Peromyscus maniculatus*)
Burrowing owl (*Athene cunicularia*)	Southern grasshopper mouse (*Onychomys torridus*)
Western kingbird (*Tyrannus verticalis*)	Desert woodrat (*Neotoma lepida*)
Say's phoebe (*Sayornis saya*)	California vole (*Microtus californicus*)
Horned lark (*Eremophila alpestris*)	Black-tailed hare (*Lepus californicus*)
Loggerhead shrike (*Lanius ludovicianus*)	Desert cottontail (*Sylvilagus audubonii*)
Lark sparrow (*Chondestes grammacus*)	Pronghorn antelope (*Antilocapra americana*)
Grasshopper sparrow (*Ammodramus savannarum*)	
Savannah sparrow (*Passerculus sandwichensis*)	
Western meadowlark (*Sturnella neglecta*)	
Mountain plover (*Charadrius montanus*)	

no particular species mentioned or described in detail. Still, understanding this vegetation is important in its own right. Plants provided the food base, shelter, nest sites, and a diversity of other habitat attributes for an ecosystem full of resident and migratory prairie animals. Botanically meaningful information can be gleaned from a few of the early postsettlement accounts. For instance, Pedro Font described the San Gabriel Valley as "a country very level in all directions, which we found very green in places, the flowers already bursting into bloom." A few days later he used a bit more botanical detail to further portray the region: "[T]he road is almost level, except for some hills about halfway on the journey, and all very green and covered with grass and various herbs, among which is found a species of small wild onion which in shape and taste is the same as the garden onion, and some of which I ate at the mission of San Gabriel." The wild onions that Font referred to were plants of the genus Allium. They, and other edible-bulb-producing plants such as blue dicks (*Dichelostemma capitatum*), were common constituents of early Los Angeles. So, while the precise species composition of the vegetation described by Font is not completely clear, his accounts provide a vision of prairie vegetation with wildflowers, grasses, and bulbs growing on the flat terrain.[18]

Fages's descriptions of plants growing on the Los Angeles Plain and valleys were generally less clear than Font's, although he did refer often to areas as being "well-grassed." Characterizations such as "good grass," "luxuriant grass," and similar attributes were employed by many observers when describing the vegetation of the valleys and plains.[19] In this context, however, the meaning of the word grass is rather nebulous and should not be interpreted too literally. In nearly all cases, early environmental commentators used grass as a collective term to describe green swards of short-stature plants that could serve as livestock forage rather than as a reference to plants of a particular botanical taxonomy. A diversity of nongrass species (such as wildflowers, sedges, and bulbs) were typically included as grass. The extent of this imprecision is apparent in a comment made by journalist Edwin Bryant in 1847: "The varieties of grass are greater than on the Atlantic side of the continent, and far more nutritious. I have seen seven different kinds of clover, several of them in a dry state, depositing seed upon the ground so abundant as to cover it, which is lapped up by the cattle and horses and other animals as corn or oats, when threshed would be with us."[20] Although native clovers (*Trifolium* spp.) and grasses both grew in the California prairies that Bryant explored, he erroneously viewed them as the same thing; in actuality they were two completely different and unrelated botanical taxa.

A comparison of LeRoy Abrams's *Flora of Los Angeles and Vicinity* (a published comprehensive listing of native and naturalized plants in the region in 1917) with the known species compositions of nearby modern relict prairie fragments is another approach to assessing the historical species composition of Los Angeles' prairie vegetation. This relict analysis suggests that the few extant patches of prairie still resemble the historical vegetation. Carrizo Plain National Monument, a 250,000-acre preserve in the southeastern corner of San Luis Obispo County, contains the largest remaining fragment of prairie in the state of California. Its vegetation includes more than two hundred native plants. Of these species, more than 60 percent were also part of the historical vegetation of Los Angeles, according to Abrams's *Flora*. Another relict prairie can be found at the Santa Rosa Plateau Ecological Reserve in southwestern Riverside County. More than five hundred native plant species are part of the vegetation at that 8,300-acre preserve. As with the Carrizo Plain, more than 60 percent of the Santa Rosa Plateau species were also historically present in the Los Angeles region. While species overlap between the extant and historical floras is only partial, it indicates that the fragments of prairie that still exist today in the Southern California region are informative windows into the ecological past.[21]

Interestingly, more than half the relict prairie species with known historical presences in the Los Angeles flora were annual forbs and wildflowers. This finding corresponds well with descriptions of the Los Angeles Plain, such as Font's comment that an area near the Los Angeles River "was very green and flower-strewn." These annual forbs and wildflowers were probably the most spatially dominant members of the prairie vegetation. In the spring, vibrant ephemeral carpets of goldfields (*Lasthenia californica*), pink owl's clover (*Castilleja exserta*), orange fiddleneck (*Amsinckia menziesii*), and baby blue eyes (*Nemophila menziesii*) commonly covered Southern California's flatlands.[22] The lifestyle of annual plants was very adaptive in the Mediterranean climate and environment of Southern California. Seeds were stimulated to germinate by winter rainfall, and the subsequent plants went on to grow, flower, produce seeds of their own, and die over a period of weeks or months. Their entire life cycle was completed before the onset of summer heat and drought. This attribute, along with the fact that seeds of many of California's annuals had the ability to remain dormant in the soil for years, meant that these native plants were able to persist and thrive despite the region's wide year-to-year fluctuations in rainfall.[23] In addition, many of these native annuals were weedy or otherwise opportunistic. Such life-history traits would have been adaptive in a wild presettlement prairie that was constantly being dug up by rodents, grizzly bears, and other animals.[24]

Why a Prairie Disappeared

European settlement of Southern California led to significant changes in the region's disturbance regime. Fire was among the most important tools employed by the Tongva to manipulate their environment. By purposefully burning vegetation they were able to promote and maintain habitats for native game animals, including rabbits, a variety of rodents, antelope, and mule deer (*Odocoileus hemionus*). Burning was also employed to enhance the productivity of important food plants, including prairie wildflowers such as chia (*Salvia columbariae*), red maids (*Calandrinia ciliata*), clovers, and bulbs. It is likely that these people also promoted the productivity of other useful native plants through small-scale cultivation, broadcast seeding, and coppicing. By manipulating the mix and abundance of native plant and animal species present in the ecosystem, the Tongva were able to exert control over the vertical structure of the region's vegetation and over a diversity of natural processes.[25] Aspects of the environment that would have been directly or indirectly affected by these human manipulations include numeric ratios of predator species (such as coyotes and hawks) to their smaller prey (that is, rodents, small birds, and insects).[26] Intensities of interspecies competition among organisms with similar needs for limited environmental resources, such as water or habitat space, would also have been affected. All of this ceased when Europeans displaced Tongva culture.

Although quite significant, the manner and magnitude of Tongva manipulations of the environment were in no way comparable to the massive and lasting ecological effects initiated by European settlement.[27] The ecological transformation that led to the disappearance of the Los Angeles prairie began in the 1770s when mission settlements were established and the vast surrounding flatlands of the plains and valleys were swiftly converted to agricultural uses. Livestock grazing became the region's most widely established agricultural practice, and its effects on the natural environment were irreversible. For the first century following European settlement, herbivory and domesticated livestock, by far the dominant organisms, governed the region's ecological processes.

Robert Glass Cleland noted that the pastures controlled by the Spanish missions were of "gargantuan size" and that the lands of the San Fernando Mission alone covered an area of 350 square miles. These mission lands were stocked with very large numbers of free-ranging livestock, particularly cattle. By 1817 the Rancho San Rafael in the San Gabriel Valley "was pasturing 1800 large cattle, 1000 calves, 600 unbroken horses, seventy tame horses and seventy mules" and "twelve years later the number of cattle had almost doubled." In 1847 Bryant observed that "large herds of cattle and sheep were grazing upon the plain in sight of the [San Fernando] mission." A traveler, William Manly, was astonished to find "cattle and horses everywhere but no sign of human habitation" on the lands of the San Gabriel Mission in 1849. As time passed and the region became more settled, the number of livestock grew even larger. In an 1860 journal entry Brewer described the Los Angeles Plain as "only wanting water to make it of the greatest fertility. Now during the rainy season it is most green and lovely, thousands (probably thirty thousand to fifty thousand) of horses and cattle are grazing there." In another entry Brewer described the ranches of the San Fernando Valley as having "no fences, the cattle are half wild, and require many horses to keep them and tend them. A ranch with a thousand head of cattle will have a hundred horses." Numerous sheep and hogs also foraged in these pastures. Prairie vegetation was the food base for all of these animals.[28]

At the time of European settlement, the fauna of the region's wild flatlands already included a significant diversity of native herbivores. Antelope, the ubiquitous ground squirrels and gophers, rabbits, deer, mice (*Peromyscus maniculatus* and *Reithrodontomys megalotis*), and voles (*Microtus californicus*) were found throughout the landscape, but the most abundant native foliage eaters were probably grasshoppers. Entomologist Charles L. Hogue noted that the Los Angeles region was, as it continues to be, habitat for numerous native grasshopper species and that "the hopping activity of these insects prompted early Los Angeles residents to name what is now South Figueroa Street 'Calle de las Chapules' (Spanish for 'Street of the Grasshoppers')."[29]

The effects of Southern California's many wild native herbivores on the natural vegetation bore very little functional resemblance to the effects of introduced European livestock animals. Native herbivory was not continuous all year round. Rather, it varied from season to season and from year to year as native animals responded to climatic fluctuations and other sorts of environmental variability. Native herbivores also differed from livestock in that they did not intensively graze in large herds. In addition, native animals ate narrower and more idiosyncratic sets of plants than were consumed by the considerably less choosy domesticated livestock. Given the large numbers of domesticated animals that became established on the flatlands of Southern California and their significant feeding differences, it is clear that the introduction of livestock grazing produced a disturbance regime that was novel and extremely ecologically disruptive.[30]

Moreover, because the recent (post-Pleistocene) evolutionary development of the region's native vegetation did not include exposure to intensive grazing by herds of large herbivores, many native plants apparently lacked sufficient adaptations for coping with the scale of biological damage caused by prolonged and continuous exposure to large grazing animals. In addition, the region's highly variable annual rainfall resulted in variability in forage production. In some years the landscape was overgrazed, and in drought years the effects of this overgrazing were catastrophic. According to observations compiled by cowboy chronicler Dane Coolidge, "in 1805, thirty-five years after the first herd was brought in, they were killing cattle in the San Fernando Valley because they were destroying the grass." The Los Angeles region's livestock industry recovered but collapsed again in the 1860s when Southern California experienced devastating floods and then prolonged drought. Because all organisms in this ecosystem were interconnected by an intricate web of mutual dependencies, competitive interactions, and predator-prey relationships, the negative impacts of overgrazing, magnified by the natural stresses of floods and drought, cascaded through the entire system, affecting the native flora and fauna in unexpected and damaging ways.[31]

Simultaneous to European settlement and the establishment of the livestock industry were the introduction and rapid naturalization of a suite of invasive plants, most of which originated in the Mediterranean region. These species included yellow mustards (*Brassica nigra* and *Hirschfeldia incana*), filaree (*Erodium cicutarium*), and—perhaps most importantly—annual grasses, including wild oats (*Avena barbata* and *A. fatua*) and red brome (*Bromus madritensis*). Today, these Mediterranean species dominate Southern California's few remaining prairie fragments and occur in other natural ecosystems as well. In the vast majority of cases these invasive species were transported inadvertently to California as seed contaminants of ship ballast, crop seed, or nursery stock or through adherence to imported livestock fur.[32] However, the presence of European plant seeds such as filaree, wild oats, curly dock (*Rumex crispus*), and burr clover (*Medicago polymorpha*) in adobe bricks of early Spanish mission structures strongly suggests that at least a few invader species had actually arrived prior to the 1769 initial settlement of Alta California. These species apparently invaded when European explorers left their ships to make brief visits to coastal California or via overland dispersal from Spanish settlements in Baja California by native animals.[33]

Like many of the soil disturbance–adapted native prairie species, most of the new alien invaders were ruderal annuals. Because they originated in the Mediterranean region, not only were the invaders preadapted to Southern California's Mediterranean-type climate, they were also adapted to the effects of livestock grazing and other environmental changes introduced by the Spanish and later settlers. In fact, it is quite likely that livestock herds in Southern California's prairies facilitated the spread and naturalization of these alien species. A recent study demonstrated that a single grazing cow can consume and later disperse three hundred thousand viable seeds per day in its dung.[34] In addition, some of these invading ruderals were derived from domesticated crops (e.g., *Avena fatua*) or simply had recent Mediterranean evolutionary histories that included prolonged exposure to agricultural soil cultivation. When disturbance-adapted alien plants arrived in the Los Angeles prairie, they probably readily colonized the diggings and burrows of grizzly bears and rodents that perforated the Los Angeles landscape. Moreover, these alien ruderals likely thrived and spread in areas where settlers cultivated the soil for row crops, vineyards, and orchards.[35] Because these annual invaders had short generation times and large reproductive outputs (seeds), their spread throughout California was extremely rapid. In fact, their widespread naturalization happened so quickly that apparently no one noticed or bothered to document the process.

It is hard to imagine how such a massive biological invasion could have gone undetected. But it did. Except during the spring, when colorful wildflowers were in abundance, the broad flat prairies composed a subtle landscape lacking the obvious visual drama of California's rocky Pacific coast and majestic mountain ranges; the prairies may have elicited less attention. Early settlers were not naturalists. They viewed Los Angeles' valleys and plains as a resource to be exploited. They saw little intrinsic value in this new environment and were so driven to dominate it that they failed to notice regional changes in vegetation and ecology. Whatever the reason, the early settlers exhibited a high degree of "verbal (and visual) blindness." Because of the absence of records chronicling the invasion by Mediterranean plants, modern ecological scientists are working to reconstruct vegetation dynamics at the time of European contact to gain insight into the processes by which alien species invaded and became integrated into this and other ecosystems. It is probable that the invading species had resource requirements that were very similar to those of native prairie plants. These invaders, which were apparently better able to survive exposure to heavy livestock grazing and chronic soil disturbance than were native prairie plants, outcompeted native plants for limited resources such as water, nutrients, and space. The displacement of natives by aliens means that the few relict prairies in California are thoroughly contaminated by Mediterranean annuals.[36]

Prairie to Urban Woodland

The vast flat plains and valleys of the Los Angeles region once supported a unique and biologically diverse prairie ecosystem. The massive environmental changes wrought by European settlement transformed this largely treeless prairie terrain into an agricultural and livestock landscape that was soon polluted by invasive weeds. More recently the region has been transformed yet again, this time as an imported, ornamental, urban woodland of eucalyptus, oleander, Canary Island pine, and jacaranda. Land that supported a low-stature, almost two-dimensional native prairie is now habitat to a taller and much more three-dimensional synthetic woodland.

This new ecosystem is a poor substitute for the complex and dynamic pre-settlement prairie. While the structure and species composition of the new vegetation bear no resemblance to the historical prairie, today's prairie is, nonetheless, inhabited by many animals (see table 2.2). This suite of animal species differs radically from the prairie dwellers that once roamed these same locales (table 2.1). Several are alien invaders, but, interestingly, Southern California natives constitute the majority of the faunal species that are now common on the flatlands of Los Angeles. These species are recent immigrants from the natural chaparral and woodlands on the hillsides and in the canyons adjacent to the urbanized plains and valleys. They are ecological opportunists that have successfully expanded their habitat use to include the ornamental shrubs and trees of the new urban woodland. Because of their recent range expansions, some of these native animal species are probably more widespread today than they were at the time of European contact, when prairie, rather than urban woodland, covered the flatlands.

The Los Angeles prairie is gone, but significant wildlands remain in the hills and mountains that surround the city. Although these lands are not as wild as they once were, the biodiversity that they support is an important and irreplaceable component of Los Angeles' natural heritage; it deserves to be protected and restored. With uncompromising and ecologically responsible stewardship, the region's chaparral, coastal sage scrub, oak, and walnut woodlands and riparian corridors can be saved from fates like the one that befell the Los Angeles prairie.

TABLE 2.2
Opportunistic immigrant bird and mammal species

BIRDS	MAMMALS
Rock dove[a] (feral pigeon, *Columbia livia*)	Virginia opossum[a] (*Didelphis virginiana*)
Great horned owl (*Bubo virginianus*)	Raccoon (*Procyon lotor*)
Anna's hummingbird (*Calypte anna*)	Striped skunk (*Mephistis mephistis*)
Acorn woodpecker (*Melanerpes formicivorus*)	Fox squirrel[a] (*Sciurus niger*)
Downy woodpecker (*Picoides pubescens*)	Norway rat[a] (*Rattus norvegicus*)
Western scrub-jay (*Aphelocoma californica*)	Black rat[a] (*Rattus rattus*)
American crow (*Corvus brachyrhynchos*)	House mouse[a] (*Mus musculus*)
Bushtit (*Psaltriparus minimus*)	
Northern mockingbird (*Mimus polyglottos*)	
European starling[a] (*Sturnus vulgaris*)	
Yellow-rumped warbler (*Dendroica coronata*)	
House sparrow[a] (*Passer domesticus*)	

Note: These species are native to Southern California's chaparral and woodlands, except where noted. They commonly inhabit the ornamental urban woodlands that now exist on flatlands where Los Angeles prairie historically existed.

[a] Invasive alien species.

3

Ranchos and the Politics of Land Claims

KAREN CLAY AND WERNER TROESKEN

Most accounts of land and property in Southern California decry as unfair the 1851 California Land Act that governed the transition in property rights between Mexico and the United States. These stories of loss, although compelling, fail to tell us how widespread the loss was, what precisely the losses were, or why these costs occurred. In short, the literature devoted to land claims fails to provide an adequate metric against which loss can be measured and then interpreted.[1]

In comparing how Los Angeles–area claims fared relative to other California land claims, we have examined the specific costs Los Angeles claimants bore and the political constraints that led to the passage of the Land Act. We have also tried to compare the outcome of the claims process in California to the outcome in acquired territory.

Land and Property in Nineteenth-Century Los Angeles

Spanish settlement began in the late eighteenth century with the establishment of Roman Catholic missions and military presidios along the California coast. Missions were expected to be largely self-sustaining, and the Spanish government granted control over large tracts of land. A small number of grants were made to individuals as a reward for service (see figure 3.1).

After independence in 1821, the Mexican government continued and expanded the practice of granting land to citizens.[2] Until the 1830s, the Roman Catholic missions controlled most of the desirable coastal land. Because the priests actively resisted the granting of lands, only a small number of grants were made in most years. In the mid-1830s, the Mexican central government secularized the missions, reducing them to the status of parish churches and stripping them of virtually all of their lands. In the process of secularization, the Catholic Church was given ownership rights in small parcels that encompassed the mission buildings, and government officials awarded certain Native Americans rights to use lands near various missions.

Secularization opened up huge tracts of land at a time when the external market for cattle products was growing. Up to the 1820s, Latin America had

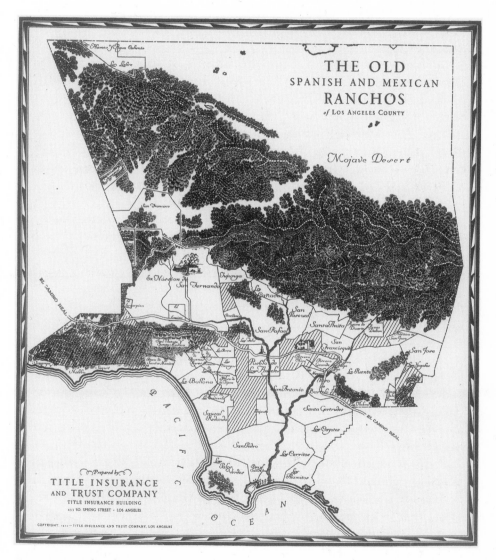

Figure 3.1. Spanish and Mexican land grants in California. Public domain.

been the primary supplier of hides and tallow for world markets. Political instability forced traders to seek alternative sources of supply, and one place they looked was California. Cattle that ran wild on land near the California coast that had been of little value suddenly became a commodity that could be exchanged for foreign goods such as fabric, luxury foodstuffs, and religious goods. Multiyear contracts offered by traders indicated that the hide and tallow trade would be an ongoing proposition. Secularization and the continued strength of the foreign market in turn drove an economy centered on ranchos (large ranches) and gave increased prominence to rancheros (the holders of titles to these properties).[3]

Since nearly all the grants of land in Southern California were made by the Mexican government, it is useful to examine the process by which individuals could obtain grants under that system. Mexican land law stated that citizens could apply to the governor of California and receive grants of up to eleven leagues (about forty-eight thousand acres) of land. The procedure was relatively straightforward: the applicant sent a petition to the governor that included the request for land and the reason for the request, a description and sketch of the land, and personal information. The governor sent these materials to a local official, the *alcalde* (mayor), who attested to the petitioner's standing in the community and verified that the land was unoccupied. If the alcalde's report was positive, the governor would usually make the concession, and the alcalde would put the grantee in formal possession of his land. This typically involved conducting a survey of the land in the presence of neighbors. Once occupation and improvement conditions had been met, grantees submitted their request to the territorial legislature for approval, which, if granted, finalized the transfer.

Prior to the American takeover in July 1846, governors had made approximately 750 land grants.[4] These property holders had rights, and these were guaranteed protection under the 1848 Treaty of Guadalupe Hidalgo at the close of the Mexican-American War. At the time of the treaty, the U.S. Congress recognized the need for an institution to govern the transition but waited until after the Compromise of 1850 had guaranteed California's admission as a state to take action on property rights.

In the aftermath of the compromise, Congress faced a backlog of legislation as well as eighteen bills on California. The issue of land titles in the new state nevertheless received immediate attention, in the form of the California Land Act. The heart of the act was the requirement that "each and every person claiming lands in California by virtue of any right or title derived from the Spanish or Mexican government, shall present the same . . . together with such documentary evidence and testimony of witnesses as the said claimant relies upon in support of such claims." Individuals had to present these claims to a three-person land commission that would investigate and decide their validity. The act provided for the appointment of an agent whose duty it was to "superintend the interests of the United States." Both sides—the claimant and the U.S. government—had the right of appeal from the land commission to the U.S. district courts in California and from there to the U.S. Supreme Court. If the highest court that a claim reached confirmed its validity, the next step was to have the claim surveyed and resolve any boundary disputes. Once this was complete, the owner of the claim could receive a patent, which definitively established property rights under U.S. statutes.[5]

The Fate of Los Angeles Land Claims

The act gave owners two years to submit their claims to the land commission. Filing gave grantees the option, but not the obligation, of pursing their claim once the commission began hearing cases. Filing a claim was free. It appears that virtually everyone who held a grant filed a claim. By the March 1852 deadline, 813 land claims had been filed.[6]

An examination of statistical evidence for four Los Angeles–area land claims, San Pedro, Ballona, Alamos y Agua Caliente, and Jurupa, sheds light on the fate of such claims under the California Land Act. These claims represent a variety of grant dates, sizes, and outcomes. For two of the claims, there is additional evidence from partition suits in the 1860s. San Pedro, a Spanish grant to Juan Jose Dominguez of ten leagues in Los Angeles County, was regranted to Cristobal Dominguez, Juan Jose's nephew, in December 1822. Jurupa, seven leagues in Riverside County, was granted to Juan Bandini in September 1838. La Ballona, about three leagues in Los Angeles County, was granted to Agustin Machado, Ignacio Machado, Felipe Talamantes, and Tomas Talamantes in November 1839. Interestingly, the Ballona grantees had been in possession of the land for nearly two decades prior to the granting. Finally, Los Alamos, six leagues in Los Angeles County, was granted to Pedro Carrillo in October 1843.[7]

The outcome of the claims process was eventually favorable for three of the four claims. The land commission confirmed San Pedro, Ballona, and Jurupa. Confirmation meant that if there were no appeals, claimants could have their property surveyed and patented. The commission rejected Alamos y Agua Caliente because of nonperformance of the conditions of the grant, a common reason for rejecting a grant. The federal government appealed all three of the successful claims, and the federal district courts again confirmed each. The federal government appealed two of the three claims (San Pedro and Ballona) to the Supreme Court. In 1857, the government dropped its appeals in the San Pedro and Ballona cases. The government issued patents for San Pedro in 1858, Ballona in 1873, and Jurupa in 1879.

Table 3.1 presents evidence on how the size and grant date of Los Angeles–area land claims compared with other California land claims. Los Angeles County grants, desirable because of their proximity to the village and the port, were significantly smaller on average than grants elsewhere in the basin. And Los Angeles–area grants were smaller than other California land grants. The timing of these grants, however, was typical of California as a whole. Within the area, grants of land in Ventura County were made somewhat earlier than average, and grants of land in Riverside County were made somewhat later than average. This is a reflection of the fact that Riverside was considered to be

TABLE 3.1
Size and timing of land grants

Size	All	LA area	Los Angeles	Orange	Riverside	San Bernardino	Ventura
Number	802	145	88	18	13	7	19
SIZE IN SQUARE LEAGUES							
Smallest	0.00004	0.00004	0.00004	0.0036	0.5	1	0.0064
Largest	400	25	20	17	11	8	25
Average	4.4	3.6	2.7	5.6	4.6	4.3	5.6
Median	2.3	2	1	4.5	4	3	4
YEAR							
Earliest	1778	1781	1781	1784	1818	1838	1795
Latest	1846	1846	1846	1846	1846	1846	1846
Average	1839.2	1835.8	1837.5	1827.2	1842.2	1841.1	1836.2
Median	1841	1842	1843	1841	1844	1841	1837
Granted in 1840s	61%	61%	66%	56%	85%	57%	42%

Note: Grants that were ultimately patented under the California Land Act were assigned to modern counties based on the location of the majority of the acreage of the grant. So, for instance, a grant where 90 percent of the acreage was located in Los Angeles County and 10 percent in Orange County would be listed as located in Los Angeles County. Grants that were not patented were assigned to counties based on the best available information about location. Data on the original grants are based on R. H. Avina, "Spanish and Mexican Land Grants in California" (master's thesis, University of California, 1932); J. N. Bowman, "Index of the Spanish-Mexican Private Land Grant Records and Cases of California," Bancroft Library, 1958; O. Hoffman, "Reports of Land Cases Determined in the United States District Court for the Northern District of California, June Term 1853 to June Term 1858, Inclusive," San Francisco, 1862.

TABLE 3.2
Outcomes under the California Land Act

Confirmations	All	LA area	Los Angeles	Orange	Riverside	San Bernardino	Ventura
			LAND COMMISSION				
Total heard	788	144	87	18	13	7	19
Number confirmed	512	98	59	16	6	5	12
Percentage	65	68	68	89	46	71	63
			FEDERAL DISTRICT COURTS				
Total heard	591	110	58	16	12	7	17
Number confirmed	526	103	54	15	12	6	16
Percentage	89	94	93	94	100	86	94
			U.S. SUPREME COURT				
Total heard	92	8	4	1	3	0	0
Number confirmed	44	4	2	0	2	0	0
Percentage	48	50	50	0	67	NA	NA
			PATENTS				
Total	788	144	87	18	13	7	19
Number patented	627	120	67	16	12	6	19
Percentage	80	83	77	89	92	85	100

Note: Data based on J. N. Bowman, "Index of the Spanish-Mexican Private Land Grant Records and Cases of California," Bancroft Library, 1958; O. Hoffman, Reports of Land Cases Determined in the United States District Court for the Northern District of California, June Term 1853 to June Term 1858, Inclusive, San Francisco; with additional information on Supreme Court decisions from United States Supreme Court Reporters (various years).

relatively remote. Los Ángeles County had average timing, because individuals continued to request and receive grants that were further inland over time.

Table 3.2 documents the outcome of the land claims process for Los Angeles–area land claims and other California claims. The land commission confirmed roughly two-thirds of the cases both in the Los Angeles area and overall. Alamos y Agua Caliente was rejected because of nonperformance of the conditions of the grant. Other claims were rejected either because the original grant was made in violation of Mexican land law or because there was no evidence that a grant had been made. A large number of the commission's decisions were appealed; district courts confirmed 89 percent of all claims and 94 percent of the Los Angeles–area claims. The relative success of the claimants in Los Angeles County may be a reflection of the higher quality of the claims on average.

Southern district judge Isaac Ogier was, however, reputed to be more lenient than the northern district judge, Ogden Hoffman, so the success of Los Angeles claimants may be a reflection of judicial preference as well.[8]

While a number of decisions were appealed, the majority of these were dropped prior to being heard by the Supreme Court. Although Los Angeles–area claimants fared about as well as their counterparts in other sections of the state at the Supreme Court level, many fewer Los Angeles–area cases than average reached the Supreme Court. Los Angeles–area cases represented 18 percent of the land commission cases and 19 percent of the district court cases but only 9 percent of the Supreme Court cases. Thus Los Angeles–area landowners were more often spared the difficulty and expense of pursuing a land claim thousands of miles away in Washington DC.

Eighty percent of the claims in California were ultimately patented, and the Los Angeles area, at 83 percent, did slightly better than average. The patent rate varied from a high of 100 percent in Ventura County to a low of 77 percent in Los Angeles County. The lower percentage in Los Angeles County most likely reflects a number of factors, including the size of grants, the year granted, and whether the claimants had an *expediente* (a document of record for the grant issued by the Spanish or Mexican governor). In particular, because of the high value of some real estate in Los Angeles County, it might have been more attractive for individuals to pursue doubtful land claims than in the outlying counties. The salient point is that Los Angeles–area land claims fared about the same as other California land claims under the California Land Act.

The Burden of the Act on Los Angeles–Area Claimants

Although Los Angeles–area land claims fared reasonably well under the California Land Act, claimants were not so fortunate. To protect what claimants viewed as rightfully theirs, they had to undertake costly and time-consuming litigation. Some claimants, faced with lucrative offers or burdensome debts, sold part or all of their land. Those that persevered faced the threat of squatters. For those claimants who survived or escaped squatters, an agricultural depression of the early 1860s and the imposition of property taxes imposed additional hardship.

The average claim spent five years in litigation, appearing during that time before both the land commission and the federal district court. Legal fees for bringing a claim before the land commission typically fell between five hundred and fifteen hundred dollars. Appeals to the federal district courts cost one hundred to five hundred dollars. Lawyers sometimes agreed to work on a contingency basis, with the typical fee being one-quarter of the land to carry the claim through the land commission and the district court. For those claims that were appealed to the Supreme Court, legal fees were another six hundred to one thousand dollars. In addition to the lawyers' fees in land or money, claimants had to pay for other litigation expenses, the survey, and any boundary litigation, which necessarily added to an often high total expenditure. For instance, the Dominguez family incurred a total cost of more than twenty thousand dollars in obtaining a patent for Rancho San Pedro.[9]

As land became an increasingly marketable asset, some original grantees wanted or needed to realize that increment of value. Sale for profit or for necessity raises a problem when interpreting property transfers since these transfers may or may not have been a result of the Land Act. Nineteenth-century historian Theodore Hittell alleged that 40 percent of the land in Los Angeles County was alienated to meet the costs of litigation under the act. Some claimants undoubtedly did have to mortgage their property or sell undivided shares of their ranches to outsiders to fund litigation. Evidence on this point is sketchy and inconclusive, however.[10]

One form of evidence helps to clarify land transfers: partition-suit records. Prior to patenting and partition, individuals bought and sold undivided shares of an entire claim. At some point either before or after a patent was awarded, a partition suit was often brought in the local state district court to allow division of the land among multiple owners. Table 3.3 provides new evidence on ownership in the mid-to-late 1860s for five grants: Tajauta, Ballona, Cienega, San Pedro (all in Los Angeles County), and Valle de San Jose (in Alameda County). Documents related to these five partition suits were uncovered in the course of research on the California land grants.

The extent to which the families of the original grantees retained ownership of the land is striking. Indeed, the finding is so striking that it is worth questioning the results. One possibility is that the partition suits were conducted in family members' names although those individuals no longer owned the land. This seems unlikely, however, since all five partition suits contain at least one name that clearly belongs to an outsider.[11] Another possibility is that these five ranches are not representative of the experience of the 551 patents. Without a full search of the legal and historical archives for partition suits, it is impossible to determine how representative these five suits are. A priori, however, there is no reason to believe that they are not representative. The evidence suggests that in the mid-to-late 1860s grantees and their heirs may still have controlled a significant portion of the land then in private ownership in Los Angeles County and perhaps in California as a whole.

In some cases owners had to defend their property rights against the federal government, holding off encroachment from squatters. The majority of the

TABLE 3.3
Evidence from partition suits

Name	Share	Cumulative (percent)	Name	Share	Cumulative (percent)
RANCHO TAJAUTA (AKA LOS CUERVOS), JUNE 14, 1867 (PATENTED 1873)					
Jose Maria Abila	11/70	15.71	Emilina Mellus	1/210	87.62
Henrique Abila	11/70	31.43	Josephina Mellus	1/210	88.10
Felipe Abila	2/35	37.14	Edward Mellus	1/210	88.57
Juan Abila	2/35	42.86	Tomas Alvarado	1/70	90.00
Carnelio Abila	2/35	48.57	Delores Alvarado	1/70	91.43
Petra Abila	2/35	54.29	Andrea Alvarado	1/70	92.86
Louisa Abila	2/35	60.00	Lugardu Alvarado		
Juana Maria Abila	2/35	65.71	de Palomares	1/70	94.29
Soledad Abila	2/35	71.43	Julio Valenzuela	2/245	95.10
Vincente Elisalda	2/35	77.14	Nervio Valenzuela	2/245	95.92
L. D. Philips	2/35	82.86	Ascension Valenzuela	2/245	96.73
A. Dalidu, J. Alexander	1/35	85.71	Tomasa Valenzuela	2/245	97.55
Francis Mellus	1/210	86.19	Alfundo Valenzuela	2/245	98.37
James J. Mellus	1/210	86.67	Maria Valenzuela	2/245	99.18
A. Dalidu Mellus	1/210	87.14	Felipe Valenzuela	2/245	100
RANCHO LA BALLONA, MAY 1868 (PATENTED 1873)					
Estate of Aug. Machado	17/56	30.36	Fr. and Dal. Machado	1/48	92.86
A., J. A., R., C. Machado	7/32	52.23	Benina Talamantes	1/84	94.05
John D. Young	1/8	64.73	Gregoria Talamantes	1/84	95.24
Maced Aguilar	3/32	74.11	Tomasa Talamantes	1/84	96.43
Geo. Ad. Sanford	1/16	80.36	Pedro Talamantes	1/84	97.62
Elen. Young et al.	1/16	86.61	Jacinto Talamantes	1/84	98.81
Laurinao Talamantes	1/48	88.69	Jesus Talamantes	1/84	100
Manuel Valenzuela	1/48	90.77			
RANCHO LA CIENEGA, DEC. 1866 (PATENTED 1871)					
Henry H. Gird	1/5	20.00	Elizabeth Dalton	1/20	83.75
Francisca Abila			James A. Vandenburg	1/32	86.88
de Rimpau	1/5	40.00	John G. Carpenter	1/32	90.00
Januario Abila	1/5	60.00	William Andres	1/40	92.50
Antonio Urquidy	3/40	67.50	James H. Whitworth	1/40	95.00
Thomas Gray	1/16	73.75	Mariano Chavis	1/40	97.50
Matthew Lanfranco	1/20	78.75	Francisco Alvarado	1/40	100

TABLE 3.3
Evidence from partition suits

Name	Share	Cumulative (percent)	Name	Share	Cumulative (percent)
RANCHO SAN PEDRO, DEC. 1855, 1862, 1885 (PATENTED 1858)					
Manuel Dominguez	0.596	59.61	H. R. Myles	1/6	66.67
Conception R. de			P. Banning	1/6	83.33
Rodriguez & J. A. Aguirre	0.260	85.62	J. P. McFarland	1/12	91.67
Pedro & Maria de Jesus			J. G. Downey	1/12	100
Dominguez	0.105	96.12	Subdivision of 22,222 acres of Manuel		
Antonio M. Rocha	0.020	98.12	Dominguez's share, 1885		
Maria Rocha de Macado	0.019	100	One-sixth each to Ana Josefa D. de		
Subdivision of 2,423 acres of Manuel			Guyer, Guadalupe Dominguez, Maria		
Dominguez's share, Oct. 1862			D. D. de Watson, Victoria D. de Carson,		
B. D. Wilson	1/3	33.33	Susana Dominguez, and Maria de los		
M. Dominguez	1/6	50.00	Reyes Dominguez		

Name	Share	Cumulative (percent)	Name	Share	Cumulative (percent)
RANCHO EL VALLE DE SAN JOSE, 1868 (PATENTED 1865)					
Antonio Sunol	0.214	21.38	Jose Bernal	0.023	74.03
Leonard Hill +			Charles Duerr & Louis		
Martin Ambrose	0.054	26.82	Nusbaumer	0.023	76.30
Rafaela Felis y Bernal	0.045	31.35	John Botts	0.018	78.08
James Pedie	0.044	35.71	N. G. Patterson	0.017	79.83
Juan Pablo Bernal	0.036	39.28	William Mendenhall	0.014	81.26
Guadalupe Bernal	0.036	42.85	Juan Bernal, Junior	0.014	82.69
Lafayette Lagrange	0.036	46.42	A. Baker & Alex. Esdon	0.014	84.12
Juana Higuera Bernal	0.034	49.83	Dyonisio Bernal	0.014	85.55
Teresa Bernal Livermore	0.033	53.15	Delfina Bernal	0.014	86.98
Refugia Bernal Kottinger	0.026	55.72	Rita Bernal	0.014	88.41
Michael Rogan	0.024	58.12	Martin Mendenhall	0.013	89.71
Augustine Bernal	0.023	60.39	Thomas Hart	0.013	91.02
Maria Antonio Bernal	0.023	62.66	Abalino Bernal	0.011	92.16
Augustine Bernal Jr.	0.023	64.94	Presentacion Bernal	0.011	93.29
Maurice Bernal	0.023	67.21	Charles G. Garthwart	0.011	94.43
Jose Reyes Bernal	0.023	69.48	And 11 others	0.45	98.88
Angelina Bernal Neil	0.023	71.75			

Note: All five partition suits are located at the Huntington Library, San Marino, CA. Tajauta is 1200 (microfilm); Ballona, Cienega, and San Pedro are in the Solano-Reeve Collection; Valle de San Jose is 306995.

squatting took place in or near San Francisco, but Los Angeles–area grants suffered incursions as well. For instance, in 1855 Mission San Gabriel in Los Angeles County reportedly had between three hundred and five hundred squatters. In the late 1850s and early 1860s, Jurupa and San Bernardino were both sites for squatters who took up land. Then in the late 1860s and early 1870s, squatters staked claims on land held by the Mission San Buenaventura and Sespe in Ventura County. These are merely the cases that were reported in the popular press and likely represent but a fraction of the instances of squatting.[12]

To compound problems of adjudicating land titles, Southern California experienced an agricultural depression in the early 1860s. Drought, combined with a diminishing market for cattle, combined to leave some owners land poor. To pay taxes, service existing debt, and maintain their lifestyles, many formerly well-off owners mortgaged their properties, betting that the downturn was only temporary. Unfortunately, the drought continued and cattle died off (in some cases faster than they could be slaughtered for hides and tallow). Cattle that survived were sold at low prices as everyone tried to salvage what they could. Land, previously a source of income and a store of value that could be borrowed against, suddenly produced little or no income.

Tax obligations were roughly 2 percent of total wealth measured as real estate and personal property (chiefly cattle). Between 1852 and 1862, grazing lands in Los Angeles County and much of Southern California were valued for tax purposes at a standard $0.25/acre, with the value falling to $0.125 and then to $0.10 over the next two years. Cattle, previously valued for tax purposes at $4.50/head, fell to $3.00 and then to between $1.00 and $2.50. Prior to the drought, an average Los Angeles–area ranch of eighteen thousand acres (about four leagues) with two thousand cattle and $1,000 worth of horses and other taxable improvements required a tax payment of $290. Once the drought began, this figure fell to $185 and then to around $140. According to historian Robert G. Cleland, more than 85 percent of the property owners in 1864 Los Angeles were delinquent in paying taxes. Compared to litigation expenses for the ranches and probably the household expenses of many owners, tax payments were small, but finding any cash at all during the depression was problematic.[13]

The Fairness of the Land Act

The California Land Act was probably the only politically tenable solution to the problem of California land claims. Millions of acres of prime coastal and valley land were at stake in California. Two types of problems complicated the resolution of property rights. The first was the difficulty in determining whether property rights had been established under Mexican law. Grants were provisional, and few had complied with all of the conditions of their grants. Further, many grants had been made in violation of one or more tenets of Mexican land law. The second problem was the difficulty in determining boundaries of the land grants. When individuals applied for grants, they appended a *diseño* (a rough sketch) of the land. An 1849 report on land titles noted, "These sketches frequently contain double the amount of land included in the grants; and even now very few of these grants have been surveyed or their boundaries

TABLE 3.4
Property rights in acquired territory

Territorial acquisition	Acreage acquired	State	Confirmed claims	Confirmed acreage	Average size
Old Northwest and Old Southwest	525,452,800	Illinois	936	185,774	198
		Indiana	962	188,303	196
		Michigan	942	280,769	298
		Ohio	111	51,161	461
		Wisconsin	175	32,778	187
		Alabama	448	251,602	562
		Mississippi	1,154	773,087	670
Louisiana Purchase	523,446,400	Iowa	1	5,760	5,760
		Louisiana	9,302	4,347,891	467
		Missouri	3,748	1,130,051	302
		Arkansas	248	110,090	444
Florida	43,342,720	Florida	869	2,711,290	3,120
Texas	247,060,480	Texas			
Oregon Compromise	180,644,480	Oregon	7,432	2,614,082	352
		Washington	1,011	306,795	303
Treaty of Guadalupe Hidalgo	334,479,360	California	588	8,850,144	15,051
Gadsden Purchase	18,961,920	Arizona	95	295,212	3,107
		Colorado	6	1,397,885	232,981
		New Mexico	504	9,899,021	19,641

Source: Report of the Public Lands Commission, 1904, cited in P. W. Gates, *History of Public Land Law Development* (Washington DC: Zenger, 1978), 86, 92, 113, 118, 119.

fixed." The high quality of the land, the possibility of gold, and the large number of Americans who wanted land guaranteed that debate would be litigious and extensive.[14]

Aware of these problems, Congress considered several approaches to the land claims issue. Senator Thomas Benton, the father-in-law of John Fremont, owner of one of the most valuable claims in California, relentlessly championed confirmation. Confirming invalid claims would have been costly for Congress both in political and economic terms since it involved a government grant of additional land—land that was of high quality and possibly contained gold. Confirmation also carried the risk of widespread violence since many grants were already overrun with American squatters who believed, wishfully or otherwise, that the land was theirs for the taking.[15]

Three approaches were given more serious consideration. Using a land claims commission with a right of appeal to Congress, as Congress had done before, was likely to lead to delay and lobbying. The resolution of property rights under this system had been time consuming and could be unnecessarily protracted.[16] An appealing alternative was to retain a land claims commission and designate federal courts to hear appeals. Congress had not previously made district and supreme courts the only forums for appeal.[17] In doing so, Congress freed itself from much of the burden of confirmation and sharply limited the number of appeals that claimants could conduct. This freedom came at a cost—Congress had to pay for judges, defense, and other expenses, and it would not have the final word on the validity of land claims. The Committee on the Judiciary, which shaped the final bill, also discussed a hybrid approach that would have limited government appeals for claims smaller than 640 acres. Ultimately, the costs of fraud loomed too large. Senator John M. Berrien noted the committee had decided against adopting this approach because even claims of 640 acres could be extremely valuable if they encompassed mineral deposits.[18] The California Land Act, although imperfect, represented a politically expedient solution to a difficult problem.

This politically expedient solution also meant that land claimants in California fared well relative to other individuals holding grants to land that had been made by foreign governments. Table 3.4 shows the number of claims, the total number of acres claimed, and the average claim size for all such territory. Although California had comparatively few land claims, the size of the average claim, at 15,051 acres, was forty or fifty times larger than those of claims in most other states. Only Florida, at 3,120 acres, and Iowa, at 5,760 acres, had claim sizes that were even close. Land claims resulting from the Treaty of Guadalupe Hidalgo and the Gadsden Purchase also covered a larger portion of the acquired territory than did claims resulting from all other acquisitions except Florida. Despite this, 80 percent of California land claims were ultimately confirmed and patented.

Statistics have not been compiled on how rapidly claims were patented prior to the California cases. Anecdotal evidence suggests, however, that claimants of similar-sized grants elsewhere had spent decades before Congress and in the courts pressing their claims. In contrast, in California the average time from the filing of a land claim to the awarding of a patent was seventeen years. Thus an average claim had received a patent by 1870, or about twenty years after the passage of the California Land Act. The resolution of property rights was adjudicated in-state for 88 percent of the claims, not thousands of miles away in Congress or before the U.S. Supreme Court.

Following its experience in California, Congress abandoned the commission and court system. In New Mexico it required the surveyor general of the territory to investigate claims and make recommendations on confirmation to Congress. The surveyor general was not, however, given either the personnel or the budget to carry out this mandate. In the first annual report he observed that "the present law has utterly failed to secure the object for which it was intended." This approach proved so ineffectual in resolving property rights that Congress found it necessary in 1891—nearly forty years after acquisition—to establish a Court of Private Land Claims. This court finished its work in 1904. About 24 percent of New Mexican land claimed was eventually confirmed and patented. This rate was about one-third that of California, and the resolution of property rights took decades longer.[19]

One hundred twenty of the 144 Los Angeles–area claims submitted under the California Land Act—or 83 percent—were ultimately patented. This patent rate compares favorably with the overall patent rate in California of 80 percent. The claims process was both expensive and time consuming. Squatters, taxes, and a severe drought compounded claimant hardship. Scholars have long believed that the combined effect led many owners to sell their land or lose it through taxes or mortgages, but the evidence from partition suits indicates that land loss up to the mid-1860s may have been significantly smaller than previously reported.

The fairness of the California Land Act depends on the counterfactual scenario. If without the act, all claims would have been confirmed immediately and at no cost to the claimant, then the act was not fair. But this conjecture disregards key problems: many land claims overlapped, and in these cases confirmation would have led to protracted boundary litigation, possibly forcing one party to choose land elsewhere. Squatters, on the verge of rioting under the

California Land Act, could easily have staged a full-scale rebellion. Congress might have lost the revenue from the roughly 3 million acres that were not confirmed under the act.

If the California case is compared to the land claims processes that applied in other acquired territory, the California Land Act looks a bit better. The act resolved claims more quickly than had previous land acts. Whether the outcomes for California land claims would have been more favorable under previous acts is difficult to tell because only a small number of claims greater than five thousand acres had ever been submitted under previous acts. Given the high patent rate in California, it seems unlikely that outcomes there would have been better. The more relevant comparison for California may be New Mexico. New Mexico was acquired during the same period and was also covered with large grants; its claims process moved extremely slowly and had a much less favorable outcome. In any event, one aspect of this complex and important chapter in the history of Southern California is that environmental issues, especially the deleterious effects of drought, played an undoubtedly critical role in undermining what the California Land Act of 1851 seemingly, if briefly, upheld: the legitimacy of property rights established during previous national, and ethnic, regimes.

PART TWO
Land Use and Governance

By the end of the nineteenth century, greater Los Angeles had clearly come up against environmental limitations in profound ways. Sustainable development would not be a phrase with any meaning for nearly another century, yet it had become clear to individuals and institutions (public, civic, and commercial) that environmental obstacles posed actual obstacles to growth and that ongoing change in the present would structure visions of the future.

To be sure, systems of environmental control, which are the focus of this section, sprang from fairly straightforward understandings, and even convictions, of nature as obstacle. Aesthetic appreciation of natural beauty or perceptions of the necessity of open space within city boundaries—viewpoints which can be found in early-twentieth-century Los Angeles—were undoubtedly secondary to the primacy of controlling nature.

On the one hand, this is historically understandable. Los Angeles was, as both Blake Gumprecht and Jared Orsi illustrate, a pueblo, village, town, and then city with a tempestuous relationship with local watersheds. Given the geological shape of the Los Angeles basin (a feature John McPhee discusses explicitly), the region's rivers had difficult jobs to do. In periods of heavy winter rains, the Los Angeles River, the major riparian artery on the landscape, must carry significant amounts of water to the sea, and it must do so on a landscape veritably tipped up so that stream flow and velocity are maximized by fifty miles of gravitational pull. Gumprecht and Orsi describe the region's love-hate relationship with the mercurial Los Angeles River. Periodic floods have enlarged the river's channel and on occasion altered its course. Urban growth and metropolitan expansion have accelerated the costs attendant to property damage and related destruction. Orsi and Gumprecht explore in detail the increasing complexity of environmental problems at the scale of a regional system.

Nineteenth-century contests over the control of land and its use continued into the twentieth century as investors, boosters, and entrepreneurs strove to shape development in a rapidly growing metropolis. As Daniel Johnson argues, a historical understanding of air quality issues and rising regional awareness of changing atmospheric conditions requires scholarly sensitivity to class realities within the urban core of turn-of-the-century Los Angeles. Avoiding the oft-resorted-to tendency simply to name an arrival date for Los Angeles smog, Johnson examines municipal policy and electoral politics in the working-class wards of Los Angeles to track the impacts of (and responses to) the omnipresent environmental degradation in an industrializing economy. His analysis reveals the unfortunate and seemingly inevitable conflict over differential patterns of environmental threats in the form of various airborne and other toxic assaults and the long history of what we now call environmental inequity.

By the 1920s, industrial Los Angeles had become synonymous with oil. Paul Sabin explores in detail the various ways in which oil companies and their allies worked around, or often simply in the face of, legal restrictions designed to protect the California coastline from the environmental damage caused by oil exploration and processing. His chapter is a reminder that more recent California battles over the intersection of commerce and environment, whether the focus is water, forests, property rights, or air quality, have a long and complex history, especially in the greater Los Angeles region.

It was in the 1910s and 1920s that Los Angeles physician John Randolph Haynes rose to prominence in the progressive juggernaut of regional reform. Tom Sitton examines the role the Haynes Foundation, a philanthropic institution begun by Haynes and the oldest such entity in Los Angeles, has played in Southern California and state politics through its ongoing investment in research and scholarship into land use that could be put to effective political use. Haynes, who died in the 1930s, would not have known the term sustainable development, but he would have understood it, and Sitton suggests that his foundation has done significant work since the founder's death precisely in that realm.

Christopher Boone provides a late-twentieth-century bookend to Johnson's account of pollution, politics, and power. Boone's study of land use regulation, specifically zoning, and the siting of manufacturing in the Industrial East Side of Los Angeles examines the origins of environmental inequity. He examines the factors that might explain a correlation between hazardous facilities and the housing of specific racial/ethnic groups living in conditions of relative poverty. Boone's account reveals the processes that produced current patterns of "toxic racism." This knowledge, he contends, is foundational for crafting policy that might address past inequity and ensure equity in the future.

The last word in this section belongs to John McPhee. His investigation of the debris flow problem in the San Gabriel Mountains above the Los Angeles basin, aside from being one of the inspirations for this book, acts as a comment on the forays into flood control and watershed management by Gumprecht and Orsi.

This section begins with a different kind of case study. Terry Harkness's imaginative place study reveals processes of environmental change at a single site along the San Gabriel foothills and offers an accessible venue by which to understand the interaction of place, time, and landscape.

Folio Two: Lost Landscapes/Past Lives

TERRY HARKNESS

This visual history of Southern California citrus culture identifies significant structures and processes that have defined the Southern California landscape in imagination, experience, and place, a distillation of the physical setting: the powerful earthquake, the wild chaparral fire, the mudslide and debris torrent, the ever present reality of millennial geology in a semiarid Mediterranean climate.

California has been a dramatic stage and host to a myriad of competing ideologies, myths, dreams, and aspirations. It has been the setting of economic, material, and practical conflict for native and immigrant generations. The playing out of this history has occupied an imaginative center for Californians as well as all other Americans. Recent and massive landscape alterations to Southern California have erased many local landscapes that spoke to many competing issues and experiences about human aspirations and their physical expression on the landscapes of California. One persistent and powerful American dream as acted out in Southern California was of a life of direct, productive work; modest material comfort; and earned leisure and culture, where one could afford a piece of land with a home and garden and secure the independence to achieve these. Another reality paralleled this life in California, a physical history of gradual and catastrophic natural regimes; a semiarid Mediterranean climate of sun, drought, and winter rainstorm; mountain building; erosion and debris flows; intermittent and unexpected earthquakes and wildfires. This folio is an interpretative dialogue of landscape and lives, place and personal history, focusing on the agrarian expression of Southern California citrus culture from 1870 to 1940, located on the uplands fronting the San Gabriel, San Bernardino, and San Jacinto mountain ranges from Pasadena to Redlands, a seventy-five-mile visual, natural, and cultural transect.

Along the semiarid San Gabriel front, the native inhabitants and lightning burned the grasslands, firing thousands of acres of mountain chaparral in fall and spring. Innumerable mud and boulder slides slipped across the precipitous mountain slopes and buried the lands directly below. Ranchers settled and guarded the foothill canyons to capture and collect the trickling water that in flood times became a torrent of liquefied mud and boulders. During times of drought, residents of the ranchos in the basin went to the canyon ravines to harvest water in wagons. When the railroads arrived, a second California gold rush triggered a frenzy of speculation and spawned a unique orchard culture of small family farms of ten to twenty acres that soon covered thousands of acres of alluvial fans below the San Gabriel mountain range. By the 1890s agricultural groves and the dispersed citrus communities had developed to such an extent that the red cars of the Pacific Electric interurban lines had linked all the valley and foothill communities of the Los Angeles basin.

By the 1930s naturalist recluses had established themselves in the canyon mouths and glens above the citrus communities, their mountain stations a short hike from the communities below. These canyon hideaways were settled by the local John Muirs and John Burroughs of the adjacent foothill towns. Settlement at the edge of the mountain ridges and valley fans was a contrast of escapist scenes of pines, California sycamores, and live oaks clustered along steep, shaded canyon glens. Living high on the ridges, foothill residents looked out across valley panoramas extending all the way to the ocean and the Channel Islands beyond. Even on the hottest summer nights, refreshing breezes flowed off the mountain faces to cool the canyon ravines. Pearl Harbor and World War II brought an end to the San Gabriel foothill citrus culture and the landscape of windbreaks, orchards, and towns. The land consumption for housing development diffused over the entire valley of orange groves, stretching right up to the mountain front. As if overnight a megalopolis was in place; an urban or suburban landscape had replaced an agrarian culture of citrus, vineyards, and small service towns.

The place and paradoxes are astonishing; the region is a tracery of faults. The San Gabriels are battered and crumbling from mountain building, earthquakes, and mass erosion. The Santa Ana winds and chaparral fires on steep slopes followed by spring rains bring catastrophic mudslides and debris flows.

These graphic reconstructions remind us of physical elements and histories of rapid change, contested visions, entangled experience, and memory that are common to our varied pasts and evolving futures.

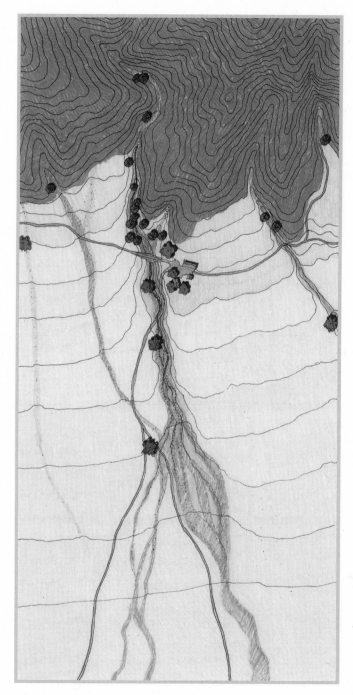

Gabrielino/Mission/Rancho Landscape 1770–1850.

Dry Farming/Grazing/Dry Fruit Culture 1850–1870.

Early Citrus Orchard Culture 1875–1885.

High Citrus Orchard Culture 1890–1910.

Urban/Suburban Land Conversion 1920–1985.

4

Pollution and Public Policy at the Turn of the Twentieth Century

DANIEL JOHNSON

I N April 1907 businessman J. W. Eddy addressed the Los Angeles City Club. He warned its members that air pollution had become "an aggressive nuisance and unless dealt with radically and heroically [it] will soon become unbearable." He urged municipal leaders to take action so that future generations could enjoy "our pure air and clear skies uncontaminated with soot and grime, or nauseating and poisonous fumes."[1] Eddy's comments provide both an uncomfortably accurate prediction of the future and an indication of how very early in the city's history pollution became a matter of public policy debate.

At the turn of the century there was a growing awareness of the environmental degradation caused by economic and demographic growth. Important steps were taken to grapple with this issue, most notably the institution of zoning laws that segregated industrial and residential districts. However, efforts to create effective pollution controls were often curtailed by economic, political, and social considerations. Calls for municipal action were checked by the influence of corporations, the ardent desire of civic boosters for rapid economic diversification, and the drive for frugal government. The result was public policy that often focused primarily on encouraging economic growth rather than preserving the city's environment and that all too readily subordinated the interests of Los Angeles' poorer citizens to the goals and ambitions of the wealthy and powerful.

For those who envisioned Los Angeles as a major metropolis, there was much to cheer about in the first decade of the century. As late as the 1870s, Los Angeles was a relatively small city, its economy dominated by cattle raising and wine making. In the 1880s, however, the city's population began to expand, as people flocked to Southern California to enjoy its salubrious climate. Between 1900 and 1910 this growth became explosive, with the city's population tripling from 102,479 to 319,198. This demographic flood fueled a tremendous building boom and an economy driven by real estate development and tourism. At the same time, many civic elites and business interests became convinced that the city's future would not be secure without the ability to diversify and expand the economy through industrial development. Their aspirations quickly began to be realized. Between 1899 and 1904 the total value added by manufacturing grew from $7,046,000 to $16,125,000, and by 1909 it would nearly double again to $29,673,000.[2]

Both demographic growth and industrial expansion produced significant environmental problems. The amount of garbage produced by this swelling population, for instance, quickly overwhelmed the antiquated disposal system, while rising demands for liquid gas led to the expansion of petroleum-fired plants that spewed smoke and soot over the city. Industrial smoke stacks and noxious industries similarly soiled Los Angeles' fabled climate, creating health hazards, damaging property values, and touching off a fierce debate over public policy and pollution controls. Citizens whose economic fortunes were vested in traditional residential real estate development and homeowners interested in preserving the health and economic value of their neighborhoods clashed with those invested in diversifying the economy.

The city's political system often proved inadequate to deal with the environmental challenges created by growth. In the first few years of the century, Los Angeles' government was still dominated by machine politicians whose desire for personal profit or the political support of public utilities and industrial corporations frequently trumped any concern for the welfare of their constituents. Even in instances where corruption did not play an overt role in shaping their environmental policies, these politicians generally favored economic expansion, regardless of the cost to residential districts. By 1906 a growing progressive reform movement had begun to reshape the city's political system. While some significant efforts were made by reform administrations to grapple with pollution problems, these efforts were also limited. Middle-class reformers often proved as eager to promote industrial development as had machine politicians. Moreover, while they were less likely to be influenced by corruption, their vision of cost-effective city government unfortunately also meant that environmental considerations sometimes took second place to fiscal prudence.

These debates over public policy and the management of environmental problems took place within the context of certain social realities. In general terms, the city was geographically divided between affluent middle-class West

Side neighborhoods and the less wealthy residential areas of blue-collar workers and lower-middle-class citizens to the east (see table 4.1).[3] Local newspapers commonly noted this distinction, referring to the working-class section as "east of Main Street." The only significant exception was the predominately blue-collar Second Ward, lying west of Main Street. Most of the industrial development in this era, and the pollution that accompanied it, took root in the East Side, with its easy access to transportation facilities and a ready labor supply.

While industrial development benefited working people by providing jobs, two factors tended to moderate their enthusiasm. High levels of home ownership meant that many workers had a direct economic stake in preserving their neighborhoods. Quite aside from concerns over lifestyle and health, workers protested the presence of polluting factories and public infrastructure because it directly threatened the value of their homes. Also, because of the real estate boom, unemployment remained fairly low during this period, with the exception of a recession in 1908.[4] Thus, for blue-collar workers whose neighborhoods and homes were being crowded by emergent industries, the protection of their neighborhoods from pollution may well have taken precedence over job creation. This ambivalence or outright hostility toward industrial development frequently put them at odds with public policy makers and civic elites eager for economic growth (see table 4.2).

TABLE 4.1
Occupations of male citizens, by wards, 1900 (percent)

	East Side wards					West Side wards			
Occupation	Sixth	Seventh	Eighth	Ninth	First	Second	Third	Fourth	Fifth
Skilled	37	50	44	33	43	40	29	23	23
Unskilled	10	9	28	17	12	13	4	4	7
Blue collar	47	59	72	50	55	53	33	27	30
Clerical	17	15	6	16	11	15	22	24	19
Managerial	3	2	2	3	4	4	2	3	7
Professional	6	3	1	4	6	6	11	11	10
Proprietor	17	14	11	11	13	13	19	20	17
White collar	43	34	20	34	34	38	54	58	53
Not given/ other	11	7	7	16	12	9	13	14	17

Source: U.S. Bureau of the Census, *Twelfth Census of the United States: 1900* (Washington DC: Government Printing Office, 1901). Figures based on a 20 percent sampling of the manuscript census.

The contradiction between economic diversification and preservation of residential districts first became evident during the oil boom of the 1890s. Residents of Los Angeles had long been aware of the region's petroleum resources. Native Americans had sometimes waterproofed their basketry with locally occurring tar, while the Spanish and Mexican *pobladores* (settlers) had used this *brea* to seal their roofs. It was not until the 1890s, however, that American entrepreneurs such as Edward Doheny began to systematically exploit the city's natural oil reserves. By 1897 the area bounded by Figueroa, First, Union, and Temple streets was home to more than five hundred wells, while another two thousand dotted a broad swath of the northern part of the Second Ward, stretching from Elysian Park to Vermont Avenue. Many civic boosters eagerly greeted this bonanza. The city was just emerging from the depression of the early 1890s, and concerns about Los Angeles' economic future ran high. It was argued that exploitation of local oil supplies would not only directly stimulate the economy, but also aid in attracting industrial development by providing an abundant source of cheap energy.[5]

While some viewed the petroleum industry as a possible new basis for the city's economy, others noted its capacity for destruction. As Charles Lockwood describes it, "The oil boom had ruined one street after another in Los Angeles. Entire neighborhoods had vanished under the forest of wooden derricks and a grimy film of oil, and the roar of escaping natural gas and the ump-um-ump-um . . . never ceased." Writing in 1944, at a time when Los Angeles was being rapidly industrialized by the war, a longtime resident of the city recalled that "I lived thru the period of former oil drilling campaigns and saw beautiful sections of this city ruined and I hope that such will never come again. . . . Human greed and avarice, unless restrained, would destroy our beautiful beaches, our residential areas, without any compunction." Indeed, the primitive drilling technology of the era ensured the proliferation of problems. Excess crude from uncapped wells frequently poured out onto the streets, flowing down gutters into the residential sections. Prior to the turn of the century these problems

TABLE 4.2
Home ownership, by ward, 1900 (percent)

East Side wards					West Side wards			
Sixth	Seventh	Eighth	Ninth	First	Second	Third	Fourth	Fifth
59	29	18	52	55	35	25	44	56

Source: U.S. Bureau of the Census, *Twelfth Census of the United States: 1900*, vol. 1, pt. 2 (Washington DC, Government Printing Office, 1903), 702.

went largely unchecked. Recognizing the potential importance of petroleum production for the local economy, city officials were reluctant to interfere. As Mayor Meredith P. Snyder observed in 1897, "This is one of the leading industries in the city, and all legislation bearing on it should be liberal."[6]

After 1900 efforts to regulate the oil industry met with somewhat greater success. In part this was due to the collapse of oil prices in 1901 and a new cycle of real estate speculation. With petroleum considered less crucial for the economy, there were calls to beautify the city and tear down the hundreds of abandoned derricks littering the landscape and to halt the flooding from uncapped wells. Such interest came not only from the blue-collar and lower-middle-class white-collar inhabitants of the Second Ward, which housed most of these drilling operations, but also from homeowners in the silk stocking wards to the south, who were aghast at the odorous black crude traveling down to their exclusive neighborhoods. The city council ordered nonfunctioning derricks to be torn down and charged its oil supervisor with the task of cracking down on the problem of runoff. Unfortunately, these regulations proved less than effective. In 1907, for instance, the oil inspector attempted to cite twenty owners of

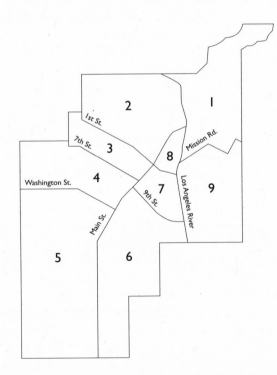

Figure 4.1. Los Angeles wards, 1908. Courtesy Daniel Johnson.

derelict wells, only to have the cases thrown out by the court, which ruled that the original ordinance was unconstitutional (see figure 4.1).[7]

The social, economic, and political circumstances surrounding the city's regulation of the gas industry were even more complicated. During the late nineteenth and early twentieth centuries, most gas used in lighting and heating was produced in plants that converted coal or petroleum into a gaseous form. This process produced significant pollution problems. Some by-products were transitory, such as smoke and soot, while others were more permanent, such as the tarry residue left over from the conversion process. Despite these problems, the industry continued to expand. A boom in residential construction enlarged the market for gas. The LA Gas and Electric Company met much of this demand. Residents of the working-class Eighth Ward had long complained about the air pollution produced by the LA Gas and Electric Company's plant on Aliso Street. In their 1903 petition to the council, they graphically described the problem: "Great clouds of dense black smoke, charged with greasy soot and cinders, and noxious, ill-smelling gases, constantly arise from the many short smokestacks maintained by the company. This smoke and all its oily dirt and filth settles and is driven by the winds from all directions over our places of residence or business and into our houses, warehouses and factories, through doors, windows, and even through cracks in the walls, permeating and soiling our clothes, household goods and manufactured articles and making it a burden to live or do business in the section."[8]

The neighborhood suffered as well from other problems attendant on the gas plant. Explosions resulting from the gas-making process rocked the area, shaking nearby homes hard enough to crack the plaster from their walls; streets were frequently reduced to a pitiful condition, as oil and lampblack from leaking carts mixed with mud to create a slippery mess; and the nearby Los Angeles River, into which the company dumped its refuse, became choked with a greasy stream of oily residue, which flowed south into the blue-collar Seventh and Sixth wards. Protests proved of little avail, in large part because of the company's close ties to neighborhood political machines. Ward representatives often depended on the company to provide the money, patronage, and campaign workers to retain their power. In return, the council often ignored the complaints leveled against the company and worked to shut out competitors, giving LA Gas and Electric a near monopoly on local markets.[9]

Ironically, in other instances the close relationship between the LA Gas and Electric Company and municipal politicians worked to the advantage of working-class residents. The company's poor service and inability to rapidly expand to meet new demand infuriated many people, including civic elites, who wished to encourage, at any cost, the development of competition. Those blue-

collar citizens whose neighborhoods were directly threatened by these new
plants did not necessarily agree. The horrendous problems associated with this
industry created an understandable antipathy amongst the residents of the East
Side toward the creation of new gasworks in their neighborhoods.

One of the most intense battles was fought over the establishment of the
Suburban Gas Company in the Eighth Ward. When the company presented its
proposal to establish a plant on St. John Street near the river, it was greeted
with delight by local manufacturers interested in the supply of cheap coke fuel
that would result from the gas-making process and, more generally, by civic
boosters who wished to break the LA Gas and Electric Company's monopoly
control of the industry.[10]

The residents of the affected area were of a decidedly different mind. As the
city's fire commission began consideration of the company's permit on November 15, 1901, nearly one hundred men and women, mostly small homeowners,
crowded into the room to protest against the plant. A week later the room was
similarly crammed by spectators waiting to hear the commission's decision.
When it voted to allow the permit, the crowd reacted with a brief, stunned
silence, and then, according to local newspaper coverage, erupted into
protest.[11]

> A hum arose all over the room, which quickly developed into a rumble
> and then into an indignant outpouring of speech on the part of Eighth
> Warders. Excited women made surreptitious grabs towards the com-
> missioners' hair while they muttered maledictions upon the men whom
> they accused of betraying the public trust. The men were louder and
> more boisterous in protest. 'So that means that this board will take away
> our property and our homes from us,' declared an elderly man with a
> patriarchal white beard. "I can hardly believe it possible that such men
> as you would . . ." and the old man turned his head away to hide emo-
> tion.[12]

This kind of response, coupled with substantial political pressure from the
established gas monopoly, ultimately convinced the city council to overturn
the fire commission's decision. They redrew the zone in which gasworks could
be constructed, effectively banishing the rival company from the city. Despite
the council's action, Suburban Gas refused to stop construction, arguing that
the fire commission permit was sufficient. The battle between the Eighth Ward
residents and Suburban Gas continued until April 1902, when both federal and
local courts ruled against the company.[13]

The rejection of new gasworks by working-class residents and machine
politicians provoked considerable agitation in the press. With their potential

competitors shut out, the LA Gas and Electric Company easily maintained its monopoly, a monopoly that potentially threatened to constrict a booming real estate market dependent on rapid and efficient expansion of public utility infrastructures. Refusing to give any legitimacy to protests emanating from the affected areas, the *Los Angeles Express*, a reform newspaper, asserted that "citizens are clamoring for a liberal policy toward the corporations that are seeking to secure a foothold in Los Angeles." The *Times* similarly dismissed claims that manufacturing would lead to pollution problems: "It would certainly be unpleasant to see Los Angeles overhung with a mantle of smoke from factory chimneys, but then, in the first place, we can make the factories consume their smoke, and in the second place, with trolley cars running 100 miles an hour or so, we can easily get out into the open." These optimistic assessments reflected a far different perspective than that voiced by residents whose lives would be affected.[14]

Class, political corruption, and larger economic concerns also emerged as key themes in the struggle over the expansion of the meatpacking industry in Los Angeles. Packers chose to set up plants in the city to meet the growing demand of a local market. The smells and effluent of this industry sparked protests in the working-class neighborhoods that had been designated as a meatpacking district. These concerns came to a head in 1904 when Julius Hauser, a local meatpacking magnate, began construction of a new slaughterhouse in the Sixth Ward, on East Twenty-ninth Street near Lemon. The sudden appearance of Hauser's construction crews shocked residents, since the entire ward was beyond the boundaries of the slaughterhouse district—or so they thought. In fact, in April the council had hurried through an ordinance extending the district to this site, without discussion or notice to adjacent residents. At the same time, the council's board of public works abandoned several streets to the Hauser Company. Outrage against the new plant spread beyond the Sixth Ward, since its location ensured that it would also affect blue-collar neighborhoods in the Seventh and Ninth wards. Public indignation was sparked by revelations that several councilmen had personally profited from the Hauser deal. The most obvious mark of this could be found on the huge piles of lumber that littered the construction site, all of them bearing the label of Nofziger & Brothers Lumberyard, the business owned by the councilman for the Ninth Ward.[15]

A few weeks earlier construction had begun on two slaughterhouses in the Eighth Ward. The sections affected had long been within the established district, and in fact one of the plants was a replacement for a building that burned down in May 1904. Nonetheless, the ward's citizens desired surcease from the ghastly pollution caused by the slaughterhouse operations, particularly since one of the proposed sites lay close to a school attended by six hundred children.[16]

This building spurt led to increased political activism by the residents of the four working-class wards. At the council's June 26 meeting, protesters packed city hall, seeking relief from these encroachments. As the *Los Angeles Record* sympathetically reported, "The lobby was filled with men and women whose years of toil have been productive of ownership of small cottages. They came to fight for the preservation of those little homes, all that they had. They knew that the smells of the slaughter houses, the dying cries of the animals, the stench and filth would drive them from those cottages which represented the work of years. Opposed was the power of enormous wealth behind the millionaire butchers. Contrasted with the set, determined faces of the workmen were the suave smiles of the highly paid attorneys who laughed at the feeble efforts of the property owners."[17]

Faced with the prospect of political protest, the council ordered the owners of the slaughterhouses to cease construction until a resolution could be achieved. Both Bob Todd, councilman for the Eighth Ward, and James Davenport of the Sixth concurred with this move, though Davenport, perhaps unwisely, complained that his constituents were responsible for not objecting earlier and that he regretted "that the matter should come up in this shape for the reason that we want to encourage manufacturers to locate in the Sixth Ward. The territory lying east of Alameda street makes an ideal manufacturing district."[18]

The political firestorm had only just begun. Night after night hundreds and thousands of citizens in the affected wards met to issue proclamations and lambaste the council. A mass meeting of the residents from the Sixth, Seventh, Eighth, and Ninth wards contemptuously dismissed council arguments that the new factories would bring wealth and new jobs to the city, and passed resolutions attacking their actions: "Resolved, By the citizens of Los Angeles in mass meeting assembled, that we condemn in unmeasured terms our city council for fastening upon our citizens an unmitigated nuisance in defiance of the interests of the city and the wishes of the people." In the Ninth Ward, the voters had long tolerated the machinations of ward boss E. L. Blanchard and his disciple, Councilman O. E. Nofizger, but the angry assemblies mustered there threatened to "wreck the Blanchard political machine if it is used to put men in office who confiscate homes for the purpose of increasing lumber sales." In the Sixth, several hundred residents proposed to invoke the initiative and "carry their cause to the citizens generally and ask, in the name of justice, that their homes be protected."[19]

Resistance to slaughterhouses quickly became entangled with a concurrent political development: the effort to recall James Davenport, the councilman from the Sixth Ward. Labor unionists angry at Davenport's services to corporate employers had begun the campaign, but it had also attracted the financial and institutional support of the middle-class reform movement just beginning to arise in Los Angeles. This latter group was interested in the recall for two reasons: the removal of Davenport, a typical machine politician, would serve as a powerful demonstration of the recently enacted recall provisions, and Davenport's actions in awarding the city printing contract to the *Los Angeles Times* had infuriated E. T. Earl, owner and publisher of the *Los Angeles Express* (the journalistic flagship of the progressive reform movement). The alliance of unionists and middle-class reformers sought to capitalize on the high emotions surrounding the slaughterhouse issue by accusing Davenport of being a key figure in the effort to bring slaughterhouses to the Sixth Ward. The *Los Angeles Times*, an archconservative paper that backed the beleaguered councilman, complained that his opponents "harped upon [the slaughterhouse issue] continually, magnifying it beyond all reason and endeavoring to create a sentiment against Davenport among his own people." This strategy worked perfectly, and in September 1904 James Davenport suffered the first recall of a public official in U.S. history.[20]

Thoroughly frightened by Davenport's recall, the council finally agreed to the removal of the Hauser plant from the Sixth Ward, though not gracefully. As one councilman, Owen McAleer, bitterly noted, "because a few people of the Sixth and Seventh wards, who, I doubt if they are even citizens of the United States who live on sand lots worth probably $75 each, come here and cry against the proposed building of a great industry in the city, we are stampeded and want to shut out every business."[21]

While the Hauser plant in the Sixth Ward had been successfully halted, the other slaughterhouses being constructed in the Eighth Ward continued to arouse controversy. Unable to rouse the council to ban these facilities as well, angry East Side residents began an initiative campaign to put a measure on the 1904 ballot barring slaughterhouses from the city entirely. Although successful in collecting sufficient signatures for their measure, they also faced mounting resistance from the city's business interests. On July 18 fifty merchants and manufacturers filed a counterpetition with the council asking that the slaughterhouse district remain untouched, arguing that "Los Angeles is a fast growing city—not a backwoods village."[22]

Both the reform-minded *Express* and the conservative *Times* shared this opinion. Eager to see Davenport recalled, the *Express* had supported efforts to halt the construction of the Sixth Ward plant. It drew the line, however, at further obstruction of manufacturing interests, arguing, "The conditions governing are by no means the same as in the Sixth Ward instance. In one case the slaughterhouses were on the ground first and those who have bought property and built houses in the vicinity of such plants have done so with their eyes open." The *Times* was even more adamant, enthusiastically backing the successful efforts of meatpackers to put their own initiative measures on the ballot, including one sponsored by the Hauser company that would reopen the Sixth Ward slaughterhouse district, a position supported as well by the Chamber of Commerce and the powerful Merchants' and Manufacturers' Association.[23]

Abandoned by its middle-class allies and facing well-organized opposition from the business community and the local political machines, the working-class effort to ban the slaughterhouses faltered. While all but one East Side ward passed the measure to bar these institutions from the city, the silk stocking wards of the West Side overwhelmingly voted the measure down. Of the four slaughterhouse propositions placed on the ballot, only one passed: the measure that not only affirmed their presence in the Eighth Ward, but also reopened the area claimed by the Hauser interests in the Sixth Ward. The movement's organizers commented on the bitter sentiment among their followers toward the residents of the silk stocking Fourth and Fifth wards, "who live in fine homes and apparently are willing to have the slaughterhouses located in other districts."[24]

In the period following the slaughterhouse protests, East Side residents intensified their activism. The pace of industrial development quickened between 1904 and 1907, advanced in part by the flight of capital from San Francisco following the 1906 earthquake. Working-class residents greeted these developments with mixed emotions. While they benefited from the overall prosperity of the city, they also suffered unpleasant ramifications. By 1906, for instance, many homeowners had been forced to leave the Eighth Ward, driven out by the pollution that accompanied industrialization. Similar encroachments were taking place in the Sixth and Seventh wards and in the western sections of the First and Ninth.[25]

Concerned about the destruction of their neighborhoods, the residents of these areas vigorously resisted the introduction of polluting industries. The primary arena for this political opposition was the city's fire commission. The commission granted permits to operate steam and gasoline engines and acted as an informal zoning commission, a power that often placed the commissioners in the uncomfortable position of deciding between industrial development and citizens' desire to preserve the quality and value of their homes. Early in 1905, for instance, the residents of Gless Street in the Ninth Ward appeared before this body to protest the creation of a small brass foundry in the middle of a residential district. These men and women, mostly owners of small dwellings, were given short shrift by the commission. Frustrated by their inability to secure relief, the protesters continued their efforts with a campaign of direct harassment against the owners, including showers of rocks directed at the offending plant.[26]

The city's business elite complained that the work of the Merchants' and Manufacturers' Association and the Chamber of Commerce in bringing industrial concerns to Los Angeles was being undermined by such protests. "Capital is always timid," a business leader warned. "A business man expects strong inducements before he embarks in a new enterprise. There is a wide and fertile field here for development along manufacturing lines, but it is the people themselves who appear to hamper it most." One real estate developer similarly criticized this opposition, observing that "this talk of 'soiling the atmosphere' is 'country all over,' and a lot of nonsense. Such a thing wouldn't happen, but if it did happen it would be better to soil the atmosphere and be a great metropolis, even if one had to chop one's way through it downtown every day."[27]

Business interests received a sympathetic ear from Mayor Owen McAleer. McAleer, elected in 1904, was a classic machine politician. A supervisor at a local iron foundry, he hailed from the blue-collar First Ward and became something of a hero to working-class voters because of his opposition to Henry Huntington, the local streetcar magnate. However, in almost all other instances McAleer firmly tied himself to the interests of business. He opposed labor unions, agreed on the need to encourage capital investment, and dismissed the protesters who mobbed the fire commission, noting scornfully, "Everybody fancies he lives in a choice residence district." McAleer ordered the commission to favor industrial development whenever possible. The effort to enforce this edict fell to Martin Betkouski, the principal spokesman for the commission. Betkouski himself hailed from the working-class Second Ward—another district being rapidly transformed—and was a key figure in that district's Democratic political machine. His decisions, however, reflected his own interests as an industrialist and the concerns of the business community, rather than those of his working-class constituents: in almost every instance he supported the mayor's liberal policies toward manufacturing, regardless of the cost to local communities.[28]

The unresponsiveness of machine politicians to environmental concerns was also evident in sanitation policies, particularly in the collection and disposal of garbage. Residents of all sections of the city as well as prominent business interests had complained for years about the quality of the service a private contractor provided. In 1905 the board of health investigated and found that less than five tons of garbage was burned daily. Cities with a similar population burned eighty tons on average. The board of health attributed the relatively low volume to a failure to collect garbage and the contractor's practice of selling edible trash to local hog farmers. Most of the odiferous piggeries were located in the city of Vernon southeast of the Sixth Ward. Despite a flagrant violation of his contract, the noisome conditions caused by these practices, and the vociferous protests of health officials, the city council refused to discipline the garbage contractor. Many believed his close ties to the council not only won him the contract but enabled him to manipulate its terms. As one health commissioner bitterly complained, "This whole garbage business smells to high heaven, and all we can do is sit here with folded hands and pass resolutions."[29]

Ultimately the council agreed to build a city-owned crematory to dispose of garbage; the construction process was again shaped by politics. In a controversial decision, the council approved a contract with the Decarle Manufacturing Company for the construction of an incinerator. Councilman Arthur Houghton, who represented the Sixth Ward and was an independent elected in 1904 by organized labor, warned that Los Angeles was being charged twice what Atlanta had paid for a comparable facility and that Decarle incinerators did not have a good reputation. His colleagues ignored him. Many observers noted that all the contracts for the metal work went to the Baker Iron Works, a firm that had kept Owen McAleer on its salary as a superintendent despite his two years as a councilman and subsequent election as mayor. As one newspaper sardonically observed, "The deal has passed into municipal history as one of the queerest of all queer deals."[30]

While all segments of the city suffered from poor garbage collection, the East Side suffered the solution. Three wards were considered for the new incinerator: the Sixth, Seventh, and Eighth. In each ward property owners and residents protested strenuously against the placing of the noisome facility in their neighborhood. Ultimately, the council chose the Sixth Ward, represented by political outsider Arthur Houghton. By April 1906, after innumerable delays, which provoked fresh charges of corruption, the new structure was finally completed and the burning of garbage began, to the dismay of the ward's residents.[31]

The various struggles over industrial development and municipal garbage collection during this period clearly illustrate the deficiencies of environmental policies shaped by machine-style government. These policies all too often were influenced by personal interest and the desire to placate politically powerful corporations. Even in those instances where immediate political gain did not play a large part, elected officials demonstrated an eagerness to promote economic development despite the potential costs to their constituents. At times public pressure did force them to modify their tactics, and in other instances their immediate political interests coincided with those of their constituents, but on the whole they proved unresponsive to growing public concern over pollution issues—concerns particularly apparent in working-class districts.

By 1906, however, the structure of Los Angeles government had begun to change. In 1902 reformers secured passage of civil service and direct-democracy measures and followed this in 1904 with a successful drive to create an independent board of public works. In the election of 1906, candidates sworn to support political reform gained a majority on the council. The reformers had pledged to eliminate political corruption and to create a government more attuned to the needs of the people. Their promises offered hope to citizens who had found machine politicians unresponsive to their demands, and in several cases city government did become more active in addressing pollution issues.

There was certainly a growing political awareness of these issues. The Republican and Democratic candidates for mayor promised to make Los Angeles the "Paris of the West" and address the growing smoke problem created by the expansion of industries in the urban core. Even the *Los Angeles Times*, long a supporter of rapid industrial development, expressed alarm: "Sunshine and pure air have been potent factors in the growth of Los Angeles. There was a time when the city could boast truly of its healthful climate, but of late that boast has been an empty mockery. Too often the sun shines upon Los Angeles through a pall of dim smoke, and except when strong winds blow from the ocean, the air is poisoned with acrid fumes and choking dust. . . . We are ruining the climate of Los Angeles by poisoning the air with soot and dust."[32]

This statement highlights a key dilemma: industrial pollution had begun to tarnish the city's long-standing reputation as a healthful retreat for tourists, invalids, and others seeking to trade harsh conditions in the Midwest and East for life in an American Mediterranean. The potential damage to the city's housing market and tourist industries softened business opposition to environmental regulation. Indeed, the Los Angeles Chamber of Commerce added its voice to the groundswell of support for governmental intervention.[33]

Equally important were the voices of professional and reform institutions that joined together to demand action. These included the city's board of health, the Pure Food Commission of the LA County Medical Board, the state medical society, and various women's clubs. The overwhelming show of support for restrictive legislation forced the council to act. Even Barney Healy, the Eighth Ward councilman who had long been a political ally of the gas company (the heaviest polluter in the city), dared not oppose the antismoke ordinance, lest he suffer the wrath of his long-suffering constituents. A new law, passed in October 1907, created a system for classifying smoke density and established fines for stacks producing the most offensive form of smoke—"the thick, sooty kind that has made Pittsburgh famous"—for more than ten minutes per hour. East Side residents "rejoiced that a measure of relief is at hand."[34]

Residents of the working-class East Side could also take some comfort in the city's attempt to rationalize industrial zoning. Prior to 1908 Los Angeles regulated the placement of polluting enterprises through the decisions of the fire commission and a patchwork system of ordinances that created districts for specific industries. In 1908, however, a court challenge had overturned the commission's ability to restrict industrial development on grounds other than safety. This, coupled with the evident conflict between industrial and residential real estate development, inspired the council to pass an ordinance in 1909 making the entire city a residential district, except for specifically established industrial zones. This law was intended not only to protect homeowners from the encroachment of factories, but also to create districts where the right of industrialists to build their plants would go undisputed. Yet, neither the new zoning regulations nor the antismoke ordinance fully solved the endemic conflict over industrialization.[35]

To a great extent, business concern over environmental issues proved to be transitory. The *Los Angeles Times*, which published editorials about a smoke problem in 1907, once again promoted the need for industry during the recession of 1908. "We have heard so much about blue skies, mocking birds and the fragrance of the roses or the glory of the poppy bed that we resent any presence which casts a bit of smoke athwart the sunlight, or makes a noise to frighten the lark on the fence. We must realize that a community cannot eat sunshine, satisfy its hunger on the song of the bird, or make a salad out of poppies. The climate and its natural accompaniments have done wonders in making the city what it is, and their influence is abiding. But they have done so much we must now supplement them with manufacturing industries as props to sustain that already in existence."[36]

Henceforth it would remain steadfastly on the side of industrial development, at almost any cost. Moreover, despite the good intentions of the antismoke ordinance, the little evidence that exists suggests it was applied selectively. Enforcement was left to the overburdened police department, and newspapers reported that few companies were making any effort to comply.[37]

The new zoning ordinance similarly ran into problems. Which districts should become industrial and which residential quickly became a contested issue. Large sections of the city that already housed industries, such as the Eighth Ward, were simply confirmed in their status, but there were also efforts to add new industrial zones. These attempts often met with fierce resistance from local residents, a development viewed with considerable disgust by the *Los Angeles Times*. It editorialized, "While other cities and towns are encouraging manufacturers and even offering them bonuses to locate, the City Council of Los Angeles virtually says that a manufacturer cannot do business in this city without putting up a fight for the privilege—and with every advantage given to the opposition. The always-ready croakers against smokestacks and whirring wheels need not prove that the manufacturing proposition is objectionable; the burden of proof is placed on the would-be manufacturer. Unfair, silly and destructive to growth!"[38]

It soon became apparent that the *Times* was not alone in this sentiment. Within a few months of the ordinances' passage the city's business interests began pushing hard for concessions to manufacturing concerns. In October 1909 the council met with representatives from the Chamber of Commerce, the Merchants' and Manufacturers' Association, and the realty board to discuss the liberalization of the zoning law. The *Times* reported that the joint committee's purpose was to "dedicate a much larger area than is now set apart for industrial purposes so that factories seeking to establish themselves here may not first be required to run the gauntlet of rapacious property owners, as has been the case recently." Despite this lobbying, an effort to add five new industrial districts in June of the following year faltered under a deluge of protests, and ultimately only one additional industrial zone was created.[39]

In 1910, under continued pressure from the business community, the council, now firmly controlled by progressive reformers, agreed to revise the zoning law. A variety of organizations were consulted on the planned changes, including a special committee created at the request of the council, consisting of representatives from the Chamber of Commerce, the Merchants' and Manufacturers' Association, and the realty board. Their report, while cognizant of the need to protect residential districts, recommended the creation of a more flexible and liberal system that would accommodate the expansion of manufacturing and place "no obstacles in the way of industrial concerns desiring to locate here." One industrialist bluntly urged the council, "If it came to a choice between the smoke of industries or their cessation in Cleveland or Pittsburgh, the people would vote for the smoke." Another businessmen, when asked if he thought that this plan would "sacrifice the homes of the thrifty," replied that "there might be some cases of this sort but the industrial progress of the city could hardly be stopped by such considerations." East Side residents did not greet the plan to open new regions to manufacturing with great enthusiasm. An East Side councilman (one of the few remaining on the council after the reformers ended the old ward system of representation in 1909), bitterly attacked the suggested revision, observing that "if this is carried out . . . it will mean that the capitalist class will be in control of the question, men like Mr. Andrews who live in quarter million dollar houses in the Bonnie Brae district and who do not consider the sacredness of the residence districts of the workingmen." His opposition proved fruitless. In June of 1911 the council approved a new zoning ordinance that expanded the areas of the city available to industry.[40] This decision underscored the class and economic biases of the new progressive government. Most of the reform leaders were middle class, often with close ties to the city's business interests. When faced with the choice of favoring industrial developers or preserving the homes of blue-collar residents, all too often their natural inclination was to support the former over the latter.

By the end of the decade there had been some significant changes in how public policy makers in Los Angeles addressed the problem of pollution. Pressure was growing on city government to find viable ways to curb or accommodate the environmental degradation caused by industrial development and demographic expansion. Affected residents, mostly on the city's East Side, raised their voices in urgent protest, and in many instances public health officials echoed their concerns. As problems such as air pollution from industrial smokestacks became increasingly pervasive, some business interests chimed in as well, concerned about the impact on the city as a whole, particularly the threat to the vital real estate trade. At the same time, the shifting political structure of the city produced important improvements. The replacement of machine politicians with progressive reformers lessened the impact of direct corruption on the regulatory process, while under the more efficient government installed by the reformers, the city also implemented the beginning of systematic zoning to segregate residential and industrial districts.

Yet, in many ways efforts to rein in pollution remained quite limited. If East Side residents had suffered from the corrupt manner in which machine politicians handled the garbage crisis, they suffered equally from the fiscal penny pinching of the reformers. Similarly, while the new reform government rationalized the process of separating industrial and residential districts, this did not actually reduce pollution, but rather confirmed its segregation to poorer neighborhoods. Public policy makers confirmed a trend: the policies and practices of machine and reform administrations were more or less consistent. Both were biased toward economic growth and promoted industrialization despite the effects on health and housing values in the city's less affluent districts. Countering this bias was left to the affected residents, who often spoke out against unrestricted development.

These issues would emerge again and again in the coming decades. Over the course of the twentieth century, civic boosters and developers would continue to push for industrial development, new administrations would still seek cheaper ways to deal with garbage and other pollution problems, and ordinary citizens would persistently raise their voices in protest. The ultimate question would remain the same: who would ultimately pay the price for Los Angeles' growth?

5

Beaches versus Oil
in Greater Los Angeles

PAUL SABIN

THE California government dominated major transformations occurring in the state's oil economy in the first decades of the twentieth century. Geology and previous political decisions framed the period's controversies regarding state petroleum properties. The terms of federal land grants for educational purposes, for instance, specifically barred the states from receiving mineral lands. By chance and error, California received several parcels with significant oil deposits. But by the 1920s the state had sold the promising oil properties to individuals or companies. The school land grants thus did not provide the state with an extensive domain of oil and gas deposits, and virtually all of California's onshore oil fields lay in the federal public domain or in private ownership.

Along the Pacific coast, however, rich pools of oil, totaling more than 5 billion barrels, stretched from Huntington Beach to north of Santa Barbara. The Wilmington field, one of the four largest oil fields in the United States, contained 1.5 billion barrels under tidelands in the Long Beach and Los Angeles harbors. Major petroleum deposits also abutted the coastal towns of Huntington Beach, Santa Barbara, and Ventura. California's offshore fields would encompass 19 percent of the state's total petroleum reserves as of the late 1990s (see figure 5.1).[1]

Mounting pressure in the 1920s to develop these promising coastal fields forced California's state and local governments to confront questions similar to those that previously had preoccupied federal agencies and decision makers. Who would gain the right to profit from the state's natural resources? How fast would oil operators and the state develop state-owned petroleum deposits and how would the production revenues be spent? There was also a new set of questions: Would beaches trump oil in a struggle for political dominance? What kind of environmental protections would state and local lawmakers enact to protect California's valuable coastal beaches? Control over the oil deposits also turned on questions of state and federal law: where did coastal tidelands begin, and who owned them?

Aggressive targeting of the state-owned coastal petroleum lands began in earnest in 1927. Small-scale operations had flourished at nearby Summerland since the 1890s, but these early efforts had produced little oil and had not adequately tested the potential of the coastal fields. Now oil operators demanded prospecting permits under the 1921 California mineral leasing act. As oil operations moved toward the Pacific near Santa Barbara, Venice, Huntington Beach, and Long Beach, public attention turned to state management of the coast. The controversy over coastal drilling moved in waves along the shore. It first crashed fiercely in Santa Barbara County in the late 1920s. Then, in the

Figure 5.1. Panoramic view of Summerland oil derricks near Santa Barbara, undated. Security Pacific Collection, Los Angeles Public Library.

key 1928 decision of *Boone v. Kingsbury*, the California Supreme Court undermined the political success of beach conservationists by forcing the state government to issue oil drilling permits for coastal lands. After the legislature responded by banning further coastal oil development, a high-stakes political clash broke out at the Huntington Beach field. Throughout the protracted conflict, the oil industry's relationship with beachfront recreation, home ownership, and tourism remained central.

Battling the Drilling Front at Santa Barbara, Venice, and Huntington Beach

When oil operators began rushing to the coast of Santa Barbara and Ventura in 1927, post–World War I prosperity had already attracted residential and commercial interests to the area's beautiful coastline. Two competing economies in the state clashed over the use of coastal resources. Was the Pacific coastline a site for the extraction of raw materials, commercial harbors, and shipping or a serene place of relaxation, recreation, and realty? This simple polarity breaks down, to be sure, since oil development itself enabled the beachfront economy by fueling the sprawling automobile-dependent settlements of the Los Angeles basin and the state's increasing automobile tourism. But on the coast itself, the two sets of interests clashed. Wealthy coastal landowners and real estate developers fought industrial encroachment, and Save the Beaches groups, particularly powerful near Santa Barbara, denounced oil pollution and the ugliness of coastal oil operations.

California surveyor general W. S. Kingsbury at first granted coastal oil prospecting permits as requested, but then he reversed course and sought to block the oil development, declaring that oil would ruin California's spectacular coastline.[2] As upland wells yielded substantial petroleum, thwarted tidelands oil operators, who had filed permit applications to drill the entire Santa Barbara County coast, and sympathetic observers attacked Kingsbury as an obstructionist. Following several oil strikes at Seacliff near Santa Barbara on private lands, Howard Kegley, petroleum correspondent for the *Los Angeles Times*, criticized naive "petroleum experts" who stopped issuing drilling permits for the public tidelands. In addition to blocking important new development, California was forfeiting valuable oil royalties, Kegley argued. The state could now only "sit idly by and watch private land owners drain the oil from under State lands." The Ventura County Chamber of Commerce sponsored traveling speakers to build support for tidelands oil development and the business activity associated with it. According to the *Los Angeles Times*, the chamber was "disseminating the truth" about the safety and importance of beach drilling by sponsoring local speakers to talk before trade groups and organizations throughout Southern California. The *Times* forcefully advocated coastal oil development in its editorial and news coverage—except when oil operations threatened coastal recreation and real estate development in the Los Angeles basin. The local Oil Workers' Union in Ventura similarly passed a resolution calling for beach oil development, as did the Ventura County Building Trades Council and the Merchants' Credit Association of Ventura.[3]

Frustrated oil operators also mounted a legal offensive by suing under the 1921 leasing law to compel the state to issue permits and leases. Yet Republican governor Clement C. Young firmly supported Kingsbury.[4] Governor Young, who won office in 1927 after serving eight years as lieutenant governor and previously as Speaker of the California Assembly, was a former high school English teacher and real estate developer in northern California. An active member of the Sierra Club, Young favored conservation of scenic areas and natural resources. In 1927, he signed legislation creating the California State Parks Commission, to which voters would allocate 6 million dollars in bond funding in June 1928.

California attorney general Ulysses S. Webb joined Governor Young in aggressively defending Kingsbury's cautious, discretionary approach to coastal drilling. An avid hunter and fisherman, Webb believed passionately that public trust doctrine protected the California coast for public navigation, fisheries, and recreation, and he sued to protect the public's rights. Webb now questioned the constitutionality of California's oil leasing laws. For more than a thousand years, Webb argued in the key case *Boone v. Kingsbury*, "all civilized governments" had recognized an enduring public interest in tidelands. He called it common knowledge that the oil wells would pollute the water, making it uninhabitable for fish, and that a "forest of derricks" would make the coastline unattractive, "except to the individual who is profiting." Responding to criticism by oil operators of these "aesthetic grounds" for blocking oil permits, Webb denounced their "spur of greed . . . to seize that which has been stored for years and kept and safeguarded as the people's right."[5]

Webb dismissed warnings that California would lose significant revenue if it failed to grant the leases, noting accusatorily that the mineral leasing act stipulated a royalty of only 5 percent. Edward Doheny had obtained his preferential Elk Hills naval reserve lease from Albert Fall "through fraud, hypocrisy and deceit and crime," Webb observed, yet even that lease retained for the federal government 37 percent of the oil. "Drawn, I do not know by whom, nor do I know at whose instance," California's mineral leasing bill had been "an inconsiderate legislative act." Before the California Supreme Court, Webb wondered plaintively, "Why did the legislature do this?"[6]

But the California Supreme Court majority scoffed at Kingsbury and

Webb's reasoning. In a major victory for the oil companies, the court ruled that the surveyor general lacked the legitimate power to reject permit applications.[7] The court struck down on technical grounds 1923 amendments that granted discretion to the surveyor general. The court also dismissed Kingsbury and Webb's public trust arguments in language steeped in awe of oil's "enormous" significance to commerce, industry, and "the comfort of the race." The state legislature, the court said, "recognized the use of gasoline and oil to be practically indispensable to the needs of rapid, expanding industry and commerce." Allying the state with what it regarded as prodevelopment federal policy, the court invoked the federal government's recent laws as providing "the most liberal terms" to induce its citizens to explore for mineral resources. "In fact," the court declared, "the development of the mineral resources, of which oil and gas are among the most important, is the settled policy of state and nation, and the courts should not hamper this manifest policy except upon the existence of most practical and substantial grounds."[8]

The California court's ruling in *Boone* swept aside administrative discretion and opened to prospecting all coastal lands not dedicated to public purposes. The high court had authorized a "Tidelands Oil Hunt," according to the *San Francisco Chronicle*. Within a short time, operators who obtained permits under the ruling would erect piers and drilling islands off the coast of Santa Barbara County, between Goleta and Ventura.[9]

The *Boone* case exposed complex tensions between differing conceptions of the public good and the different economic and political interests embraced by the state court and the legislature. *Boone* galvanized state politicians to contain the spreading oil front. In January 1929, one month after the court ruling, the legislature barred any new tidelands prospecting permits until September 1. This urgency measure allowed the legislature to craft a new tidelands oil policy. During the spring legislative session an assemblyman from Carpinteria, a seaside town twelve miles south of Santa Barbara, pushed through a bill that explicitly prohibited further state oil permits for state beaches or tidelands. As he signed the bill in May, Governor Young declared that the measure preserved for the people "the highest use that our beach lands can be put, namely—recreation." With the new law in hand, the Young administration cut off new access to coastal oil. The state rejected seventy-two out of seventy-three applications in the fall of 1929 to prospect for oil and gas on state lands at Huntington Beach. The state's Huntington Beach oil field would be preserved for the future, announced finance director Alexander R. Heron. At the same time, Surveyor General Kingsbury continued his campaign against beach drilling and used legal technicalities to cancel as many as possible of the coastal permits that the *Boone* ruling had forced him to issue.[10]

The administration's restrictive policy appropriately matched market conditions in the state oil industry overall. Competition among California oil operators for access to common pools had compelled the operators to extract oil rapidly during the 1920s, driving down crude oil prices and per-barrel profits. The same day that Alexander Heron announced the seventy-two rejected Huntington Beach applications, Herbert Macmillan, president of the California Oil and Gas Association, declared overproduction "the most important problem confronting the oil industry." The state's major oil companies, and many smaller enterprises, urged voluntary cutbacks in production by California oil operators to boost prices. By restricting development of the coastal oil fields and helping to curtail production from existing wells, the Young administration thus sought to tighten the spigot that continued to gush California oil in the face of low market prices.[11]

This administrative and legislative activity, together with the specter of a hemorrhaging flow of cheap oil, persuaded the California courts to adjust to the new legislative mandate in the years following *Boone*. Instead of emphasizing petroleum's overwhelming importance to modern society, an appellate court in 1933 upheld the 1929 restrictions in language that echoed Kingsbury and Webb's position. The ruling deferred to the state legislature's decision to preserve the scenic beauty of the beaches and waterfronts against "an unsightly forest of oil-well derricks" and the "obnoxious fumes from overflowing crude oil." The court observed that: "the legislature has a right to assume that it is wise and profitable to preserve the valuable minerals of the public domain for the benefit of the state. It may be reasonably assumed it would be profligate for the legislature to abandon valuable mineral resources of the state to the exploitation of private interests."[12]

These "reasonable" assumptions reversed the tone and premises of *Boone*, acknowledging the aesthetic disadvantages of coastal drilling as well as the potential economic loss of valuable natural resources. The appellate court also endorsed the urgency stipulation of the January 1929 prohibition on prospecting permits. Shortly following the *Boone* decision in December 1928, Kingsbury had received a flood of inquiries from oil operators eager to develop coastal lands. The appellate court concluded that only the legislature's speedy action had prevented a new round of prospecting permits.

These new political and legal developments, however, could not undo *Boone's* pro-oil impact. Development proceeded apace on the coastal permits that the California Supreme Court had forced Kingsbury to grant in Santa Barbara County. The *San Francisco Chronicle* soon described the Ellwood field as the "most spectacular tideland development to date." A drilling race ensued in the fall of 1929, with seven new producing wells built in the open ocean on state-controlled lands. The wells were prolific producers of high-quality oil, with low development and transportation costs. At Goleta, Carpinteria, and Capitan, oil operators also drilled twenty-six new wells, further promising to map out the Santa Barbara County region's oil pools. Reports from Ellwood described wells such as that of the General Petroleum Company, which broke loose "roaring like a giant blast furnace," spouting nearly 1 billion cubic feet of gas daily, "enough to supply the need of nearly half the state." Pacific Western brought in a well producing thirty-five hundred barrels per day of high-gravity oil, from a point located about twelve hundred feet from shore.[13] The single well produced seventy-six thousand dollars of oil and gas in the last month and a half of 1929 alone. Eleven months later, in September 1930, the Barnsdall Oil Corporation brought in another Ellwood tidelands well that flowed thirteen thousand barrels per day, the largest in California at the time.

Many observers thought these drilling successes made the case for opening the coastal oil fields more widely to development. Ever the enthusiast for the money that flowed from oil, Howard Kegley of the *Los Angeles Times* thought the money pouring in "likely to rebuke the politicians who steadfastly opposed further tideland drilling." Kegley wrote, "It is the impression of many an oil man that the State cheated itself out of vast fortunes in royalties by withdrawing the tidelands from drilling." Yet California had little need for a new source of oil in 1929 and 1930. The state scrambled to find ways to limit production to sustain oil prices, which had fallen sharply during the 1920s. The owners of the Barnsdall well, like the owners of other new producing wells along the Santa Barbara coast, immediately curtailed production to 30 percent of the well's potential, in accordance with a statewide curtailment program. If Kingsbury had prevailed in his opposition, oil operators would not have drilled tideland wells in Santa Barbara County at all. And legislative restrictions on new coastal prospecting permits held firm in the face of the extraordinary petroleum wealth.[14]

With the political conflict over state tidelands in Santa Barbara County temporarily resolved by *Boone* and the legislative ban on new leases, the coastal controversy shifted to municipal lands at Venice and Huntington Beach. The Los Angeles Playground Commission, which controlled the municipal beach, proposed to lease the Venice beachfront for oil operations in 1930. As oil operators drilled private lands nearby, development associations and chambers of commerce along the coast fought to save the beaches of Santa Monica Bay for swimming and other recreation (see figure 5.2).[15]

A lawsuit by Lewis Stone, a popular movie actor whose residence faced the ocean on the Venice beach, ultimately blocked the beach development plan in October 1930. The California appellate court concluded that the municipality could not issue oil leases on lands granted by the state for harbor purposes. To the *Los Angeles Times*, which opposed tidelands drilling in the Los Angeles basin even though it supported drilling in Santa Barbara and Ventura, the court decision was a hollow victory. The city council had granted city permits to drill private property immediately contiguous to the beach and on the beach itself, in some places right down to the high-tide mark. Active drilling rigs hemmed the public beach on all three land sides. Given these incursions, it was a fair question, the *Times* declared, "whether the city should not accept the consequences and get the public something in return" by using oil royalties to purchase a new beach. Otherwise, the *Times* predicted, the city would lose the oil royalty revenue, earmarked by the Los Angeles Playground Commission to purchase another public beach elsewhere; see its own oil drained away by near-by private wells; and leave the public with only a ruined beach.[16]

The complex forces of beach protection, oil development, and the public's financial interest in oil—all driven by the rule of capture in common oil pools—would continue to clash through the 1930s as private oil operators encroached on the shoreline at Huntington Beach and Long Beach. The state government increasingly recognized oil royalties as a potential source of rev-

Figure 5.2. Oil derricks behind houses in Venice, undated. Security Pacific Collection, Los Angeles Public Library.

enue, despite continuing restrictions on tidelands drilling and California's low 5 percent royalty rate. The pursuit of revenues derived partly from two sources: the institutional interest of state employees in the capture of resources and the increasingly grim financial position of California as the Great Depression buffeted the state (see figure 5.3).

At Huntington Beach, state financial interests heightened by the Great Depression came into sharp conflict with the government's mandate to protect the beaches and California's complex political and business alliances. Development of the offshore field at Huntington Beach followed the rapid rise and fall of an onshore field in the city, which had occurred in the preceding decade. This town-lot field, which surged in production along with Long Beach's Signal Hill field and nearby Santa Fe Springs in the early 1920s, was situated principally under small, privately owned properties. The rule of capture had propelled an orgy of oil production as landowners and their lessees rushed to claim common subsurface petroleum deposits. Competing landowners had demanded aggressive development by lessees to offset neighboring producers. Where Standard Oil preferred to space wells one to every eight to ten acres on

Figure 5.3. Huntington Beach oil field, ca. 1940s. Security Pacific Collection, Los Angeles Public Library.

its larger holdings, oil operators at Huntington Beach, Signal Hill, and Santa
Fe Springs often crowded one well onto every one and a half to two acres on
the small town lots. These production methods quickly depleted oil reserves
and wasted capital, and the town-lot field at Huntington Beach was in permanent decline by the end of the 1920s.[17]

Huntington Beach thus seemed in 1928 to be moving toward the beach-
based economy of recreation and real estate that lay in its future. The state
stepped in to control oil pollution resulting from haphazard production methods. The State Fish and Game Commission successfully sued seventy oil operators to stop them from letting oil run through the Huntington Beach street
gutters into the sea. The *Los Angeles Times* began to envision a more recreational and residential economy at Huntington Beach. Ocean bathers would
"cavort and gambol in the breakers and come out glistening with drops of pure
salt water instead of having their bodies smeared with oil."[18]

Oil operators did not abandon Huntington Beach, but instead shifted their
sights toward the beach and tidelands. In 1927, the Standard Oil Company of
California purchased rights from the Pacific Electric Land Company to a narrow strip of land between the highway and the beach. Standard Oil then built
a fifteen-hundred-foot retaining wall parallel to the bluff along the beach, filling the space between the bluff and the wall to create a solid base on which to
erect oil derricks.[19] Many of the wells along this narrow strip drifted through
an underground fault into the state-owned tidelands oil pool that started at the
beach and went out into the ocean, but did not actually lie directly beneath the
Standard Oil property. As the town-lot field played out, other companies
sought to follow Standard Oil onto the beach and tidelands, and Standard Oil
maneuvered to protect its privileged access (see figure 5.4).

As they sought to develop the coastal oil fields, the companies ran into laws
that barred tidelands drilling there. The 1921 state mineral leasing act specifically prohibited the leasing of state tidelands or submerged lands fronting on a city.
In 1928, aspiring oil operators tried to circumvent the 1921 restrictions by arguing for an exemption for the Huntington Beach tidelands. Surveyor General
Kingsbury rejected their argument, declaring the tideland area off-limits to oil
development. As in the Santa Barbara region, oil operators sued Kingsbury to
force him to issue the coastal permits. Attorney General Webb continued his
strong support of Kingsbury and personally appeared in the Orange County
courthouse to oppose the petitions. Webb conceded that the city beach already
had been "despoiled" by oil wells, instead arguing against a precedent-setting
decision that might undermine the law against tideland drilling. The California
appellate courts agreed with Kingsbury and Webb's position and rejected the
permit demands. In contrast to the judicial reasoning in *Boone*, which described

the legislature as eager to help industry tap state oil reserves, the courts now identified a "trend of the legislative mind" toward beach protection.[20]

Defeated in court, the oil companies next pursued a political solution in alliance with local governments that had close ties to oil operators and depended on the industry for tax revenues and commercial activity. If the state leasing act would not allow the oil operators to develop the offshore field, then the cities would fight alongside the operators to change the law. In the spring of 1931, their political allies in the legislature pushed a bill through to transfer to Huntington Beach all tidelands fronting on the coastal town. At first presented as a beach development measure, it quickly became clear that the bill's true aim was to spur oil development. The Huntington Beach city attorney declared that modern devices could prevent pollution and that the field's low gas pressure would prevent dangerous gushers. He attacked his opponents as shills for Standard Oil, protecting its exclusive access to the tideland oil pool from the beach bluff and bolstering its dominance of the California industry generally. The Santa Ana City Council, the Orange County Board of Supervisors, and the Los Angeles County Board of Supervisors passed resolutions urging Gov-

Figure 5.4. Huntington Beach oil field, ca. 1940s. Security Pacific Collection, Los Angeles Public Library.

ernor James Rolph, who succeeded Clement C. Young in 1930, to approve the
bill. In this new political alignment, local governments believed they were protecting the public interest against a state legislature that was under the sway of
Standard Oil and was keeping revenues out of public coffers.[21]

The public and private records of these proceedings display the opaque
combinations of interests and principles in play. In private meetings in the state
capitol, lawyers and lobbyists for Standard Oil of California quietly opposed
the bill. William Randolph Hearst, said to be protecting his immense coastline
estate as well as carrying the battle for Standard Oil, publicly denounced
coastal oil development. At a contentious June hearing in Sacramento, private
property owners along the beaches near Huntington Beach protested coastal oil
drilling. Governor Rolph concluded the June hearing by warning against the
"evil of oil drilling" on the tidelands. "I am opposed to drilling for oil on the
beaches and I think the people of the entire State are opposed to it," Rolph
said. Unlike Clement C. Young or Ulysses S. Webb, "Sunny Jim" Rolph had
no clear track record favoring conservation and beach protection. Rumors circulated that Standard Oil paid for Rolph's veto. What is known is that the
mayor and city attorney of Huntington Beach and Standard Oil's Sacramento
lobbyist milled around the governor's office until midnight on June 19, the last
day on which Rolph could sign the bill, and that the governor vetoed it. The
coalition of those opposed to tidelands drilling had prevailed.[22]

Governor Rolph's alliance with Standard Oil and the Southern California
property owners forced the independent oil operators and their local political
allies to go directly to California voters with a ballot referendum, hoping to
strike down the legal obstacles to drilling the Huntington Beach oil lands. In a
ballot information pamphlet circulated to voters, the mayor and city attorney
of Huntington Beach denounced Standard Oil by implication and appealed in
blunt terms to the public's interest in tax revenue and fairness:

> Private interests are opposed to the leasing of such State-owned land.
> They want to take oil from under State lands without paying the State
> anything for it.
>   These private interests are trying to create a smoke screen by yelling
> "protect our beaches." These same companies are now producing mil-
> lions of barrels of oil within a stone's throw of such state-owned land.
> Where this has occurred the beach has already been ruined.[23]

But California voters rejected these appeals in May 1932 by a vote of 59 to
41 percent, embracing instead the counterargument that the beaches should be
preserved for the people of the State.

Determined because of the money at stake, the Huntington Beach City

Council tried again in November with Proposition 11, a proposed constitutional amendment to transfer the tidelands to the city for development purposes. At the same time, the Huntington Beach City Council negotiated a number of leases with local operators whose successful wells would offset Standard Oil's domination of the tidelands field. The council granted a thirty-year oceanfront lease to the Pacific Exploration Company, which promised to spend 2 million dollars to offset seventeen upland Standard Oil Company wells by building fourteen piers and drilling fifteen new offshore wells. Several prominent local oil operators led Pacific Exploration, including Roy Maggart, whose previous tidelands permit application had been rejected by the courts. Maggart and his colleagues sought to reverse their legal defeat through further political maneuvering.[24]

The Huntington Beach City Council also worked with other rejected permit applicants to try to offset Standard Oil's upland wells from the onshore side. To get as close as possible to Standard's strip of land on the bluff above the beach, the city attempted to lease part of the coastal highway to the local Carr Oil Company. Like Roy Maggart, the Carr Company's president, Arthur Carr, had recently had his permit application rejected in state court. Carr proposed to dig large underground pits beneath the highway, to place all the producing machinery there once the wells had been drilled, and then to reinstate the highway above the pumping wells. The following spring, the city council similarly tried to give the Signal Oil and Gas Company access to twenty-four-foot strips down the center of beachfront streets in exchange for a 20 percent royalty. Tens of millions of dollars rode on the validity of the leases and the city's control of the tidelands field. The city council demonstrated its determination to open the offshore field to local oil operators through its embrace of these unusual highway deals.[25]

Local business and political leaders split on these efforts to develop Huntington Beach's coastal oil. On the day that the city council granted the tidelands lease to the Pacific Oil Company, the Huntington Beach Chamber of Commerce adopted a resolution protesting the plan. The small businesses represented by the chamber wanted the city to control the coast for the benefit of recreational and commercial development, not oil.[26] In the ballot arguments presented to voters, the Huntington Beach Chamber of Commerce and the Beach Protective Association called the "spoilation of our beaches" a "tragic public sacrifice." Other Southern California civic associations and business groups also organized a Save the Beaches movement to mobilize opposition statewide. In nearby Los Angeles, the city's Chamber of Commerce declared that tidelands drilling would "desecrate the beaches," potentially ruining the coast from San Pedro to San Diego.[27]

Governor Rolph and other statewide organizations strongly allied with the beach protection groups. Before a gathering of the California Real Estate Association, Rolph blamed the oil industry and its precipitously low prices for the general economic demoralization of the state. "The oil industry has already prostituted itself," Rolph said. "Let us not allow it to prostitute our beaches." Following Rolph's address, the association joined the attack, arguing that coastal drilling "tends to destroy real estate values" and pollute beaches so that they cannot be used for recreation. The association denounced this "opening wedge" that would extend oil drilling up and down the California coast. The Mineral Resources Section of San Francisco's elite Commonwealth Club similarly opposed the November ballot proposition. In light of the general state of overproduction in the petroleum industry and considerable reserves available in the state's other oil fields, the Commonwealth group urged that the state conserve the Huntington Beach petroleum. San Francisco mayor Angelo J. Rossi and the San Francisco Board of Supervisors agreed and urged voters to reject the coastal drilling proposition.[28]

These appeals to protect coastal beaches from the "Spoilers and Oilers" resonated with California voters, who defeated the November 1932 proposition, again by a margin of 60 to 40 percent.[29] Once more, the broad beach protection alliance had denied oil operators access to the Huntington Beach offshore field. Despite enormous political pressure on the state government to allow tidelands drilling at Huntington Beach, the 1921 and 1929 prohibitions held firm, specifically barring prospecting leases on coastal lands fronting municipalities and more generally blocking new tidelands leases. The Huntington Beach tidelands field was to remain untapped except for drainage by Standard Oil Company wells on the beach bluff. But local oil operators would not let the oil lie.

Breaking the Ban, and the Law, at Huntington Beach

Frustrated on the political front, Huntington Beach oil operators illegally bypassed state restrictions.[30] Recent technological advances enabled oil operators to better control their drills underground. Pioneering operators located in Huntington Beach's town-lot field, for example, could tilt their drilling shafts toward the Pacific, sending diagonal oil wells out through Standard Oil's beach-bluff property into the tidelands oil pool. The technology intensified the controversy around coastal drilling restrictions by giving small operators the capability to bend regulations in surprising ways.

W. E. McCaslin had confounded expectations in 1931 when he developed a commercial well at 7,700 feet in depth, three blocks from the ocean. A closely watched test well by Superior Oil several months earlier had produced only water, confirming for many that at Huntington Beach, unlike Signal Hill, no deep oil zone would replace the rapidly tapped higher oil strata. But McCaslin's well now suggested otherwise. Other Huntington Beach operators eagerly began to redrill and deepen old wells in the summer of 1932. Statistics indicate a steady decline in Huntington Beach production in the late 1920s and early 1930s and then a sharp increase in 1932: the operators had tapped a new source of oil. In the summer of 1933, Huntington Beach oil operators regularly reported major new producing wells, frequently drilled with the same derricks situated above diminished older wells. Wells that had been only "small strippers" from 1926 to 1930, and then abandoned, now produced a princely one thousand barrels per day.

Huntington Beach was enjoying an oil boom—one that the combination of geology and California leasing laws did not allow for.[31] A fault running along the coast sharply separated the declining onshore field from the tidelands pool, neatly preventing drainage into older Huntington Beach wells. To produce from the offshore pool, a well had to breach the fault. But except for Standard Oil's wells perched directly above the fault on the beach bluff, and a lone permit north of the city limits that had been granted under *Boone*, no oil company could legally do so. The mineral leasing act of 1921 specifically prohibited the leasing of tidelands fronting on an incorporated municipality. The 1929 legislative changes further barred any tidelands leases for the entire California coast.

The large sums of money generated by the drillings that defied restrictions impressed onlookers as much as did the environmental threat or the sheer illegality of the activity. Reports that operators were slanting wells in the summer of 1933 led W. S. Kingsbury, now the chief of the new Division of State Lands in the department of finance, to send Arthur Alexander, a state petroleum production inspector, to investigate. Alexander rented binoculars from a local store and set up, at some distance away, to survey drilling activity. In subsequent litigation, he described how at 4 a.m. on August 1, 1933, he observed the Termo Company preparing to drill a well in the town-lot area. At that time, the drilling rig was open so that "all operations could be clearly observed from the street." But upon his return at 10 a.m., drilling had begun and "the rig was carefully covered for approximately eighteen feet from the ground." Even so, above the covered part of the rig Alexander could see that the drill pointed toward the tidelands. During the next two days, Alexander saw drill pipe placed and removed at an angle from the well. A veteran driller, C. M. Potter, confirmed Alexander's observations, adding in an affidavit that he had "never seen or heard of" a deliberately angled well before working at Huntington Beach. Potter recalled that the operators had taken "unusual precautions . . . to conceal operations by carefully enclosing the derricks."[32]

When the Huntington Beach story burst into full public view, the scandal focused on the economic losses to state coffers, rather than beach protection, since the new wells were not on the beach. "In the face of some denials and diplomatic silence elsewhere," the *San Francisco Chronicle* reported in September 1933, "extreme perturbation exists in high State offices over oil drilling conditions at Huntington Beach." Oil operators had extracted thousands of barrels per day from slanted wells. The state's losses, which ran to millions, continued "to pile up." Attorney General Webb vowed to restrain illegal production and to seek damages for the drainage of state oil. His office filed suits in Orange County Superior Court seeking court permission to determine whether operators had drilled diagonal shafts to extract oil from state-owned tidelands.[33]

Governor Rolph's director of finance, Rolland Vandegrift, initially joined this push to crack down on trespassers. Born in Pennsylvania in 1893, Vandegrift had served as a military officer in World War I, then moved to California, where he studied and taught California history and governmental affairs. A California booster who collected old California branding irons and early-American pressed glass, Vandegrift had entered the political fray as director of research for the California Taxation Improvement Association and then the California Taxpayers Association. Attracted to Vandegrift's reputation as a budget hawk and antitax conservative, Governor Rolph had appointed him finance director.[34]

In response to growing publicity about the Huntington Beach situation, Vandegrift announced that the state would use "every legal means" to prosecute trespassers and recoup lost revenues. Vandegrift also asked corporation commissioner Harry Daugherty to scrutinize permit applications carefully to protect investors from buying shares of companies producing oil that "belongs to the State of California." Vandegrift, in early November 1933, called the state's oil litigation "the biggest suit in the United States," involving "$300,000,000 worth of oil," adding, "The interested operators are moving heaven and earth to stop us."[35]

Vandegrift's early positioning and brazen defiance soon yielded to preferential legal treatment and political acquiescence. Vandegrift reversed his public position twelve days after his bold threats, announcing that California would settle with the operators who had begun drilling before November 13. His policy shift reflected heavy lobbying by associates of Governor Rolph and legislative leaders. Trespassing operators formed the Huntington Beach Townsite Association and hired J. M. Jefferson, a lobbyist for small loan interests and a major supporter of Orange County assemblyman and Speaker Edward Craig. Subsequently, any oil operators hoping to settle with the state government were forced to join this Townsite Association as a precondition. Another lobbyist, supposedly close to Governor Rolph and his son, allegedly contracted with Huntington Beach producers "to receive $100,000 for securing a contract with the State on a five or six percent royalty basis."[36]

Although eager to satisfy these powerful economic interests by letting them extract the state's oil, the Rolph administration still hungrily eyed oil royalties from the Huntington Beach field. California was mired in the Great Depression and chronically short of revenue. A major fight over how to deal with California's fiscal crisis had roiled the statehouse during the previous June. Legislators imposed a new sales tax, slashed property taxes, and debated a new income tax and the shift of highway revenues from road construction and maintenance to the general fund. Finance director Vandegrift looked to royalties from the Huntington Beach trespassers to help make up the state budget shortfall. But this financial imperative did not dominate Rolph administration policy. Vandegrift agreed to low royalty arrangements that benefited the Huntington Beach oil operators who were lobbying the administration heavily. But his eagerness to obtain some royalties from the Huntington Beach field foreshadowed the fiscal arguments that liberal Democratic and Republican lawmakers would make, beginning in 1935, on behalf of much tougher royalty arrangements.[37]

Uncertain legal authority and the steadfast opposition of Attorney General Webb hampered Rolph and Vandegrift's plans to settle with the oil operators. The legal dispute centered on whether California could grant easements and arrange to get royalties from slanted wells that were illegal given the continuing ban on beach and offshore drilling. Webb contended that it could not. The state legislature had authorized agreements when adjacent wells drained oil from a common oil pool, he thought, but not when illegal wells tapped oil under state lands. The Huntington Beach oil operators worked closely with Vandegrift to challenge Webb's administrative ruling with a test case in Sacramento Superior Court. With Vandegrift's blessing, James B. Utt, an assemblyman from Orange County, sued Vandegrift to force him to settle with the oil operators. Judge Malcolm Glenn, who previously had ruled against Webb and Kingsbury's efforts to block coastal drilling, now concluded that the dire situation at Huntington Beach threatened California's ability to manage its petroleum resources. Without addressing Webb's concerns about accommodating illegal trespassers, Judge Glenn authorized Vandegrift to settle with the oil operators.[38]

Ruling in hand, Vandegrift proposed a royalty schedule for operators tapping the Huntington Beach offshore field. Under a sliding scale based on price and output, wells producing fifty barrels per day at a price of $0.50 per barrel would pay the minimum royalty of 5 percent. Those producing a high three thousand barrels per day at the unlikely price of $1.75 would pay a maximum royalty of 66 percent. Vandegrift predicted average royalties of 15 percent and annual net state revenues of around $1 million. He called the schedule "fair" and the state's "last word." California then sued to force unwilling Huntington Beach trespassers to sign the royalty agreements. The evidence was overwhelming—officials of the Termo Company confessed—and the cases proceeded smoothly, resulting in royalty settlements. When some operators resisted royalty agreements, Vandegrift threatened to close trespassing wells and transfer all oil profits to the state.[39]

Orange County politicians urged the state government to leave the local oil operators alone. Lawyers for the city of Huntington Beach sued to stop California from pursuing its litigation, complaining that it undermined the local property tax base. The city argued that local operators were entitled to take the tidelands oil. Oil in the tidelands pool was simply "free to anyone who can reduce it to possession, provided he commences to drill his well on his own land." The real villain, Huntington Beach argued, was Standard Oil, which stood to benefit most from the state's litigation. As early as 1927, the lawyers reminded the superior court, the *Standard Oil Bulletin* had printed pictures of company wells "actually drilled on the Beach." Stopping the local oil operators would leave Standard Oil all the oil and with no obligation to compensate the state. The strategy of cracking down on the local oil operators thus was vulnerable to the charge of pandering to Standard Oil.[40]

To shift the focus away from local oil operators, Huntington Beach claimed that state officials had known for years that Standard and others had pumped state oil from coastal wells, extracting more than 6 million barrels without compensating the state. The city council's aggressive counterattack, which sought to force the state to back away from its suits, dovetailed with the personal interest of at least one of its members. City councilman John Marion's Huntington Beach Oil Company faced suits over two wells that demanded three hundred thousand dollars in damages.[41]

California's coupling of generous royalty terms with the threat of litigation persuaded the final independent operator, the W. K. Company of Los Angeles—the sixty-sixth company the state had sued—to settle in December 1934. Webb Shadle, attorney for the Division of State Lands, estimated that the agreements together would yield about $100,000 a month. The state also would receive an additional $850,000 for oil and gas extracted earlier. A calculation done several years later indicated that the royalties averaged a little below 12 percent, above the 5 percent minimum prospecting royalty rate stipulated in the state mineral leasing act, but far below the 30 to 40 percent royalties proposed in the legislature soon afterwards.[42]

Even as the independent oil operators paid the state, their complaints drew Standard Oil into the controversy. An investigation of connections between the government and Standard Oil found no collusion, but suggested that several beach-bluff wells did drain from the tidelands. Arlin Stockburger, Vandegrift's successor in the department of finance, moved quickly to make royalty arrangements with Standard Oil on the same terms as with the independent operators at Huntington Beach. The oil companies "should all be treated alike," Stockburger maintained, using egalitarian rhetoric to protect Standard Oil's privileged position.[43]

Being treated alike meant, at bottom, paying the state little. If California had been a private landowner, it would never have allowed the trespassers to keep most of what they stole. The state's capitulation underscored the mix of politics and law that shaped the management of publicly owned natural resources. The state gave the companies a sweetheart deal despite political and legal factors that weighed against accommodation. No industry consensus supported the companies that slanted their wells under the tidelands. Many members of the California oil industry vocally disapproved. Proposed revisions to an August 1933 document on regulating oil production in California, for example, distanced statewide oil industry committees from the unethical behavior of the Huntington Beach operators. One key subsection underscored the fundamental point that "subsurface equities are coincident in extent with surface ownerships and have the same inalienable and inviolable rights as property." In other words, diagonal drilling violated clear property rights and constituted unlawful trespass. Another subsection specifically attacked the slanted drilling practices at Huntington Beach, declaring that the "abnormal and unconventional development of any field such as is now occurring in the Huntington Beach ocean front area . . . is so contrary to any conceivable code of ethics or regulation as to merit the utmost condemnation."[44]

The California courts similarly rejected slanted drilling. In contemporaneous cases involving private parties, state courts protected landowners and lessees from trespassers who penetrated their land through slanted wells. When landowners filed suit to stop slanted-well trespass, they asked for monetary damages equal to the quantity of oil extracted from beneath their lands. Landowners such as the Union Oil Company and Pacific Western Oil Company prevailed on virtually all accounts. The case against slanted drilling, in short, was an easy one to win in court.[45]

The courts' willingness to protect the rights of private landowners strongly indicates that the state government easily could have won injunctions to close the Huntington Beach slanted wells and collect damages equal to the value of the oil extracted. Nathan Newby, a losing defendant in a Union Oil case, complained bitterly that Standard Oil had not been held to the same 100 percent damages standard. Attorney General U. S. Webb had brought criminal charges against the company that trespassed on Pacific Western's property. Yet Rolland Vandegrift only sued Huntington Beach trespassers for full damages and an injunction when they refused to pay low royalties, and he dropped the suits as soon as he achieved settlements.[46]

The Rolph administration had its reasons for settling for such low royalties. Vandegrift and Governor Rolph trod a fine line with their Huntington Beach policy. On the one hand, they favored the politically powerful operators and their political contributions, and they wanted the boost that oil royalties, though low, would bring to the state budget. On the other hand, oil operators elsewhere in the state, as well as public officials, pointed out that Huntington Beach crude was contributing to the overproduction and low oil prices that plagued the state oil industry during the 1930s. Huntington Beach operators were among the chief offenders in disregarding state oil quotas, complained Ralph Lloyd, the head of the state conservation committee that sought to reduce output and boost prices. Vandegrift also could not completely ignore the 1921 prohibition on tidelands leasing near municipalities and the 1929 law barring leases along the coast. To allow some production, but not too much, Vandegrift struck deals with operators who had begun drilling wells illegally by November 1933. But Vandegrift would not negotiate with those who began trying to drill beneath the tidelands only after he had signaled, through the settlements, that it could be legal to do so. Vandegrift's solution rewarded oil operators guilty of trespass and theft while freezing out those who obeyed the law.[47]

California's struggle over coastal oil drilling in the 1920s and early 1930s underscored the increasingly uneasy relationship between coastal extractive industry and the booming tourist, recreational, and residential economy. The controversy also deepened the conflict over who would reap the economic benefit of California's rich coastal oil fields—local oil operators, Standard Oil, or the state government—and when that development would occur. The outcome of the struggles to develop California's coastal oil was determined not by the market, but instead by fierce political struggle among competing interests. In the end, slanted drilling from the uplands largely protected the coastal waters from pollution. But the trespassing and royalty agreements state officials crafted did little to capture revenue for the state government or to speed Huntington Beach's transition to its future beach economy.

6

Who Killed the Los Angeles River?

BLAKE GUMPRECHT

Tʜʀᴏᴜɢʜ much of its course, the Los Angeles River is hard to imagine as a river at all. Its channel is artificial, its bed and banks constructed of concrete, reinforced with steel. Little water flows in the river except during storms. At other times the flow is mostly treated sewage, discharged into the channel from three plants in the San Fernando Valley. The river was built to accommodate storm surges twenty thousand times its dry-season flow, yet the bulk of the water it carries nine months out of the year is confined to a much smaller, low-flow channel cut through the center of its wide bed. Most often the river is a broad swath of dry pavement that looks like nothing so much as a deserted freeway.

Homes, businesses, and streets have replaced the marshes, vineyards, and orange groves once nourished by the river's waters. Chain-link fence and barbed wire stand guard where willow and cottonwood trees once rose. Shopping carts rest in midstream where grizzly bears roamed in search of food, Indians trapped waterfowl, and young boys collected nettles for playground pranks. Styrofoam cups are now more abundant than fish in a river where steelhead once spawned. As these images suggest, perhaps nothing symbolizes the environmental transformation of Los Angeles more than the destruction of the Los Angeles River, that thing, ironically, to which the city owes its life (see figures 6.1 and 6.2).[1]

Government flood control officials in general and the U.S. Army Corps of Engineers in particular are often blamed for turning the Los Angeles River into an ugly concrete ditch. In recent years, an increasingly potent coalition of environmentalists, landscape architects, planners, and politicians has developed to promote the revitalization of the river. These advocates have been quick to con-

demn as short sighted, unimaginative, and even corrupt the engineers who
they say turned the "once-enchanted" river into something else. Some have
taken to calling contemporary flood control officials who have been slow to
support efforts to green the river "a concrete cult." At one level, of course, the

Figure 6.1. Corpse found in the concrete river channel by Los Angeles police in 1955 symbolizes
how thoroughly the image of the river changed during the twentieth century. Los Angeles Police
Department Archives.

flood control agencies were responsible. The river of today was largely constructed under the direction of the U.S. Army Corps of Engineers between 1935 and 1959, after the federal government took over a local flood control program that had proved incapable of satisfactorily limiting the flood hazard in a rapidly growing metropolis. Construction crews working under contract to the Corps of Engineers enlarged the river's channel, straightened its course, and lined its bed and banks with 3 million barrels of concrete. They created the fifty-one-mile storm drain that is still flatteringly called the Los Angeles River.[2]

In truth, however, the destruction of the river was more gradual and complex, and flood control officials were little more than undertakers, closing the coffin on a river that was by then almost dead. The transformation of the river began a half century before the first concrete was poured, when American settlers from more humid eastern states, unaccustomed to the climate and hydrology of Southern California and unimpressed by the little stream that barely flowed most of the year, drained the river dry and turned it into an industrial site and a dumping ground. By the time a coordinated, regional flood control program began to be viewed as a necessity, the river had been so deprived of its surface flow and defiled by the growing population along its banks that few cared if it was covered with concrete. The nature of development and the price

Figure 6.2. The artificial channel of the Los Angeles River in the San Fernando Valley, 1995. Courtesy Blake Gumprecht.

of real estate along the river, moreover, largely limited the flood control strategies that government officials could consider.

The Importance of Perceptions

Nothing doomed the Los Angeles River more than the physical environment that created it and human perceptions of that environment. Although
some mountain peaks in the area receive forty inches of rain and snow a year,
coastal Los Angeles County receives but fifteen inches of precipitation on average, and, because of the erratic nature of the region's climate, even that number exaggerates what can be expected in most years. Rainfall, moreover, is
largely limited to three winter months and seldom falls during the peak growing season, so if settlers wanted to plant crops, they had to transport water to
their fields from one of the few surface water sources that existed. Because of
its particular geology, the Los Angeles River was one of the only streams in the
region to flow year-round. Consequently, the earliest villages, aboriginal and
European, tended to be located nearby. At least two dozen Indian villages were
located along various courses of the river. When Spain, in the eighteenth century, decided to establish an agricultural settlement in the area to supply food
to its military operations on the coast, it too chose a location beside the river,
founding the pueblo that became Los Angeles in 1781. The river and its underground supply would be the city's sole source of water until 1913.[3]

For its first century, Los Angeles remained a small agricultural village, and
the river proved a satisfactory source of water for both irrigation and domestic
use. It was not until the first transcontinental railroad line to Southern California was completed in 1876, and increasing numbers of Americans moved to
the region, that the water supply began to pose a problem. Elsewhere, the environmental limitations presented might have naturally slowed settlement, but
here the other physical attractions were so great that such shortcomings were
easily overlooked (see figure 6.3).

The same climate that produced minimal rainfall, and left most stream
channels dry much of the year, also had positive attributes. The sun shone (and
shines) nearly every day. Winter never came, at least not in the sense that the
Iowan or New Englander knew it. Tall mountains rose majestically nearby, and,
for an alternative view, the beach was a trolley ride away. Real estate promoters
capitalized on such conditions, and the mass migration of people to Southern
California continued unabated for decades. Even today, with its earthquakes,
pollution, traffic, and gangs, Los Angeles retains a powerful pull on people
from places that are mountainless, beachless, cloudy for months on end, and
hostage to the grip of winter. But the Los Angeles River, even before it was
paved, was not seen as part of the benefits package. To emigrants from the east-

ern United States, it was hardly a river at all; it was little different from the nameless creek or brook they knew back home.

Unusual though the Los Angeles River was in the semiarid region, the fact remained that it was a relatively small stream and a limited source of water compared with those possessed by other urban areas. Thus, as hundreds of thousands of newcomers poured into Southern California, the river did not stand a chance. River water carried through numerous open irrigation ditches, or *zanjas*, that wound through the city had helped to make Los Angeles the earliest wine center in the West and one of the most productive agricultural regions in the nation (see figure 6.4). The first oranges shipped east from California were also irrigated with river water. The river, furthermore, was instrumental in creating the verdant landscape that charmed travelers and settlers from eastern states and contributed greatly to the development of the region's reputation as a garden paradise. But as the population grew, agricultural interests lost out in the competition for the river water supply. Vineyards and orange groves were subdivided for homes and businesses. The zanjas were gradually filled in and built over. Completion of a second cross-country railroad

Figure 6.3. The Los Angeles River near downtown, ca. 1900. Seaver Center for Western History Research, Natural History Museum of Los Angeles County.

line in 1886 spurred a fare war that inspired an even greater population boom. Eventually, the river would prove unable to meet the city's water needs.[4]

Officials of the private water company that supplied water to Los Angeles residents in their homes first showed concern over the volume of water in the river about the time the second railroad line came to town. Between 1883 and 1892, the number of customers supplied by the company grew from nineteen hundred to nine thousand. In response to the increased demand, the water company sought to conserve more of the river's surface flow by enlarging its only reservoir, increasing its capacity from 1 million to 13 million gallons in 1884. Despite the added storage, the surface flow of the river soon became insufficient to supply the needs of the growing city. To increase the amount of water available to it, the water company in 1886 installed a double line of perforated pipes—a device known as an infiltration gallery—ten to fourteen feet below the river bottom to capture the river's underground flow. Water pumped from the infiltration gallery provided an additional 10 million gallons of water a day. The significance of this innovation to the future of the river was even greater. Before long, the river would be drained dry by such developments and Los Angeles would turn its back on the stream that was the city's reason for being.[5]

As more and more water was required to meet domestic needs, the city of Los Angeles, which maintained control of the irrigation system, became less able to accommodate the water requirements of farmers. By 1886, the network of zanjas had grown in size to irrigate more than eleven thousand acres in and around Los Angeles. More than a dozen named zanjas meandered fifty miles within the corporate boundaries of the city and extended several miles south of its limits. As late as 1894, the city official who oversaw the irrigation system commented that "there is plenty of water in the river." But by 1897, following three winters of subnormal rainfall, his successor warned that a shortage was developing. "Irrigators are clamoring for water," he said, "and it seems impossible for me to furnish the same to them." In 1899, the city water overseer complained that the private water company was "at times taking almost all the water in the river." As a result, the city was occasionally unable to supply water it had contracted to deliver to irrigators and for which it had already been paid. The situation became so serious in 1900 that Los Angeles was forced to spend seventeen hundred dollars to hurriedly install three pumping plants in the river to tap still more of its underground flow, this time to meet irrigation needs. The Los Angeles River, meanwhile, was beginning to resemble a desert watercourse.[6]

The city of Los Angeles gained control of the domestic water system in 1902 after a decade-long legal battle. About that time, city engineers calculated

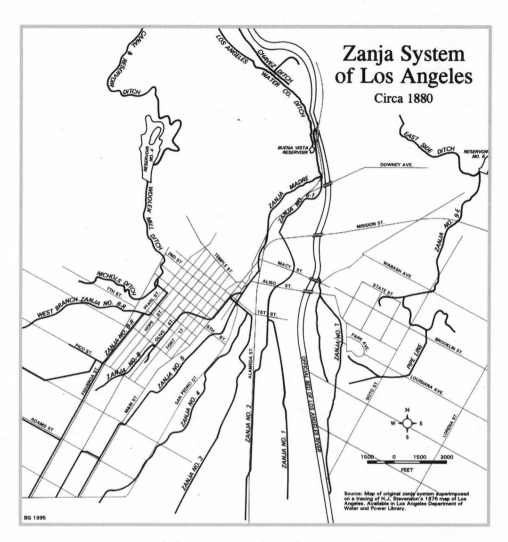

Figure 6.4. An extensive network of zanjas transported water from the Los Angeles River to nearby vineyards and orange groves, undated. Courtesy Blake Gumprecht.

that the river, under normal conditions, could be expected to provide at least 45 to 50 million gallons of water a day, even during the summer. At the then current rate of consumption, that was enough water to supply a city of perhaps 150,000 residents. If the Los Angeles River was to continue to resemble a river, it would not be capable of providing even that much water. But as Los Angeles filled up with homes, the notion that the native character of the river should be preserved never entered the public debate. City officials faced the more pressing problem of how they would supply water to a city that was growing so fast. Aesthetic concerns have little chance when basic human needs are threatened; government officials, moreover, had no mechanism for stemming the tide of newcomers. When the city took over the water system, Los Angeles had a population of about 128,000, and hundreds more were arriving every week. Four years earlier, city officials had begun to investigate options for augmenting the river's supply, and, in 1907, construction would begin on an aqueduct to transport water to Los Angeles from the eastern slopes of the Sierra Nevada, more than two hundred miles away. In the interim, however, they had to take immediate action to prevent faucets from running dry.[7]

Facing imminent crisis, city officials sought to curb individual consumption through the installation of thousands of water meters and to conserve existing resources by building new reservoirs, but they also sought to drain every last drop of water from the river. Wells were driven into the river at three different points north of downtown, increasing the city's water supply by 15 million gallons a day. New infiltration galleries were also installed. In 1904, a 1,178-foot tunnel was driven into bedrock 115 feet beneath the river bed near the outlet of the Arroyo Seco. Nine wells were then drilled in the river to allow water to percolate into the tunnel. Additional infiltration galleries were installed across from Burbank in 1905, and, the following year, the infiltration galleries constructed by the private water company in 1886 were extended two thousand feet. By removing the subsurface flow of the river, the wells and infiltration devices sucked the river dry. A series of photos taken a few years later by county flood control officials dramatically illustrates the impact such developments had on the character of the river. One shows the river near Griffith Park, upstream from most diversions from its channel, its flow ample, its banks lined with brush and willows. In another, taken "200 feet below (the) filtration galleries," the river is dry, a puddle in midstream the only reminder of its former state.[8]

The population of Los Angeles rose to nearly a half million by the time the Owens River aqueduct delivered its first water in 1913. The only way the city was able to prevent a shortfall of water in the meantime was by cutting per capita consumption in half, enlarging storage space by nearly a billion gallons, and increasing its use of water from underground sources. The river that had been a magnet for settlement for thousands of years and had nurtured the city for more than a century was destroyed in the process. The once ample stream became a local joke. A turn-of-the-century newspaper columnist later remarked that its channel was "so dry eight months out of the year that a pollywog would have to stand on his head to get enough moisture to soothe a headache." Even booster publications began to find humor at its expense. One such publication referred to the river in quotes. "This 'river'—as the tourist scoffingly emphasizes it—generally only flows underground," it said.[9]

The Owens River aqueduct increased the volume of water destined for the Los Angeles River because irrigation water applied to fields percolated underground and eventually returned to the surface in its channel. Still, as urban development spread along the river, pollution began to threaten its surface flow. As a result, the stated goal of the city in managing the river was to keep any water from flowing in its channel. The city water department sought instead to intercept any water destined for the river while it was still underground and clean, pumping it from the groundwater basins that were its natural source.

Expansion of two infiltration galleries enabled the city in 1917 to halt all surface diversions from the river and discontinue use of two chlorination plants. When aqueduct deliveries were later increased, however, 5 million gallons of water a day again flowed in the river east of downtown. To prevent water from traveling that far, a new set of infiltration galleries was constructed in 1920. Then, in 1925, twenty-four wells were drilled in the San Fernando Valley, the huge natural reservoir that was the source of most of the river's flow. In 1930, ten more wells were installed. "The object of these wells," said a report of the Los Angeles Board of Water and Power Commissioners, "is to lower water levels enough to prevent any surface water from flowing under the Dayton Avenue bridge, except during flood periods."[10] Such statements made clear that the Los Angeles River had become a river in name only (see figure 6.5).

Economics versus Aesthetics

Vital as the river was to the growth of Los Angeles, its significance was always more economic than aesthetic. Though the utility of the river was certainly appreciated, its appearance rarely seems to have been. For the most part, in fact, the river was ignored. It was never the center of local life as some modern-day environmentalists have supposed. The earliest commentaries about Los Angeles rarely mention it, except when it turned vicious and overflowed its banks. Promotional publications marveled at the bountiful harvests its water produced, but said little about the river itself, except in brief historical passages. Guidebooks may have sent tourists this way and that across its channel, to visit picturesque vineyards or steep mountain slopes, but the river seldom received even passing notice. Despite its utilitarian importance, the river also seems to have been one of the least photographed landmarks in early Los Angeles. In the hundreds of images that chart the development of the city in the nineteenth century, the river is almost never seen, except far in the background.

As the Southern California landscape was transformed following the arrival of the railroads, the character of the river was significantly altered, and soon it was as much deplored as it was ignored. The river, indeed, became the antithesis of the Arcadian ideal so central to the promotion of the region, despite its role in creating that image. Elsewhere, palm trees were planted to confirm the region's reputation as a Mediterranean paradise. Homes and gardens became inseparable. People could sleep outside year-round, or so the popular songs said.[11] But even in the enlightened metropolis, an industrial base had to be developed and the refuse of urban life had to go somewhere. Like so many urban waterways, the Los Angeles River became a dumping ground. But in other ways its plight was unique. Because it carried so little water on much of

Figure 6.5. The dry, sandy bed of the Los Angeles River near downtown Los Angeles, ca. 1930, shows that efforts to prevent any water from flowing on the surface of the river during the dry season were successful. Department of Special Collections, University of Southern California, California Historical Society Collection.

its course, its use as a dump was more conspicuous, and the other uses of its channel unique. People actually lived in its bed. Not only was the river lined with industry, it became an industrial site itself.

In Los Angeles, as in other cities, industrial development followed stream courses, though in Southern California this did not occur for all the usual reasons. Elsewhere, rivers provided a means to transport industrial products. They supplied the water that powered turbines and provided a convenient way to dispose of liquid wastes. The flow of the Los Angeles River, however, was too insignificant and irregular to enable waterborne commerce. By the time industry became widespread in Los Angeles, moreover, the river had been so deprived of its surface flow that power generation was not a possibility. The river also had limited potential as an outlet for sewage because there was too little water in its channel to dilute effluents or wash them downstream.

In Los Angeles, industry developed along the river because it was there that the earliest railroads were built, probably because the riverfront lands were prone to flooding and were therefore less desirable for other uses. Southern California's first railroad, the Los Angeles and San Pedro, built in 1869 to link Los Angeles and its future port, constructed its depot one half mile west of the river. Though the impact of this railroad on development was less dramatic than that of the national lines that arrived a few years later, it did inspire the first significant industrial building in the city. Warehouses, lumber yards, blacksmith shops, foundries, and wagon factories began to displace the vineyards and orchards near its station.[12]

When the Southern Pacific Railroad came to Los Angeles in 1876, it took over the tracks of the Los Angeles and San Pedro. The Southern Pacific built its line from San Francisco along the eastern edge of the San Fernando Valley, then south to Los Angeles along the east bank of the river. Its tracks crossed the river near its confluence with the Arroyo Seco and ran south though present-day Chinatown to its meeting with the old Los Angeles and San Pedro. The Southern Pacific constructed its first station a quarter mile south of the Los Angeles and San Pedro depot. Within a few years, a small manufacturing district made up of a gas plant, flour mills, slaughterhouses, and freight yards developed in the vicinity. Railroad development along the river intensified in 1886 when the Los Angeles City Council gave the Atchison, Topeka & Santa Fe a fifty-foot right-of-way on the west bank of the river for its tracks. Before long, spur lines crisscrossed the former agricultural lands adjacent to the river. Industry was most heavily concentrated in the area between Alameda Street and its channel. This area was home to planing mills, foundries, lumberyards, fuel plants, food and beverage manufacturers, warehouses, and the like. Devel-

opment of the downtown riverfront was completed in 1891 when the Los Angeles Terminal Railroad built a line to San Pedro on the east bank of the river.[13]

Railroad and industrial development so changed the landscape beside the
river near downtown that as the stream channel was gradually robbed of most
of its surface flow there was little demand for its care or improvement. Perception of the river had been so altered that in 1887, when eighty horses were killed
in a stable fire, their carcasses were dumped in the river bed. Thus, as Los Angeles city officials wrestled with the problem of what to do about the growing volume of sewage produced in the city, many thought it only logical that the city's
liquid wastes be discharged into the river. Perhaps realizing that the river would
do little to carry the sewage away, city engineers proposed instead that a comprehensive sewer system be built at a cost of 1 million dollars. The proposal
called for the construction of an outfall sewer to transport the city's sewage fifteen miles across the coastal plain to the Pacific Ocean. Some saw this as an
unnecessary expenditure with the river so close. The *Los Angeles Times*, in an
editorial, said, "A fair investigation will make it apparent to all reasonable persons that the building of the outfall sewer would involve a needless expense.
The river route . . . is the natural route."[14]

The ocean outfall sewer was eventually approved by voters in 1892, but that
did little to prevent degradation of the river. In 1896, for example, the city
council received complaints that rubbish was being dumped in its bed. A few
years later, the board of health reported that the river channel was becoming a
health hazard because of "pollution by pigeons and other species of fowls," a
reference to a large pigeon farm that existed beside the river (though it may
seem strange by today's standards, the pigeon farm was a far more popular
attraction than the river). In 1904, five local residents complained to the council that large amounts of tar and oil dumped in the river bed posed a threat to
humans and livestock. So much tar and oil had been dumped in the river, one
man testified, that a pool had formed that he said was two to ten feet deep and
covered an area thirty by eighty feet. Because a thin layer of dust sat atop the
pool, he added, it was largely invisible and, as a result, several men and animals
had become stuck in it. Four cows, in fact, had to be rescued when they became
trapped in the sludge and sank up to their necks. "Only about four to six inches of the cows were visible above the tar," the man said. "In order to save them
from perishing it was necessary to fasten ropes to their heads and with the aid
of about forty men, and a team of horses, the animals were dragged from the
deposit."[15]

With so little water in its bed near downtown, the river also became home
to increasing numbers of transients. The *Los Angeles Times* in 1901 featured a
long article on the "ever shifting class that inhabits the river bed." They includ-

ed thieves, "men of morose disposition with ambition dead," a drug "fiend," and even an ex-millionaire. Three photos published with the article show that some of their dwellings were remarkably permanent looking. One looks two stories tall, perhaps to enable its owner to survive high water. In 1903, the city health officer complained that "manure, garbage, etc." left by "squatters" living in the river threatened the health of local residents, and recommended that the city council enact an ordinance prohibiting people from living in the river channel. Just such an ordinance was approved in 1911, but people continued to live in the river, particularly during hard times. Folk singer Woody Guthrie, commenting on a song he wrote about a deadly 1934 flood in Los Angeles, claimed that many more people were killed than were counted in official death tolls—dirt-poor "Okies" living in the river bed.[16]

As industrial development spread along its banks, the most common use of

Figure 6.6. Mule-drawn teams haul sand and gravel from the riverbed near downtown Los Angeles in the 1920s. After the river was sucked dry by water developments, the most visible use of its channel was as a source of sand and gravel for construction crews. Los Angeles Public Library, Security Pacific Collection.

the river was as a source of sand and gravel for construction crews (see figure 6.6). City council records from the late nineteenth and early twentieth centuries are filled with requests from contractors seeking permission to remove sand and gravel from pits in the river bed. In 1901, the council even approved the construction of a bridge into the bed of the river at Aliso Street to make it easier for teams to haul gravel from its channel. City officials reported in 1907 that one thousand to twelve hundred truckloads of sand and gravel were being removed from the riverbed every day. So much sand was hauled from the river that a city street superintendent warned that the stability of bridge supports and levees built along the river was being threatened.[17]

The Los Angeles City Council in 1910 sought to gain some control over activity in the river when it enacted an ordinance prohibiting the dumping of refuse and rubbish in its channel. The law, however, was clearly a failure. Even city officials ignored it. Two years after passage of the ordinance, a Los Angeles parks commissioner remarked that the river was "unsightly to the extreme." He reported that not only were huge volumes of sand and gravel being hauled from the river, but that "teams engaged in removing gravel frequently haul back

Figure 6.7. Smoldering Los Angeles city dump protrudes into the river near downtown Los Angeles, 1923. Water Resources Center Archives, Joseph Barlow Lippincott Collection, University of California, Berkeley.

trash and dump it into the river bed." The parks department conducted a survey of such activity in 1912 and reported that an average of twenty-seven truckloads of rubbish were being dumped in the river each day. Adding to the unsightly and unsanitary character of the river through downtown was a huge city dump that sat on the west bank of the river and projected into its channel. City council records indicate that, despite the 1910 ordinance, the city continued dumping refuse into the riverside dump until at least 1925 (see figure 6.7).[18]

There were occasional proposals not only to clean up the river but to beautify its channel, but these appear to have been isolated suggestions, the most sweeping of which, perhaps not coincidentally, were made by nonresidents and relative newcomers, whose ideas about the river may not have been shaped by local attitudes. None of these proposals made it past the idea stage, moreover, which probably reflects the lack of care Angelinos had for their river. The earliest proposal to improve the river was made by Dana Bartlett, a New England–raised minister and settlement-house director, who suggested in 1906 that "despite the fact that its banks are lined with factories and the river bed itself is sought by utilitarian corporations," the river could be "made into a line of beauty." In 1910, another easterner, Charles Mulford Robinson, a proponent for City Beautiful planning, recommended that the river be cleared of trash and that trees be planted on its banks. Even he acknowledged "the river presents a very serious problem, and one which cannot be solved with entire aesthetic satisfaction. A river bed that for most of the year is dry and that has on both of its banks a railroad is not an attractive object."[19]

The nature of still other proposals, moreover, suggests much about local perceptions of the river. Joseph Mesmer, an influential local merchant, recommended about 1910 that the river, the "most unsightly sight in the city" in the words of an article describing his plan, be transformed into a series of parks, lakes, and esplanades. To men such as Mesmer, the improvement of the river was an economic issue because the river was the first thing many out-of-town visitors saw when they arrived in Los Angeles by train. More interesting, though, was what Mesmer proposed to do to the river. To create a park six miles long, he recommended that the river's bed and sides be "lined solidly with concrete." About the same time, a member of the Los Angeles Board of Park Commissioners made a more modest proposal, recommending only that quarrying activities in the river be regulated and that steps be taken to prevent further dumping in the riverbed. His comments are even more telling. "It would be expensive and difficult, if not impossible, ever to make the river bed a thing of beauty," he said, "but it is not necessary to have it so ugly and unsanitary."[20]

Real Estate and the River

The geographic dimensions of settlement in Los Angeles in the late nine-teenth and early twentieth centuries also strongly influenced the future treat-ment of the river. The city's original Spanish and Mexican settlers, like the Indians before them, understood the erratic nature of streams in arid regions and built their homes far enough from the river to, for the most part, assure their safety in times of flood. Despite its reputation as a land of perpetual sun-shine and little rain, Southern California faces a greater hazard from cata-strophic floods than probably any other metropolitan area in the nation.

Los Angeles is naturally flood prone because of the region's climate and topography. Tall mountains ring the valleys and coastal plain, trapping storms and speeding runoff. Some of the most concentrated rainfall ever recorded in the United States occurred in the San Gabriel Mountains, which rise more than ten thousand feet above Los Angeles. Before their channels were remade by humans, the rivers and streams of the lowlands were ill equipped to carry the great quantities of water, mud, rocks, and trees that cascaded from these moun-tains during storms. The Los Angeles River overflowed its banks at least ten times in the first one hundred years after Los Angeles was founded. It also changed courses repeatedly and, during one great flood in 1825, shifted its mouth twenty miles down the coast, cutting an entirely new channel directly south after leaving Los Angeles.[21]

Until the boom of the 1880s led to the rapid subdivision of agricultural lands and increased urban development throughout Southern California, how-ever, floods were usually relatively benign and were seen by many as beneficial because they restored moisture and nutrients to soils. "A flood might be a tem-porary evil," remarked one early observer, "but like the overflow of the Nile, a year of plenty always followed." There was also less potential for damage from floods before the arrival of the railroads because most of the land near the river was still devoted to farming and few structures had been built on the most flood-prone lands. Maps show that as late as 1876 nearly all of the land within a half mile of the river was still under cultivation. The earliest residential areas in Los Angeles were laid out on the benchlands further from the river and on the terraces east of its channel. This helps explain why, after a flood in 1862 that may have been the most extensive in the history of Southern California, a local newspaper commented that "the losses . . . on the whole . . . have been quite insignificant."[22]

The new class of settlers who moved to Los Angeles after the arrival of the Southern Pacific had a very different attitude toward the river, however. Not only did they fail to appreciate the river aesthetically, but they had little respect for its potential dangers. Urban development, as a result, began to seriously encroach on the floodplain. The first significant subdivision of agricultural lands had begun a few years earlier, when the Los Angeles and San Pedro Railroad had built its depot one half mile west of the river. This had spurred a small property boom in the area, and before long home lots began to be sold in the vicinity. Development intensified when the Southern Pacific took over the Los Angeles and San Pedro. Warehouses and factories were constructed near its depot, and the area immediately surrounding the incipient industrial complex was subdivided for residences to provide homes for laborers in the area. Within a few years, much of the area between Alameda Street and the river was occupied by small houses. By the late 1880s, residential development had spread north and south on both sides of its channel (see figure 6.8).[23]

As Los Angeles grew, few paid much attention to the stream that flowed gingerly through the center of the city. Most probably laughed at the Los Angeles River when they thought of the "real" rivers back home. One who did take

Figure 6.8. Taken from a balloon looking east across the river in 1887, this photograph shows the encroachment of urban development on the west side of the river, east of downtown Los Angeles. Seaver Center for Western History Research, Los Angeles County Museum of Natural History.

the river seriously was J. J. Warner, an early Los Angeles newspaperman who had arrived in Southern California in 1831. As development moved ever closer to the river, he warned in a series of letters published in the *Los Angeles Times* in 1882 "of the risk to which many . . . are exposing themselves, their property and their families in the selection of places upon which to build their dwellings." Warner, who had witnessed major floods in 1832, 1859, 1862, and 1868, wrote, "There are many now living in Los Angeles who do not know the magnitude of the volume of water which flows through this city when the river is flooded." He castigated the "reckless and crafty" real estate agents who had sold property along the river and cautioned that if a flood of the magnitude of previous floods occurred again, it "would destroy a large part of the property situated in that part of the city."[24]

Such warnings did little to deter newcomers from buying lots in the area, some of them scoffing at the idea that the harmless-looking river could possibly be a threat. The case of Alfred Moore is especially telling. Moore arrived in Los Angeles in 1876, the same year as the Southern Pacific, and bought a large lot a few hundred yards west of the river, where he built a house. An auctioneer by trade, Moore eventually bought several other lots in the neighborhood. Some he sold, but he built small homes on others and began renting them. After Warner's letters were published, Moore responded with a letter of his own, thumbing his nose at the danger. "We need not, I think, feel at all alarmed about a flood," he said. "I have lived on the Aliso Tract . . . for the past eight years and never saw a flood yet." He boasted that he had sold six lots "within a few feet of the river" to a woman who was "plucky enough" to disregard the warnings of her neighbors about the possibility of an overflow. "I am selling bottom land lots, so-called, rapidly ever since," he wrote. As it turned out, Moore would be among the hardest hit when Los Angeles experienced a series of major floods beginning two years later. He lost at least eight houses and by the following decade had moved away from the riverfront.[25]

Still, because long dry periods usually separated the great floods, a characteristic of the region's Mediterranean-type climate, and thousands of newcomers oblivious to the flood risk continued to move to the region, urban development began to line the river up and down its course in succeeding decades. The cities of Burbank and Glendale, located along the river in the San Fernando Valley, and Long Beach, astride the river's mouth, were founded during the Boom of the Eighties and grew rapidly after commuter rail lines were built to them from Los Angeles just after the turn of the century. The first leg of the Pacific Electric commuter railroad was built from Los Angeles to Long Beach in 1902. The line became an immediate success and helped Long Beach grow from a small town to the third largest city in the county by the end of the decade. The Pacific Electric extended its tracks to Glendale in 1904 and Burbank in 1911, and both those towns grew rapidly thereafter as well.

The opening of the Owens River aqueduct in 1913 spurred increased urban development beside the river in the San Fernando Valley. Towns also began to spring up near the river along the Pacific Electric line from Los Angeles to Long Beach. Emblematic of the amnesia Los Angeles had about the danger posed by the river was the fact that two of these cities, Vernon and Huntington Park, were platted directly in the former channel of the river, as it had existed until a flood in 1889 caused it to shift its course sharply east. Within a few years, a large petroleum plant was built right in the old bed of the river.[26]

Government officials were largely powerless to prevent development on the flood-prone lands adjacent to the river. When the first large-scale flood control program in Los Angeles was initiated in 1915, legal instruments such as flood-plain zoning, designed to prevent development in high-risk areas, did not yet exist. Such strategies were still considered to be on shaky legal ground thirty years later, after the federal government had taken over the flood control program.

Further limiting the power of planners was the fact that ownership of much of the river channel itself was in private hands. Elsewhere in the United States, navigable rivers had been set aside as public property, but this was not the case in Southern California since the river carried too little water on most of its course to float a boat. Consequently, as the county flood control program was getting under way, engineers were limited in the strategies they could consider. The cost of land along the river south of Los Angeles, for example, prevented them from giving the river a wide berth and allowing more of its natural character to be maintained. "Land is here so valuable that it is advisable to keep the right of way as narrow as possible," wrote a member of a county flood control planning board in 1915. By the 1930s, the nature of development along the river made it virtually impossible for government officials to consider more ecologically sensitive approaches for preventing floods.[27] In truth, however, there seems to have been little public sentiment at the time that such approaches were even desirable. Significant environmental concern for the river is a modern phenomenon.[28]

It is important to remember, too, that all development in the watershed of the river, not only that in its floodplain, increased runoff, heightened the flood hazard, and ultimately contributed to the remaking of the river. Every new house, driveway, shopping center, and parking lot further transforms the hydrology of the region. Contemporary environmentalists, many of them living outside the area that is considered most susceptible to floods today, have been critical of those living beside the river along its lower reaches who have fought mandatory flood insurance and have supported efforts to increase structural flood protections along its channel. Such people fail to acknowledge that they, like all Southern Californians, have contributed to the flood risk, that the homes in which they live, the roads on which they drive, the places they work, and the stores where they shop were built atop a landscape that once absorbed and stored most of the seasonal rains. By their very presence in Southern California, they are complicit with the flood control engineers with whom they are so often at odds.

We must resist the temptation, furthermore, to judge history and those who shaped it by contemporary standards. It is essential to consider the context in which people from an earlier time made their decisions. The Los Angeles River, like other urban rivers in the late nineteenth and early twentieth centuries, was viewed as a resource and little else. Residents took from it all they needed to survive until its channel was drained dry. And then they took some more. Flood control projects are generally blamed for turning the river into an eyesore, but in truth it was the city's increasing reliance on the river for its water supply that first transformed it from a thing of beauty (albeit seldom appreciated as such) into an object of ridicule. Urban development further remade the river, so that even before the first extensive flood control projects were begun, it was rarely viewed as an asset, as something to be saved. Rather, it was an occasional hazard that had to be controlled. Concrete channels merely became the coffin for a river that had already been sapped of nearly all its life.

7

Flood Control Engineering in the Urban Ecosystem

JARED ORSI

WINTER storm rolled onshore at Los Angeles on February 13, 1980. A second storm followed a day later, then a third and a fourth and a fifth. A sixth storm brought the heaviest rains yet, swelling the Los Angeles River to its levee tops. Meanwhile, weather forecasters spotted a seventh storm brewing out on the Pacific. As water rose in the dark that night, the swamped electronic stream gauges stopped functioning, and the technicians at the flood control headquarters lost track of how high the water was running. If the river were to spill over its walls, it would eat away at the levees from the landward side. They would crumble, and the torrents would gush into adjacent neighborhoods. No one knew if the channels could handle one more storm. Fortunately, the rain stopped that night, and the seventh storm never materialized. When the sun rose the next morning, inspectors from the Los Angeles County Flood Control District (LACFCD) found flood debris strewn atop the levees near the Wardlow Road overpass in Long Beach. Apparently it had been a very close call.[1]

The levees at Wardlow Road and other Southern California flood defenses have enjoyed much success. They have prevented more than 4 billion dollars of damage since 1917 and saved an untold number of lives. As the troubling debris atop the levee attests, however, the flood danger persists. Although the levees held in 1980, the storm produced 270 million dollars in property damages, and the brush with catastrophe led the Federal Emergency Management Administration to contemplate raising flood insurance rates and strengthening building codes for property owners along the lower Los Angeles River. By 1987, the Los Angeles District of the U.S. Army Corps of Engineers declared the levee system inadequate. Three times in the 1990s floods damaged more than 100 million dollars of property, and the corps feared a potential 2-billion-dollar flood should a storm just larger than 1980's strike. Today, after seventy-five years and more than a billion dollars of flood control engineering in Southern California, the flood threat still looms. The source of these problems lies in the design of the structures but also in the institution of flood control itself.

Since its inception in 1914, institutionalized flood control in Southern California has been technocratic.[2] After February 1914, when the rivers leapt their banks to ravage agricultural fields, inundate city neighborhoods, and choke the newly built harbor with silt, Los Angeles County officials appointed a team of engineers to redesign the rivers. Since then, a special public agency, the LACFCD, which was later joined by the Army Corps of Engineers, has vested power in technical experts to design physical structures to replace nature's hydrology with human technology. Technical considerations have, in theory at least, guided almost all policy making, and officials have generally assumed that experts' diagnoses of the rivers and corrective designs would translate without alteration into construction and operation of flood control devices. By the 1970s, one of the institution's critics noted, the flood controllers had "developed a mentality . . . that flowing water should only be dealt with by engineers and solely as an engineering problem." Meanwhile, flood control's political and other nontechnical facets have been cast as outside the scope of the problem. "We don't play politics," one army engineer snapped in response to a journalist's 1994 question, "we're engineers."[3]

In practice, however, taming Southern California's rivers has indeed involved politics. Political institutions, like ecosystems, have their own internal logic that interacts with external influences to produce change that is not always straightforward or predictable. In Southern California's twentieth-century flood control institutions, political structure—that is, law and bureaucratic jurisdictions—determined which individuals and organizations did and did not have authority to carry out flood control and specified what types of projects they could undertake. Political will, forged by conflict among interested parties and their supporters, often overrode the technical merits of designs in influencing which projects would gain public support. And political culture—public memory, visions of the future, and prevalent ideas about nature, science, and public policy—delimited the range of possibilities that could even be imagined. Thus flood control became not merely a technical exercise in modeling the rivers' flood pattern and building physical structures to contain it. Rather, through politics, all the messy, irrational, and contingent factors that make the unfolding of history so dynamic and unpredictable impinged on the flood control calculus and thus entered the mix of factors influencing where, when, and how water flowed in Los Angeles. Flood control engineering, it turned out, was disorderly and unpredictable, not unlike the rivers the flood controllers sought to tame.

Flood controllers, however, have generally overlooked this disorder that politics has injected into the process of river taming. Ironically, the technical orientation of flood control in Southern California owes its very existence to the disorder of dynamic, contingent history. It originated as a logical product of the political culture of the Progressive Era but failed to provide much flood protection in the face of political conflict in the 1920s. Despite two decades of floundering, the program appeared so compelling under the historical circumstances of the Great Depression that it rendered alternative flood control strategies virtually invisible.

Through the midcentury decades, political and climatic conditions continued to favor technically oriented flood control, and a federal-local partnership produced the flood defenses that fortify Los Angeles today. Both the transience of these conditions and their indispensability to the success of flood control, however, became apparent in the 1970s, when minor floods caused major damage and environmentalists began challenging the assumption that paved riverbeds were good for the community. Remarkably, throughout most of this saga, flood controllers were working with substantially the same technical blueprint, the LACFCD's 1931 Comprehensive Plan. Something more than technics, therefore, must explain the ups and downs of institutionalized flood control in Southern California. Debris topped the levees in 1980 because flood control in Los Angeles was much more than an engineering problem.

Centralized Authority and a Comprehensive Plan

The flood control technocracy was born when the waters of the great 1914 flood mixed with the political culture of the Progressive Era. That experience—the first large flood in a quarter of a century—alerted people to a problem, and progressivism told them what to do about it. Roughly spanning the late 1890s into the 1920s, the Progressive Era was a time when, nationwide, societal problems, especially those concerning the environment, were coming to be seen as ever larger and more complex, requiring more elaborate organizations for combating them.[4] People formed private organizations and government agencies to pool their resources to attack problems that they shared an inability to solve as individuals. Most frequently, they turned these problems over to experts. With objective expert management, everything in society, it seemed, from Gifford Pinchot's national forests to Henry Ford's assembly lines, could be made to function systematically and efficiently. It was this obsession with system and expertise that linked progressives of different professions, social backgrounds, and ideological bents. Through a progressive lens, the sludge that the flood deposited in the Los Angeles Harbor, the disrupted business, and the unforeseen costs of repairs did not appear to be exceptional events in a usually benevolent natural environment. Instead, they were disruptions to a system. Order had broken down.

With fashionable Progressive Era confidence in experts, the 250 delegates to a Los Angeles County flood control convention in 1914 resolved that "control of the flood waters of the County should be vested in a centralized authority and should be in accordance with a comprehensive plan." Over the next year, a specially appointed team of engineers surveyed, measured, projected, predicted, and calculated until they compiled a three-hundred-page proposal for controlling the water from the mountains to the sea. They would dam the water, store it, spread it, confine it, and divert it until the rivers functioned with the same efficiency and mechanical predictability that Ford had achieved at factories and that Pinchot had extracted from forests. With 16.5 million dollars and five years of construction, the engineers promised, these devices would "permanently relieve the people of Los Angeles county from the menace of future floods."[5]

To implement this comprehensive plan, Southern Californians created the LACFCD.[6] Heading the agency was a chief engineer who directed the design and construction of flood control structures. The district would submit plans to the county board of supervisors, who would place the proposals on the election ballot. Voters would ratify the plans and approve bond measures to finance them. Thereafter, all power would return to the engineers. In an attempt to curb undue influence by contractors seeking to manipulate designs to get more lucrative contracts, the law creating the district prohibited any changes to engineering plans once voters approved them.[7] Together, the centralized authority and the comprehensive plan reduced flood control to an engineering problem to be dealt with primarily by engineers.

Twenty years and 50 million dollars later, however, the flood control program lay in shambles. Between 1917 and 1924 the LACFCD's visionary first chief engineer James W. Reagan transformed the initially modest proposals of the board of engineers into a program of gargantuan concrete mountain dams, some of which were planned to be taller than any previously built anywhere in the world. The new plans reignited earlier conflict between parties who favored small dams and reforestation and those who preferred the big new dams. Although both sides, of course, marshaled engineering experts to plead the technical merits of their cases, the ostensibly technical debates invariably masked struggles over who would pay for flood control structures, who would oversee their construction, and who would control water rights to the redesigned rivers. In 1924, a severe drought and the conversion of rural land to urban uses combined to bolster the popularity of the big-dam program (which promised to resolve the problems of both water shortage and surplus), and Reagan's dams won a record majority in the election to approve their financing. But controversy continued to rage through the 1920s, and Reagan resigned in 1927 amidst attacks on his engineering expertise. Two years later, the canyon walls collapsed at the construction site of San Gabriel Dam, the largest of the projects, and a graft scandal involving a county supervisor surfaced.

Reagan's less flamboyant successor, E. C. Eaton, embarked on a more methodical plan to survey the flood control needs of the entire county and to undertake construction on a cost-benefit basis. So unpopular had the LACFCD become, however, that even in the aftermath of a flood that produced devastating debris on New Year's Eve 1933, the discredited agency could not muster enough voter support to pass a bond measure to finance Eaton's Comprehensive Plan, which he had unveiled in 1931. By the early 1930s, then, the flood danger in the ever expanding Los Angeles metropolitan area was growing faster than the flood defenses, and the LACFCD had no money and no credibility.

Ironically, the emergence, early promise, and subsequent failure of locally led flood control in Southern California had little to do with the technical merits of the proposals and much to do with historical timing, political disputes, and public relations. Flood control engineering turned out to be less an exercise in replacing a disorderly natural hydrology with an orderly engineered one than in substituting the disorder of nature for the disorder of artifice.

Paths Not Taken

Hypothetically at least, the flood control failures of the early 1930s might have sparked a reevaluation of the program's engineering emphasis and pointed flood controllers down a new path. But that did not happen. During the Depression decade, a few tentative efforts to integrate less technical alternatives into flood control surfaced. Many conservationists advocated so-called upstream flood control measures—fire prevention, reforestation, soil and water conservation, and check-dam building. An urban planning firm proposed combining parks and recreation with flood control. And a few people even dared to suggest hazard zoning to limit development of the flood plains. None of these alternatives, however, got very far. In fact, most failed even to come up for serious public discussion. Instead, the structure and culture of flood control politics in 1930s Los Angeles rendered these alternatives virtually invisible.

Perhaps the most intriguing possibility was hazard zoning. Through exercise of the police power, cities and counties in California had authority to limit or prohibit development in flood-prone areas. Although more than 2 million people inhabited Los Angeles County in the 1930s, many of the areas that are today threatened with flooding were still undeveloped at the time. A 1942 State Planning Board report recommended that zoning to limit future development in flood plains would often be more cost effective than erection of dams and channels to protect places from inundation.[8]

It was widely recognized by the 1930s that development aggravated the flood danger—both by augmenting the runoff that storms produced and by placing more people and property in harm's way. Moreover, engineering works to control floods often created a sense of security that induced more development, which in turn necessitated more flood control works. A few people in the 1930s sought to break this cycle with hazard zoning. The State Planning Board, the Municipal League, and an urban planning firm hired by the Los Angeles Chamber of Commerce all made little-noticed recommendations for using zoning to prevent flood damage, and Los Angeles County actually amended its zoning ordinance in 1940 to prohibit new residential construction in a pair of small flood-prone areas a few miles southwest of downtown. None of these initiatives, however, developed into anything remotely resembling systematic hazard zoning.[9]

This was partly due to the power structure that vested flood control decision-making authority in technical bodies. The engineers, to whom flood control had been entrusted, were builders, not planners, and they defined the nontechnical aspects of flood control as outside the scope of their work. For example, in response to attempts to get the district to landscape its facilities and to open them to boating, fishing, swimming, and sightseeing, the agency's officials maintained that it was neither "our duty" nor "even legal" to spend district money on such matters. Similarly, federal engineers often chided city planners for failure to prevent development of flood-prone zones, but Congress did not authorize those engineers to assist local authorities with floodplain zoning until 1960. Meanwhile, local engineers did not seem particularly interested in hazard zoning. Eaton, among others, believed that development had proceeded too far to make zoning an effective option. Thus, although both federal and local engineers recognized that uncontrolled land use had aggravated the flood threat, they considered coordinated planning to be somebody else's responsibility. Consequently, any challenges to the engineering focus of Los Angeles flood control had to come from outside the system.[10]

The biggest obstacle to the emergence of such alternatives was a political culture that worshipped growth and development. For decades Southern California boosters celebrated towns that did not yet exist, water that had not yet arrived, and people who did not yet live there. Much of the region's development was driven by promises of future growth. Not surprisingly, when the Los Angeles Chamber of Commerce commissioned a study of parks and recreation in the region in 1927 and the report came back in 1930 not only with a proposal for riparian parkways that would double as overflow zones during periods of high water but also with plans to enlarge municipal property ownership and to use hazard zoning to control real estate speculation in riparian zones, the chamber's leaders balked at what they perceived as a radical threat to future property development in Los Angeles. Moreover, many chamber leaders found the proposal's call for a new municipal authority with sweeping jurisdiction that included parks, roads, flood control, and other infrastructure, in the words of one director, "terrifying." Fearing the new authority would infringe on some of their own informally exercised power, the chamber's directors never acted on the report.[11]

Similarly, when the Municipal League proposed hazard zoning as a flood control strategy in 1938, the idea went nowhere. Although Los Angeles by that time boasted some of the first and toughest zoning regulations in the country, these earlier initiatives had been intended to protect existing property interests. To use zoning to limit future development was a leap that the business leaders of 1930s Los Angeles were not prepared to make. In fact, some Chamber of Commerce directors were so uneasy about any sort of government interference with private property rights that they balked even at federal funding for flood control, for fear of allowing "the Federal Government to become so intimate in our affairs." As one director snorted in 1936, "We objected under the NRA [National Recovery Administration] to all of that and now we are inviting them back in through another door." Consequently, in contemplating the various flood control alternatives in the 1930s, the chamber appears not to have considered zoning at all. Nor did the authors of a 1941 book connect zoning and flood control when advocating a master plan for Los Angeles. The flood control section in that book barely mentioned zoning, and the zoning chapter completely ignored flood control. Despite the engineers' twenty-year inability to keep floods away from people, the possibility of using zoning or parks to keep people away from the floods remained too threatening to receive extensive consideration.[12]

Meanwhile, engineering remained a compelling flood control strategy. Not only did it beckon with the allure of public works employment to reduce the region's swelling relief rolls, but it also promised federal money for local needs. In March 1936, as the corps held public hearings on proposed federal legislation authorizing it to undertake flood control engineering in Los Angeles, fear arose that local dissension might induce Congress, as one official later put it, to "spend the money where they aren't so fussy." The board of supervisors chair, Herbert Legg, directed the Chamber of Commerce and other organizations to offer their unconditional support for the pending legislation.[13]

A Southern California congressman admonished John Anson Ford, the lone dissenting supervisor, that "local opposition would almost to a certainty kill it." Although Ford persisted in mild objections to the army's plans, almost everyone else fell into line. After much bickering, the Chamber of Commerce supported the plan "in every detail," as did a majority of the board of supervisors, the region's congressional delegation, and, of course, the LACFCD officials. Even the Municipal League, which had long been critical of flood control engineering, muted its objections during the mid-1930s, maintaining that despite certain flaws in the proposal, "these army engineers did do a good job." Thus, pressure for local unity limited the objections that arose to the proposed federal engineering program and dampened enthusiasm for seeking alternatives.[14]

Despite the engineering program's previous failures, then, no viable alternatives emerged in the 1930s. The power structure that charged engineers with initiating flood control policy, the political culture that had for decades celebrated unhampered urban development, and the imperatives for seeking federal aid combined to render nontechnical approaches virtually unimaginable and prevented them from entering serious public debate. The gap between the recognition of previous flood control engineering failures and the articulation of new sorts of strategies is illustrated by an exchange between the LACFCD's chief engineer, E. C. Eaton, and Donald Baker, the former president of the Los Angeles City Planning Commission. Although he was an engineer himself, Baker considered flood control to be "preeminently a problem of economic and human nature, with construction and hydraulics secondary." In a 1935 roundtable discussion published in the *Transactions of the American Society of Civil Engineers*, Baker contended that the "physical, meteorological, hydrological, recreational, cultural, historical, financial, and political" aspects of flood control all contributed to the danger. He called for a comprehensive plan in which "all the various phases and aspects of the problem" would be coordinated. Until Los Angeles County adopted such an approach, he warned, floods would recur.[15]

But Baker's proposition, that managing water also meant managing politics, the economy, and society, was simply too foreign even to be heard. In dismissing Baker's comment, Eaton responded in the same issue of *Transactions* that the county had in fact already produced a Comprehensive Plan.[16] He was referring, of course, to the LACFCD's 1931 manifesto outlining the most urgently needed engineering works. So different were the premises behind Baker's comprehensive plan and Eaton's Comprehensive Plan that they misunderstood one another despite using the very same words.

The Sun Is Shining over Southern California

Any doubts about the need for flood control engineering drowned in March 1938, as the greatest recorded deluge in Los Angeles took fifty-nine lives and damaged 62 million dollars worth of property. When the famed Southern California sun returned after the storm, the ever optimistic Los Angeles mayor Frank Shaw took to the radio. "The sun is shining over Southern California today," he reassured listeners, and "Los Angeles is still smiling."[17] (See figure 7.1.)

For the next thirty years, the mayor's optimism proved well founded. In contrast to the earlier local flood control efforts, the army corps managed to build whatever it designed. Before it could harm the fortified metropolis, a flood striking at the end of the 1960s would have had to fill the 106 mountain

Figure 7.1. Los Angeles River overflowing its banks, 1938. University of Southern California, California Historical Society Collection.

debris basins, spill over the five valley flood control dams, or make a breach somewhere along the 350 miles of concrete river channels. If these defenses had been in place in 1938, the corps's Colonel John Dillard declared in 1965, the disaster would not have occurred.[18] Indeed the path of the water from sky to sea had radically changed since the 1930s. One thing that had not changed, however, was the influence of human history on that path. Just as the failures of the local program had stemmed in large part from nontechnical factors, the federal program owed much of its success to the favorable political, economic, and cultural conditions that prevailed at midcentury. These conditions, along with the fact that they coincided with a long period free from severe flooding, enabled the corps to make substantial progress on a plan that was technically similar to the one that the LACFCD had been unable to launch in the 1930s.

Political quiescence accounted for the ease with which flood controllers turned blueprints into infrastructure between 1938 and 1969. After several moderate appropriations in the late 1930s, Congress approved 270 million dollars in 1941 for the army to embark on a comprehensive flood control program, the Los Angeles County Drainage Area Project (LACDA). Although similar to the 1931 Comprehensive Plan, which the LACFCD had been unable to build support for in the early 1930s, LACDA sparked almost no controversy for nearly three decades. A 1963 book on Southern California government cited flood control as one of the few metropolitan issues on which there was substantial consensus across the region. The most important source of this midcentury quiescence was the fact that the federal government was picking up the check. As Chamber of Commerce president William Rosecrans noted in 1938, a million dollars "is a lot of money if yours, but if it is Government money it is not very much." Local leaders such as Rosecrans were reluctant to look the gift horse of federal engineering in the mouth.[19]

A second source of quiescence in flood control politics was a general ideological consensus that stemmed from the national emergencies of World War II and the cold war. Like other high-tech, capital-intensive federal projects, from the space program to the interstate highway system, flood control in Southern California was tinged with the rhetoric of national security. As airplane factories and other industrial endeavors proliferated in Los Angeles, local and federal officials increasingly worried about the flood threat. In approving LACDA, one engineering journal noted in 1941, Congress was contracting for "insurance that the vital defense industries around the city would not lose time on account of wet feet." During World War II, armed soldiers guarded the flood control sites. No saboteurs showed up to menace the defenses, though hundreds of thousands of visitors flocked annually to swim at the reservoirs and gawk at the imposing structures.[20]

Even after the war, national defense concerns persisted, with citizens supporting flood control on the grounds that it would protect the region's water supply in the event of "a war, earthquake, or other catastrophe," and that "jeopardy to Coastal Plain Naval installations could affect the national defense of this country." Amidst such concerns, the district and the corps were able to portray flood control as the will of the people and to represent the few dissenters as voices of minority special interests whose goals deviated from the good of the many. As a result, one observer noted at the end of the 1950s, "local political warfare . . . has in the past twenty years more or less disappeared from the scene."[21]

The result of the federal money and the widespread consensus was to limit flood control debate to technical issues—locations, dimensions, and other specifications of individual projects. Unlike the local program of the 1920s, which had often lacked meaningful mechanisms for resolving even technical disputes, the army corps's hierarchical organization structure helped diffuse what little disagreement did arise. The only project to generate substantial controversy during the midcentury years was Whittier Narrows Dam, which was proposed to lie between the towns of El Monte and Whittier in eastern Los Angeles County. While acknowledging the need for flood control engineering in general, El Monte citizens objected to Whittier Narrows Dam in particular because its reservoir would have at times submerged a portion of the town. Not only did they lobby Congress vigorously to deny funding for the dam, they also hired a team of engineers, including the former flood control chief Reagan, to formulate alternative engineering strategies that would yield the dam's benefits while preserving the town from inundation. Unlike the controversy over San Gabriel Dam, however, the Whittier Narrows dispute never spun out of control to hamper the rest of the flood control efforts.

Approval of corps projects such as Whittier Narrows Dam required that designs move up and down a chain of command from the desk of local engineers through regional and national offices to the Secretary of War and back down to the local level for revisions. Ultimately, Congress had to approve funding once the army approved the design. This hierarchy provided plenty of opportunity at each level for dissent but confined it to technical questions. In response to El Monte's opposition to the dam, the corps abandoned, reinstituted, and modified the project many times in the 1930s and 1940s. Finally in 1948, a version of the project that all sides could support emerged when Richard Nixon, then a congressman from the area and an aspiring Senate candidate hoping to resolve this conflict that divided his constituency, brokered a compromise to lower the dam's height and move its proposed location downstream to avoid flooding El Monte. Thus, even the most contentious flood control debate centered on how, not whether, to reengineer the rivers.[22]

A final factor favorable to engineering works was the prolonged climatic quiescence that coincided with the political calm. The few floods that struck during the postwar years hardly matched the fury of the storms of 1914, 1916, 1934, and 1938 that had undermined confidence in existing flood control practices. In fact, as an *Engineering News-Record* editor put it in 1956, Los Angeles has been "extremely lucky" to have escaped the past fifteen years of explosive growth and only partial completion of the flood control works without a major storm. Flooding did occur in 1952, 1954, and 1956, but the combined damage from these three storms did not approach the devastation of 1938. Had there been no flood control works, the combined damage costs likely would not have exceeded that of the 1938 deluge. Furthermore, damage was localized in areas where LACDA structures were planned but not yet completed, which tended to confirm the value of what was already being done. After each flood, officials touted statistics indicating how much damage the existing structures had prevented: 20 million dollars in 1952, 55 million dollars in 1956.[23] Completion of other works already on the drawing board, officials promised, would head off even more destruction. The only thing wrong with the flood control system, it appeared, was that it was not yet completed (see figure 7.2).[24]

Figure 7.2. Los Angeles River channel construction, the San Fernando Valley, 1955. National Archives.

Midcentury flood controllers, then, benefited not only from political quiescence, but also from a prolonged period of calm waters. Technocratic flood
control as it had developed in its first decade of existence required that experts
gather data on local hydrology, predict future conditions, design protective
structures, secure public approval and financing, and then construct those
structures. Thus it required that nature and society be predictable, that politics
be calm, and that devices function as planned. All of these conditions prevailed
in the thirty years after the involvement of the federal government. It is little
wonder, then, that the army corps and the LACFCD accomplished everything
that they planned between the 1930s and 1960s: there was nothing in nature or
society to stop them (see figure 7.3).

Flip Buckets and Other Uncertainties

The engineers' optimism was seemingly borne out in 1969 when LACDA
prevented more than 1 billion dollars of damage during record-breaking
storms. "The Los Angeles County drainage area project," the army corps
declared, "protected the Los Angeles metropolitan area from what otherwise
would have been unprecedented damage." By 1987, however, the euphoria had

Figure 7.3. Channel construction near downtown, 1954. National Archives.

faded, as the corps distributed a brochure warning that "Disastrous Flooding Could Return to Los Angeles County."[25] Understanding the causes of this shift underscores how integral midcentury political and climatic quiescence was to the success of flood control during the period. Since 1969, neither politics nor nature has been quiescent, and the results in flood control contrast sharply with the apparent successes of the midcentury years.

Moderate storms in 1978 and 1980 surprised flood controllers by triggering severe flooding, even in areas they had thought were protected. A partial explanation can be attributed to the historic underestimation of both frequency and severity of flooding in Southern California. Flood control requires engineers to predict the frequency and severity of potential floods. Flooding water, it turned out, was anything but predictable. The fifty-year flood, which engineers designed infrastructure to withstand, was a hypothetical event with a 2 percent chance of occurring in any given year—a rare but severe event. Nature, however, did not package its storms in discrete fifty- and one-hundred-year units. Instead, each storm was an amalgam of varying intensities. In twenty-five-year storms, such as the one that roared up the slopes of the western San Gabriel Mountains in 1978, some canyons would get a drizzle while the slopes just over the hill would get a fifty-year drenching. Four times between 1969 and 1983, some part or other of the basin suffered fifty-year flooding, even though no storm as a whole surpassed that magnitude.[26]

Adding to the unpredictability, urbanization made the so-called fifty-year floods ever more likely. When engineers designed the flood control system in the 1940s, they expected the region to remain at least partly agricultural. As asphalt covered roads and subdivisions replaced farms, the surface of the Los Angeles basin grew nearly impervious to water. Runoff no longer spread out or soaked into the ground.[27] By 1980, when the orange groves and walnut orchards had all but disappeared, urban runoff had increased 25 percent, and the flood control designs had grown inadequate to protect the strip malls, subdivisions, and freeways that had replaced the farms. It took less rain in 1980 to make a flood.[28]

Even when predictions were correct, structures did not always work as intended. Since the 1930s, the district and the army corps had dug enormous basins in the foothills to capture the debris that rumbled out of the canyons during heavy rains. In 1978, these debris basins became, in the words of one district official, giant "flip buckets" that hurled debris into the neighborhoods they were supposed to protect. Partly, these strange fluid dynamics resulted from bad luck. The debris flows clogged drains and tossed boulders into outlets, causing the muck to overflow the basins. The failures also stemmed from complex interactions among the water, mud, and flood control works themselves. The designers had anticipated debris flowing at regular rates and settling into the basins. In the 1978 storm, however, the sludge flowed in surges, crested the dams, and sloshed into downstream neighborhoods before the basins had completely filled. Thus the uncertainty of fluid dynamics and the misfortune of rolling boulders rendered debris basins unable to catch the amount of material they were designed to contain.[29]

Politics proved no more predictable. Between the 1962 publication of Rachel Carson's *Silent Spring* and Earth Day in 1970, environmentalism evolved from the fringe ideology of a handful of wilderness lovers into a mainstream, middle-class movement with an impact on almost every facet of American life, including Southern California's concrete rivers. Beginning in the late 1960s, environmentalists prodded the LACFCD into adding bicycle paths and landscaping to the river levees and even managed to block or modify a few flood control projects. In 1987, a group of artists founded Friends of the Los Angeles River (FoLAR), which went on to stage river cleanups; produce a technically sophisticated alternative vision for the Los Angeles River that included parks, paths, and groundwater recharge; and challenge engineers' attempts to clear brush from river channels and to raise the walls along the lower Los Angeles River near Wardlow Road.[30]

While FoLAR's successes in "greening the rivers" were limited, they substantially altered the flood control process by injecting nontechnical concerns for wildlife, open space, aesthetics, parks and recreation, and neighborhood revitalization into the flood control debate.[31] As a result, in contrast to the mid-century decades, the army corps and the LACFCD could no longer build without taking into account the environmental impact of and the public response to the proposed projects. By 1997, for example, before the district could undertake even as simple a task as clearing brush that had sprouted in the soft-bottomed portions of the channels, it had to secure the approval of no fewer than eight federal and state agencies and face the public outcry of environmentalists who considered the volunteer vegetation to be vestiges of the primordial landscape springing up to reclaim the river. And environmental and community well-being along the rivers became part of the public discussion surrounding the 2001 Los Angeles mayoral election. Through the efforts of FoLAR and other groups, much public attention focused on the issue of river management in Los Angeles in the 1990s, and in combination with the 1978 and 1980 storms, the environmentalist critique has, for the first time since 1914, reopened the question of how to control the floods.

Necessary but Not Sufficient

During the 1980 flood, levees along the San Jacinto River failed at only 25 percent of their design capacity, diverting the torrents down Main Street of a small desert town on the eastern edge of the metropolitan area. The official corps report blamed the disaster on unforeseen fluid dynamics and upstream flood control works—yet another example of water and flood control devices interacting in strange ways to aggravate flooding. One engineer who studied the failures, however, concluded that the structures' collapse likely had something to do with bureaucracy as well. The levees' design called for construction with local rock, which turned out not to meet construction standards. But the bureaucracy had no mechanism for modifying the project once under way, without, as the engineer put it, "someone's head rolling." Consequently, builders forged ahead with the inadequate local materials, which eventually contributed to the undermining of the levee banks. Even when prediction, design, and public ratification went off as planned, bureaucracy could lead to faulty construction and disaster.[32]

Along the San Jacinto River and all over Southern California during the twentieth century, politics determined the flow of water just as much as precipitation and engineers' designs. Politics influenced what could be imagined—and what could not. It influenced what could get built—and what could not. And it influenced whether or not the structures that could be imagined and that were built would actually work, as was discovered at San Jacinto, where bureaucracy helped turn a good design into a catastrophe. Finally, the politics of changing American environmental values has guaranteed that quite apart from whether or not the flood control program works, it may still arouse conflict over the purposes and style of flood control engineering and indeed over whether it is desirable at all. The lower Los Angeles River levees, after all, have not failed since the discovery of their inadequacy in 1980, but they have nevertheless been the object of much rancor and a flash point for debate over technically oriented flood control.

One possible, but erroneous, conclusion that might be drawn from the influence of politics over flood control is that the public should give engineers the funding and get out of the way. One obvious problem with that interpretation is that in a democratic society, politics is a necessary and desirable aspect of decision making. Another problem is that even the seemingly technical aspects of flooding have proved just as unpredictable and messy as politics. A twenty-five-year storm, such as that of 1978, is not just a twenty-five-year storm. Well-designed debris basins inexplicably turn into flip buckets. Protective levees redirect the flow of water to undermine themselves. Precipitation records are too short and land use changes too rapid to make reliable predictions about future hydrology. All of this has made it difficult, and perhaps impossible, to achieve the precision of prediction that flood control engineering seems to require for success. Moreover, Southern Californians ask much more of their flood control today than they did at midcentury. They ask that structures be beautiful, that they bring people and neighborhoods together, and that they allow native willows and yellow-billed cuckoos to thrive. These are not primarily technical questions (see figure 7.4).

Thus the breach in the San Jacinto levee is twentieth-century Southern California flood control in microcosm. It is a failure born of the interaction between unpredictable and messy engineering and unpredictable and messy politics. In Los Angeles, systems for imposing the order of engineering on unruly nature have often failed because both engineering and nature are unruly. Flood control has, therefore, become an exercise in substituting one disorderly system for another. This does not require abandoning engineering efforts—they have saved billions of dollars and numerous lives in the past eight decades. It does mean, however, heeding the insight of the Caltech scientist who concluded in 1982 that engineering structures by themselves are "necessary but not sufficient."[33]

Figure 7.4. Debris basin with spillway, 2000. Courtesy Jared Orsi.

8

Private Sector Planning
for the Environment

TOM SITTON

OVER the past one hundred years, private organizations expanded their role in the planning of American cities. Business leaders, academics, homeowners, professional planners, and environmentalists as well as civic reform associations, philanthropic foundations, and other nongovernmental agencies with a stake in changing urban environments sought to influence planning to suit their particular interests—economic, social, altruistic, and otherwise. This became especially apparent in metropolitan areas, where individuals and interest groups large and small organized coalitions to participate in planning decisions and in implementing (or halting) major development projects.[1]

The process was notably evident in Los Angeles, where voluntary organizations became increasingly active in influencing public policy affecting all aspects of the region's environment. Business organizations such as the Chamber of Commerce, the realty board, and to a lesser extent the several downtown merchants' associations lobbied for planning measures to protect private enterprise and increase business opportunity, frequently at the expense of the natural environment. These organizations were especially active in the first decades of the twentieth century, when contemporary Los Angeles took form. Business and commercial groups were the spearheads of industrial and residential growth. The city's entrepreneurial leadership, present on the boards of many commercial groups, and the Automobile Club of Southern California helped to establish the Los Angeles Traffic Commission in 1922 to reorder the city and county street grid. The auto club sponsored a parkway plan in 1937 that set the basic pattern for the region's freeway system. The Chamber of Commerce led the ambitious initiative culminating in the 1930 Olmsted-Bartholomew plan that would have created parks and recreational facilities throughout the county.[2]

Besides these business-oriented associations, a number of other private organizations also participated in the planning process. Civic reform organizations such as the Municipal League in the first half of the century and Government Research Inc. and the short-lived Citizen's Research Inc. in the 1940s, whose primary interests were muckraking and structural alterations of municipal government, joined in the planning process when government actions might affect natural and human-built resources. Labor unions, associations of property owners, and other interest groups also entered the debates on environmental issues. These organizations, for the most part, represented their members' concerns, and those concerns often clashed with the goals and objectives advanced by other economic, social, and political groups.

With such competition to influence planning policy and environmental change, the small and often beleaguered city planning department turned to private organizations committed to rational planning for assistance. In a most critical era for such service, from the late 1930s to the early 1950s, the John Randolph Haynes and Dora Haynes Foundation was the most effective such agency. Created in 1926 as Los Angeles' first private, general-purpose foundation by two of Southern California's prominent Social Democrats, the Haynes Foundation was initially established to further their political and social reform objectives, including direct legislation, public ownership and management of natural resources (particularly water and hydroelectric power), improvement of the living conditions and protection of the rights of workers and American Indians, and modernization of municipal government structures and functions.[3]

Upon the death of founder John R. Haynes in late October 1937, the remaining trustees began discussing the foundation's future direction and major funding commitments. Composed at that time primarily of progressive reform activists such as state senator Herbert C. Jones, political writer Franklin Hichborn, U.S. commissioner of Indian affairs John Collier, and other prominent individuals who shared many of Dr. and Mrs. Haynes's political objectives, the majority of the board of trustees agreed to an initial concentration on one major program while funding other favorite projects on a smaller scale. Consensus on the major project was difficult to reach as the board divided into two camps. One group demanded direct political action, hoping to mold the foundation into a "pioneering shock troop agency" for social reform. A more conservative faction argued for a passive program of academic research geared toward influencing public policy and governmental procedures. Trustees favoring the more restrained approach prevailed, and a project aimed at analyzing regional planning dilemmas and aiding local planning agencies to meet these challenges became the principal avenue for advocacy.[4] In time, under the auspices of Charles Eliot II, the foundation assumed a significant role in the region, funding numerous studies devoted to resource management, open space and recreation, and related subjects central to environmental planning.

At the time, the need for promoting and coordinating local planning was evident. By 1939, the Los Angeles area had been the scene of landmark planning accomplishments in the legal sense but marked deficiencies in implementation. Efforts by progressives in the early part of the century to devise methods to ameliorate urban social problems and protect the local landscape by regulating industrial and residential development came to fruition in 1920, when a city planning commission with limited powers was established. Municipal planners in Los Angeles County cities led by G. Gordon Whitnall then campaigned for the 1923 creation of the Regional Planning Commission, the first in the nation. Four years later Los Angeles County implemented the nation's first county zoning ordinance, and state legislation passed that year and in 1929 established the legal foundation for further planning endeavors. But lax enforcement of the ordinances during a decade of booming real estate development and rapidly changing transportation patterns in the 1920s subverted some of these accomplishments.

In the 1930s the city planning department went into decline as its commissioners were accused of corruption during the Frank Shaw administration scandals and as the city engineer acquired control of construction of federally funded infrastructure and authority over subdivision regulation. Other municipalities in the county determined their suburban expansion with little regard for its overall effect on the region, especially for its largest city. Urban planning, whether public or private sector, was not coordinated to promote rational development in the region or to meet residents' concerns about the nature of environmental and ecological change.[5]

Regional planning, with its emphasis on managing changes to the natural and human-built environments, fit neatly into John and Dora Haynes's conception of a rational approach to solving some of the social ills facing metropolitan and surrounding areas. Besides his overtly political and economic interests in reform, Dr. Haynes was a staunch supporter of G. Gordon Whitnall's efforts to establish a city planning program in Los Angeles throughout the second decade of the century. The doctor was also a member of the National Housing Association and countless other organizations concerned with improved living and working conditions for American workers, a more democratic process for regulating land use, and public control of natural resources.

Though not as controversial as some of the passions of this Social Democrat, regional planning advocacy was still a politically charged issue that offered the trustees an opportunity to further some of the founders' goals on a large scale at a particularly critical moment.[6]

The Haynes trust was not the first philanthropic foundation to enter this field. Almost two decades earlier the Russell Sage Foundation made regional planning in New York one of its chief concerns. Believing that "the physical environment exerted a profound influence on social life," the Russell Sage trustees modeled their effort on Paul Kellogg's surveys of Pittsburgh and initiated a decade-long project resulting in the publication of the *Regional Survey and Plan of New York and Environs*, and in financing for the independent Regional Plan Association of New York. (Kellogg had received financial support in several endeavors from Dr. Haynes.) Several other U.S. foundations had taken part in various urban planning projects, particularly model housing developments. The most noteworthy among these endeavors was Chatham Village, a demonstration project of multifamily housing constructed in Pittsburgh with funding from the Buhl Foundation. Haynes trustees active in this field were well aware of these and similar projects in Chicago and elsewhere. Their intent was to use these as possible prototypes for the new program.[7]

Occidental College president and Haynes trustee Dr. Remsen D. Bird initially suggested the regional planning program and was the key proponent on the board. Described as "widely known as a planning prophet after the best prophetic tradition," Bird had been interested in planning for quite some time. In November 1938, he was appointed to the Los Angeles City Planning Commission by reform mayor Fletcher Bowron, who had recently replaced Frank Shaw after a recall election.. Bird was one of many Bowron commissioners charged with rooting corruption out of city government; Bird's brief was also to set the city on a more rational path of planned development. His primary interest was in the use of master planning to establish order in regional growth. Along with fellow planning commissioner William Schuchardt he worked feverishly to strengthen the powers of the department and change commission procedures to focus more time and resources on master planning and less on spot planning and variances. His May 1939 speech before the Chamber of Commerce proselytizing for a regional master plan was an official announcement of a campaign that would result in one of the Haynes Foundation's most significant accomplishments and lead the city planning department in a new direction.[8]

Shortly after he joined the city planning commission, Bird approached the officers of the Pacific Southwest Academy (PSA) about aiding his city planning campaign. This West Coast division of the American Academy for Political and

Social Science consisted of a number of local academics and Haynes Founda-tion trustees. The PSA leaders enthusiastically agreed to cooperate and in sev-eral meetings held in early 1939 helped Bird to formulate a plan for the foundation and to identify a planning expert to carry it out. A small Commit-tee of Inquiry was formed to further the project. Bird hoped that the group would expand with representatives of business and other interests and become an institution similar to the Regional Plan Association of New York.[9]

With prodding from Bird, the PSA, and trustee Charles Grove Haines, the regional planning proposal was approved in May 1939 and initiated immedi-ately. California State Planning Board official L. Deming Tilton, a former pro-fessor, professional planner, and consultant to national, state, and municipal agencies, was hired on a half-time basis as the foundation's counselor on plan-ning. Guided by a trustee advisory committee, Tilton was charged with sur-veying the local planning situation; making recommendations for a program of investigation, research, and action; and promoting cooperation with govern-ment agencies at all levels to accomplish the trustees' objectives. Central to this commitment was the foundation's aim to "render aid to the extent of its avail-able resources toward completion of those phases of regional and city planning which are deemed most significant for the political, social, and cultural devel-opment of the region in which Los Angeles is the center." As the trustees assert-ed in the foundation's public statement regarding the new program, they would take "one approach to a large and complex problem which must be attacked from many angles—economic, sociological, governmental and educational." They asserted that their desire was "to assist in making this great city a safer, more healthful place in which to live and work; to secure a plan for a metro-politan region offering larger opportunities for human development."[10]

Although he would have considerable support from trustees and others, Tilton's task was formidable. As he set out to address the deficiencies in region-al planning, he found that his most pressing challenge and potentially his most effective achievement was to be coordinating the efforts of a multitude of inter-ested groups and individuals. Tilton immediately made himself and his mission known to local officials and the general public. Mayor Bowron appointed him to the city housing authority and to the Civic Center Authority, a group of design professionals devising a plan for the siting and design of a complex of government buildings in the area north of downtown. He became an adviser to the city planning department for department reorganization, review of housing project sites, master planning, and transportation and water problems. He also served as a consultant to the Los Angeles County Regional Planning Commission for shoreline issues and for the master plan for airports and trans-portation systems. On the fourth day of his Haynes employment, he was the featured speaker at the closing banquet of a county conference on conservation in which numerous city and county officials, planners, and engineers presented papers on regional environmental issues.[11]

Working as a liaison between municipal and county planning agencies and private groups such as the Chamber of Commerce, Town Hall, and the University of Southern California on conservation and traffic programs and planning conferences became a priority for Tilton. Downtown merchants were particularly alarmed by the dispersion of retailers out into the suburban hinterlands of Los Angeles County. These businessmen hoped to have a hand in crafting policies and plans intended to prop up the declining central city. Chamber of Commerce leaders were concerned about regional economic opportunities for industry and small businesses that might be constrained by zoning regulations and other planning decisions. These groups and other representatives from the private sector found it expedient to cooperate with Tilton, who sought their support in working toward a consensus in regional development.[12]

Tilton's most ambitious and successful endeavor was an analysis of the Los Angeles region that surveyed its geography, land use, population, economy, energy sources, infrastructure, and other features to identify problems and opportunities, a prelude, as he understood it, to drafting a much-needed regional master plan. This project evolved from the spring 1939 meetings of Remsen Bird and the PSA social scientists who encouraged the foundation's consideration of this program. Bird, Tilton, and the PSA academics agreed to pursue such a study and enlisted social scientists, government officials, and experts in fields such as architecture and housing (Richard Neutra) and street systems (E. E. East of the Automobile Club of Southern California). PSA editor George W. Robbins and Tilton edited the essays over the next year, and the Haynes Foundation financed the entire publication.[13]

The product of this effort, *Los Angeles: Preface to a Master Plan*, appeared in 1941. Hailed since as a "provocative view of what the prewar metropolis was and could have been," the collection of essays connected the natural and human-built features of the region to economic and social concerns in a plea for the compilation of a master plan to guide intelligent growth. Tilton's contribution, "The Master Plan," was the unifying essay. It began with a reference to the New York Regional Plan and went on to trace local initiatives and then assert the case for the advantages of regional planning and of carrying out any program for change on a countywide basis. The onset of World War II would limit the utility of this volume. During the war urban planners turned their attention to more pressing national defense matters in partnership with federal planners; they had little opportunity to shape development when shortages of capital and building materials precluded the construction of large-scale residential and business developments. The book, however, established a reference point for postwar planning, became an invaluable reference work in city planning departments over the next two decades, and remains an important historical document for analyzing the environmental concerns and planning strategies of that moment.[14]

While working on these projects, Tilton also participated in the revision of the Los Angeles city charter as technical adviser for the sections related to planning. One of the original charges to the Haynes Foundation trustees was to assist governments in charter revision, and modernizing the section on planning to give it more direction and increased powers was interpreted as part of that change. Mayor Bowron appointed Tilton to the 1940 committee along with trustee Anne M. Mumford, and the two Haynes Foundation figures worked diligently on the planning and zoning subcommittees. Their efforts resulted in charter amendments that strengthened the planning department and added a zoning commissioner and board of appeals. City voters approved the amendments in the May 1941 municipal election, and a more modern and professional city department soon emerged. Of particular importance were a redefinition of the qualifications of department personnel and a change in procedure that removed minor zoning reclassifications from planning commission agendas to provide more time for commissioners and staff to devote to master planning, testimony to the work of trustee Remson Bird.[15]

Tilton's half-time service to the foundation netted positive results on specific projects, as well as placing the Haynes name in the forefront of local planning. But with limited time and funding, his accomplishments were difficult for some of the trustees to evaluate. Tilton's belief that the "principal function and value of the work of the Foundation in the last analysis is probably that of providing a center, detached from political and financial controls, around which citizens of integrity and social consciousness can gather and through which they can make effective contributions to the development and government of this great urban region"—a major accomplishment in itself—could not justify the rapidly growing expense of his program.[16]

In late 1940 the trustees decided to curtail the regional planning program and shift foundation funds to another project. Tilton continued his work at a gradually reduced level until July 1942, when he accepted the position of planning director for the city and county of San Francisco. During that period he continued to consult with local planning agencies and initiated the transformation of *Los Angeles: Preface to a Master Plan* into a high-school-level text, *Cities Are For People* (1942). This popular volume urged students to consider the benefits of planning as a social and environmental necessity for a better city.

It was written by former newspaper reporter Mel Scott, produced for the Pacific Southwest Academy by the Haynes Foundation, and illustrated with images from an exhibition devoted to the promise of planning held at the Los Angeles County Museum of History, Science, and Art.[17]

With the decision to phase out Tilton's regional planning program, the Haynes trustees considered several possibilities and decided to devote most of the foundation's funds to a housing survey of Los Angeles. This Metropolitan Area Studies Program would analyze housing stock, urban blight, transportation patterns, racial accommodation, economic readjustments, and other issues that affected public planning decisions. The research would be carried out by Dr. Frank M. Stewart and his staff at the University of California, Los Angeles, Bureau of Governmental Research, which had already received some Haynes funding for specific research studies on campus. The new program, however, would be undertaken at the Haynes Foundation headquarters and supervised by a committee of trustees. With the initiation of this project the foundation began its experiment in operating as a social science think tank along the lines of the Russell Sage Foundation and the Brookings Institution, albeit on a much smaller scale.[18]

The Metropolitan Area Studies Program was initiated in mid-1942 as the Haynes staff began its housing study with data drawn from the 1940 U.S. census, the first census enumeration to report extensively on housing conditions. The research design linked some thirty-five variables, such as the dwelling's structural condition, whether or not a household owned or rented, and the occupants' ethnicity and household income, to determine their association with housing and neighborhood deterioration. Once the data had been collected and analyzed, the research team put together proposals to remedy the conditions they uncovered. The study, *Los Angeles: Its People and Its Homes* (1944) was a monumental compendium of facts and correlations of the city's demography. It served as a vital planning tool at the time and as the source for city reports and projections, especially by the Los Angeles City Housing Authority, and has been a valuable reference guide for social scientists and historians ever since. In addition, the program staff worked closely with local planners, academics, students, social welfare agencies, and ethnic and racial groups in related programs for community improvement. The success of this program spurred the Haynes trustees to expand it by creating complementary projects on a smaller scale in the areas of race relations and economic development, while approving several modest grants related to broader regional planning.[19]

With this growing flurry of activity the board decided that it could better coordinate its mushrooming think-tank efforts by hiring an expert to direct the operation. In late 1943 the trustees chose Charles W. Eliot II, grandson and namesake of the late Harvard University president and nephew of a noted partner in the firm of landscape architect Frederick Law Olmsted. A landscape planner in Boston, Eliot then served as the head of several national planning agencies before he became executive officer of the National Resources Planning Board. When Congress abolished the board in 1943, Eliot became available for the Haynes position and accepted it at two-thirds time to allow him to teach and consult on other projects. His service would relieve the Haynes trustees, several of whom were absent because of wartime service for the U.S. government, of the day-to-day details of operating the in-house research projects.[20]

Beginning in January 1944, Eliot organized the overall research program, providing short-range and long-range goals. He continued to refine the foundation's principal methods of operation, which were analyzing problems through social science research conducted by experts, organizing government officials and community forces to mobilize support for intelligent solutions to those problems, and educating the public to the need for these programs with a vigorous public relations and publication strategy. Besides increasing the output of research monographs, he added a new Haynes pamphlet series consisting of brief restatements of the scholarly research monographs in a format that would engage a lay audience.[21]

Eliot also brought order to the various research projects by consolidating them into four units, three of which were conducted by other staff members under Eliot's overall direction. They included an economic unit concerned with an industrial survey of the area, a governmental organization section that focused on intergovernmental relations and regional public works projects, and a social meaning section analyzing social demographics and race relations with emphasis on neighborhood composition and development. The heads of these departments and most of their assistants worked full time in the Haynes Foundation office and produced a remarkable number of publications of their research while working with government agencies, other academics, and community groups.[22]

The fourth section, physical development, was the successor to Tilton's regional planning program and was primarily concerned with environmental conservation in greater Los Angeles. Eliot himself supervised this section, having specialized in this field while heading the National Resources Planning Board. Like Tilton, he devoted much of his time during his tenure at the Haynes Foundation to serving as a member of organizations such as the Shoreline Planning Association of California; the Los Angeles County Citizens Committee on Parks, Beaches, and Recreational Facilities; and similar agencies devoted to natural resource management.[23]

Although the physical development section would be small in terms of staffing, its work became increasingly timely and important in light of the massive degradation of Los Angeles' natural setting during World War II. Industrial development in support of the defense effort brought new manufactories to the region and the need for financing and emergency policies for the rapid expansion of existing plant. These defense-related industries poured dangerous waste in Southland waterways and spewed noxious chemicals into the air, cloaking the industrial and downtown areas in a blanket of smog. Oil drilling near the coastline to supply war needs speeded the rate of land subsidence, while new oil wells in residential areas ruined the landscape and enraged the neighbors. Beach erosion caused by faulty breakwater construction necessitated the introduction of tons of replacement sand. The exploding population of immigrant war workers and their families increased the demand for temporary housing, schools, and recreation facilities. The population influx also further taxed the already overtaxed sewer system, resulting in the dumping of nearly untreated sewage into the Santa Monica Bay, a quarantine of many of the surrounding beaches, and a state lawsuit filed against the city in 1943. By that year the region was clearly in the throes of a critical assault on all of its physical features, and the county and municipal governments needed help.[24]

Under Eliot's guidance, the physical development section produced three important studies that developed some of the general strategies of *Los Angeles: Preface to a Master Plan* into more specific recommendations. The first was *Plans and Action for the Development of the Los Angeles Metropolitan Coastline*, written by Donald F. Griffin, who synthesized the recommendations of numerous public entities regarding conservation and development along the Southland coast. Concerned with recreational facilities, public access, transportation links and parking, pollution, and sand erosion, Griffin's work illustrated the best available plans devised for the area. He made specific recommendations for a state park from Topanga Canyon to San Pedro to restore this stretch of beaches, for measures to stop breakwater blockage of littoral drift and to decrease the trapping of sand from flood control projects, for better freeway access to beaches, and for the acquisition of more beach property for public use (two-thirds of the acreage was privately owned at the time). Produced as an educational tool and intended for mass distribution, this monograph reminded citizens that it was their responsibility to demand that local government clean, preserve, and provide greater access to the local coastline. A large gathering of planners and city and county officials celebrated the release of this report at the foundation office near the end of 1944, as Griffin set out to secure funding for his recommended projects.[25]

The second publication was a county-generated report for a group chaired

by Eliot and appointed by the board of supervisors with the charge of survey-
ing existing recreation facilities throughout the county. Eliot, Griffin, and
other Haynes staff members prepared, printed, and distributed the 1945 *Report
of the Citizens Committee on Parks, Beaches, and Recreational Facilities*. Using as
its basis the neglected 1930 Olmsted-Bartholomew comprehensive plan for
more than fifteen hundred square miles of the Southland (sponsored and then
rejected by the Chamber of Commerce), the committee identified existing
resources and the need to create additional facilities based on expanding population and the dearth of parkland in some county areas. It recommended that
the board take action to remedy the situation by acquiring more land for recreational use, with further planning based on this document. A survey by the
Haynes staff of metropolitan recreation programs in counties throughout the
nation was appended to provide possible models for a Los Angeles organization. The foundation's printing and wide distribution of this report helped to
fulfill its mission in making these inadequacies known to the public.[26]

Waterlines—Key to Development of Metropolitan Los Angeles, released in
1946, was the third major product of the physical development section. Griffin
did much of the research, and he and Eliot then composed this publication,
which was intended to educate the general public on the problems and opportunities of growth related to streams and watercourses in Los Angeles County.
Eliot described some of the flood control problems in the area caused by too
much water and the agricultural and recreational deficiencies resulting from
too little. In documenting past projects and those on the drawing board he
demonstrated how multiple-use projects along water lines could combine to
serve additional functions while protecting the quantity and quality of water
resources for drinking, recreation, and irrigation. As with many such Haynes
reports, this one also called for citizen action to support intelligent projects and
more planning to ensure protection of resources and rational development.[27]

Under Eliot's direction the think tank produced a wealth of research
reports, monographs, and pamphlets on subjects studied in the four sections,
as well as a far-reaching public relations campaign to publicize the Haynes contributions to analyzing possible directions for Los Angeles' growth. He helped
to make the foundation a major coordinating center for a variety of groups
involved in planning and implementation of public projects and an important
ally for the city and county planning departments. During his tenure the foundation could claim significant responsibility for steering the city planning
department toward its major 1940s successes in creating district master plans,
a comprehensive zoning ordinance (1946), a shoreline development plan
(1945), and community redevelopment legislation, and its participation in the
Civic Center Authority. Eliot's personal relationships with his trustees, staff,

and some government officials, however, were not as blissful and, along with his ever ballooning budget requests, eventually led to his departure in 1945. The trustees decided not to replace him as director of research but to place supervision of the in-house research apparatus in the hands of a triumvirate of social scientists. When Donald Griffin left the foundation in 1946, the trustees decided that the physical development section had served its purpose, and it was replaced by a labor-relations project.[28]

In the latter half of the 1940s, the Haynes Foundation think tank concentrated on local topics as defined by the economics, sociology, and government (regional administration) sections. Many of the subjects under review touched on relationships between economic, social, and administrative forces and their effects on the environment, although for the most part only indirectly. The government section was involved in analyzing structural features and functional operations of municipal administration, but it also developed a major program closely related to previous studies of regional planning and changes to the landscape in examining the interrelationships of all forms of local government services within the metropolitan area. Edwin A. Cottrell, a former Stanford University political scientist and recent Haynes trustee, initiated this ambitious program while overseeing other grant projects related to regional government administration.[29]

Metropolitan Los Angeles: A Study in Integration eventually consisted of sixteen volumes published between 1952 and 1955 and researched and written by Haynes Foundation trustees, staff, and outside contributors. Cottrell based the series on a number of similar studies already produced by the University of California, Los Angeles, Bureau of Governmental Research that had been partially financed by the Haynes Foundation. His major objective was to examine the multiplicity of overlapping government services and the use of available resources to eliminate duplication of functions and waste of precious resources. Individual volumes addressed environmental issues such as sanitation, fire protection, highway placement and construction, water supply, recreation and parks, and overall regional planning as well as more administrative matters related to law enforcement, schools, libraries, and municipal finance. Each contributor investigated the historical background of the subject within the entire region, described current problems and opportunities, and suggested possible consolidation of functions for more simplified and efficient service delivery. The overall plan, as summarized in the final installment, was hailed in the foreword by a confident Gordon C. Watkins as one that "political logic and civic experience are quite likely to bring to pass." Finally completed after Cottrell's death, the series served as the basis for future efforts to streamline the metropolitan network of local governments, as well as becoming yet another major contribution to regional planning analysis and resource management.[30]

The Haynes Foundation trustees gradually reduced the size of the think tank during the late 1940s as they began funding an increasing number of grant projects performed at outside institutions. One was a study for the city's newly established Community Redevelopment Agency for its first major projects. The proposal was advanced by trustee Reginald D. Johnson, a former architect and progressive housing advocate who, like his associates Catherine Bauer and Mel Scott, supported the concept of redevelopment of blighted areas as a means to revitalize depressed communities and improve the living conditions of residents. Johnson shared Bauer and Scott's wariness regarding the use of this process by private entrepreneurs. The Haynes Foundation had already supplied funding for a 1944 research project by former Los Angeles city planner G. Gordon Whitnall to determine the legal basis for redevelopment law.[31]

Johnson hoped to keep the foundation in the forefront of this activity as the Community Redevelopment Agency embarked on its initial projects on Bunker Hill and in Chavez Ravine. Architect Robert Alexander and planner Drayton Bryant conducted the Haynes study of these sites and proposed a mix of uses, combining residences with commercial uses. More critically, they argued for redevelopment agency construction of replacement housing for Bunker Hill residents and those living in Chavez Ravine who would be displaced by redevelopment. The study raised some concern with a few Haynes trustees because of its recommendation that the public housing projects be designed for an economically and racially mixed population but was finally published unchanged by the foundation as *Rebuilding A City* in 1950.[32]

The massive transformation of the city's natural and human-built landscape on Bunker Hill and in Chavez Ravine took place, though not as Alexander and Bryant envisioned. Their call for coupling new public housing with the redevelopment of blighted areas ensured that their study became embroiled in the acrimonious campaign against "socialist" housing waged by real estate and allied interests nationwide, a political battle that was as divisive in Los Angeles as it was in other American cities. Those challenging city and state intervention into housing provision were finally victorious in reducing the city's commitment to public housing when Mayor Fletcher Bowron, defender of the city's federal contract to provide ten thousand units of such housing, was defeated by the private development alliance in 1953. Chavez Ravine became another kind of park when Dodger Stadium was built there a decade later, and Bunker Hill gradually evolved into a corporate acropolis of midrise residential towers and high-rise office buildings.[33]

In the early 1950s a number of factors moved the Haynes trustees to rethink the foundation's mission. The departure of much of the Haynes research staff and its most progressive trustees, cold war–era concerns over the political affiliations of staff members and grantees, and the imminent demolition of the Haynes headquarters to make room for another freeway prodded the trustees to abandon the internal research apparatus altogether, simplify the foundation's operating procedures, and commit it to funding outside organizations and educational institutions. Beginning in 1953 the foundation gradually shifted its spending to academic scholarships and a general research program of projects conducted mostly by local social scientists. Research grants were awarded for investigations of a wide assortment of subjects, some of state and even national scope and many the special interest of particular trustees. For several decades very few of the projects had a direct relationship to local environmental conditions. Ironically, this came at a time when more and more U.S. foundations were becoming involved in studies of the urban environment.[34]

Since the 1980s the Haynes Foundation has once again approved a substantial number of grants concerned with the Southern California environment. The foundation has supported research on water quality and distribution, traffic congestion and highway building, air pollution, housing, toxic-waste management, regional planning, and growth control; in many cases the analysis linked the political, social, and economic ramifications of changes to issues of natural and human-built resources. For the most part, these projects have been conducted independently, with little relationship to each other. While each is important in itself, the sum of the parts does not have the benefit of coordination and mutual study that characterized the work of the Haynes think-tank researchers of the 1940s. A 2003 symposium on the sustainability of the Los Angeles environment, which was organized and sponsored by the foundation, was closer in its organization and objectives to the projects of the World War II era.[35]

The legacy of the Haynes Foundation's investment in regional planning and natural resource management since the 1940s is difficult to measure. The research publications produced by Haynes staff on a multiplicity of topics, including environmental quality and change from a regional perspective, provided planners and decision makers with the data these professionals needed to understand current dilemmas and make rational choices for the future. Whether or not the proper choice was made is another matter, one in which Haynes Foundation analysts exerted no control. With the benefit of hindsight, many critics have argued that inappropriate choices were made on many occasions. But some of the same critics give due credit to the work of the Haynes think tank for its promotion of the rationalization of metropolitan government and resource management, for creating the knowledge necessary for making choices about the course of development at a critical moment for the Los Angeles environment, and for its support of public planning agencies.

As an influential private organization, elite directed like most others at its level, the foundation analyzed environmental problems and systems, suggested alternative directions, educated the public to the consequences of those choices, and called for citizen action to support rational choices and protect resources, all while attempting to accommodate continued growth. Present observers might lament that a particular road was not traveled. It is nevertheless important to recognize that more damage might have been done to the landscape and the natural environment in Southern California had midcentury urban planners been deprived of this corpus of research and analysis, research supported by, and in many ways organized by, a private organization.[36]

9

Zoning and Environmental Inequity in the Industrial East Side

CHRISTOPHER G. BOONE

I N 1997, the municipal council of Commerce in Los Angeles County denied a recycling firm the right to construct a multimillion dollar facility, despite the substantial sums it would have contributed to city revenues. The council objected to the noise and traffic the plant would generate and to possible deleterious health effects on nearby residents. The decision was in keeping with a national pattern of concern over issues of environmental inequity, the disproportionate concentration of toxic and waste facilities in minority communities. The population of Commerce is more than 90 percent Latino, and the city has one of the highest concentrations of toxic sites in Los Angeles County. Commerce is, in a sense, a poster child for environmental inequity. The council's refusal to grant the waste recycling facility a conditional-use permit was one step in its efforts to curtail environmental inequity. A year later, it drafted and passed an ordinance to prohibit any waste processing facility from locating in the city, incorporating explicit environmental justice language into the text.[1]

The city council had the wherewithal to forbid toxic industries since its incorporation in 1960. The Environmental Quality Act of 1970 provided the legislative means, but for most of the city's brief history, elected officials, business leaders, and residents strove to create a model city, a place where industrialists and residents worked and lived together. From 1960 to 1990, the council and planning commission imposed few limits on industry, other than cosmetic regulations to install and maintain landscaping and provide adequate off-street parking. The twelve thousand people living in Commerce had to share space with as many as seventy thousand others who commuted to the city for work, and not surprisingly, parking was an important item on the planning commission's agenda. But the challenges residents faced extended beyond parking. They lived next to hazardous facilities, such as a DDT manufacturer, and had to survive the hazards of industrial accidents that in some cases sent people to the hospital. The dangers of living close to industry are well known and well documented, but the planning commission and city council did little, at least until the 1990s, to check these hazards.[2]

Industry is the dominant land use in Commerce. It accounts for 68 percent of the land and is the raison d'être of the city. The Lakewood Plan of 1954 permitted easy and inexpensive incorporation by allowing new municipalities to purchase services from the county, and the Bradley-Burns Act of 1956 allowed the return of a portion of state sales tax revenues to municipalities; both paved the way for the incorporation of Commerce as an industrial and residential city. In exchange, the city promised residents that no property taxes would be levied on dwellings or businesses and that operating funds for the municipality would come primarily from sales tax returns, promises the council has been able to keep. Residents receive a number of services without charge in return. As a consequence, industry has been treated well in Commerce. Before the city incorporated, the area was almost entirely built up, with a mixture of residential, commercial, and industrial uses. The planning commission placed few limits on industry, as it was working primarily with inherited land use. In other words, the commission had little need to draw up a comprehensive diagram for land use. It could regulate existing land use, grant variances, and deny building applications, but the body had little opportunity to shape fundamental aspects of the city's future.[3]

A historical examination of how this area of Los Angeles County became an industrial region and a center of toxic facilities can reveal the process of creating an industrial community in twentieth-century Southern California. It also explains a pattern of environmental inequity that exists in this part of eastern Los Angeles County. The key factor was a series of zoning decisions the Regional Planning Commission (RPC) authorized in the 1920s.

Toxic Release Inventory and Environmental Justice

The environmental justice movement has a long history, but it gained momentum in 1987 with the introduction of the Environmental Protection Agency's Toxic Release Inventory. For the first time, interested parties had access to a national database of industries that released toxic substances into the environment. Since that time, the number of chemicals included in the Toxic Release Inventory database has expanded, and the data have been placed on the Internet in a format accessible to nonexperts. The database has been an important source of information for academics, local governments, and community organizations engaged in environmental justice research and action. The data have been used to demonstrate, in many cases, the disproportionate number of toxic sites located in minority communities. Differing statistical methods and geographic spatial scales have produced contradictory results, and refinement of analysis continues. But in the case of Los Angeles County, four studies of environmental equity arrived at similar findings: census tracts with a high proportion of minorities, especially Latinos, possess a disproportionately high concentration of hazardous facilities.[4]

One of the charges those active in the environmental justice movement have made is that industries deliberately locate their facilities in minority communities. Firms believe that minority groups with limited opportunity will not protest the decision because they need jobs, they lack political power, and the housing adjacent or close to industrial sites is already valued lower than comparable housing in other locales. The term environmental racism was coined to highlight this apparent injustice, suggesting that the spatial correlation between minorities and noxious industries is the product of deliberate actions.[5]

One method of investigating this theory and these allegations is historical inquiry: searching out which came to an area first, industry or residents. If industries were built and residents later moved in, the reasoning goes, a concentration of minorities is not the result of deliberate environmental racism by industry; it was instead the result of an individual or family decision to be close to work, to secure less expensive housing, or other reasons. Some scholars take a broader view of the term and suggest that regardless of motive, the result— the geographic correlation of minorities and toxic sites—is a product of institutional racism, a body of practices that systematically disadvantages minority communities. Restrictive covenants, for example, have restricted access to housing and therefore limited where racial and ethnic minorities might live. If minorities moved into an area after industry was established, it may have been because they were legally barred from other locations. Regardless of how environmental racism is defined, most scholars agree that to understand current patterns of inequity, or the documented proximity of minority communities to toxic sites, a historical examination of place-specific cases is needed. An examination of the past is necessary to comprehend a process that led to current patterns and hence to create a policy that might address these inequities.[6]

Role of Zoning in Creating an Industrial East Side

Present patterns of toxic sites in eastern Los Angeles County are largely the legacy of zoning decisions made by the RPC in the late 1920s. The RPC was charged with the regulation and coordination of land use in unincorporated areas. Zoning was not new to the Los Angeles area: the city approved land use districts, a rudimentary form of zoning, in 1908 and passed actual zoning regulations in 1921. The push for zoning came mainly from the members of the realty business, who desired a mechanism to stabilize land values. From their perspective, securing and maintaining value in residential land and property meant industries would not, or could not, be located nearby. Realtors saw the greatest profit potential for housing in the West Side of Los Angeles (city and county) and lobbied to designate this section residential, leaving by default the East Side for industrial use.[7]

Zoning at the county level was made possible in 1927 after the county board of supervisors passed an ordinance allowing the county to regulate land use, an extension of its police powers. The RPC zoning section looked after the details of a coordinated and comprehensive land use plan within the county. Developing such a plan required the RPC to balance property rights with community rights. To address this tension, the commission tried to leave the initiative for planning in the hands of the community. "Before any attempt is made to recommend that certain districts be zoned," a report by the zoning section stated, "a substantial number of citizens in that district petition the Regional Planning Commission to proceed with the necessary studies and the holding of public hearings."[8] As much as it would have liked to impose a carefully planned zoning code for the entire county, the commission deemed it necessary to respect the wishes of the majority of property owners. That the City of Los Angeles already had zoning in place likely helped the RPC in its efforts to zone land use. But overcoming the uneasiness of individual property owners about giving up some of their rights was a serious and delicate concern.

To demonstrate the wisdom of zoning, the commission used humor in its publications. One comic strip in a report shows two men walking along a sidewalk, one complaining to the other about the zoning plan: "Wot right they got to say whether I build a house or a factory on my own property I'd like to know!" When he arrives home he sees a signboard on the lot next door announcing the construction of a funeral home. The last frame shows a "red hot" letter of protest addressed to the Honorable Board of Supervisors. The commission used this type of publication and other means to convince the public that zoning could protect their properties, and especially their property values, in an effort to secure cooperation. In a pamphlet describing the duties of the zoning division, the commission emphasized that zoning was meant to be "*protective*, rather than a *restrictive* measure."[9] (See figure 9.1.)

The idea that zoning was protective was surely a hard sell, since the term *restricted* was used in the zone classifications, but the booklet tried to emphasize the logic as well as the cost-saving benefits of planning. "There will come

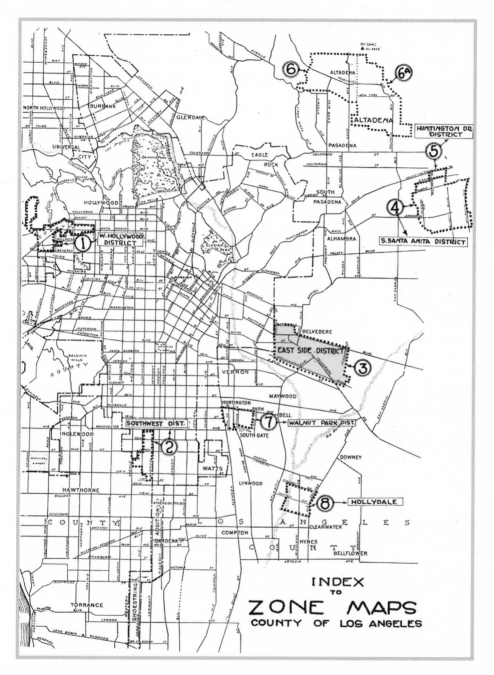

Figure 9.1. Los Angeles zone map of 1930. The East Side district (shown in gray) was unique in its designation as an industrial zone. All other districts were zoned primarily residential. Huntington Library, San Marino, California.

a time in the life of any growing community when further uncontrolled growth or expansion cannot be continued without inviting social and economic disaster, and when the lack of a comprehensive and far-reaching plan for the development and building control will necessitate costly and wasteful improvements." If the RPC could not appeal to the community spirit of property owners, it believed it could appeal to their pocketbooks. "Zoning in its final analysis," the RPC concluded, "means assured property values, and eliminates to a large degree *mistaken judgment in the purchase of land.* Wrong uses of land in any community spell economic loss."[10]

Zoning also served to separate incompatible land uses, particularly industry and residences. There was a simple logic for separating these land uses. The most obvious reason was the wish to keep noxious industries away from residences. The rapid expansion of cities in the nineteenth century brought housing into proximity with factories, often with deleterious consequences. Planners and civic leaders in Los Angeles were well aware of the squalor to be found in old industrial cities, both in Europe and on the East Coast of the United States. Indeed, Los Angeles was promoted for what it was not as much as for what it was. The Los Angeles Chamber of Commerce promoted the region as "Nature's Workshop," an ideal place for workers and capitalists alike. Chamber publications depict a gardenlike setting with a temperate year-round climate that would keep worker and manager happy and content (and the former union free). A detached dwelling away from the smoke and dust of the factory was one means for keeping Los Angeles from becoming Chicago's Back of the Yards or the bleak industrial townscapes on the English Midlands. Zoning, in this sense, served an important role in social engineering.[11]

Although zoning was promoted as a means to keep factories away from garden homes, the commission made it clear that industry would benefit from the separation, as it would avoid injunctions and lawsuits by keeping its distance from residential districts. For industries this had to be balanced with the need to tap a local labor market. Too great a distance might discourage workers from seeking employment. Those traveling greater distances would incur higher transportation costs, putting pressure on wages. Panorama City, in the San Fernando Valley, was a working example of the economics of clustering industry and residences. Similar suburban clusters of industry and housing constructed during and after World War II were critical elements in defining the multinucleated urban region that now characterizes Los Angeles County. Industry had a clear interest in locating close to residential areas, but the commission did its best to sell zoning or separation of land uses to industry as a cost saver. In the final analysis, the desire to separate land uses favored homeowners and the real estate industry over factory owners.[12]

Protection of property values appears to have been the primary concern of the RPC planners, who paid less attention to the environmental hazards of industry in residential areas. Zoning laws did make some provision to keep the most noxious and dangerous industries away from residences, relegating these to M3 zones and granting permits only after a review. A permit was required to establish refineries, abattoirs, tanneries, smelters, garbage dumps, and acid plants (among others) in M3 zones. The zoning regulations stipulated that no more than twenty residences could be located within a half mile of the proposed industry or activity. Nor could the industry or activity be within one half mile of a zone other than M3. If these conditions were met, the RPC was required to hold a public meeting to determine if the activity would "be a menace to, or endanger, public health, safety, or welfare."[13] A half mile may have been sufficient distance to keep away the stench of a meatpacking plant from a residential district (assuming favorable winds), but maybe not for the harmful effects of chemicals. Residents of the City of Commerce have been hospitalized after industrial accidents, so perhaps the buffer established between dangerous and hazardous facilities is insufficient.

By 1930, the RPC had completed zoning studies and prepared maps for eight areas, primarily east of Los Angeles. Examination of the zoning maps shows that the majority of land was zoned residential. The exception was the aptly named Industrial East Side. Here the RPC had mapped a mixture of industrial, residential, and commercial parcels. As with other areas, it reflected to a large degree existing or proposed land uses. Residential subdivisions had already been platted by the 1920s, although few houses had been built by that time. For the major thoroughfares, the commission set aside parcels for commercial use. Other subdivided parcels were designated R4, or unlimited residential use (permitting apartments). The remainder of the land was divided into manufacturing parcels, mostly M2, or light manufacturing.

Why the RPC permitted industrial land use here and so little elsewhere is an important question, since it helps to explain both the number and the concentration of industries in Commerce and the consequences of these decisions, high levels of toxic releases. In the late 1920s, the area was largely unsettled. Aerial photographs from the late 1930s show agriculture and fields, including numerous truck farms operated by Japanese families. A system of residential streets was in place on the north side of the district, but few houses had been built. A few manufactories, such as the Simons brick factory, were in place, but for the most part, the area consisted of open fields. What must have caught the planning commission's attention were the railroad lines—the Southern Pacific, Santa Fe, and Union Pacific—that passed through the area. Each had been completed long before the zoning decisions were made; their location informed the commission as it drew up its land use plan.[14]

Railway lines and spurs attract industry because access to transport is a key factor for production and distribution. Before the East Side was zoned, one enterprise, the Central Manufacturing District, had developed industrial properties based on these principles. Modeling the area after an industrial district in Chicago, the developers of the Central Manufacturing District platted industrial parcels connected by rail spurs to the Los Angeles Junction Railway, a service that provided a direct connection to the lines of the Union Pacific, Santa Fe, and Southern Pacific. The Chicago capitalists who developed the district recognized what the RPC realized—that the East Side would attract manufacturers if it were zoned for industry, since there was sufficient land available and more important, that land was served by the railroads.[15]

The RPC understood the need to zone land for industrial development. To gauge the amount of available industrial land in the county, it ordered the zoning office to map and compute the acreage of all land within one mile of railway tracks. Because of the space requirements of industry, the commission also asked the zoning section to calculate the number of large lots available along railway corridors. If land along the identified corridors was "being broken down into townsite lots," the RPC argued, that land would be "unavailable for industrial purposes." The commission carried out the study to illustrate that "good industrial property lying within a reasonable distance from rail service is scarce, and that some concerted action will be necessary to prevent the breaking down into small parcels of much needed industrial land." To the RPC, industrial properties were best defined as large parcels of vacant land that were close to railway tracks and away from housing. Because the Industrial East Side satisfied three of the four criteria (part of the area had already been platted for housing), it was a prime target for industrial zoning.[16]

The Los Angeles Chamber of Commerce also argued in favor of designating land for industry and worked closely with the RPC to see that this objective was achieved. In a 1950 study on industrial location, the chamber included information it thought important for prospective firms, including size of markets; availability of labor, raw materials, fuel, and water; and available sites. Anticipating the apprehensions of prospective firms, it emphasized that the county was proactively setting aside industrial land close to railway tracks. "In [the] establishment of all major industrial areas," the study concluded, "planning administrators have endeavored to distribute industrial zones along the railroad right of ways and other strategic locations." One of the chamber's ongoing concerns was the inadequacy of accessible industrial land. In a later survey of industrial firms in Los Angeles County, the RPC reported similar findings regarding the shortage of industrial land, especially close to the central core of the city. Those firms that responded reported that their principal dissatisfaction with conducting business in Los Angeles County was insufficient space. In an era when the chamber and the RPC worried about the lack of available industrial land, the area that would be incorporated as the City of Commerce appeared highly suitable to fill that need. The East Side would become the Industrial East Side.[17]

Because the East Side was an attractive location for industry, the RPC worked hard to make sure that land in this area would be zoned industrial. It is telling that the East Side was the only unincorporated district that did not request zoning. In West Hollywood, Altadena, Temple, Florence, Downey, and Glendale, local government, citizen associations, or chambers of commerce asked the RPC for assistance in the preparation of land use plans and zoning.[18] Zoning the Industrial East Side district, the RPC indicated in its annual report, was a difficult process. Over eighteen months, planners studied different scenarios for a mix of housing, industrial, and commercial activities. "Many conferences and public hearings were held, the most difficult problem being to bring about a harmonious spirit between the numerous local organizations," the commission reported. Eventually consensus was reached at a public meeting "without one dissenting vote being cast." For the RPC, the zoning plan was a victory, given the pressures to zone land for industrial development.[19] Although the public eventually agreed to the plan, it was the RPC that developed the land use plan and zoning regulations for the East Side. The result was a mixed industrial-commercial-residential district—a perfect combination for exposing people to pollution. In other words, the RPC's objective, the creation of an industrial and residential East Side, set the pattern for environmental inequity.

Environmental Inequity and the Multinucleated Region

Current patterns of environmental inequity are partly a product of the spatial structure of greater Los Angeles. The region's history of residential and industrial location differs in some respects from that of eastern cities. As eastern cities industrialized in the nineteenth century, the tendency was for industry to remain close to the central business district to take advantage of markets and to minimize transportation costs of goods and workers. At the same time, housing shifted toward the periphery, particularly for people of means, who could afford new forms of public transportation such as the streetcar. Prior to 1920, Los Angeles was mainly a commercial city, and many easterners remarked on the lack of industry for a city of its size.[20]

Between 1920 and 1940, the pattern began to change. Los Angeles added more industrial jobs in that period than any city in the country except Detroit. By the time industry began to stake a foothold in Los Angeles, locational priorities were different. New transportation technologies, larger scales of production, rising land prices in the central city, and suburbanizing workers made peripheral locations attractive to industry. Most of the new towns that incorporated in the 1920s and 1930s were in the industrial zones in the southwest and eastern parts of the county. As the growth of Los Angeles accelerated after World War II (6 million people have been added to the city's population since 1940), industries and residences continued to shift to the suburbs, in some cases with industry leading and planning the way. The simultaneous establishment of industry and residences in the suburbs meant that the two land uses would exist side by side.[21]

The timing of growth in manufacturing and population, predominantly after the Second World War, meant that Los Angeles would conform more to the multinucleated model of spatial structure than did older, established eastern cities. Besides the timing of growth, two historical circumstances aided in the creation of multinucleated Los Angeles. The first was massive land speculation in the 1880s and 1920s, which created far-flung towns miles beyond Los Angeles. While many failed, others later became the nodes in the web of Los Angeles' urban and suburban expansion, pulled together by the red car system.[22]

A second factor was Los Angeles' particular settlement history, specifically its location twenty miles inland from the ocean. Most cities in the East were established near the coast or adjacent to waterways. These locations offered water for manufacturing and cooling and access to far-flung markets and supplies. In most cases, the waterfront was adjacent to the central business district. By the time Los Angeles began to industrialize, the locational advantages of waterfront locations were already known, but its waterfront was at a distance from the city's commercial center. A decentralization of industry was therefore necessary to take advantage of waterfront locations. In combination, these factors helped to make Los Angeles the multinucleated city par excellence, ensuring that industry would be found together with residences in suburban locations and not restricted to a central core.

To a certain degree, the RPC's decision to zone the East Side industrial reflects the realities of industrial dispersion. Its decision acted as a stamp of approval on an inevitable migration of industry east of the Los Angeles River. The industrialization of Vernon, just to the west of Commerce, was already under way when the commission drafted its plans. Industry had begun to disperse from the traditional core of Los Angeles, and the East Side was one direction of decentralization. The Commerce area was literally in the path of industrial expansion. In other words, Commerce might have become industrial even in the absence of zoning. Indeed, without zoning, the region might have become completely industrial, pushing out residential land use. The experience of Vernon, where industry slowly took over most of the land in the city, might have occurred in Commerce as well. In this sense, zoning may have amplified future problems of environmental inequity because it protected some of the land in Commerce for housing, ensuring that people would live close to toxic industries. Eighty years later, residents of Commerce must live with the environmental legacies of the growth of a multinucleated region coupled with the RPC's concerted efforts to zone the East Side of Los Angeles County as a mixed industrial and residential area.

Environmental Inequity

Residents in the City of Commerce, mostly Latino, live close to a large number of toxic facilities. This case of environmental inequity is largely the result of the RPC's decision to zone the area as mixed industrial-commercial-residential in the late 1920s. The historical question is whether the commission took into account the ethnicity of the population in surrounding areas (since within the region there were few residents) when it made its decision.[23] No evidence remains to support it, but given explicitly racist sentiments at the time, it was likely a factor in the minds of commissioners or the zoning division staff who studied maps in search of sites for industrial development. In a 1924 information packet for General Motors, for example, the Chamber of Commerce's Industrial Division reported that most of the workers in Los Angeles were "American" but that on the East Side there were more than fifty thousand "Mexican" workers, men suitable for common labor and women "from a race of people who have been workers in textiles, laces and embroideries for centuries . . . naturally adept in the use of their hands" for apparel industries. An added bonus, unskilled American labor would cost an employer forty cents an hour, while Mexican labor would cost only thirty cents an hour.[24] The prevailing notions about what kind of work Latinos would perform and for how much might have played a part in the commission's decision to zone the East Side industrial. But the open land with large parcels served by three railways was also a critical factor in the decision-making process.

Regardless of intent or motive, the result of the zoning decisions was to create the conditions for environmental inequity in eastern Los Angeles County. By the Second World War, the Industrial East Side was becoming what the commissioners envisioned. More than a hundred plants were manufacturing war-related items, and as they converted to peacetime factories, moderately priced homes were built in the neighborhoods set aside in the zoning plan. During the post–World War II boom, Latinos began to move into the area in larger numbers. By 1960, more than 40 percent of the population was Latino, but within a decade the figure had jumped to more than 70 percent. As an East Side community, the City of Commerce was in the general direction of growth for Latino neighborhoods. It also offered good wages in industrial jobs and moderately priced homes. Industrial restructuring and decentralization of industry in the late 1970s and early 1980s eliminated some of the employment just as the Latino population grew in size. In the first decade of the twenty-first century, Commerce is relatively poorer and has a higher concentration of Latinos than in 1970. On top of these changes, it remains one of the most polluted communities in the county. The current pattern is the result of numerous decisions over the course of eighty years by individuals, institutions, and industries, as well as larger structural changes to the economy of Southern California.

Identifying and analyzing environmental justice, this historical case study demonstrates, requires an examination of myriad factors, including the institutions (such as zoning) that worked to prescribe the current patterns of land use and therefore the potential for environmental inequity. An evaluation of the RPC's decisions suggests that zoning was a root cause for current patterns of environmental inequity. Zoning prohibited manufacturing elsewhere as it encouraged the location of industry on the East Side. Ironically, without zoning a more dispersed pattern of industry might have developed, thereby spreading the burden of toxins over a broader area and reducing the acute concentration of toxic wastes and a legacy of environmental injustice in Los Angeles County.

10

Los Angeles Against the Mountains

JOHN McPHEE

I n Los Angeles versus the San Gabriel Mountains, it is not always clear which side is losing. For example, the Genofiles, Bob and Jackie, can claim to have lost and won. They live on an acre of ground so high that they look across their pool and past the trunks of big pines at an aerial view over Glendale and across Los Angeles to the Pacific bays. The setting, in cool dry air, is serene and Mediterranean. It has not been everlastingly serene.

On a February night some years ago, the Genofiles were awakened by a crash of thunder—lightning striking the mountain front. Ordinarily, in their quiet neighborhood, only the creek beside them was likely to make much sound, dropping steeply out of Shields Canyon on its way to the Los Angeles River. The creek, like every component of all the river systems across the city from mountains to ocean, had not been left to nature. Its banks were concrete. Its bed was concrete. When boulders were running there, they sounded like a rolling freight. On a night like this, the boulders should have been running. The creek should have been a torrent. Its unnatural sound was unnaturally absent. There was, and had been, a lot of rain.

The Genofiles had two teen-age children, whose rooms were on the uphill side of the one-story house. The window in Scott's room looked straight up Pine Cone Road, a cul-de-sac, which, with hundreds like it, defined the northern limit of the city, the confrontation of the urban and the wild. Los Angeles is overmatched on one side by the Pacific Ocean and on the other by very high mountains. With respect to these principal boundaries, Los Angeles is done sprawling. The San Gabriels, in their state of tectonic youth, are rising as rapidly as any range on earth. Their loose inimical slopes flout the tolerance of the angle of repose. Rising straight up out of the megalopolis, they stand ten thousand feet above the nearby sea, and they are not kidding with this city. Shedding, spalling, self-destructing, they are disintegrating at a rate that is also among the fastest in the world. The phalanxed communities of Los Angeles have pushed themselves hard against these mountains, an aggression that requires a deep defense budget to contend with the results. Kimberlee Genofile called to her mother, who joined her in Scott's room as they looked up the street. From its high turnaround, Pine Cone Road plunges downhill like a ski run, bending left and then right and then left and then right in steep christiania turns for half a mile above a three-hundred-foot straightaway that aims directly at the Genofiles' house. Not far below the turnaround, Shields Creek passes under the street, and there a kink in its concrete profile had been plugged by a six-foot boulder. Hence the silence of the creek. The water was now spreading over the street. It descended in heavy sheets. As the young Genofiles and their mother glimpsed it in the all but total darkness, the scene was suddenly illuminated by a blue electrical flash. In the blue light they saw a massive blackness, moving. It was not a landslide, not a mudslide, not a rock avalanche; nor by any means was it the front of a conventional flood. In Jackie's words, "It was just one big black thing coming at us, rolling, rolling with a lot of water in front of it, pushing the water, this big black thing. It was just one big black hill coming toward us."

In geology, it would be known as a debris flow. Debris flows amass in stream valleys and more or less resemble fresh concrete. They consist of water mixed with a good deal of solid material, most of which is above sand size. Some of it is Chevrolet size. Boulders bigger than cars ride long distances in debris flows. Boulders grouped like fish eggs pour downhill in debris flows. The dark material coming toward the Genofiles was not only full of boulders; it was so full of automobiles it was like bread dough mixed with raisins. On its way down Pine Cone Road, it plucked up cars from driveways and the street. When it crashed into the Genofiles' house, the shattering of safety glass made terrific explosive sounds. A door burst open. Mud and boulders poured into the hall. We're going to go, Jackie thought. Oh, my God, what a hell of a way for the four of us to die together.

The parents' bedroom was on the far side of the house. Bob Genofile was in there kicking through white satin draperies at the panelled glass, smashing it to provide an outlet for water, when the three others ran in to join him. The walls of the house neither moved nor shook. As a general contractor, Bob had built dams, department stores, hospitals, six schools, seven churches, and this house. It was made of concrete block with steel reinforcement, sixteen inches on center. His wife had said it was stronger than any dam in California. His crew had called it "the fort." In those days, twenty years before, the Genofiles' acre was close by the edge of the mountain brush, but a developer had come along since then and knocked down thousands of trees and put Pine Cone Road up the slope. Now Bob Genofile was thinking, I hope the roof holds. I hope the roof is strong enough to hold. Debris was flowing over it. He told Scott to shut the bedroom door. No sooner was the door closed than it was battered down and fell into the room. Mud, rock, water poured in. It pushed everybody against the far wall. "Jump on the bed," Bob said. The bed began to rise. Kneeling on it—on a gold velvet spread—they could soon press their palms against the ceiling. The bed also moved toward the glass wall. The two teenagers got off, to try to control the motion, and were pinned between the bed's brass railing and the wall. Boulders went up against the railing, pressed it into their legs, and held them fast. Bob dived into the muck to try to move the boulders, but he failed. The debris flow, entering through windows as well as doors, continued to rise. Escape was still possible for the parents but not for the children. The parents looked at each other and did not stir. Each reached for and held one of the children. Their mother felt suddenly resigned, sure that her son and daughter would die and she and her husband would quickly follow. The house became buried to the eaves. Boulders sat on the roof. Thirteen automobiles were packed around the building, including five in the pool. A din of rocks kept banging against them. The stuck horn of a buried car was blaring. The family in the darkness in their fixed tableau watched one another by the light of a directional signal, endlessly blinking. The house had filled up in six minutes, and the mud stopped rising near the children's chins.

Stories like that do not always have such happy endings. A man went outside to pick up his newspaper one morning, heard a sound, turned, and died of a heart attack as he saw his house crushed to pieces with his wife and two children inside. People have been buried alive in their beds. But such cases are infrequent. Debris flows generally are much less destructive of life than of property. People get out of the way.

If they try to escape by automobile, they have made an obvious but imperfect choice. Norman Reid backed his Pontiac into the street one January morning and was caught from behind by rock porridge. It embedded the car to the chrome strips. Fifty years of archival news photographs show cars of every vintage standing like hippos in chunky muck. The upper halves of their headlights peep above the surface. The late Roland Case Ross, an emeritus professor at California State University, told me of a day in the early thirties when he watched a couple rushing to escape by car. She got in first. While her husband was going around to get in his side, she got out and ran into the house for more silverware. When the car at last putt-putted downhill, a wall of debris was nudging the bumper. The debris stayed on the vehicle's heels all the way to Foothill Boulevard, where the car turned left.

※

A metropolis that exists in a semidesert, imports water three hundred miles, has inveterate flash floods, is at the grinding edges of two tectonic plates, and has a microclimate tenacious of noxious oxides will have its priorities among the aspects of its environment that it attempts to control. For example, Los Angeles makes money catching water. In a few days in 1983, it caught twenty-eight million dollars' worth of water. In one period of twenty-four hours, however, the ocean hit the city with twenty-foot waves, a tornado made its own freeway, debris flows poured from the San Gabriel front, and an earthquake shook the region. Nature's invoice was forty million dollars. Later, twenty million more was spent dealing with the mountain debris.

There were those who would be quick—and correct—in saying that were it not for the alert unflinching manner and imaginative strategies by which Los Angeles outwits the mountains, nature's invoices at such times would run into the billions. The rear-guard defenses are spread throughout the city and include more than two thousand miles of underground conduits and concrete-lined open stream channels—a web of engineering that does not so much reinforce as replace the natural river systems. The front line of battle is where the people meet the mountains—up the steep slopes where the subdivisions stop and the brush begins.

Strung out along the San Gabriel front are at least a hundred and twenty bowl-shaped excavations that resemble football stadiums and are often as large. Years ago, when a big storm left back yards and boulevards five feet deep in scree, one neighborhood came through amazingly unscathed, because it happened to surround a gravel pit that had filled up instead. A tungsten filament went on somewhere above Los Angeles. The county began digging pits to catch debris. They were quarries, in a sense, but exceedingly bizarre quarries, in that the rock was meant to come to them. They are known as debris basins. Blocked at their downstream ends with earthfill or concrete constructions, they are also known as debris dams. With clean spillways and empty reservoirs, they stand ready to capture rivers of boulders—these deep dry craters, lying close above the properties they protect. In the overflowing abundance of urban nomenclature, the individual names of such basins are obscure, until a day when they appear in a headline in the *Los Angeles Times*: Harrow, Englewild, Zachau, Dunsmuir, Shields, Big Dalton, Hog, Hook East, Hook West, Limekiln, Starfall, Sawpit, Santa Anita. For fifty miles, they mark the wild boundary like bulbs beside a mirror. Behind chain links, their idle ovate forms more than suggest defense. They are separated, on the average, by seven hundred yards. In aggregate, they are worth hundreds of millions of dollars. All this to keep the mountains from falling on Johnny Carson.

The principal agency that developed the debris basins was the hopefully named Los Angeles County Flood Control District, known familiarly through the region as Flood Control, and even more intimately as Flood. ("When I was at Flood, one of our dams filled with debris overnight," a former employee remarked to me. "If any more rain came, we were going to have to evacuate the whole of Pasadena.") There has been a semantic readjustment, obviously intended to acknowledge that when a flood pours out of the mountains it might be half rock. The debris basins are now in the charge of the newly titled Sedimentation Section of the Hydraulic Division of the Los Angeles County Department of Public Works. People still call it Flood. By whatever name the agency is called, its essential tactic remains unaltered. This was summarized for me in a few words by an engineer named Donald Nichols, who pointed out that eight million people live below the mountains on the urban coastal plain, within an area large enough to accommodate Philadelphia, Detroit, Chicago, St. Louis, Boston, and New York. He said, "To make the area inhabitable, you had to put in lined channels on the plain and halt the debris at the front. If you don't take it out at the front, it will come out in the plain, filling up channels. A filled channel won't carry diddly-boo."

To stabilize mountain streambeds and stop descending rocks even before they reach the debris basins, numerous crib structures (barriers made of concrete slats) have been emplaced in high canyons—the idea being to convert plunging streams into boulder staircases, and hypothetically cause erosion to work against itself. Farther into the mountains, a dozen dams of some magnitude were built in the nineteen-twenties and thirties to control floods and conserve water. Because they are in the San Gabriels, they inadvertently trap large volumes of debris. One of them—the San Gabriel Dam, in the San Gabriel River—was actually built as a debris-control structure. Its reservoir, which is regularly cleaned out, contained, just then, twenty million tons of mountain.

The San Gabriel River, the Los Angeles River, and the Big Tujunga (Bigta Hung-ga) are the principal streams that enter the urban plain, where a channel that filled with rock wouldn't carry diddly-boo. Three colossal debris basins— as different in style as in magnitude from those on the mountain front—have been constructed on the plain to greet these rivers. Where the San Gabriel goes past Azusa on its way to Alamitos Bay, the Army Corps of Engineers completed in the late nineteen-forties a dam ninety-two feet high and twenty-four thousand feet wide—this to stop a river that is often dry, and trickles most of the year. Santa Fe Dam, as it is called, gives up at a glance its own story, for it is made of boulders that are shaped like potatoes and are generally the size of watermelons. They imply a large volume of water flowing with high energy. They are stream-propelled, stream-rounded boulders, and the San Gabriel is the stream. In Santa Fe Basin, behind the dam, the dry bed of the San Gabriel is half a mile wide. The boulderstrewn basin in its entirety is four times as wide as that. It occupies eighteen hundred acres in all, nearly three square miles, of what would be prime real estate were it not for the recurrent arrival of rocks. The scene could have been radioed home from Mars, whose cobbly face is in part the result of debris flows dating to a time when Mars had surface water.

✳

People of Gardena, Inglewood, and Watts no less than Azusa and Altadena pay for the defense of the mountain front, the rationale being that debris trapped near its source will not move down and choke the channels of the inner city, causing urban floods. The political City of Los Angeles—in its vague and tentacular configuration—actually abuts the San Gabriels for twenty miles or so, in much the way that it extends to touch the ocean in widely separated places like Venice, San Pedro, and Pacific Palisades. Los Angeles County reaches across the mountains and far into the Mojave Desert. The words "Los Angeles" as generally used here refer neither to the political city nor to the county but to the multinamed urban integrity that has a street in it seventy miles long (Sepulveda Boulevard) and, from the Pacific Ocean at least to Pomona, moves north against the mountains as a comprehensive town.

The debris basins vary greatly in size—not, of course, in relation to the populations they defend but in relation to the watersheds and washes above them in the mountains. For the most part, they are associated with small catchments, and the excavated basins are commensurately modest, with capacities under a hundred thousand cubic yards. In a typical empty reservoir—whatever its over-all dimensions may be—stands a columnar tower that resembles a campanile. Full of holes, it is known as a perforated riser. As the basin fills with a thickflowing slurry of water, mud, and rock, the water goes into the tower and is drawn off below. The county calls this water harvesting.

Like the freeways, the debris-control system ordinarily functions but occasionally jams. When the Genofiles' swimming pool filled with cars, debris flows descended into other neighborhoods along that part of the front. One hit a culvert, plugged the culvert, crossed a road in a bouldery wave, flattened fences, filled a debris basin, went over the spillway, and spread among houses lying below, shoving them off their foundations. The debris basins have caught as much as six hundred thousand cubic yards in one storm. Over time, they have trapped some twenty million tons of mud and rock. Inevitably, sometimes something gets away.

At Devils Gate—just above the Rose Bowl, in Pasadena—a dam was built in 1920 with control of water its only objective. Yet its reservoir, with a surface of more than a hundred acres, has filled to the brim with four million tons of rock, gravel, and sand. A private operator has set up a sand-and-gravel quarry in the reservoir. Almost exactly, he takes out what the mountains put in. As one engineer has described it, "he pays Flood, and Flood makes out like a champ."

※

I have not been specific about the dates of the stories so far recounted. This was to create the impression that debris pours forth from the mountains continually, perennially, perpetually—which it does and does not, there being a great temporal disparity between the pace at which the mountains behave and the way people think. Debris flows do not occur in every possible season. When they do happen, they don't just spew from any canyon but come in certain places on the mountain front. The places change. Volumes differ. There are vintage years. The four most prominent in this century have been 1934, 1938, 1969, and 1978. Exceptional flows have occurred at least once a decade, and lesser ones in greater numbers. Exceptional flows are frequent, in other words, but not frequent enough to deter people from building pantiled mansions in the war zone, dingbats in the line of fire.

Why the debris moves when it does or where it does is not attributable to a single agent. The parent rock has been extensively broken up by earthquakes, but that alone will not make it flow. Heavy rainfall, the obvious factor, is not as obvious as it may seem. In 1980, some of the most intense storms ever measured in Los Angeles failed to produce debris flows of more than minimal size. The setting up of a debris flow is a little like the charging of an eighteenth-century muzzleloader: the ramrod, the powder, the wadding, the shot. Nothing much would happen in the absence of any one component. In sequence and proportion each had to be correct.

On the geologic time scale, debris flows in the San Gabriel Mountains can be looked upon as constant. With all due respect, though, the geologic time scale doesn't mean a whole lot in a place like Los Angeles. In Los Angeles, even the Los Angeles time scale does not arouse general interest. A superevent in 1934? In 1938? In 1969? In 1978? Who is going to remember that? A relatively major outpouring—somewhere in fifty miles—about once every decade?

Mountain time and city time appear to be bifocal. Even with a geology functioning at such remarkably short intervals, the people have ample time to forget it.

In February of 1978, while debris was still hardening in the home of the Genofiles, Wade Wells, of the United States Forest Service, went up and down Pine Cone Road knocking on doors, asking how long the people had lived there. He wondered who remembered, nine years back, the debris-flow inundations of Glendora and Azusa, scarcely twenty miles away. Only two did. Everyone else had arrived since 1969.

Wells is a hydrologist who works in the mountains, principally in San Dimas Experimental Forest, where he does research on erosion and sedimentation—the story of assembling debris. With a specialist's eye, he notes the mountain front, and in its passivity can see the tension: "These guys here, they should be nervous when it rains. Their houses are living on borrowed time. See that dry ledge? It's a waterfall. I've seen hundreds of tons of rock falling over it." More often, though, he is thousands of feet above the nearest house, on slopes so steep he sometimes tumbles and rolls. With his colleagues, he performs experiments with plants, rock, water, fire. When I first became interested in Los Angeles' battle with debris flows, I went up there with them a number of times. The mountains, after all, are where the rocks come from. The mountains shape the charge that will advance upon the city. People come from odder places than the East Coast to see this situation. One day, a couple of scientists arrived from the Cordillera Cantabrica, in northwestern Spain. When they saw how rapidly the San Gabriels were disintegrating, one of them said he felt sorry for Wells, who would soon be out of work. When Wells told him that the mountains were rising even faster than they were coming down, the man said, "*Muy interesante. Sí, señor.*"

From below, one look at the San Gabriels will suggest their advantage. The look is sometimes hard to come by. You might be driving up the San Gabriel River Freeway in the morning, heading straight at the mountains at point-blank range, and not be able to see them. A voice on KNX tells you that the day is clear. There's not a cloud in the sky, as the blue straight up confirms. A long incline rises into mist, not all of which is smog. From time immemorial, this pocket of the coast has been full of sea fog and persistent vapors. The early Spaniards called it the Bay of Smokes. Smog, the action of sunlight on nitrogen oxides, has only contributed to a preexisting veil. Sometimes you don't see the San Gabriels until the streets stop and the mountains start. The veil suddenly thins, and there they are, in height and magnitude overwhelming. You plunge into a canyon flanked with soaring slopes before you realize you are out of town. The San Gabriel Mountains are as rugged as any terrain in America, and their extraordinary proximity to the city, the abruptness of the transition from the one milieu to the other, cannot be exaggerated. A lone hiker in the San Gabriels one winter—exhausted, snow blinded, hypothermic—staggered down a ridgeline out of the snow and directly into the parking lot of a shopping center, where he crawled to a phone booth, called 911 and slumped against the glass until an ambulance came to save him.

Hang-glider pilots go up the San Gabriels, step off crags, and, after a period of time proportional to their skills, land somewhere in the city. The San Gabriels are nearly twice as high as Mt. Katahdin or Mt. Washington, and are much closer to the sea. From base platform to summit, the San Gabriels are three thousand feet higher than the Rockies. To be up in the San Gabriels is to be both above and beside urban Los Angeles, only minutes from the streets, and to look north from ridge to dry ridge above deeply cut valleys filled with gulfs of clear air. Beyond the interior valleys—some fifty thousand feet away and a vertical mile above you—are the summits of Mt. Baldy, Mt. Hawkins, Mt. Baden-Powell. They are so clearly visible in the dry blue sky that just below their ridgelines you can almost count the boulders that are bunched there like grapes.

If you turn and face south, you look out over something like soft slate that reaches fifty miles to an imprecise horizon. The whole of Los Angeles is spread below you, and none of it is visible. It is lost absolutely in the slate-gray sea, grayer than a minesweeper, this climatic wonder, this megalopolitan featherbed a thousand feet thick, known as "the marine layer." Early in the day, it is for the most part the natural sea fog. As you watch it from above through the morning and into the afternoon, it turns yellow, and then ochre, and then brown, and sometimes nearly black—like butter darkening in a skillet.

*

In millennia before Los Angeles settled its plain, the chaparral burned every thirty years or so, as the chaparral does now. The burns of prehistory, in their natural mosaic, were smaller than the ones today. With cleared fire lanes, chemical retardants, and other means of suppressing what is not beyond control, people have conserved fuel in large acreages. When the inevitable fires come, they burn hotter, higher, faster than they ever did in a state of unhindered nature. When the fires end, there is nothing much left on the mountainsides but a thin blanket of ash. The burns are vast and bare. On the sheer declivities where the surface soils were held by chaparral, there is no chaparral.

Fine material tumbles downslope and collects in the waterless beds of streams. It forms large and bulky cones there, to some extent filling the canyons. Under green chaparral, the gravitational movement of bits of soil, particles of sand, and other loose debris goes on month after month, year after year, especially in oversteepened environments, where it can represent more than half of all erosion. After a burn, though, it increases exponentially. It may increase twentyfold, fortyfold, even sixtyfold. This steady tumbling descent of unconsolidated mountain crumbs is known as dry ravel. After a burn, so much dry ravel and other debris becomes piled up and ready to go that to live under one of those canyons is (as many have said) to look up the barrel of a gun.

One would imagine that the first rain would set the whole thing off, but it doesn't. The early-winter rains-and sometimes the rains of a whole season—are not enough to make the great bulk move. Actually, they add to it.

If you walk in a rainstorm on a freshly burned chaparral slope, you notice as you step on the wet ground that the tracks you are making are prints of dry dust. In the course of a conflagration, chaparral soil, which is not much for soaking up water in the first place, experiences a chemical change and, a little below its surface, becomes waterproof. In a Forest Service building at the foot of the mountains Wade Wells keeps some petri dishes and soil samples in order to demonstrate this phenomenon to passing unbelievers. In one dish he puts unburned chaparral soil. It is golden brown. He drips water on it from an eye-dropper. The water beads up, stands there for a while, then collapses and spreads into the soil. Why the water hesitates is not well understood but is a great deal more credible than what happens next. Wells fills a dish with a dark soil from burned chaparral. He fills the eyedropper and empties it onto the soil. The water stands up in one large dome. Five minutes later, the dome is still there. Ten minutes later, the dome is still there. Sparkling, tumescent, myco-phane, the big bead of water just stands there indefinitely, on top of the imper-meable soil. Further demonstrating how waterproof this burned soil really is, Wells pours half a pound of it, like loose brown sugar, into a beaker of water.

In the slow progression of normal decay, chaparral litter seems to give up to the soil what have been vaguely described as "waxlike complexes of long-chain aliphatic hydrocarbons." These waxy substances are what make unburned chaparral soil somewhat resistant to water, or "slightly nonwettable," as Wells and his colleagues are wont to describe it. When the wildfires burn, and temperatures at the surface of the ground are six or seven hundred centi-grade degrees, the soil is so effective as an insulator that the temperature one centimetre below the surface may not be hot enough to boil water. The heavy waxlike substances vaporize at the surface and recondense in the cooler tem-peratures below. Acting like oil, they coat soil particles and establish the hydrophobic layer—one to six centimetres down. Above that layer, where the waxlike substances are gone, the veneer of burned soil is "wettable." When

Wells drips water on a dishful of that, the water soaks in as if the dish were full of Kleenex. When rain falls on burned and denuded ground, it soaks the very thin upper layer but can penetrate no farther. Hiking boots strike hard enough to break through into the dust, but the rain is repelled and goes down the slope. Of all the assembling factors that eventually send debris flows rumbling down the canyons, none is more detonative than the waterproof soil.

In the first rains after a fire, water quickly saturates the thin permeable layer, and liquefied soil drips downhill like runs of excess paint. These miniature debris flows stripe the mountainsides with miniature streambeds—countless scarlike rills that are soon the predominant characteristic of the burned terrain. As more rain comes, each rill is going to deliver a little more debris to the accumulating load in the canyon below. But, more to the point, each rill— its natural levees framing its impermeable bed—will increase the speed of the surface water. As rain sheds off a mountainside like water off a tin roof, the rill network, as it is called, may actually triple the speed, and therefore greatly enhance the power of the runoff. The transport capacity of the watershed— how much bulk it can move—may increase a thousandfold. The rill network is prepared to deliver water with enough force and volume to mobilize the deposits lying in the canyons below. With the appearance of the rills, almost all prerequisites have now sequentially occurred. The muzzle-loader is charged. For a fullscale flat-out debris flow to burst forth from the mountains, the final requirement is a special-intensity storm.

Some of the most concentrated rainfall in the history of the United States has occurred in the San Gabriel Mountains. The oddity of this is about as intense as the rain. Months—seasons—go by in Los Angeles without a fallen drop. Los Angeles is one of the least-rained-upon places in the Western Hemisphere. The mountains are so dry they hum. Erosion by dry ravel greatly exceeds erosion by water. The celebrated Mediterranean climate of Los Angeles owes itself to aridity. While Seattle is receiving its average rainfall of thirty-nine inches a year, Chicago thirty-three, the District of Columbia thirty-nine, and New York City forty-four, Los Angeles is doing well if it gets fifteen. In one year out of every four over the past century, rainfall in Los Angeles has been under ten inches, and once or twice it was around five. That is pure Gobi. When certain storm systems approach Los Angeles, though—storms that come in on a very long reach from far out in the Pacific—they will pick up huge quantities of water from the ocean and just pump it into the mountains. These are by no means annual events, but when they occur they will stir even hydrologists to bandy the name of Noah. In January, 1969, for example, more rain than New York City sees in a year fell in the San Gabriels in nine days. In January, 1943, twenty-six inches fell in twenty-four hours. In February, 1978, just before the Genofiles' house filled with debris, nearly an inch and a half of rain fell in twenty-five minutes. On April 5, 1926, a rain gauge in the San Gabriels collected one inch in one minute.

The really big events result from two, three, four, five storms in a row coming in off the Pacific. In 1980, there were six storms in nine days. Mystically, unnervingly, the heaviest downpours always occur on the watersheds most recently burned. Why this is so is a question that has not been answered. Meteorologists and hydrologists speculate about ash-particle nuclei and heat reflection, but they don't know. The storm cells are extremely compact, deluging typically about ten miles by ten. One inch of rain on a patch that size is seven million two hundred and thirty-two thousand tons of water. In most years, in most places, a winter rain will actually stabilize a mountainside. The water's surface tension helps to hold the slope together. Where there is antecedent fire, water that would otherwise become a binding force hits the rill network, caroms off the soil's waterproof layer, and rides the steep slopes in cataracts into the nearest canyon. It is now a lubricant, its binding properties repelled, its volume concentrating into great hydraulic power. The vintage years present themselves when at least five days of rain put seven inches on the country and immediately thereafter comes the heaviest rainfall of the series. That is when the flint hits the steel, when the sparks fly into the flashpan. On that day, the debris mobilizes.

※

"The ultimate origin of the debris flows," [geologist Leon Silver] said, "is the continuous tectonic front that has made this one of the steepest mountain fronts in North America and produced a wilderness situation not a hundred metres from people's houses."

The continuous tectonic front is where the North American and Pacific Plates are sliding past each other—where Bakersfield moves toward Mexico City while Burbank heads for Alaska. Between Bakersfield and Burbank lie the San Gabriel Mountains. With the San Bernardino Mountains east of them, they trend east-west, forming a kink in the coastal ranges that come down from San Francisco and go on to Baja California. The kink conforms to a bend in the San Andreas Fault, which runs along the inland base of the mountains. The kink looks like this:

It could be a tiptoeing h. It resembles a prize-winning chair. Los Angeles is like a wad of gum stuck to the bottom of the chair. The mountains are one continuous system, but its segments are variously named. The upper stretch is called the Coast Ranges. The lower leg is called the Peninsular Ranges. The kink is called the Transverse Ranges.

My hieroglyph represents, of course, not only the mountains but the flanking San Andreas Fault, which comes up from the Gulf of California, bends left around Los Angeles, then goes on to San Francisco and north below the sea. As if this regional context were not large enough, Silver now placed it in a larger one. The East Pacific Rise, the ocean-basin spreading center away from which the Pacific Plate and other plates are moving, sinuously makes its way from the latitude of Tierra del Fuego all the way north to Mexico, where it enters the Gulf of California. The East Pacific Rise has splintered Mexico and carried Baja California away from the mainland—much as the Carlsberg Ridge has cracked open the deserts of Afro-Arabia and made the Red Sea. Baja is not moving due west, as one might guess from a glance at a map, but north by northwest, with the rest of the Pacific Plate. The cumulative power of this northward motion presses on the kink in the San Andreas, helping the mountains rise.

That much has long seemed obvious: as the two sides of the San Andreas slide by each other, they compress the landscape at the kink. It has been considerably less obvious that a compressional force accompanies the great fault wherever it goes. In the past, the building of the Coast Ranges and the Peninsular Ranges was in no way attributed to the San Andreas Fault. A paper published in *Science* in November, 1987—and signed by enough geologists to make a quorum at the Rose Bowl—offers evidence that the San Andreas has folded its flanking country, much as a moving boat crossing calm waters will send off lateral waves. The great compression at the kink is withal the most intense. The Coast Ranges and the Peninsular Ranges are generally smaller than the Transverse Ranges. The San Gabriels are being compressed about a tenth of an inch a year.

Why the kink is there in the first place is "not well understood." Just to the northeast, though, in the Great Basin of Utah and Nevada, the earth's mantle is close, the earth's crust is thin and stretching. In the past few million years, the geographic coordinates of Reno and Salt Lake—at the western and eastern extremes of the Great Basin—have moved apart sixty miles. This large new subdivision of the regional tectonics is in every way as entrancing as it is enigmatic. Almost all of California may be headed out to sea. Already, the east-west stretching of the Great Basin has put Reno west of Los Angeles, and it may be what has bent the San Andreas Fault.

Some of the rock of the San Gabriels is two hundred times as old as the San Andreas Fault, which has been in existence for less than a five-hundredth of the history of the world. Plates come and go—splitting, welding, changing through time, travelling long distances. Before the present North American and Pacific Plates began to work on this particular rock, Silver said, it may have been "bashed around in Mexico twice and perhaps across the Pacific before that." He continued, "It's a bedrock ridge up there. It's a weirdo wonderful block of rocks, the most complicated mountain range in North America. It includes the oldest rocks on the West Coast. The San Gabes look like a flake kicked around on plate boundaries for hundreds of millions of years."

*

The San Gabriels were rising faster than they were disintegrating, Silver said. The debris basins had given geomorphologists an unparalleled opportunity to calculate erosion rates. They could even determine how much mountain is removed by a single storm. On the average, about seven tons disappear from each acre each year—coming off the mountains and heading for town.

Between the geology-department roof and the San Gabriels, the city gradually rose. A very long, ramplike, and remarkably consistent incline ended in the sheerness of the mountain wall. This broad uniform slope is where the seven tons an acre had emerged from the mountains, year upon year for a number of millions of years—accumulating as detrital cones, also known as fans. Broad at the bottom, narrow at the top, the fans were like spilled grain piling up at the edge of a bin. There were so many of them, coming down from stream after stream, that they had long since coalesced, forming a tilted platform, which the Spaniards had called the bajada.

"I used to live on the mountain front," Silver said. "By Devils Gate, at the mouth of Arroyo Seco. We could hear the big knockers go by—the three-metre boulders. The whole front face of the San Gabes is processed."

"Processed?"

"Shattered and broken. It is therefore vulnerable to landsliding, to undercutting by the streams, to acceleration by local earthquakes, to debris flows."

"Why does anybody live there?"

"They're not well informed. Most folks don't know the story of the fireflood sequence. When it happens in the next canyon, they say, 'Thank God it didn't happen here.'"

"Why would a geologist live there?"

"It's a calculated risk. The higher you build, the cooler it is. There are great views. And at night, up there, the cool air off the mountains flows down and pushes the dirty air masses back. The head of our seismological laboratory lives on the mountain front. In fact, most of the Caltech geology department lives on the mountain front."

"Where do you live?"

"Way out on the fan."

✳

Before the citrus, there were ranches; before the ranches, Indians; before the Indians, the primeval scene: huge unencumbered alluvial fans leaning into the fast-rising mountains beside the hazy plain—the broadest coastal lowland in all of California. Despite the sea fog and the general lack of more concentrated water, the climate was so congenial that when people discovered it they were willing to struggle to live in it. The people of Asuksangna were among the first. Their village has become Azusa. For agricultural purposes, they burned grass-lands in spring. Inadvertently, they torched untold acreages of chaparral and set up innumerable debris flows. Lightning ignited what the Indians missed. Eas-ily, they adapted to the consequent flows. Ranchers, when they came, settled by the canyons to guard the trickling water, and shot one another over rights to the water, which occasionally carried loads big enough to kill them all. Huge contiguous ranches lined the San Gabriel front—Rancho San José, Rancho Azusa de Duarte, Rancho Santa Anita, Rancho La Cañada, Rancho Tujunga, Rancho Ex-Mission de San Fernando. During the long drought of the eighteen-sixties, horses and mules went into the mountains to bring out water in tanks. The effort notwithstanding, the bones of parched cattle were scattered about the plain. The message was clear: this environment was no less hostile than it was appealing. When the railroads arrived (1876, 1885), they set off a population splurge that has since become known as California's second gold rush. The people rushing in were farmers, and the gold was oranges. From Kansas City, the fare to Los Angeles was for a brief time a dollar. The citrus orchards were established in small units, [forest manager Charles] Colver said, "ten to fifteen acres each—all that one man could tend to." There were soon a hundred thousand acres of citrus. Ditches from the mountains irri-gated the trees. Once in a while, the ditches filled with debris. In 1884, in the aftermath of a fire in Soledad Canyon, debris tore away the tracks of the Southern Pacific. (In 1978, in the aftermath of fire, debris wrecked the tracks in the same place.)

In the eighteen-seventies, to connect agricultural towns, local railways had begun to climb the bajada. Long straight avenues are there now, steadily rising three and four miles. At least one railway was mule-drawn. When the mules made it to the top of the fan, they went around to the back of the train and got onto a special flatcar, on which they rode downhill. In the eighteen-nineties, electricity replaced the mules, and the street railways began to assume almost the exact pattern of the freeways that have replaced them. Under the influence of the Pacific Electric Railway, communities began to coalesce, like the alluvial fans.

For many decades, there was a moat of oranges between the built-up metropolis and the mountain front. After the wildfires of 1913 resulted in the flows of 1914, inspiring, in 1915, the creation of the Los Angeles County Flood Control District, debris was not thought of as the essence of the threat. The operating word was "Flood."

✳

In November, 1933, the chaparral burned in numerous watersheds above Pasadena, La Cañada, La Crescenta, and Montrose, and slopes were left black and bare. Rainfall in amounts that the Flood Control District called a "Noah-type storm" followed in the last days of the year, mobilizing, on January 1, 1934, a number of almost simultaneous debris flows that came out of the mountains, went through the orchards and into the towns, killed dozens of people, destroyed hundreds of houses, and left boulders the size of icebergs far down the fans. (In the middle of all this chaos, the football team of Columbia University went into the Arroyo Seco and defeated Stanford in the Rose Bowl.) Out of Pickens Canyon came a debris slug of such magnitude that it travelled all the way to Foothill Boulevard, crossed it, and passed through the business district of Montrose. A boulder eight feet in diameter came to rest on the main street of town, three miles south of the mountain front. This was the same Montrose to which Jackie Genofile would one day retreat in order to feel safe. The New Year's Day Flood, as people still refer to it, killed thirty-four in Montrose and neighboring towns, and ruined nearly five hundred houses. All over the bajada, Model A's were so deeply buried that their square roofs stuck out of the mud like rafts. Streets of La Crescenta, a mile downhill from where the Genofiles live now, were like the braided rivers of Alaska, with channels of water looping past islands of debris.

The working gravel pit that filled up and fortuitously became the prototype debris basin was in Haines Canyon, just above the village of Tujunga, whose civic infrastructure it happily preserved from otherwise certain annihilation. While the mud, sand, and boulders that were deeply spread on the alluvial fans were demonstrating that a flood of rock was a far greater menace than a flood of water, this inspirational gravel pit was showing what to do about it. With enough money—enough steam shovels, enough dump trucks, enough basins cupped beneath the falling hills—Los Angeles could defy the mountains, and append to an already impressive list one more flout in the face of nature.

After Pearl Harbor, rapidly expanding war industries drew people to Los Angeles from all over the United States. They worked mainly in the oil, steel, and aircraft industries and in plastics factories that made butadiene as a substitute for rubber. The ascending effluents of the smelters, refineries, mills, and factories added a great burden to the marine fog layer—made heavier still as the work force moved about in cars. To describe this ochre cumulus, the world's shortest portmanteau word, which had been coined around 1905, was borrowed from London.

Housing developments had to be created. The land under the orchards was an obvious choice, and a lot of citrus fell in the war. Like a spider plant or a wandering Jew, an orange tree is psychologically sensitive. Not surprisingly, a virus broke out in the orchards—a strain known to pomologists as "the quick decline."

When the war ended, the quick decline did not. As Chuck Colver well remembers, "This was a mortal blow. If a grower didn't suffer from it, he thought he would, so he sold to a developer as an easy way out. After the war, the new people stayed on, and it was readily apparent that agriculture and urbanization were not compatible. Citrus relied on smudge pots to protect the trees against freezes. It used fertilizer that was smelly. It created dust in the tilling. It bred flies. Big slow trucks went around full of oranges. Everybody had tolerated all this when oranges were the sole economy, but it was a nuisance to the newcomers. They threw garbage in the orchards. They stole oranges. And, above all, they complained. They passed laws against smelly fertilizer, against smudge smoke, against pesticides. Citrus could not compete. Water became too high-priced. Smog began to affect the trees. The size and quality of fruit deteriorated. A superior product became an inferior product."

Fifty miles of citrus disappeared as the communities coalesced and the megalopolitan census passed eight million. Los Angeles did not spread out like a blooming flower, or grow from a center, like continental ice. It grew all at once all over the plain. It filled in the mountain front. In the late winter of 1938, thirty inches of rain had fallen in six days. Publications of the United States Forest Service later described the event as "the greatest rainstorm in the recorded history of the San Gabriel Mountains." Early debris basins did not pass this test. They filled up and overflowed. They were not designed to separate rock from water. With the rise of population, and the postwar proliferation of development along the mountain front, successive debris dams and accompanying basins—each unique, fitting the conditions of its canyon—

became ever more proficient, designed to function like giant colanders. The most recent is Buena Vista Debris Basin, which was built in 1981 at the head of Norumbega Drive, in Monrovia. With its Yale bowlishness, its columnar steel trash racks, its perforated outlet tower, and its two-hundred-foot-wide rock-filled concrete dam, it represents the state of the art. The confident owner of a house just below it has landscaped his place with sandbags.

Generally, the debris basins work. People can lie peacefully in their beds and listen to the thunk of boulders heading into traps. Carter Canyon Debris Basin, in Sierra Madre, is in an extremely steep gorge under high-rising mountainsides. Carter Canyon is where Wade Wells, one arid afternoon, pointed out to me a number of rock outcroppings about thirty feet above the dry streambed and said they were the lips of falls. The debris basin was built in 1954. In the autumn of 1978, eight different fires denuded the mountains above. The Mountain Trail Fire—the one most closely related to Carter Canyon Debris Basin—consumed fifteen hundred acres. During a storm a few weeks later, Wells went to Carter Canyon and watched hundreds of tons of mud and boulders coming over one of the falls. The basin caught it all effectively. The basin was cleaned out, and trucks took away the debris. In 1980, when Carter Canyon Basin filled again, water alone went over the top.

※

In the fifty miles of the San Gabriel front, almost all levels of income are represented, from multifamily dingbats to pastury enclaves with moats and armed guards. Under isolated tufts of old citrus are electrically operated iron gates leading to palm-lined driveways between retaining walls of granodiorite debris. Relentlessly, builders go on finding tracts for new housing. They often borrow something from the precipitous slopes—a practice known as mountain-cropping. Whether an owner has a two-million-dollar house protected by nothing more than a trash rack in front of a culvert or a hundred-and-fifty-thousand-dollar hut with a large debris basin right beside it, debris-flow information is supposed to be a part of the exchange when houses are sold. For example, here's a nice little bungalow for sale pretty far up the fan in the neighborhood where Art Cook and his automobile were given a quarter-mile ride by the debris flow of 1969. Three bedrooms. A quarter of an acre. How about debris flows?

"Not that I know of," the realtor says. "I've never heard of that happening up there."

※

If Los Angeles hangs on long enough, it will cart the mountains entirely away, but already it is having difficulty figuring out where to put them. In a productive season, the debris basins will catch more than a million cubic yards. The reservoirs back in the mountains take in much more than that. Over-all cleanout costs can exceed sixty million dollars in a single year—a required expenditure if the system is to function.

The Los Angeles side of this battle is unexampled in heroic chutzpah—to a degree expressible in the volume of any fan. For a brief geologic time, debris has been pouring out of Little Santa Anita Canyon, for example, and piling up on the plain. Among the San Gabriels' alluvial fans, this is a modest one in all respects. Its toe is down at the horse track—Santa Anita—and its slope begins to rise through the Los Angeles Arboretum and then goes on rising a couple of miles, through the center of Sierra Madre and on up Baldwin Avenue to Carter Debris Basin, at the mountain front. The fan coalesces with fans on either side, but its width can be approximated at a mile and a half. Calculation shows that this one minor fan consists of about two billion cubic yards of material that has so far come off the watersheds above. Toward the middle of the twentieth century, Los Angeles undertook to replace nature as the depositor of material. Los Angeles assumed responsibility as well for at least fifty other fans on the San Gabriel front, not to mention lesser uplifts, like the Santa Monica Mountains and the Verdugo Hills.

Against the prodigious odds, Los Angeles is much more successful than it may appear to be when neighborhoods buried to the rooflines are pictured in the *Times*. To date, the debris basins have trapped twenty million tons of mountain. A small fraction of that figure has managed to get beyond them. Since the basins can fill up in a few hours, equipment has to be marshalled very swiftly to make cleanouts—and sometimes repeated cleanouts where more debris is expected. At the height of a storm, radio patrols are all over the front feeding information into the computers of the Storm Operation Center, which deploys forces from six field yards—deploys the motor graders, the backhoes, the front-end loaders, the trailer-mounted night-construction floodlight systems, the thirty-five-ton truck-mounted clamshell cranes, the forty-five-ton draglines with six-yard buckets, the six-inch pumps that can suck in and spit out rocks, the rock grapples that can pick up five-ton boulders, and, above all, the big ten-wheelers: dump trucks capable of hauling fifteen tons at a time.

Los Angeles owns some of this equipment, but Los Angeles is not an OPEC country. Los Angeles cannot afford to keep hundreds of dump trucks waiting for an annual or biennial storm. The debris is made attractive to private truckers. They are paid fifty dollars an hour for lugging mud, no overtime. Flood has used as many as three hundred private trucks in one storm. They come from all over Southern California—from Lone Pine in the Owens Valley, from San Diego. Forty trucks once came from Redding, nearly five hundred miles north, and found no work when they arrived. A call once came to the section from a heavy-equipment operator in the Midwest. He wanted the work for his cranes and large loaders, and was willing to send them two thousand miles.

Wherever there has been an antecedent fire, debris basins are likely to fill to the brim. In 1978, every basin filled for fifteen miles under the slopes burned by the Mill Fire—eighteen basins in all. In some of them, the rocks were so big that they had to be broken by dynamite before they could be removed. Dunsmuir was cleaned twice that winter, Mullally and Denivelle three times. They filled as they were being emptied. Zachau was cleaned out three times as well, but it still let boulders ten feet in diameter get away. People living below Zachau sued (unsuccessfully), claiming that the county had not maintained the basin. "We had records that showed if there was two ounces of dirt in it we took it out," [engineer] Dan Davis says, his indignation unmitigated.

Before the creation of the debris basins, mountain sands were carried to the ocean by winter floods. Now there is a beach problem. Sand is being lost to offshore canyons and is not being naturally replenished. A place that values its beaches as much as Southern California does has no choice but to buy sand. Sand has been transported by ten-wheelers from the mountains to the beaches. When thirty thousand yards of sand was put on Zuma Beach, people complained about the color contrast. Materials cleaned out of the Laurel Ridge Debris Basin, in the Santa Monica Mountains, used to be hauled over the mountains in a direction away from the ocean and dropped at the Calabasas dump. Subsequent Laurel cleanouts went onto the beach. The Sedimentation Section has been investigating the possibility of using pipeline slurries to transport debris to distant gravel pits; it could also go in pipelines to the beach. Vito Vanoni said, "I think the day will come when we grind it all up and send it to the beach. The question is: Where do we get the water for the slurry? We could use sewage. That's not so good. Possibly we could use salt water."

Years ago, in an act of lyric irony, Flood Control bought four cloud-seeding generators and set them up near reservoirs in the mountains and along the front. The cloud-seeding generators have been used almost exclusively during foul winter weather, since they would not be efficacious under the otherwise azure sky. The department is criticized for seeding clouds. On the other hand, letters appear in the *Times* attacking the department when it does not seed clouds. The generators shoot incoming weather fronts with microscopic crystals of silver iodide. This is known as "enhancing the storm." The storm is worth at least a hundred dollars an acre-foot. Los Angeles wants the water so much that it mines the storm. This requires artful judgment. The idea is to increase the volume of rain, but not to the point of mobilizing debris flows. The cloud-seeding generators were running on February 7, 1978, for example, and they ran on February 8 and February 9, but they were shut down when the proportions of the storm became apparent. The events on Pine Cone Road and at Hidden Springs and in the Verdugo Hills Cemetery, among others, occurred in the first hours of February 10. The seeding could not have added anything much to the total rainfall, but the fact remains that during the wettest week of the rainiest season of the twentieth century the cloud-seeding generators were enhancing the storm. Cheeky is the warrior who goes behind the lines to pick the enemy's pockets on the eve of battle.

*

After one season, twelve million cubic yards were removed from four of the mountain reservoirs. After one season, a million two hundred thousand yards were taken out of the debris basins. In Santa Fe Basin, the huge trap in the San Gabriel River where it meets the Los Angeles plain, the Army Corps of Engineers has fifteen million yards it wants to get rid of, but where? Disposal sites have become extremely hard to find. Every abandoned gravel pit between Tujunga and Twenty-nine Palms has already been filled with the rock of the transverse mountains, or so it seems. Chuck Colver, of Covina, who watched his orchards go down and his neighbors come up, has been around long enough to see a likely solution to the problem. "One of these days," he predicts, "they'll be buying tracts of houses to get a place to deposit the material."

Donald Nichols, of the Department of Public Works, pointed out to me one day that the word "debris" suggests sanitary landfill and odor, so debris-disposal sites are now called "sediment-placement sites" in order to get communities to accept them. "To have to stroke our folks like that kind of insults me, frankly," he said. "But disposal is a real dilemma. The Sierra Club says, 'if you put it here, you'll kill a lizard.' The Forest Service and Fish and Game also complain. Acquisition of debris-disposal areas is much slower today because of the California Environmental Quality Act. When we try to establish a new disposal area, we run into opposition from homeowners and environmentalists. The environmentalists run the gamut from the sensible ones to the crazies. They say, 'You'll kill what you put it on. You'll dislocate animals. You'll alter the land form.' That's correct. But when we're finished we'll plant vegetation. The animals will come back. The rest we have to leave to the Big Guy in the Sky, who will finally naturalize these deposits we make."

The Big Guy doesn't always do a perfect job. In Laguna Canyon years ago, some forty houses were built on old disposed debris. In 1978, the fill failed. The forty houses—worth two hundred and fifty to five hundred thousand dollars each—slid downhill like sleds.

Inevitably, someone was inspired to put the rock back up in the mountains. This elegant absurdity may be the *ne plus ultra* in telling the Big Guy who's in charge. San Gabriel Dam, a few miles upriver from Azusa, was built in the late nineteen-thirties to keep debris from clogging a reservoir just below it. More than twelve million tons of debris have been stopped behind San Gabriel Dam in one rainy season. San Gabriel catches so much mountain that it has to be more or less continuously cleaned out. Fifty or sixty trucks have lined up to lug the debris away. One place they have put it is in the tributary Burro Canyon, a haul of less than a mile, and—in elevation—six hundred feet up. "That way the engineers can have job security," Wade Wells once said to me. "They take the debris and carry it back into the mountains, where they create a potential debris flow."

"Burro will someday serve as a campground," Don Nichols said. "We have improved on nature by putting a mountain up there that doesn't come back down. Burro has debris basins in it. It has *its own* debris basins. We put fourteen million cubic yards in Burro Canyon."

Wells and I went up there one day to see this epic artifact—in clear dry air and vast silence—eight miles from Arby's. A California quail ran by, sporting its knightlike plume. In the V-shaped mountain valley, the deposit rested like an aircraft carrier in dry dock—a comparison that would be more apt if aircraft carriers were not so small. Debris basins were along its upper flank, there to *protect* the man-made deposit. Burro Creek passed under it, through a deep culvert a mile long. For twenty million dollars, Los Angeles had returned the rock to the mountains. For twenty million dollars, they had built in Burro Canyon an edifice ten times as large as the largest pyramid at Giza.

PART 🌿 THREE

Nature and Culture

Through the first decades of the twentieth century, the Los Angeles Chamber of Commerce, by far the most important advocate for merchant and business capital in the region and a potent force in local politics, often described Los Angeles as Nature's Workshop. The symbolic richness of the phrase, especially to urban and environmental historians, is tantalizing. *Nature*, we know, is a seemingly simple term that on closer inspection turns out to be an intellectual grab bag filled with meaning. A primary purpose for *Land of Sunshine* is to tease out some of that meaning in a specific region and to understand how perceptions, meaning, and values change over time. *Workshop* is equally laden with significance and meaning, conjuring up as it does arrangements and images of work, labor, and capital. The Los Angeles workshop carries special meaning for that pre–World War II era, a period that witnessed labor strife and turbulence on a tectonic scale. The so-called crime of the century, the 1910 bombing of the *Los Angeles Times* by labor saboteurs, stands out as particularly unsettling, which it was, but it occurred in a period marked by strikes, strife, and workshop tensions.

Scholars try to tease out the regional meanings of *nature* and *workshop*, placing them in deliberate juxtaposition. From the perspective of various disciplines they provide us with insight by exploring the intersection of regional, metropolitan development and attitudes toward nature. That task was given to each author in this collection, and in this final section the cultural resonance of regional responses to nature is given center stage. It is the editors' hope that this book should end with questions every bit as much as it does with answers.

This section begins with Michael Dawson's evocative folio of photographs on landscape imagery in the Los Angeles past. Images play an undoubtedly critical role in the history of perceptions in and about Los Angeles, as William McClung illustrates in his homage to the California Photogravure Company's *Art Work on Southern California*. The boosters promoting Nature's Workshop relied to a considerable extent on pictures turned loose into various streams of commercial promotion, regional advertising, and urban public relations. Dawson's essay takes us into another, less studied, realm: the photographic arena of prewar Los Angeles. Until recently, scholars studying photography and culture paid little attention to the history of photographic production in early-twentieth-century Los Angeles. Scholars such as Dawson remind us not only that this history is rich and important but that aesthetic traditions in play in Southern California had important ties to (and deviations from) regional patterns of landscape photography elsewhere. From documentary and fine art imagery of landscape we turn in the penultimate chapter to an entirely different vantage, one shaped by everyday conceptions of animals and the regional landscape.

Environmental historian and writer Jennifer Price wonders if there is nature in Los Angeles. We know the answer, but we rely on Price to remind us about the ways (at least thirteen ways) in which environments and people—nature and culture—change through time, shaping and reshaping connections and conflicts between them.

The remaking of the Los Angeles landscape, as Paula Schiffman reminds us in part one, is an ancient process, one not necessarily even tied to human intervention. Yet as Douglas Sackman points out, there is a more recent remaking of the landscape by individuals and by individual horticultural businesses, the patterns of which are familiar to contemporary residents of and visitors to Southern California today.

Jennifer Wolch and Unna Lassiter's imaginative foray into perceptions of place shaped by the changing role animals play in an urban environment offers an unusual and at the same time meaningful vantage into the varieties of environmental perception and the ways in which perception, meaning, and values are shaped by class, gender, and race/ethnicity. It is those patterns of environmental perception, environmental change, and environmental history that Robert Gottlieb reflects on in the closing chapter of this volume.

Folio Three:
Transitions in Southern California
Landscape Photography, 1900–1940

MICHAEL DAWSON

The philosophy and aesthetics of fine art photography in the United States during the first four decades of the twentieth century may suggest little or no relationship to major environmental shifts occurring in Southern California during the same period. The practice of American fine art photography grew in a number of directions between 1900 and 1940 as the discourse of photography flowed from the aesthetics of pictorialism to the plurality of modernism. Beginning with the late-nineteenth-century struggle to establish photography as a fine art, it was no longer possible to view the photograph as only a well-crafted commercial product. Rather, the photograph assumed a more tangible link to the photographer. Changing perceptions of landscape photography in the Southern California region, and particular artistic expressions of fantasy and desire, can be seen in fine art photographs depicting the landscape of Southern California. An additional link can be established between these images and the social and economic imperatives that profoundly shaped the landscape between 1900 and 1940. Some of the crucial transformations observed within Southern California landscape photography include the meteoric rise of residential and commercial development, oil drilling and refining, and the establishment of the motion picture industry.

While most of the nineteenth century was dominated by a social faith in rationalism and scientific investigation, the last two decades saw a shift from this mode of thinking toward an understanding of the power of art to enlighten and enrich daily life. Movements led by writers and artists, such as the aesthetic and symbolist movements as well as the arts and crafts tradition, had a profound influence on the visual culture of the period. For the first time, photography was discussed as a medium of artistic expression full of new promise and potential. The most prolonged and important investigations of fine art photography occurred with an elite circle of amateurs who had the time and the ability to refine their technical skill and to expand their philosophic horizons both through the practice of photography and through dialogue with other amateurs who shared an intense devotion to the medium.[1]

The rise of the pictorialist movement in the late nineteenth century highlighted the notion that photography could indeed be a forum for valid artistic expression.

The poetic or pictorial photograph did not derive its value from a literal relationship to the scene or object photographed. Rather, the photograph achieved its status as a work of art in relation to the allegorical or emotional appeal that the photographer was able to inject into the image while translating the scene before the camera onto the finished print. The interpretation of ephemeral notions of beauty through a depiction of the poetics of the natural environment became the main endeavor of sophisticated amateurs working in the landscape tradition of pictorialism. By the late 1920s the aesthetic debates began to shift under the influence of the modernist desire to explore the inherent form of the object or scene depicted removed from the sentimental interventions that had been the hallmark of pictorialism.

In his book *The History of Forgetting: Los Angeles and the Erasure of Memory*, Norman Klein discusses the concept of the social imaginary in a manner that provides a crucial link between the expression of fine art photography in Southern California and the environmental history of the region between 1900 and 1940. Several philosophers and film theorists originally used the term social imaginary in the 1960s to explain the illusion of social discourse constructed in Hollywood cinema. Klein astutely observes that the collective construction and definition of a living fiction, which never happened but is nonetheless believed as fact, is at the heart of any study of the growth and development of twentieth-century Southern California.[2] Given this context, the photographs discussed here are open to interpretation as sophisticated social imaginaries forming a unique bond between an emerging discourse of art photography in the United States and a sophisticated visual language describing the profound transformation of the Southern California landscape.

A distilled vision of the social imaginary shared by the middle and upper class of Anglo-Americans migrating to Southern California was expounded in a host of guidebooks, magazines, and tourist brochures produced in the late nineteenth and early twentieth century. While this literary industry had variety of style and nuance, the message was clear and consistent. Southern California was a healthy and temperate climate waiting for the establishment of a broad-based and preeminent Anglo-Saxon culture, a culture that supported the illusion of a class-free society and the dream of an economic livelihood free from the increasingly dangerous and bureaucratic life of urban centers in the eastern United States. Southern California was perceived as simultaneously exotic and familiar, a vacationland of comfort and ease located securely within the borders of the United States.[3]

Herve Friend produced some of the first artistic photographs in Southern California. His photographs depict the pristine quality of the mountains, deserts, and beaches of late-nineteenth-century Southern California, while his attention to the subtleties of composition and the arrangement of light and shadow enhance the meditative and symbolic qualities of his imagery. Beginning in the 1880s, commercial photographers in Southern California supplied the growing tourist trade with photographs of the local hotels, mansions, and gardens, as well as the beach and mountain scenery. This genre of commercial photography tended to document rather than interpret and failed to bring the viewer into an emotional and spiritual bond with the landscape, a bond that created a critical link in understanding the Southern California landscape as a distinct and beautiful environment.

A large body of Friend's meditative landscape photographs can be found in *Art Work on Southern California*, published in 1900. Issued in twelve separate parts, with text by Lou Chapin, it was produced in the large format of a magazine and bound in red paper whose texture simulated alligator skin. "Scene near Hollywood" is an example of the representations of Southern California scenery that employ carefully composed elements of line, tonality, and mass that accentuate the meditative power of photographic landscape work. It appears that Friend intuitively understood the rhetorical rules of pictorial landscape photography articulated and disseminated through books and magazines soon after Friend completed this body of work in the late 1880s and early 1890s.[4]

Perhaps the most successful merging of visual and rhetorical strategies for staging the preeminence of the Southern California landscape and climate took place on the pages of *Land of Sunshine: An Illustrated Monthly Descriptive of Southern California*. The editorial board of the magazine was closely allied with the Los Angeles Chamber of

Scene near Hollywood, attributed to Herve Friend. From *Art Work on Southern California*, 1900.

Front cover of the magazine *Land of Sunshine*, August 1894. Courtesy Southwest Museum.

Commerce and was keenly aware of the stakes involved in promoting Southern California to the right class of people. *Land of Sunshine* began publication in June 1894 and immediately exhibited a sophisticated sense of design. The covers of the magazine's initial volumes illustrate the publisher's sense of the role that visual representation of place played in booster vocabulary, as well as the importance of the photograph within the overall scheme of presentation. The elaborate masthead of the magazine may be dismissed as playful fantasy, but few readers could deny the lure of the compelling vignette of seaside life, skillfully rendered by an amateur photographer on holiday with the family.

In January of 1895, Charles Lummis became the editor of *Land of Sunshine*. Lummis was already a nationally known figure as well as preeminent resident of Southern California. It was felt that Lummis would add a literary and intellectual rigor to the magazine and would increase the visibility of the publication in other parts of the country, particularly in the banking and investment communities of the Northeast.[5] Lummis often included amateur photographs on the pages of the magazine because

Coast at the Foot of Topanga Canyon, Will Connell, 1926. Department of Special Collections, Charles E. Young Research Library, University of California, Los Angeles.

he believed that this regional artistic vision would provide a soft-sell testimony as a buffer to the inflated business rhetoric that filled his booster magazine.

No discussion of the transitional currents of Southern California landscape photography would be complete without a brief examination of the early work of Will Connell. Connell not only followed the shift of fine art photography from pictorialism to modernism but also moved freely between the intellectual communities of the Los Angeles art world and the practical demands of commercial photography. As a young man in the mid-1920s Connell traveled out of Los Angeles to photograph the Southern California landscape. Connell visited the salon exhibitions in Southern California and began to associate with members of the Camera Pictorialists of Los Angeles. By 1928, Connell had decided to make a living as a photographer. He found that his artistic views of the Southern California landscape aroused the interest of editors such as Phil Hanna at *Touring Topics* magazine.

Concurrent with the rise of activity in fine art photography circles in Southern California during the 1920s was the exploitation of the pictorialist vision in several magazines promoting tourism in the region. The most sophisticated example of this exploitation was found on the pages of *Touring Topics* (later *Westways*). A regular feature of the monthly magazine was a rotogravure section touting some mountain, desert, or coastal vista in California by a noted Southern California pictorialist photographer. *Touring Topics* was a publication of the Automobile Club of Southern California, and every effort was made to get readers into their cars and out on the road. Although *Touring Topics'* main trajectory was the stimulation of tourist travel by automobile within California, the editorial vision of Phil Townsend Hanna nurtured a magazine that satisfied the immediate goals of the publisher but also exposed his readership to well-written and scholarly treatments of important issues of nineteenth- and twentieth-century California history. Connell's photograph of the beach at Topanga Canyon taken in 1928 was displayed in the photographic salons of the United States and Europe as well as the rotogravure pages of the automobile club publication.

A 1921 photograph by Kaye Shimojima is typical of the lyrical landscape work produced in Southern California during this period. By the mid-1920s, photographers began to discuss the idea of abstract pictorialism.[6] At this time, fine art photographers began to simplify their compositions and flatten the depth of the image. These photographs exhibit the qualities that define one of the most rigorous and abstract styles of pictorialism. They invite viewers to meditate on the tone and texture of the photograph while contemplating their own memories of—and relation to—the regional landscape. These images bear none of the literary or allegorical associations that were so prevalent in pictorialism around the turn of the century. Interestingly, this photograph captures the end of an era begun in the mid-nineteenth century, when domestic cattle and sheep production was a staple of the Southern California

economy. By the early 1920s sheep herding in the foothill regions of Southern California was severely curtailed by the explosion of residential development and the
severe effects of erosion caused by overgrazing.

By 1925, European and American photographic art journals were discussing the
work of a core group of Japanese American photographers working on the Pacific
Coast, especially in Seattle, San Francisco, and Los Angeles. These artists, particularly a prolific group located in Southern California, are credited with the rise of
abstract pictorialism, a movement that brought landscape photography to a new
realm. Photographs such as K. Nakamura's "Along the Pacific Coast" are the first
examples of fine art photography depicting the Southern California landscape that
did not flow seamlessly between the commercial imperatives of booster photography and the artistic vision of pictorialism. Photographers such as Nakamura rejected
the carefully honed symbols of pictorial photography exploited by the tourism
industry that were explored by an earlier generation of fine art photographers.[7]

Japanese American photographers were among the first to come to terms with
the increasing urbanization of Southern California. A photograph by Shigemi Uyeda

Dusty Trail, Kaye Shimojima, 1921. Dennis Reed collection.

was one of the most well-known compositions of the late 1920s and managed to attract the attention of the avant-garde in Europe. It is also a subtle marker of the imaginary landscape of Southern California. At the time, the photograph was praised for its subtle beauty and the delicate interplay of light and shadow. A comparison of the tightly cropped version of Uyeda's "Oil Ditch" (widely exhibited and published from the late 1920s through the late 1930s) with a more distanced view of the same landscape reveals that Uyeda photographed a pond in one of the many regional oil fields discharging excess crude into a regional waterway. It appears to have been a singular Southern California achievement to extract art from oil pollution.

Pictorial California and the Pacific began publication in January 1926. The magazine consisted of numerous photographs reproduced in the high-quality rotogravure process, with a minimum of text. Pictorial California promoted the booster vision of Southern California with the same fervor as Land of Sunshine had thirty years earlier. By this time, the editors understood that photographs constructed the fantasy much more effectively than pages of purple prose. Unlike Phil Hanna at Touring Topics, the editor of Pictorial California did not use the images of Southern California fine art photographers but instead obtained images from the Keystone Photo Service to capture desired scenes in a style that was perceived as artistic. Pictorial California continued publication in the same style and format until the late 1960s, long after the pictorial aesthetic had lost any vestige of artistic currency. In 1970, a new editor took over the magazine and changed the title to California, having deemed the former title an "archaic mouthful." One of the first articles to appear in the new edition was a lengthy expose on pollution in California, which ran under the furtive headline "Keep California Pictorial." It appears that the readership of Pictorial California had nurtured and supported this fantasy over the previous decades and did not take kindly to the new editor bursting the bubble. California magazine was out of business within a year of changing its format.

As Will Connell's commercial career began to flourish in the late 1920s, (he held accounts with Sunkist Corporation and the booster All-Year Club), his intellectual and artistic vision expanded. Phil Hanna introduced Connell to Los Angeles book dealer Jake Zeitlin, whose bookshop was a magnet for a small, energetic community that published a literary and visual arts magazine and generally supported one another's work. Inspired by these artists, Connell increasingly began to adopt the sharply focused aesthetic championed by modern photographers active in Berlin and Paris. While Connell managed to keep his experimental vision in line with the demands of his customers, his work with the technique of photomontage might have been a bit harder to sell to the tourist industry.

It is difficult to imagine what Charles Lummis would have made of Connell's montage of California mission scenes, completed as an experiment for the endpapers of a book of his photographs published by Hasting House in 1941. It is striking to com-

Along the Pacific Coast, front cover of *Photo Era Magazine*, March 1932, K. Nakamura.

Oil Ditch, Shigemi Uyeda, ca. 1928. Dennis Reed Collection.

pare such an image with those of the Lummis era—how far the regional vision had come since the nostalgia of the crumbling walls, ancient natives, and solemn padres.[8]

Edward Weston has been widely recognized as one of the most important photographic artists of the twentieth century. His work had a seminal influence on the development of fine art photography in California, but it is a curious fact that Weston

Front cover of *Pictorial California and the Pacific*, December 1927. Courtesy Huntington Library, San Marino, California.

Untitled church montage, Will Connell, ca. 1940. Department of Special Collections, Charles E. Young Research Library, University of California, Los Angeles.

did not begin a serious investigation of the California landscape until the latter years of his prolific career. By the late 1930s, Weston began an extended investigation of the California landscape. Funded by a grant from the Guggenheim Foundation, Weston was able to travel throughout the state between 1937 and 1939. During this period Weston exposed nearly fifteen hundred negatives in an experimental style, which he termed mass production seeing. Not surprisingly, very few of these negatives appear to have been made in the urban areas of Southern California. A photograph of the Hollywood Reservoir is one of the few images that were not taken in the desert or non-urban coastal regions of Southern California. Weston's notion of mass production seeing involved the capturing on film of the inspiration he felt from the landscape at hand.[9] As he was particularly uninspired by the rapid residential and industrial growth of the Los Angeles area, it is not surprising that he took very few photographs in this region.

For annotated road maps to the quiet and unspoiled regions of the state, Weston turned to his old friend Phil Townsend Hanna at the automobile club to guide the way. Hanna had become acquainted with Weston in the late 1920s through mutual association in the Jake Zeitlin circle of artists and intellectuals. Hanna had published a number of Weston's photographs in *Westways* and also agreed to support Weston's landscape project of the late 1930s. Hanna supported Weston by agreeing to purchase eight to ten photographs a month as well as a brief text for the images provided by Weston's companion Charis Wilson.

After the images appeared as monthly installments in the magazine, Hanna gathered the material together in a 1939 publication, *Seeing California with Edward Weston*. For Weston, this landscape work represented the apex of his modernist vision. A lifetime of work had perfected his craft and technique so that the operation of the camera required little thought or toil. There is an ironic contradiction in the fact that Weston's modernist vision of the California landscape first appeared on the pages of the automobile club publication. Squashed in crude geometric patterns along the printed page, Weston's dream vision seamlessly flows into a tourist spectacle of sublime consumption.

In November 1940 Edward Weston spent an afternoon on the back lot of Twentieth Century Fox studio. While he found little of interest to photograph in the urban core of Southern California, he delighted in the absurd juxtapositions of half-built cabins, twisted groves of synthetic trees, and cheaply made plaster statues that contradicted the monumentality of the figures. In this composition, Weston frames a cowboy statue under the arabesque arch of a wooden gazebo poised to begin his march into the sunset along an asphalt road disappearing into the distance. Weston's acerbic comment on the culmination of westward expansion and Manifest Destiny is clearly articulated in this image. Weston arrived in Southern California in 1906 to a far

Lake Hollywood, Edward Weston, 1936. © Center for Creative Photography, Arizona Board of Regents.

different landscape than the one he photographed in 1940. The rapid industrialization of the 1920s contributed to Weston's increasing disdain for the region. In a letter composed to his friend Merle Armitage, Weston reflected that "Los Angeles would kill anyone. The real estate boys raped the southland, heavy industry killed it. The Mexicans would have done much better. They at least understood living."[10]

Page layout for *Seeing California with Edward Weston*, 1939.

Twentieth Century Fox, Edward Weston, 1940. © Center for Creative Photography, Arizona Board of Regents.

A photograph by California-born photojournalist Peter Stackpole taken on the back lot of the MGM studios again points to the enormous economic and environmental changes occurring in Southern California during the first four decades of the twentieth century. Stackpole's comments concerning the photograph are worth recounting: "I took this just at noontime when I'd been spending the morning on a set at MGM. I thought I'd just go for a walk on a back lot. I wanted to see what the props were that they were throwing away. I thought these were kind of incongruous, a throwaway Buddha and oil wells. Nothing but money in sight. If they fail at movies, they've got oil."[11]

The imaginary pictured here has its origins in the jaundiced eye of the new truth seeker of the 1930s: the photojournalist. This image is of course humorous and indiscreet; like the portrait of a movie star caught in a situation that compromises the illusion of her purity. It is the image of a landscape groaning under the weight of a fantasy that was forced on it. During the past thirty years the land and people of Southern California have suffered from the collapse of this fantasy but have only recently begun to unravel the social imaginaries that precipitated such an enormous amount of environmental degradation. Exploring the complex relationship between

Discarded Buddha, Back Lot MGM, Peter Stackpole, ca. 1938. Oakland Museum of California.

art photography in Southern California and the economic imperatives of growth and expansion that coalesced during the first four decades of the twentieth century reveals the profound environmental transformation and degradation of the Southern California landscape. These changes and that transformation give rise to the problems those living in the region face today.

11

Thirteen Ways of Seeing Nature in LA

JENNIFER PRICE

This other Eden, demi-Paradise, this precious stone
set in the silver sea, this earth, this realm, this Los Angeles.

Steve Martin (and Shakespeare), *L.A. Story*

The entire world seems to be rooting for Los Angeles to slide into
the Pacific or be swallowed by the San Andreas Fault.

Mike Davis, *Ecology of Fear*

Experience the beauty . . . of another culture
while learning more about wastewater treatment and reuse.

Brochure for the combination water reclamation plant and
. Japanese garden in the San Fernando Valley

Prologue: From Walden to LA

THERE are many places in LA you can go to think about the city, and
my own favorite has become the Los Angeles River—a deeply para-
doxical river, most famous for being forgotten, that looks and functions like an oversized concrete sewer. It flows fifty-one miles through the heart
of LA County, and is currently enjoying an explosion of efforts to revitalize it,
but commuters who have driven over it five days a week for ten years cannot
tell you where it is. Along the river, the rough midpoint lies at the confluence
with the Arroyo Seco, a couple miles north of downtown. LA was founded here
in 1781: the confluence offered the most reliable above-ground supply of fresh
water in the LA basin. It's a miserable spot now, an unmarked wasteland of
empty lots, railroad tracks, freeway-overpass pylons, fences, and trash: it looks

like a *Blade Runner* set that a crew disassembled and then put back together wrong. It's not the most scenic place to visit the river, but this may be the finest spot on the river to think about LA. Thinking about LA is a kind of national pastime. And thinking about LA in print is a rite of passage for an LA writer.[1]

So many writers who move to this city—and I arrived in 1998—seem to succumb to an overwhelming urge to share their quirky adventures here with the reading public. You can love LA, or hate LA, or both. LA must be "the most mediated town in America," in architect Michael Sorkin's widely quoted words.[2] Few people feel ambivalent, and most writers seem to feel compelled eventually to weigh in on what it all means. The standard procedure has been to evaluate one's own love-hate relationship with LA to make sweeping and incisive judgments about American dreams and American life. And whether you proclaim that LA is the American dream or nightmare, the tradition offers writers a combination of navel gazing and arm waving that is incredibly hard to resist.

However, I am a nature writer—a brand of writer that has felt no compulsion whatsoever to write about LA, much less to move here. You could toss an apple core into the bushes and hit a nature writer in Missoula, Montana (which has to host at least a dozen screenwriters), but approximately four nature writers live among the 10 million people in LA County, and one, my friend Bill Fox, fled to Portland, Oregon, for a couple years. But I have ended up here, and Bill has just returned, because LA is an unsurpassably fantastic place to think and write about nature. More urgently, LA is the ideal place in America to completely rethink what it means to write about nature. Nature writing, that venerable American literary genre, has been begging long and desperately for a thorough overhaul. Often beautifully crafted, it also suffers a popular reputation as ponderous, high-handed, redundant. It can be so, well, boring. A devotional literature that enjoys an unusually devoted readership—so I know my friends who cherish the genre will read this critique as heresy—it seems marginal and irrelevant to far too many people. Its central and most indicative failure, I'll argue, has been its stubborn aversion to cities. Of course, the genre has become so marginal that you might not see its failures as a serious problem, but I wish to persuade you that this crisis of nature writing is a national cultural catastrophe. In the weighing in on big American stories, our nature stories should not be marginalized.[3]

Me, I love LA. I was not supposed to. I grew up in suburban St. Louis and dreamt of settling in the wilds of the southern Rockies. I was supposed to love Boulder, Colorado, where I moved in the early 1990s in the hope that it might be the perfect place, and which every day gazes approvingly in the mirror and tells itself that it is. I never did warm up to Boulder (however terrific the hiking and cross-country skiing). But from my first trip out from Colorado to visit my brother David, I was attracted to LA—the last place I had expected I would live.

This is my LA manifesto, after six years on and off the freeways. I love LA in great part because it is the single most perfect place to grapple with American nature stories: I love LA because it should in fact be one of our great national meccas for nature writing. Which is why the LA River—which hosted the chase scenes in *Grease* and *Terminator 2* and the giant mutant ants that want to take over the world in *Them!*—so quickly became my favorite place in Los Angeles. Why "Experience the beauty of another culture while learning more about wastewater treatment and reuse" has become my working motto as a nature writer. Also why so many of LA's most influential interpreters, from Nathanael West to Raymond Chandler to Joan Didion to Mike Davis, have written obsessively about nature. And why perhaps the most quoted lines in all of the fabled literature about LA are Raymond Chandler's passage on LA's fierce autumn winds: "It was one of those hot dry Santa Anas. . . . On nights like that every booze party ends in a fight. Meek little wives feel the edge of the carving knife and study their husbands' necks. Anything can happen."[4]

One Way of Seeing Nature in LA: As Nonexistent

"Is there nature in LA?"

When I tell friends, family, or anyone else that I am writing about nature in LA, they invariably ask this question—and often without sarcasm. The topic, they are thinking, should occupy one person for about ten minutes. LA, after all, has long been decried as the Anti-Nature—the American city with brown air, fouled beaches, pavement to the horizon, and a concrete river. It is sort of the Death Star to American nature lovers—the place from where the destruction of nature emanates—which is why woodsy towns such as Boulder and Missoula position themselves as the anti-LA. And this is the reigning nature story we tell in LA: there is no nature here.

A Second Way: As the Wild Things

But this story hews to a historically powerful definition of nature as only the wild things and as what and where the city is not. This way of defining nature—the great American nature story and the heart and soul of nature writing—is so firmly entrenched that it can be difficult to see nature as anything else.[5] Still, even with this definition, is there nature in LA? Absolutely. The most iconic American city also tends logically to be the most misunderstood, since the iconic and real LAs do not always match. LA symbolizes the end of nature—to use nature writer Bill McKibben's unfortunately catchy phrase—but on the ground, it actually boasts more wild corners than most cities, with three trail-crossed mountain ranges, scores of rugged canyons, and miles of beaches, where you can see coyotes, curlews, and herons in abundance as well as the occasional mountain lion.[6] The noncentralized development in Southern California has spewed forth an ungodly sprawl, but also has translated into a patchwork of wild and not-wild where you can share a rustic hillside with foxes, owls, and hawks fifteen minutes from the high-rises in downtown LA, Hollywood, or Century City.

The nature-writing anthologies often include an oddball piece—usually not two, and many have none—about wild nature in the city. And there is more than enough fodder for such stories here, if you want to write about the sunset on Broad Beach in Malibu or the soaring hawks in Griffith Park or the dolphins leaping offshore or how your heart soars like a hawk or leaps like a dolphin while you watch the sun setting.[7]

But there are so many other nature stories to tell here that are equally or more compelling. I love LA's wildness. I delight in sunsets, hawks, and dolphins as much as the next nature lover: I have a special soft spot for ducks. But the anthologies are missing about 98 percent of the possible nature stories in cities. In fact, they're missing about 98 percent of our encounters with nature generally. And the major problem with nature writing, in a few words, is that Thoreau really, really needs to get on the bus.

We have been ignoring huge, entire categories of stories. And the kinds of stories the genre tells often come with standard morals that don't seem to me very useful. To get on the bus means to tell new kinds of stories and to reinterpret the familiar ones. In LA, writers will probably opt, like most Angelenos, to get in the car instead, but however we travel around, we should be drawing up maps for a more urban and everyday landscape of nature writing. I delight that LA is a magically effective place to do this as much as I delight in the sea ducks off Broad Beach. To travel through and describe all of LA, however, could take a few decades. So, I have been scouting for a handful of especially rich nature stories—from my own encounters in the city and some that I have read about—that can suggest a blueprint for such maps.[8]

And my own favorite representative topics for a literature of nature in LA have to include, above all, mango body whips, the social geography of air, Zuzu the murdered Chihuahua, and Mapleton Drive in Bel Air. And, of course, the Los Angeles River, where all the possible kinds of nature stories in LA converge.

A Third Way: As the Resources We Use

The mango body whip story begins like this: Last April, a woman who ran into my car while it was parked at the University of Southern California left a note on the back of a receipt for a mango body whip, which she had purchased at Skinmarket at the Beverly Center mall. What's a mango body whip? I didn't know. Skin product? More perverse? I made a trip to the Beverly Center and found that it is a mango-infused thick buttery skin cream.

Nature stories abound in such an encounter. Begin with the mangoes. Follow them, and you can tell an intricate set of stories as people harvest mangoes in rural Mexico and then transport them into the LA area and into the Skinmarket factory in Simi Valley—just over the LA County line—where people use customized industrial technologies to infuse them into skin butter and then transport them out to upscale malls like the Beverly Center and then cart them away to bathrooms in nearby Beverly Hills and other cities throughout the country.

Mango body whip stories, in other words, look for and follow the nature we use and watch it move in and out of the city, to track very specifically how we transform nature into the mountains of stuff with which we literally lead and sustain our lives. It could be soap. It could be cars. It could be refrigerators, sushi, dog food, TVs, digital cameras, baseball caps, closet organizers, bracelets, concert halls, 747s, bicycles. If you tell stories that follow nature through our material lives, you will see a lot of LA—the city's warehouses, factories, commercial strips, cultural centers, and residential neighborhoods, some of which have a great deal more stuff than others.[9]

A Fourth Way: As Different to Different People

Which brings me to the social geography of air. The air in LA, if polluted, is not equally polluted everywhere. The coastal and mountain areas, which tend to be the wealthiest, enjoy the cleanest air, on average. On the inland flats, the poorest, most heavily nonwhite, and most industrial neighborhoods in LA suffer the worst air, along with alarming asthma and cancer rates. Another way to put it is that the Angelenos who work in and live near the factories that manufacture mango body whips breathe far more polluted air than the consumers who are the most likely to be the mango body whip devotees. I live on Venice Beach, on Ozone Avenue—named without irony in the clean-air early 1900s, but still one of the safest places to breathe in LA County. Twenty miles inland, Southeast LA—the most industrialized urban area in the United States, with many of LA's lowest-income and most heavily Latino neighborhoods—occupies 1 percent of the county by area but generates 18 percent of the toxic air emissions.[10]

While mango body whip stories follow nature as resources through LA, geography of air tales narrate who encounters what nature where. These tales begin with who. They ask, as an important example, who benefits most and who suffers the worst consequences as who uses and transforms nature. But they also ask who eats what and who does not and who plants what in their gardens and who lives nearest and farthest away from the city parks and who hunts and fishes and who watches birds and who chooses parrots or pit bulls or rabbits or goldfish as pets. They want to know how different people encounter nature differently.

Nature writing has ignored these two categories of stories. It has been a literary universe in which you retreat to nature from the city but never use it in the city. And the genre nearly always describes nature as a unitary thing that humans encounter and experience, that is and should mean the same to all people—but never something you encounter from a specific social position and point of view.

But such a way of seeing cannot really think about and understand—much less rethink and be responsible for—our actual place in nature and our myriad connections to it. It cannot begin to examine how our ties to nature are bound up with our connections to one another. The established nature story, which yearns for simplicity and universal meaning in this postmodern age, can explain exactly no twenty-first century encounter with nature. The modern ideal of the simple life in nature is just a refusal to see. Every encounter with nature—whether on a farm, in a wilderness area, or at the Beverly Center mall—is complex as hell. I love to go hiking in the Santa Monica Mountains. Sure, there's a typical nature story in my hikes, about communing with LA's wilds as antidote to the stress and pace and noise of a typical LA week. But to fully understand such an encounter—to place it within all the skeins of my connections to nature—I would also track and narrate the complex global travels of the petroleum, metals, and other natural resources in my Gore-Tex shell, my leather and Gore-Tex hiking boots, and the rest of my industrial high-tech gear that keeps me dry and warm and makes my closet look like an REI outlet. The hike also has to be a story about who does and does not live near the mountain parks in LA and how the particular work I do at a desk all week makes a strenuous weekend hike look attractive in the first place. And it's about how the National Park Service chooses trail routes, and how it manages fire suppression, and how it implements hundreds of rules and policies to keep both the visitors and the parklands happy.

A Fifth Way: As Landscape and Ecology We Build In and Manage

This brings me to Zuzu the murdered Chihuahua. As the *Los Angeles Times* reported, Zuzu's story begins, or ends, like this: Last fall, a coyote entered the yard of a casting director in the Silver Lake area west of downtown and ate her

Chihuahua, Zuzu. Coyotes, her husband warned bitterly, are "urban terrorists"; the bereft owner said, "I have no liberty in my front yard." Still, nature writing might typically lionize the coyote as the real victim, the noble indigenous animal encroached on by evil yippy Chihuahuas (if like me you tend to agree, then try substituting a Labrador retriever puppy for Zuzu).[11]

When you bring domestic dogs into a landscape of native animals, the resident carnivores are likely to see the pets as prey. When you use and change a landscape, the place will respond. Nature is never passive. Every place has an active, very particular ecology, climate, topography, geology, flora, fauna. Zuzu stories narrate how we change places and how they respond and how we respond back and so on and so on. They're about paving, building, bulldozing, planting, fires and fire suppression, pet keeping, earthquakes, polluting, cleaning up, water supply and management, flood control, and sewers and lawns and gardens and roads and trails and parks.

Nature writers have in fact told this kind of story—usually, however, with an evil invading Chihuahua moral, in which a destroying Man (with an absurdly small canine) enters a sacred Nature Primeval and defiles it. As a way to narrate this category of tale, evil Chihuahua ranks with urban terrorist on a scale of helpfulness: the first approach instructs us to leave nature as it is and the second to eradicate it. Neither helps us navigate how to keep pet animals in a landscape with native predators—or how to make a road or ensure a water supply or build a house. Ideally, Zuzu stories should help us think about how to create livable, sustainable cities. They should be deeply informed by knowledge of the ecology, geology, and natural history of the place. They should help us walk the essential line between doing nothing and doing whatever we want. Like mango body whip tales, they should seek to understand what our connections to nature actually are so that we can think about what our connections should look like.

These are a few topics the *Los Angeles Times* reported on in recent months: water deals in the West, discarded American computers shipped to China, dog parks, an LA landfill in the Mojave desert, the hybrid Toyota Priuses, diesel pollution in industrial south LA, battles against new developments in the outer suburbs, new parks on the Los Angeles River, high silicosis rates among Chinese trinket-factory workers, oil refineries in Venezuela, farmers' markets, the best restaurants for peach dishes, sustainable practices in Santa Monica, toxic plastics residues in polar bears in the Arctic, neighborhood lawn regulations, the fight over removing the feral peacocks who scream every morning in Palos Verdes neighborhoods, pesticides buildup in frog populations, battles for public beach access in Malibu.

These are nature topics all, about how we live in and fight about nature and about how we use it more and less fairly and sustainably and about the enormous consequences for our lives in LA and for places and people and wildlife everywhere. And nature writing has left so much of it without stories. Such topics beg for a literature—for an aesthetics, for a poetry, that can help us imagine and navigate and renavigate our connections to nature.

A Sixth Way: As a Premier Source of Human Meaning

Imagine the site of Los Angeles County four thousand years ago. The people who lived here—the Tongva, the Chumash, the Tataviam—turned birds and deer into food and clothes, and turned trees, water, rocks, and dirt into shelter, energy, tools, boats, medicine, religious objects, art. (And connections to nature back then were not easy and not simple either.) They used and changed their natural world to live. They told stories about nature to explain the world and to guide their actions within it.

What do we do in Los Angeles now? Essentially the same thing. We use nature and tell stories about it to live and understand our lives. To use nature is to be human: that's a pretty fair working definition. To tell stories is to be a human figuring things out. The stories that any people tell about nature are the most basic stories they tell. Is there nature in LA? The fact that the most basic nature story we tell in LA, as in all cities, is that there is no nature here does not make this story any less telling, powerful, or basic.

What does nature mean to us? What it means stories are one last category of story I'll suggest—and nature writing has shown great interest in this kind of story, in fact it has been the very soul of the genre. Of course, nature writers attach diverse meanings to a vast range of places, animals, and plants. Yosemite: Majesty. A sacred place. The desert: Peace. Harshness. Clarity. Songbirds: Beauty. Delicacy. Earthquakes: Fury and vengeance. Water: A metaphor for life. But nature? The overall meaning that frames all others, the ur-meaning, is wildness. The not-modern. The not-us-ness. What's out there. Refuge. Salvation. These meanings historically have reigned as exceptionally powerful American cultural assumptions. Nature writing has given them literary expression with undying tenacity, but hardly invented this way of seeing and of refusing to see. The vision of wild nature as counterpoint to a modern, corrupted civilization has always been central to American national myths and identity. (Think city on a hill, the mythic frontier, western films, and—how literal can we get?—Mount Rushmore.) To see nature as the wild things only is one of the great fantastic American stories.

It is also one of the great fantastic American denials. On Mapleton Drive in Holmby Hills (a sort of wealthy annex to the wealthy suburb Bel Air), in the Santa Monica Mountain foothills above UCLA, the TV producer Aaron Spelling built what has been publicized broadly as the starship of LA mansions—a 56,550-square-foot French limestone estate with 123 rooms, with 2 rooms for wrapping gifts, and a rose garden on top of one of four garages.[12] Here are two, generally ignored, facts about Spelling's famous homestead. First, his manse is a house of nature: it is built out of and contains fantastic quantities of oil, limestone, metals, dirt, water, and wood (a likely forest's worth of wrapping paper, to begin with). And second, there are very few maple trees on Mapleton Drive. Maybe maples grew here once, and maybe not. Either way, the street enjoys the idea of maple trees, which conjure a bucolic refuge above the smog and noise and stress of the city below. Call it maple mojo. Smaller manses of nature line the rest of Mapleton Drive, and Parkwood, Greendale, Brooklawn, Beverly Glen, and other neighboring streets. No parks, no woods, no dales, no brooks, no glens. Just the mojo of wild nature.

Mapleton Drive showcases the denial so intrinsic to the great American nature story. It's a convenient way of seeing nature if you enjoy wild things and aspire to a virtuous relationship to nature but don't want to give up any of your stuff. We embrace nature as an ideal of wildness, while losing track of the real nature around us. We say that nature is a haven from modern, high-tech, industrial urban life, but refuse to see that we madly use nature to sustain the exact life from which we seek retreat. We make sacred our encounters with wild nature, but thereby desacralize all other encounters.

If I could persuade you of any one argument, it's that our foundational nature stories should sacralize our mundane, economic, utilitarian, daily encounters with nature—so that what car you drive and how you get your water and how you build a house should be acts as sacred as hiking to the top of Red Rock Canyon in the Santa Monica Mountains and gazing out over the Pacific Ocean to watch the dolphins leap, the sea ducks float, and the sun set. True, there's terrific yearning in this nature story—for simplicity, for a slower life. There's wonder and exhilaration, too, about the natural world. There's sheer bewilderment faced with the boggling complexity of modern connectedness (how could anyone possibly keep track?). There's a large dose of real regret, for the wanton destructiveness of toxic industrialism and excessive consumerism. And there is powerful, overriding denial, in the service of powerful self-indulgence and material desire, that pushes us to imagine nature out of rather than into our lives.

Interlude: First River Trip

Just how powerful? Well, in LA, we've lost track of an entire river—not just the nature in the stuff in our houses. We cannot find LA's major waterway, which runs under ten freeways through the heart of LA County. A fifty-one-mile river in plain sight: lost.

The LA River is one of LA's central natural facts. LA inhabits a river basin, and the major river drains large portions of the three mountain ranges out to the Pacific. The LA basin, while large enough for a megalopolis, is small for such significant drainage, and the river consequently poses the greatest flood danger of any river in a major U.S. city. (Mark Twain wrote that he had fallen into a California river and "come out all dusty"—but apparently had not seen one of the Southland's raging flash floods.[13]) After a last-straw series of floods in the 1930s, which made half of LA canoeable, the city brought in the U.S. Army Corps of Engineers, who proceeded heroically to dig a concrete strait-jacket for the river—a twenty-year project that lined the river and its tributaries with 2 million cubic yards of concrete and remains the corps' largest public works project west of the Mississippi. The engineers rechristened the river the flood control channel. They decreed it was no longer a river—and to the public, the concrete channel no longer looked wild enough to count as nature. And this is how LA lost its river—not lost as in no longer had one, because LA actually did, but lost as in could no longer see or find it.

If a city is built and sustained by using and managing nature, then however you use and manage your central natural facts should have massive citywide consequences. What happens when you deny that your river is a river?

The saga of the LA River in the concrete era plays out as every brand of nature tale. And every part of this story plays largely like a tragedy. First, a what-nature-means tale: Angelenos labeled the river an unriver and imagined it out of their collective understanding of place. Also, a tale of wild things: many birds and frogs continue to use the river—they seem not to have heard it's a river no longer—but other bird and most fish species disappeared.

Also, a Zuzu story. As this city altered the landscape to control the river's floods, we largely ignored the basic hydrological processes within the place we inhabit. The reengineered river could no longer flow out into its basin, so therefore no longer replenished the aquifer with water, the soils with nutrients, and the beaches with sand. At the same time, the county directed the storm sewers into the channel, thereby turning the river into LA's grand sewer, which now gathered pesticides, motor oil, trash, dog feces, and hundreds more pollutants from driveways, lawns, roads, and parking lots across the 834-square-mile watershed and rushed them downstream and out into the Pacific Ocean. And though the channel has prevented any further flooding, the extra water from the storm sewers has dramatically increased the volume of floodwaters. In sum, the decisions that LA has made to manage its river have generated water and soil depletion, coastal erosion, higher floodwaters, and severe river, beach, and ocean pollution.[14]

This city that inhabits a piece of earth with a semiarid Mediterranean climate also chose a strategy for how to move water through the city. Here is the river's mango body whip story: LA rushed as much as possible of its free water, which it got from the sky, as fast as possible off driveways and roads into the storm sewers, which rushed the rainwater into the river and out into the Pacific—and then paid dearly to import water by aqueduct up to four hundred miles from watersheds across the West. Call it watering the ocean. And draining the West. And finally, a social geography of air story. LA may enjoy wild corners galore, but as the American city that has so consistently privileged private property over public spaces, it has also most consistently constructed the least park space per capita—a problem by far the worst in poorer neighborhoods, which not only suffer the most alarming shortages of community park space but also enjoy the least private green space and lie the farthest away from the large mountain parks. As the corps dug away, LA turned the basin's most logical site for green space, and the city's major connector, into an ugly barren scar that carved a no-man's-land through many of the most industrial and park-starved areas.

Since the late 1930s, LA has chosen to manage a major natural feature in ways that encourage vast environmental degradation, social inequities, community fragmentation, erasure of civic memory, and water imperialism. These choices, in other words, have profoundly exacerbated most of LA's notorious troubles. The good news, on the other hand, is that if managing your landscape and river poorly brings disaster and doom to the city, then managing them far more sustainably and fairly should make the city a healthier, more equitable, and all around lovelier place to live in. First, though, you have to see the river. You have to find it.

Is there nature in LA? Far more than our philosophies dream of and much more than in Portland or Boulder—more, possibly, on Mapleton Drive alone than in some small towns in Iowa. In the reinvention of nature writing, the question will seem silly, since it makes about as much sense as, is there air in the atmosphere? We'll also shun as unuseful and flat-out uninteresting, where is nature? and even, what is nature? and especially that nonsense about the end of nature, a jeremiad that offers us about as much help as declaring an end to water or plants or animals—and which bespeaks the way of thinking by which LA lost its river. The literature's powering question will become, rather, what nature is it? And then—how do we use nature? how do we change nature? how does nature react? how do we react back? how do we imagine nature? who uses and changes and imagines nature? and often the most important questions of all, how sustainably? how fairly? how well?

A Seventh Way: As Nearly Infinitely Abundant

> Who was stupid enough to erect a city on the site of Los Angeles anyway? . . . The place is rapidly . . . sinking into a *Blade Runner* dystopian futurism. . . . The air is unbreathable, the water undrinkable, the transit system impenetrable.
>
> *Time Out Los Angeles Guide* (the guide I purchased upon moving here)

> What is doubly true of America is quadruply true of Los Angeles.
> Pico Iyer, *Harper's*, 1995

Is there a more nature-intensive city than LA? LA County stretches 4,084 square miles. It is the second largest metropolitan area (after New York) by size and population: the entire four-county area has more people than each of the least populous forty-two states. LA hosts the nation's busiest port, and ranks as the largest U.S. industrial center. It is a world Valhalla for wealth and consumerism.[15] How nature moves through LA, and how we use and transform nature here, bear enormous consequences for places throughout the United States and the world.

In the literary tradition of nature writing, there has been Walden Pond, and there have been Yosemite and Tinker Creek. And there should be Los Angeles. Chicago, New York, Baltimore, Denver, Phoenix, Des Moines, and Fargo all urgently need nature writers too, and I hope people will swarm to these cities to serve. But come to LA, especially, and not only because there is just so much nature here or that this is a global center and way station for the use and movement of nature. If LA has a special relationship to nature, it also enjoys singular connections to storytelling. Above all, it enjoys a special relationship to stories about nature.

An Eighth Way: As Exceptionally Iconic

> Since the start of the '90s . . . many of us [were left] with the distinct impression that we were living through the end of civilisation . . . and that maybe the Four Horsemen were using the LA basin to warm up before riding onto the actual Apocalypse.
>
> *Time Out Los Angeles Guide*

Has any city engendered more enthusiastic storytelling? LA's special, even unstoppable—even psychotic—relationship to representation has made the meanings of nature here, like the meanings of everything else, look especially dramatic and resonant. After all, who asks, is there nature in Chicago, or is there nature in New York (much less, where is the Hudson River)? Most of us have not envisioned Manhattan or Philadelphia as major centers for nature, but as the Anti-Nature, LA represents all other cities as places where nature is not.

How have nature writers, alone in the literary community, been able to resist LA—even if they hate it? It's actually quite a lot of fun to write about LA. The rapture in the paeans is as palpable as the glee in the excoriations. Since the mid-1800s, when marketers of LA as the American Eden willed the city to prominence, LA typically has stood in as some larger story about successes and failures of American dreams: New Eden, Paradise Lost, Utopia, Dystopia, City of Angels, City of Fallen Angels, Autopia, Surfurbia, American Daydream, City of the Second Chance, and the Great Wrong Place.[16]

Whether waxing eloquent about suburban sprawl, ethnic diversity, racial violence, economic opportunity, excesses of capitalism, class warfare, sexual liberation, urban crime, self-reinvention, or moral decay, the city's storytellers have interpreted what happens in LA to define what we hope for and fear, want and don't want, and believe has gone fantastically right or wrong. "A plague has descended," the *New York Times*, the sober national paper of record, reported on the first fall rains in 2002: "It is raining in Los Angeles. People are dying on the highways. Planes are falling out of the sky." A film reviewer wrote in a recent *Entertainment Weekly*, "There's a certain kind of white, piercing empty light to the Los Angeles sky that can make a person want to commit suicide."[17] Can you imagine saying that about the rains in San Diego or investing that moral and narrative weight in the sky in Oakland? And in what other city would the informational tourist guidebooks—not just fiction, essays, op-eds, and scholarship, as well as the weather coverage—describe the place as if it were a staging ground for the apocalypse?

> Rain . . . usually [causes] massive flooding and [leaves] people stranded
> atop their vehicles or entombed in sinking homes.
>
> *National Geographic Traveler: Los Angeles*

> Near the [Santa Monica] pier, a vaguely menacing throng makes the potential
> for getting mugged almost as good as that for getting a tan.
>
> *Fodor's Upclose Los Angeles*

Even if you don't get mugged, there are . . . thieves who specialize in peering over your shoulder when you enter your PIN number.

Rough Guide Los Angeles

The oft-cited refrains American dream and American nightmare can set eyes rolling in Los Angeles itself, especially among native residents versus immigrants like me. In reality, planes do not tumble from the sky and people do not climb on their cars when it rains, and you could spend years and a small fortune on sunscreen waiting to be mugged on the Santa Monica pier. There are great walking neighborhoods here. The city is not inordinately dangerous to visit: it is not a Gotham in dire need of a bat signal. It can be frustrating to live in such a relentlessly iconic city. But proclaiming the meaning of LA will not likely fade any day soon as a national pastime. You could say—to borrow a coinage from the anthropologist Claude Levi-Strauss—that Americans have used LA to think.[18]

All of which makes LA an ideal place to reinvent one of the great American stories. If the Anti-Nature, the city that represents the city as a place without nature, is really a place of nature, then any city must be.

A Ninth Way: As a Casualty of a Larger Refusal to See Connections

Imagination is all that finally defines LA.

Michael Ventura, op-ed, *Los Angeles Times*, 2000

It is? Really?

Of course, if the real LA has not always matched up to the tales about the City of Angels, these descriptions of LA have tended to exaggerate more than to make things up. As the city with more ethnic diversity, pollution, sprawl, and inequality than most others, LA has always tended to push all things American—our trends, our narratives, our ideals—to the outer edge, and has pushed few things farther or more obsessively than an ideal of personal freedom. I read an LA is about freedom refrain nearly every week: in the month in which I am writing this, the architectural historian Robert Winter told a *Los Angeles Times* interviewer, "You have a sense of freedom here that you don't have anywhere else in the United States"; an *Entertainment Weekly* review of a new TV show set in LA declared, "Los Angeles [is] the land of reinventing yourself, of discovering new possibilities, new realities, new fantasies." LA has been the fabled city where you're supposed to be able to start over, cut loose from social constraints, and escape your past. You should generally be able to pursue the American dream of being whatever you want to be. As the astute LA writer David Ulin wrote in the *Los Angeles Times* (that same month) about a commemoration of the 1994 earthquake, "[It is] expected to be the kind of event that doesn't usually happen in Los Angeles, a conscious effort to link the present to the past." In the city so often used to articulate American stories, you can most clearly watch the association of the American Dream with private desire, and with a willful blindness to connections.[19]

> You have an inalienable right to make your real life
> conform to your dream life.
>
> *CityTripping: Los Angeles*
>
> Ultimately, L.A. is the city in me, the city
> I weave together for myself.
>
> Leo Braudy, op-ed, *Los Angeles Times*, 2002

LA has the least park space per capita and many poorer areas with almost no public park space at all. It is a notoriously fragmented city geographically and notoriously short on public spaces of all kinds that nourish public life. My adopted town is the city of the gated neighborhood. It ranks first among U.S. cities for the number of millionaires and forty-first in philanthropy. Forty-first.[20] Here, you can see how wealth and power bankroll the pursuit of private desire. You clearly view a tendency—magnified here, but hardly unique to LA—to confuse ideals of individual liberty with ideals of being free to accumulate capital and use it to do whatever you want. You can watch the failure to ballast the quest for personal freedom with other American ideals of equality and community. Here, you can watch all this translate into the willful failure to see the basic connections to people and nature that sustain life within the city.

This is the land of Proposition 13 and Proposition 187, where we want lower taxes but all the same public services. It is where affluent Angelenos want the cheapest labor but no social services for illegal immigrants, and all the economic as well as cultural benefits of ethnic diversity but gated neighborhoods to keep the diversity away from where you live, and secluded canyon homes but no responsibility for the damage after the inevitable fires and mudslides in this climate, and the freedom of car travel and the remote residential areas and pristine wilds to hike and vacation in and all the material goods you desire, but no traffic or smog or pollution and of course no industrial activity or toxic dumps near your neighborhood. Here, you can watch the great American nature story play out as part of the larger desire to benefit from all your connections to people and places and nature but refuse to make good on them.

> This is a city whose best feature is . . . [that] it does not oppress
> its citizens with a civic identity. Los Angeles lets you alone, and . . .
> forces you to consider who you . . . want to be.
>
> Robert Lloyd, *L.A. Weekly*, 2001

> Contents may have shifted during flight. . . . And remember,
> life is a work of art, designed by the one who lives it.
>
> TWA flight attendant, approach to LAX on my return trip
> from a visit to St. Louis

It's hard not to embrace the love affair with freedom here, for reasons ignoble but also admirable. I live on Venice Beach, after all, and I love that LA is a place where you can rollerblade in a thong at the beach (whether male or female) while strumming a guitar. Do you know you can buy a hot dog topped with pastrami, chili, and American cheese and wrapped in a tortilla? And I love living in a place where a friend's recent story began, "I went to Terry's house, and there was Terry, and Terry's baby, and the baby's doula, and the doula's chimp in a dress." I appreciate the greater ethnic integration, the flourishing of experimental arts, the diversity of lifestyles, and the relative porousness of social and career circles.

But individual freedom, like all such sweeping ideals, is inherently malleable and can serve a wide range of agendas, and the conviction that it means doing whatever the hell you want has to have found its most dramatic expression in the refrain that LA is, in point of fact, whatever you want it to be. It is all imagination, your dream life, yours to define. Even well-respected critics and writers repeat this shibboleth with astonishing frequency. LA, you hear, is not just a place where we tell stories. It is a story. Literally—and yours, no less, your own personal home movie. And this is the ideal of freedom gone seriously over the edge. It is the American dream on a shooting rampage. If ever a way of understanding a city and carving one's place within it were designed to lose track of connections, here it is: to say LA is whatever you want it to be authorizes you to ignore all your connections to other people, community, the past, and nature. It palpates with that same potent amalgam of material desire, overall yearning, self-indulgence, and extreme denial.

In LA, you can most clearly watch the American nature story plug into a family of sins committed in the name of the American dream.

A Tenth Way: As Especially Dangerous to Lose Track Of

On the other hand, you can see the consequences, too. In LA, it is so inarguably evident that whether you acknowledge your connections or not, they of course remain operable. Go ahead and ignore your topography, your climate, your hydrology. The air will darken, the mountains will slide into houses, and the lost river will gather toxics and trash. LA is not all imagination or your dream life. It has never been the city in me or your story to create, so watch out for the blowback—for smog, racial violence, poverty, homelessness, freeway gridlock, beach erosion, mudslides, soil depletion, sewage spills, water pollution, and the ongoing crisis in water supply. Of course, the more affluent Angelenos, who benefit most from ignoring vital connections, can evade the consequences most readily. Most of these problems will wreak far more havoc in the lives of the city's poorer residents.

This city's infamous problems can fuel an argument, as large as Los Angeles itself, for ways of seeing nature and of telling nature stories that refuse to lose track.

An Eleventh Way: As a Terrific Boon to Boulder and Missoula

None of which is to let Boulder off the hook—actually, very much the opposite. We may wish away connections in LA, but we can hardly wish away culpability for the ensuing troubles (and even affluent Angelenos encounter serious daily havoc). Boulder tends to hail itself as the anti-LA: it's the green place, the socially just place, the great good place. But you can keep your air clean more easily when the factories that manufacture your SUVs and Gore-Tex jackets lie in distant cities. You can minimize racial and class confrontations when most of you are white and affluent and most of the poor and nonwhite labor force that sustains the material life of the city actually resides far away. Nature writers have documented how cities mine the hinterlands ruthlessly for resources. But they have told us almost nothing about how urban regions, and especially the poorer areas within them, disproportionately shoulder the industrial burden of converting natural resources into our lovely wondrous stuff.

Boulder couldn't begin to be the Boulder that Boulder loves without LA (and a lot of other places like LA), just as Bel Air and Malibu couldn't be the Bel Air and Malibu people know and love minus the essential connections to nature and labor throughout LA County. Think of a defining difference between Boulder and LA as the difference between Malibu and Southeast LA writ nationally. Boulderites benefit far more, and suffer far less, from how they use nature—which I suspect is one reason why Boulder never claimed my head or heart. LA may be a land of troubles, but it is also unfairly maligned, because it is too easy to call your town the Great Right Place when you live with far fewer of the problems you create.

In other words, I don't embrace LA as the mecca for a reinvention of nature writing only because, alas, you can see the horror and fallout of the established stories so clearly here. You also can see a far larger picture of our connections to nature, and you have to live with their consequences—which is oddly heartening and makes LA feel like an honest place to think and write about nature, as well as a terrifyingly obvious place to forge fairer and more sustainable connections to nature.

A Twelfth Way: As a Focus of Great Good Work

And so many people are doing exactly that. The exorbitant costs of losing track of nature have so consistently confronted this megalopolis with the exigent need to pay attention. And when you change things in LA—where what happens has national and global ramifications, as well as metaphoric resonance—you inevitably enact change in other places too.

Angelenos ranging from elected public officials to civil engineers to urban planners to social and environmental activists have been establishing this city of troubles as a leading think tank for strategies generally to make cities more livable and more equitable, but also for recognizing the central importance of nature to such goals. And as a St. Louis friend who runs an environmental law clinic remarked to me, California is "light years ahead of the curve on environmental regulation"—in no small part due to wrestling with LA's problems. The city with the nation's worst air pollution enforces the strictest air quality regulations and maintains pioneering emissions standards for vehicles, outdoor appliances, and household products. A recent Natural Resources Defense Council (NRDC) report calls the LA area—with one out of every three beach closures in the United States—the "national epicenter" of coastal pollution. In 2000, NRDC and two local environmental groups won a landmark lawsuit against the EPA that, for the first time, requires a metropolitan area to not only prepare but adhere to the cleanup schedules mandated by the Clean Water Act—and that ideally will force other cities, too, to address their significant runoff problems.[21]

Because LA is the American city with the least park space per capita, the public agencies and nonprofits working for more parks have been pioneering methods to reclaim and green up phased-out industrial lands. In the city that suffers both extreme environmental ruin and extreme social and economic inequities, environmental justice activists have won key battles in the poorer areas of East and South LA to shut down polluters—battles that have built and strengthened the movement nationally—and have fought successfully to make the Southland's regulatory agencies the first to rewrite policies to recognize that problems such as air pollution and park-space shortages bedevil poorer and nonwhite neighborhoods disproportionately. And there can be no more cutting-edge place to work for urban transformation than on the banks of the country's most degraded urban river.[22]

LA may not be the greenest, cleanest place to be a nature writer, but it is exciting. As *L.A. Weekly* writer Judith Lewis has put it: "Los Angeles has . . . [given] me a world to battle as much as I revel in it. It has given me a life in interesting times."[23]

Interlude: Second River Trip

You almost need special glasses to see the LA River as the green and healthy river that the hundreds of people who are revitalizing it are aiming for. The project should take at least several decades—you also need great reserves of faith and patience—but it will happen if (in the early-twenty-first-century economy, admittedly a big if) the money and the political will continue to flow at the current rate.

In the mid-1980s, the first calls to revitalize the river, by the fledgling Friends of the Los Angeles River (FoLAR), seemed to push beyond what quixotic could describe. At that time, proposals to paint the concrete blue and to use the channel as a dry-season freeway for trucks met with far more serious consideration. In fact, FoLAR's proposal, after a decade of persuasion, would prove to be superb common sense before its time. By 2000, the river's restoration emerged as a major policy priority, as every imaginably relevant public and private interest—from environmentalists and social activists to neighborhood associations to urban planners and architects to the LA City Council, LA County Board of Supervisors, and LA County Department of Public Works (our quondam sun gods of flood control)—have concluded that restoring one of LA's major natural facts to health can help ameliorate the city's worst troubles.

How do you resurrect the LA River? You have to green the riverbanks. You have to clean the water. And you have to dynamite out some of the concrete. Each of these goals, it turns out, quickly becomes an act of thinking big.

To green the banks, this loose coalition of actors has set out to turn the cement scar through the heart of this park-poor, public space–starved, fragmented metropolis into a fifty-one-mile greenway and bikeway, which can become the backbone for a countywide greenway network. The LA River Greenway itself will green and connect many of the poorer neighborhoods that most desperately need new parks. FoLAR, Latino activist groups, and others also propose to turn the downtown stretch of the river in this history-averse city into a historic route with stops that commemorate key sites and events in the city's past.[24]

To clean the river—which by law the EPA must now ensure happens by 2013—you have to remove pollutants from the river itself. Even better, you want to identify where they're coming from: weed-killers, insecticides, fertilizers, paints, detergents, car waxes, gasoline, motor oil, asbestos brake linings, and the thousands more sources for your basic toxic urban street stew that washes into our soil, water, and of course our bodies. It is an overwhelming task—and some cities along the river have chosen to fight the legal decision in court instead. But to clean the river, LA will have to encourage cleaner industrial processes to manufacture products that are less toxic, more recyclable, more biodegradable.

You have to blow up some, though not every single ton, of the concrete: the Seine, after all, runs through Paris in a concrete channel. Do it today, however, and the next heavy winter rains will bring devastating floods. So the fans of concrete removal have been thinking hard about how to keep more storm water out of the river—which would require two major steps. First, you capture as much rain as possible where it falls: you can use the water right away (say, to irrigate a lawn or park), or let it sink into the aquifer (which will naturally clean the water as minerals in the soil bind toxic chemicals). Second, you divert water out of the river during floods. To capture rainfall, the county is looking to site parks, restored wetlands, and more green space wherever possible, and LA County Public Works, along with FoLAR, the River Project, TreePeople, North East Trees, and other nonprofits, has launched pilot projects for porous paving and underground cisterns and for newly designed gutters, freeway medians, and parking lots that pitch water into the ground instead of the sewers. To divert floodwaters, the county has sited the first in a projected series of diversion basins, which will double as wetlands and parks. In sum, the initial vow to remove concrete has become a springboard to rethinking more broadly how to move water through LA. It has pushed LA to consider far more carefully that the city occupies a river basin, which itself is part of a larger watershed.

Altogether, greening, cleaning, and deconcreting the river would maximize local water supplies and quality. It should prevent flooding and restore wildlife habitat. Neighborhoods throughout the LA basin will acquire much-needed park and green space, and the greenery will help clean the air. The movement to revive the river has pushed LA to the national forefront of urban watershed management. And one of LA's defining natural features has quickly become a key meeting ground within LA for the diverse efforts to enhance the equity and environmental quality of life for Angelenos.

The saga of the river now, like the tale of turning the river into a concrete sewer, is at once every category of nature story. And the river's mango body whip, Zuzu, geography of air, and wild-things tales are all now changing for the better. This story of revitalizing the river is about using essential natural resources well. It emphasizes the rewards of wild spaces in an urban setting. It's about recognizing that using nature unsustainably inevitably brings by far the most grief to poorer neighborhoods. It's about understanding the particular environment of the place you inhabit—the basic hydrology, climate, topography, ecology—and using that knowledge to guide how you change and manage that place.

A Thirteenth Way: As the Foundation of LA Stories

This is a happy land for children and all young animals. They are uniformly large, active, and healthy. They live in the pure air and sunshine.

Newton H. Chittenden, *Health Seekers' [and] Tourists' . . .*
Guide to the . . . Pacific Coast, 1884

I began by searching for the story in the streets . . . where . . .
the palm trees were high with scrawny fronds like broken pinwheels . . .
and droopy ice plant could never quite hold the earth . . . in place . . .
and an oil derrick [looked] like a rusty praying mantis, trying to suck
the last few barrels out of the dying crab grass.

Robert Towne, preface and postscript to *Chinatown* (released in 1974)

And waiting in the wings are the plague squirrels and killer bees.

Mike Davis, *Ecology of Fear*, 1998

And it should be about reimagining the place of nature in the city. But Angelenos still cannot seem to find the river and generally still doubt that the river is a real river at all. The what it means story remains uniquely stubborn. The river has not been destroyed: it is nature degraded but nature nevertheless. But amidst the epic efforts to revitalize the river, Angelenos have not yet redefined the river as natural. Despite all the great good work generally, people in and out of LA still question whether LA has any nature at all. While scientists, social scientists, historians, urban planners, landscape designers, and environmentalists have written shelves and shelves of books that describe the centrality of nature to cities, most nature writers continue to shun cities as gomorrahs of iniquitous conspiracies against nature (to overstate the case, but only a bit). And as writers in every other literary genre have tried every wild experiment imaginable, this single genre has not changed philosophically in 150 years.

In the end, this opposition of nature and cities may prove more resistant to change than the concrete in the LA River. And nowhere has this insistence flourished more powerfully than in Los Angeles—more iconically and more consequentially, but also so consistently in descriptions of the city. And here is the last, and perhaps the ultimate, reason that nature writers should flock to the City of Angels as a logical headquarters: LA, like no other metropolis, has woven the established nature story comprehensively into its stories of itself. Here, Americans have used a nature tale to think about the city they have used to think.

"To watch the front-page news out of Los Angeles during a Santa Ana is to get very close to what it is about the place," Joan Didion wrote in 1968, in a famous passage that echoes Raymond Chandler's often often quoted lines about LA's winds.[25] From the nineteenth-century marketeers to prominent LA promoter and *Land of Sunshine* editor Charles Lummis in the early twentieth century to William Faulkner and Nathanael West and the noir writers in the 1930s and 1940s to Joan Didion to Mike Davis to the current coverage in the *New York Times* and *Los Angeles Times*, describers of LA have been obsessed with sun, sea, light, sky, wind, rains, and greenery, as well as rats, cougars, killer bees, fires, cascading mud, and earthquakes. And even in the work of Davis—from whom I have learned so much about how to think about Los Angeles—the nature is fundamentally anti-urban.

Consider how nature—and this vision of it in particular—has starred in the dominant stories about LA's larger meanings. To simplify egregiously, you can parse the American dream stories into roughly three phases—dream, nightmare, and apocalypse—which, while they have coexisted almost from the start, have shifted in dominance. In the beginning, LA was the American Eden. The early descriptions emphasize the sunshine, the sea, the clean air, the diaphanous light. Nature, the dream stories promise, will make LA the uncity city, where you can escape the crowded, industrialized cities to the east, which are marked by pollution, ethnic and racial conflicts, and financial disappointments. But then, the nightmare gains on the dream. By the 1960s, LA has defaulted (inevitably) on every promise and has become paradise lost. Nightmare stories showcase the decimation of the city's natural gifts—the black sky, the fouled sea, the stolen water, the endless pavement, the dying palm trees, the concrete river—as the premier symbols of everything gone wrong. LA has become the Anti-Nature—a place with no nature at all.

And then, apocalypse: "Is the City of Angels Going to Hell?" as a 1993 cover of *Time* reads.[26] In the early 1990s, as LA reels from the Northridge earthquake, race riots, Malibu fires, mudslides, El Niño, and the O. J. Simpson trial, the reigning description of LA shifts from a place where nature no longer exists to one besieged by a nature that is quite literally anti-urban—as the city that destroyed nature becomes the city where nature comes back for revenge. The history of LA storytelling, if more complicated, basically boils down to a trilogy. Nature blesses LA. Nature flees LA. Nature returns armed.

No wonder I love LA. This city has hosted a spirited conversation about nature for 150 years. You can almost smell the obsession when you land at the LA airport. Nature stories have been far more than important stories here. They're the stories that frame the other stories. How ironic, really, that nature writers have ostracized LA so religiously. You could say that LA already has long flourished as a mecca for writing about nature—as central an American place as Yosemite, the Alaskan outback, or Walden Pond—and especially for telling the story that nature writing itself has so dedicatedly perpetuated.

This makes perfect sense, if you think about it. As in any human society, the stories we tell about nature are the most basic stories we can tell. LA has long been a place where we articulate grand American narratives. So it should not surprise us either that the foundational LA story is a nature story, or that the city with a zeitgeist of denial has used an evasive story to imagine itself. In the dream tales, nature makes LA a city where you can escape the basic social and environmental challenges of any city. The nightmare visions write LA off as a ruined city: if you utterly destroy nature, how can you possibly ever fix it? And how much farther beyond redemption could a city be that awaits imminent millennial annihilation? The apocalypse stories, too, lament the city's troubles while conveniently denying that anything can be done. Here is a city where we've dreamt brilliantly of virtue while doing spectacularly unvirtuous things. The city practically vibrates with brilliant denial in the service of spectacular yearning, self-interest, and material indulgence. And the city's foundational story is a way of seeing and defining nature that encourages and allows for all these same evasions.

To see LA—and to understand any city and how we navigate our lives within it—we need a foundational literature of nature not as the antithesis of the city but as the stuff of everyday life. Less apocalypse and avenging earthquakes and more mango body whips. Less mojo and more actual nature. We could use less "It is raining in Los Angeles. Planes are falling out of the sky," and a lot more tales that track our daily, intertwined connections to nature and to each other—such as "Experience the beauty of another culture while learning more about wastewater treatment and reuse."

I love that LA has been such an extraordinarily powerful place to tell American nature stories. But as long as LA has been a mecca for American stories, people have been calling for new ways to see the city. And nature stories have to be the logical place to start.

Postscript: The Confluence

After I found the LA River, which took me a year, I went searching for the confluence with the Arroyo Seco—the river's geographic, historic, and ecological center. Unsurprisingly, this spot can prove almost impossibly difficult to find. In the *Thomas Guide* map book, the bible for finding one's way around Los Angeles, the blue line of the Arroyo inexplicably peters out about a mile before the tributary in fact meets the river.

The day I found the river remains one of my finest days here. I started far upstream, on the sole half mile free of concrete, near the combination water reclamation plant and Japanese garden in the San Fernando Valley. I continued down to a stretch, across from Griffith Park, that boasts an inspired string of new pocket parks with native vegetation and outdoor public art. Both stretches teemed with ducks and other birds. I ended up far downstream in Southeast LA, where the channel widens out to the girth of a freeway. Black-necked stilts by the hundreds yapped and fed on algae around upturned shopping carts. A mallard shot down the swift current. The sun set spectacularly on the southwest horizon through the power lines, billboards, and smokestacks of the LA harbor. A man on a horse rode by, wearing a cowboy hat, a Mexican blanket, and a cell phone. This is LA, I thought. I was steeped so contentedly in the complex life. All day I had been marveling, there is a river in LA, a real river, what do you know, and it seemed, after a year of loving LA but not knowing why and of wanting to write about LA but not knowing how, that I was now looking at the place (duck filled, no less) that held the key to both.

With my friend Alan Loomis, an urban designer and river aficionado, I lead informal tours of the river—for friends and friends of their friends, who like to think about LA and who have heard LA has a river and want to see it. We stop at the new park sites, but also insist on a visit to the wasteland of the confluence, which I located finally on my own third try. We wander through the trash and skirt the homeless tents and lean on the massive pylons of the freeway overpasses. Here, we say, is the most hopeless as well as the most hopeful spot on the LA River. The confluence is perhaps the most extreme testament to LA's erasure of nature, community, and the past. This spot is at once the logical nexus for the proposed fifty-one-mile LA River Greenway. And the city is about to break ground on the first half acre of what should, eventually, be a great central-city park. Here, we say, is one of the best places to think about the river, which is one of the best places to think about LA—and LA historically has been one of the best places to tell stories about America. You are standing, we allow, at an American narrative vortex. This spot ideally should be swarming with Angelenos, with writers, with nature writers. And to our delight, the people on the tours say, "What a cool place." They take a great many photographs—more, usually, than at any other spot—and then we continue downstream to imagine the future of LA and the LA River Greenway, where you can drive into the river downtown.

12

A Garden of Worldly Delights

DOUGLAS C. SACKMAN

A GIRL is running through row after row of blossoming orange trees. The air is densely fragrant. But this is no dreamy scene of sun-dabbled Arcadia, no female world of plants and pleasure. The girl is furtive and desperate; she is a fugitive. Her pursuers wish to capture her and then redeem her. She is, in their eyes, wild and uncultivated. She is the desert, and they are the rain. They have the power and know-how to make her bloom and train her growth. They want to take her back to the Sherman Institute in Riverside, a boarding school established at the turn of the last century for the liberal purpose of improving Indian children. Improvement, in this case, meant making manifest to the land's conquered peoples how whites could marvelously improve the desert. As Los Angeles nurseryman and Indian agent Horatio Rust put it, "They cannot help but gain some ideas, when they go to Riverside or other thrifty towns by seeing what industry can accomplish." After studying the garden schools of Europe in which "pupils obtain an intimate knowledge of nature," Rust urged that every Indian in such schools be taught to "make, and care for, a garden . . . so that when he leaves school he shall be competent to perform all the varied labors on a farm or a garden."[1]

The girl darts across the road, and makes her way into a garden within this larger garden landscape. Here, orange trees give way to eucalyptus, lilacs, and then a more open space within. There is a trimmed yard with carefully placed ornamental plants—plants she has never seen before, from Asia and South America, from Europe and Africa. There is a red garden, full of red dahlias, peonies, dianthus, cosmos, and scarlet hollyhocks. And there is a white garden, with roses and bougainvillea. There is a Victorian house at the center of this garden and a greenhouse off to the side. All the world is here in this strange place: the garden embodies exoticism. Crawling beneath the immigrant shrubbery, the girl at last loses the battle to evade all eyes. Linnaeus's gaze fixes upon her.

Linnaeus is a monkey, brought back from the Amazon during an orchid-collecting trip made by the plant hunter Edward. The monkey saved his life, and he honors it with the name of Linnaeus, a synonym for the drive to name and thereby control all of creation. The girl, the monkey, and Edward are fictional characters from Leslie Marmon Silko's novel *Gardens in the Dunes* (1999).[2] The space they all meet in is fictional as well, though thoroughly grounded in history.

Edward is a fictional counterpart to those representatives of the Enlightenment who engaged in the conquest of the global unknown, seeking out new organisms and expanding the horizons of knowledge. His biggest dream is to have some plant named after him, to father the coming into scientific being of some organic form that had hitherto evaded the taxonomic gaze. Done in the name of value-free science, this penetration of the dark worlds of the Amazon—or, for that matter, the deserts of the American Southwest—nonetheless amounted to a global appropriation of the variety of nature as means of production. Consider the orange trees the young girl runs through. Oranges originated in Asia, but were brought to the Americas with Columbus on his second voyage. Sometime around 1810 in São Salvador de Bahia in Brazil, a mutation in an orange grove created a new and more succulent variety. In 1870, the U.S. Department of Agriculture obtained twelve seedlings of the variety from a missionary, and after these were grafted onto new rootstocks they were rechristened the Washington Navel. Three seedlings were sent to Eliza Tibbets in Riverside, and from these, millions of trees were budded. As A. D. Shamel of the U.S. Department of Agriculture explained in 1923, "Two small and apparently insignificant plant immigrants arrived in Southern California 50 years ago. . . . The introduction of these two parent trees of the Washington navel marked the beginning of the commercial growth of the citrus industry in California."[3]

Edward buys all the talk of the advancement of science and the liberation of mankind, not realizing he is but an agent of empire appropriating the world's wealth of plants and peoples. In the novel, Silko can punish him for this, and she does: his mind and body come apart in a fulfillment of a kind of Cartesian curse. Madness descends, and the cogito becomes a pathetic scramble for this man of science: he can no longer think and therefore can no longer be. Silko, having carefully researched the gardens and culture of Riverside, California, as well as the gardens and culture of the Hia C'ed O'Odham (or Sand

Papagos), has written a deeply historicized parable, an anti-colonial account of the struggle between cultures that live with nature and those that work to exploit both nature and people. She writes of people who have nourished a symbiotic relationship with the natural world (the O'Odham as well as English pagans) and of a system of capitalism whose agents penetrate every corner of the globe seeking plants that, as if by bio-alchemical magic, may be turned to gold.[4]

Gardens in the Dunes brings to the surface connections turn-of-the-century Southern Californians had to their landscape and exposes the ecological imperialism at work in the transformation of that landscape. In the late nineteenth century, Southern California also appropriated the world's store of garden literature to boost the region with the luster of Elysium. The booster literature—Southern Pacific and Chamber of Commerce pamphlets and publications, postcards, articles in magazines such as *Sunset* and *Land of Sunshine*, a sea of guidebooks—perfected the genre of Edenic travelogue. Southern California, with its mountains and sun, ocean and soils, was the most perfect garden—if not the original Eden, a simulacrum that excelled the model. For here, one could have one's fruit and eat it too.[5]

From the 1870s to the second decade of the twentieth century, the environs of Los Angeles and its people became consumed with gardening. Gardening became a source of livelihood and pride. Southern Californians grew fruit trees, and they grew ornamental trees. Their identity, and economy, became fixed to plants. This was the land of the golden orange, a place where rose parades could be held in January. Each bustling enclave—Pasadena and Ontario, Pomona and Anaheim—vied for the title of garden spot of earth.[6] The region's inhabitants, many of them newcomers who had been drawn to the place by pictures of its lush landscape, took up gardening in earnest. They planted for beauty as well as for the market and remade the landscape in Eden's image. But aesthetic delight in this cultural landscape was ultimately subordinated to a drive to turn place into profit. This is the magic that growth machines perform, turning landscape into an economic engine.[7]

Charles Saunders, who much admired the gardens of Southern California and worked hard to create his own, wrote that "Los Angeles has been a marvel of urban growth." Indeed, around the turn of the century growth and Los Angeles seemed near synonyms. Its rate of growth was rapidly catching up to that of Jack's beanstalk, one writer mused. Some observers have reveled in this growth—Los Angeles as prodigious cultural and economic metropolis incanted from mere desert. Others have reviled it, so that the old metaphor once applied to the Southern Pacific has been fixed to the city—Los Angeles as an octopus, a carcinogenic organism sprawling across the countryside. Mike Davis, for example, describes how the dominant culture of Los Angeles has malevolently remade nature in the region, creating an "ecology of fear." This turn on nature seems all the more monstrous—even matricidal—since the genesis of Los Angeles was so entwined with an appreciation of Mother Nature's unique beneficence in the region.[8]

Though all places are ultimately natural, the identity of Los Angeles has been exceptionally entangled with nature. The ecology of the region created abundant possibilities: an inviting climate, a diversity of microclimatic zones, and a rich range of soils in which all manner of plants could be grown. But the ecology did not determine the creation of the garden. For the Anglo garden to grow, that ecology had to be rearranged—water controlled and channeled, native flora and fauna displaced in favor of introductions, older claims on the land displaced and new property lines demarcated, and so on. The manifestation of the garden in Los Angeles was also an ideological process, creating a vision of the proper arrangement of nature serving a purpose easily missed amidst all of the shrubbery.

Look at all the flowering plants. Look at all the trees. They are an aesthetic delight, and their arrangements are fascinating. By the early twentieth century, Los Angeles had become "a wonderland of flowers and foliage." But the garden was no refuge from the economic sphere. Gardens functioned as economic institutions: they were either factory-like landscapes producing wealth or places of conspicuous cultivation that delineated, and legitimated, social status. The landscape was deeply infused with market forces and bound up in a web of economic, political, and ecological exchanges that spanned the globe. Plants from the four quarters of the earth were transplanted to Los Angeles, and people from the four quarters also came to harvest the plants. In Southern California, the growth of plants and the growth of the economy were linked in one vast "material dream." In short, Los Angeles became a garden of the most worldly delights.[9]

The Garden Manifest

The making of a garden is a cultural and historical project. Gardens are anthropogenic landscapes, the result of humans shaping nature into patterns that they find hospitable, inviting, and desirable. The human work of design, selection, exclusion, and cultivation goes into their creation, so that gardens are hybrid zones of human enterprise and natural expression. Gardening is "a way of bringing wildness to heel by sending it to school."[10] Any gardener knows that gardens are hardly inevitable, but the making of Los Angeles's garden around the turn of the century was often portrayed as an outcome ordained by evolution—and an outcome with lessons for the nation.

It is tempting to wonder whether Frederick Jackson Turner, that great theorist of the environmental basis of American identity and social evolution, while enjoying his thrice-daily glass of orange juice at his home at 23 Oak Knoll Gardens in Pasadena in the late 1920s felt any need to revise his frontier thesis to apply to the lush environs of Southern California. Would he have felt remiss for having failed to theorize the "fruit frontier"? Turner's 1893 essay "The Significance of the Frontier in American History" provided a powerful explanation of how American character and institutions were forged on a frontier, which he defined as the "meeting point between civilization and savagery." This meeting point was "the line of most rapid and effective Americanization." As Turner has it, the contact with the pure nature of aboriginal America stripped Europeans of all cultural baggage—including their clothes. The challenges of the environment would condition a kind of cultural molting, and Americans would emerge and discard the skins of their former selves. The environment becomes a kind of body snatcher. But the plot runs in reverse of the 1950s sci-fi classic: those who are snatched become not soulless drones but willful, independent, industrious Americans.[11]

As in the film, there is a colonial theme in Turner: the new Americans immediately go about implanting their culture and desires in the landscape that gave them new life. Miners make a mining landscape; farmers, an agrarian one; and so on, up to the city builders. Of course, Turner has been roundly criticized on a number of fronts, but there is something to his way of looking at history as a succession of landscapes, each bearing the inscription of a dominant economic actor and activity and each being written over by the next one as if the land itself were a palimpsest.[12]

What would this landscape succession of California look like? Using a broad brush, we can identify several stages. The first, predating sustained European colonialism, would be the native Californian's horticultural landscape. Often imagined as a wilderness where nature alone ruled, native Californians actually played a large role in its creation. Through a variety of land management practices, California's Indians created a garden in which a variety of useful plants were grown.[13] With the Spanish *entrada* (arrival) in the 1760s, that garden was marginalized to make way for the complex of plants and animals that the Spanish imported and sponsored—among them, olive trees, citrus, wheat, cattle, and sheep. Especially in the Mexican era, the economy, still very local in orientation, became ever more pastoral as immense flocks of sheep and herds of cattle overran the native garden.

In 1848, California became an American frontier. First, of course, was the rush for gold, which created a mining landscape. This was closely attended by the expansion of cattle ranching and the rise of bonanza wheat farming. Finally, toward the end of the 1870s, another landscape, that of horticulture, became dominant. California was remade into a garden, with oranges as the emblematic fruit. It is useful to consider this landscape succession not as natural evolution—as it was often portrayed by Americans in the nineteenth century —but as a series of conquests that remade landscapes. These landscapes each were a cocreation of a dominant social group and the environment. Each landscape was natural space made into a territory with a conventional set of rules governing human-natural relations. In these terms, we can say that landscape succession involved both deterritorialization and reterritorialization. Territories are uprooted, and then new ones, with the sanction of power and authority, are created in their place.[14]

This succession from native gardeners, to padres and vaqueros, to wheat barons, and finally to fruit growers can be portrayed as an inevitable expression of progress, and often was. Americans created such a fable of progress. In the first act, the landscape was rich and beautiful but languishing under the stewardship of lazy Californios. This was the landscape as it appeared in the narrative of Manifest Destiny, a metanarrative that "implied the domination of civilization over nature, Christianity over heathenism, progress over backwardness, and, most importantly, of white Americans over the Mexican and Indian populations that stood in their path."[15] Even after 1848, Manifest Destiny would find expression in stories contrasting a progressive nature under Americans with a stagnant nature under Mexicans. Mexicans, the stories went, locked up land in idleness while Americans put it to the best and highest use. But in Anglo-Saxon hands, the land would become better, for American agency alone could do God's will on earth and create a flourishing agrarian republic. The deterritorialization of Californios was bound closely to Americans' efforts to manifest the garden.

In the 1870s and 1880s, a number of promoters of horticulture argued that the American promise of improvement had not been fulfilled. Americans had not lived up to their potential, for miners had merely robbed the land of its wealth, and the great grain ranchers were simply "mining for wheat" in a way that would leave "the great, beautiful valleys of our State as treeless, verdureless plains."[16] Only fruit growers could create a true abundance in the state that would build community and civilization.

In a speech at the Horticultural Fair in Southern California in 1878, Dr. Ezra Carr of the University of California portrayed gardening as at once a motor and emblem of social evolution. Patriotism, he argued, could not exist before the growing of plants:

Love of country could not exist till cave and wigwam were supplanted by the hut, the permanent abode around which the vine might clamber, and the gentler races of animals gather for protection. The sour bog had to be reclaimed by the labor of the husbandman, who reclaimed the wildness of his own nature in the process, until he grew sweeter with the grasses, less savage and more generous with the fruiting fullness of his trees. The gradual transformation of the savage into the citizen may be traced in the changes in the animal and vegetable world which have accompanied it, and we may look for the greatest improvement where the close and constant relations of man and Nature are the most agreeable and permanent.[17]

E. J. Wickson, editor of the *Pacific Rural Press*, amplified this theme in his widely read book *The California Fruits and How to Grow Them* (first published in 1889). He argued that the horticultural landscape was the space of most rapid and complete Americanization. Fruit growing in particular was a "token of our advancement in one of the highest of the agricultural arts . . . [and] a demonstration of the quality of our agricultural citizenship." With an experimental outlook "free from tradition and prejudice," citrus growers in particular had created "an industry characteristically American." The California Fruit Growers Convention would sum up a generation of rhetoric when it published a pamphlet expressing in its title the fruit grower's version of Manifest Destiny: *Hand in Hand Go Horticulture and Civilization.* Horticulture, then, signified more than a branch of agriculture devoted to the production of fruits, vegetables, trees, shrubs, and flowers. "Understood as the matrix of industries surrounding fruit, flowers, and vegetables," Ian Tyrell points out, "horticulture also entailed a moral dimension."[18]

The moral of the garden stories sometimes seemed to be simply, come to California, which is Eden on earth, and you will live happily and healthily ever after. This was in fact a common theme of much booster literature, but the dominant narrative made it clear that Anglo-Saxon immigrants had work to do in California: that of reinventing Eden. In the Old Testament, Eden had been God's work and a place in which no toil was necessary. Only after the expulsion were people condemned to work. Southern Californians upended the myth and found a way to meld the Protestant work ethic with the garden idea. God had only provided a potential, in the form of Southern California's geography, soil, and climate. But the Indians had been content to live simply off the land, and the Californios had been too idle to act on the divine possibilities. It would take both work and a scientific and progressive vision to act on this potential to create a suburban wonderland. An article in *Out West* magazine expressed this belief that "the horticulturist combines city life with country pleasure and his occupation is one requiring rather more of brains than of hard labor." Providence had provided the setting, but only Anglos could complete the script for the making of a garden on earth. Rather than going back to Eden, California's forward-looking boosters felt they could fabricate it.[19]

The Edenic trope had become a cliché by the late 1880s. Pasadena was an "an earthly paradise in every sense which the term implies," and Riverside was a place where "the omnipresent orange hangs yellow with its ripened harvest . . . where Nature rejoices, birds sing and the very heart of man expands with the pleasure of living." Having made "a waste place bloom as a garden," elderly Riversiders could enjoy in their earthly surroundings a "foretaste of approaching paradise." Neologisms seemed necessary to describe the superhuman accomplishments. Governor Perkins, speaking at the fourth annual Horticultural Fair in Los Angeles in 1881, came up with a new transitive verb, *to emparadise*. Here it is in usage: "Look at the wonderful array of nature's gifts spread before us, amplified and enriched by the effort of your Association. A few short years ago and these valleys, now emparadised in fruits, cereals and flowers, raised their upturned faces in sullen, uninviting barrenness. Surely the approving smile of heaven is upon us! On every side, in valley, on hill, the happy results of your labor shows forth to gratify both heart and eye. The whole world lies before us here. That fig speaks to us of Syria; that luscious peach recalls to us the fertile land of Persia."[20]

This is a landscape that enjoys the smile of divine sanction, but it is one that has been created through artifice. It is a product of people capable of global vision and imperial reach, taking the blank slate of barren valleys (that is, deterritorialized landscapes) and enlivening it with fruity chatter from the world over (one is reminded of the grapes of Irenaeus, a second-century church father, who wrote of talking grapes[21]).

But it was not enough to have these fruits speaking of the world to Southern Californians in Southern California. They wanted to put this horticultural Babel on the road. Beginning in the 1880s, fruits were loaded onto railroad cars by the thousands to bring Southern California's garden discourse to the nation and the world. The Southern Pacific Company, recognizing the potential to increase the value of its massive land holdings as well to reap the profit of a voluminous future traffic in fruit, did much to organize the effective exhibition of California as a horticultural wonderland. It loaded preserved specimens prepared by the Los Angeles Chamber of Commerce on a traveling train called California on wheels. Inside was a collection of glass jars in which were suspended specimens of various vegetables, flowers, and fruits. In 1889 and

1890 well over a million people in the Middle West and in the South were thus exposed to a display of California jam packed with these specimens. Southern California booster organizations cooperated with the Southern Pacific and other railroads to create displays at a series of world fairs and expositions, and they even sponsored a fair devoted to citrus in Chicago in 1886. L. M. Holt, the fair's organizer, reported to the Riverside *Press and Horticulturist* that the display had worked magic on Chicagoans. Four thousand people attended daily, and ten thousand newspapers carried word of the fair. Indeed, the *Chicago Times* seemed fully convinced that California was a veritable Eden: "Its mountains and hillsides, burdened with millions of grapevines, may be described as dropping down new wine continuously, while its valleys and plains pour forth rich treasures of fruits."[22]

The fairs created grand opportunities for turning landscaping techniques into boosterism. For the World's Columbian Exposition in Chicago in 1893, the Southern California World's Fair Association, under the direction of the Los Angeles Chamber of Commerce's Frank Wiggins, sent seventy-three railroad cars full of fruits and flowers to Chicago. A fabulous array of preserved fruits went on display under glass, and fresh oranges were sculpted into spectacles of California's fecundity—an orange globe and liberty bell and a thirty-five-foot tower composed of thousands of pieces of fruit. These reified symbols of abundance were juxtaposed with living specimens. An entire garden ecosystem—living orange and lemon trees, together with palms, tropical plants, and lawns—was transplanted to Chicago. "'If your State can make such an excellent showing two thousand miles from home, you must have an incomparable climate and splendid soil,'" was a typical reaction recorded in the official report.[23] Fresh fruit was also sent in by the carload. On September 9, some 230,000 fairgoers were given a free taste of California's horticulture.

But these consumable tokens of California were supplemented by something more durable: printed material. One pamphlet, *Land of Sunshine: Southern California*, was filled with photographs of California's garden landscapes —lovely mansions with rose gardens and palm trees, citrus groves beneath snow-covered mountains, and pictures of gargantuan pumpkins. *Land of Sunshine* presented an array of reasons for the easterner to come to California. Topping the list was climate, and the fruit growing that could lead to riches as well as health. More than 70 million oranges were sold that year, bringing in 3.2 million dollars in return. The pamphlet referred to large profits of fruit growers and "the now well-established belief that the market for choice Southern California fruit, under proper methods of distribution, is practically unlimited." In fact, that year the Southern California Fruit Exchange (which would launch the Sunkist trademark) was formed; it would do much, through modern advertising, to make the market for citrus elastic.[24]

The *Los Angeles Times* was impressed by the fairs, seeing them as dynamos of growth. The fairs had awakened "fresh interest" in Southern California: "It takes no prophet nor the son of a prophet to foretell a growth within the next few years more rapid than Los Angeles has yet experienced." Indeed, the population would soar, and horticulture would continue to expand. The Boom of the Eighties followed closely on the heels of the Citrus Fair in Chicago, and though it would eventually bust, in the long run Southern California's economic and population growth would be driven by citrus and horticulture well into the twentieth century.[25]

The garden imagery would draw tourists and health seekers as well as growers who would do their part to make the open spaces of the region reflect the imagery. By 1895, I. N. Hoag (a promotional agent of the Southern Pacific Railroad) reported in the *Rural Californian* on the volume of goods flowing forth from California's cornucopia. There were eight thousand tons of deciduous fruit, thirty-nine hundred tons of dried fruit, five thousand tons of raisins, twenty-eight hundred tons of canned fruit, fifty-eight hundred tons of potatoes, fourteen thousand tons of beans, and eighty thousand tons of oranges—in total, more than 200 million pounds of produce.[26] But Southern Californians were also planting ornamental tree, shrubs, and flowers in great numbers, creating the leafy wonderland to match the Edenic landscape imagery that had lured them to the state. Nursery businesses such as those of Thomas Garey expanded, becoming virtual factories for the production of palms or citrus to complete the manifestation of the garden (see figure 12.1).

Exotics, Empire, and the Reinvention of Nature

The growing of gardens involves more than the creative manipulation of nature's forms: gardening works with the structure of society as well. As the Anglo economy developed in the boom years, a social system grew up around the production plant. Wickson and other horticultural promoters had envisioned the growth of egalitarian, and white, communities around fruit growing. In fact, the work of creating and maintaining the ornamental and fruit-bearing plants required intensive labor, which was supplied by a stream of racialized others: native Californians, Californios, and immigrants from Mexico, China, southern Europe, Japan, and the Philippines. By the early twentieth century, much of the labor of growing, maintaining, and harvesting was put in the hands of these people, who were often imagined to live beyond the boundary of the body politic. To the extent that their presence, through spatial segregation, was rendered invisible, the character of the original garden could seem to be fully achieved: it was a place removed from work. Rather than creating an organic space of democratic opportunity, the gardens of Los Angeles inscribed social hierarchy into the landscape.[27]

As Victoria Padilla explains in her invaluable study of Southern California gardens, "a man's status was symbolized by the sweep of the lawn that separated his house from the street and the number of specimen trees and palms that grew thereon." This invidious use of plants did not escape that sharp critic of conspicuous consumption Thorstein Veblen. Writing in 1899, Veblen pointed out that "some beautiful flowers pass conventionally for offensive weeds; others that can be cultivated with relative ease are accepted and admired by the lower middle class, who can afford no more expensive luxuries of this kind; but these varieties are rejected as vulgar by those people who are better able to pay for expensive flowers and are educated to a higher schedule of pecuniary beauty in the florist's products; while still other flowers, of no greater intrinsic beauty than these, are cultivated at great cost and call out much admiration from flower-lovers whose tastes have been matured under the critical guidance of a polite environment."[28]

According to Veblen's theory of the leisure class, such nonutilitarian plants performed their job of delineating social status with the utmost efficiency. Vast

Figure 12. 1. Interior of a palm nursery, undated. Huntington Library, San Marino, California.

groves of orange trees were a sign of wealth, but groves of rare trees collected from around the world—trees that produced nothing that could be sold and that required much labor to maintain—sent an even louder message about personal power and worth. Veblen's "polite environment" flourished around the turn of the century in Southern California, and the wealthiest bought exotic plants in great quantities and hired the new professional landscape gardeners to create spectacular grounds. In 1915 Walter Woehlke would sum up a generation of activity by observing that from "Pasadena eastward for sixty miles the foothills of the orange belt are being transformed by the landscape gardeners of the financial elite."[29]

The consumption and display of exotic plant materials coincided with the emergence of the United States' overseas empire. Consumption of exotics and their use as objects of display by the wealthy had long been practiced, reflected in the collection of specimens for curiosity cabinets and the development of royal botanic gardens such as that at Kew in England. One English Duchess "went so far as to have a dress designed to give her the appearance of a walking botanical garden." These botanical collections and display were intertwined with the spread of empire. In the late nineteenth century, the United States was developing its own overseas empire, particularly in the Pacific. At the same time, America's leisure class became ever more fascinated with the exotic, being consumed with what Edward Said called orientalism. The ability to appropriate the exotic became intertwined with the making of self.[30]

In California, professional horticulturists worked with the plants of the world, developing techniques and knowledge needed to acclimatize them to the foreign environment of Southern California. As Padilla explains, they "distributed these exotic plants and taught the new citizens of the state how to raise them so that the exuberance of their growth soon became world renowned." Individuals, as well as communities, put the plants to work in creating an exotic and Edenic look.[31]

By 1888, Pasadena had transformed itself into "an earthly paradise [with its] beautiful pepper and eucalyptus trees, cypress hedges and other ornamental trees and shrubs, beneath which are miles of substantial cement sidewalks, which enclose countless blocks of palatial mansions and pretty cottages of modern and unique design which are surrounded with rare flowers and semi-tropic plants." These city gardens amounted to three-dimensional advertisements for the community, confirming that this was a place where paradise could be recreated. Such gardening made California into something of a magic kingdom long before Disney razed an orange grove in Anaheim to create his fantasyland.[32]

Charles Saunders, an avid gardener and prolific writer, delighted in this global collection of plants. "It is an inestimable privilege to have the plant life of the whole world sampled to your hand," he wrote. He believed that such plants "come to us with tales of other lands and peoples, and to know all we can about them is a contribution to international good will and a help to the realization of world kinship." While this Quaker idealism is admirable, the real history of this plant importation involves as much ecological imperialism as it does pacific intercontinental enrichment. Something of the gap between plant importation and the creation of international goodwill is hinted at in Saunders's remark that "if the average Californian's taste for excluding Asiatics extended to the plants of Asia as well as to people, the gardens of the state would be poorer by many a charming tree and shrub whose presence with us we owe to that wise old continent across the Pacific." In fact, the orange trees had ultimately come from Asia, and in the late nineteenth century, much of the labor in the citrus groves was performed by Chinese. Fruit growers, though, confessed that Chinese workers were "undesirable in many respects." They were imagined to be unassimilable and harmful to the body politic—somehow beyond acclimatization.[33]

The garden as a place of conspicuous cultivation relied on imported plants, and Southern Californians incorporated an astounding range of organic others. Take, for instance, Senator Thomas Bard's garden in Hueneme. In it could be found plants from Australia, Abyssinia, Azores, Burma, the Canary Islands, China, the Cape Verde Islands, Central America, Ceylon, California, the Catalina Islands, the Caucasus Mountains, Europe, the Fiji Islands, Formosa, the Himalayas, India, Japan, Java, Korea, Mexico, Mediterranean countries, Madagascar, Madeira, Malay, New Caledonia, New Zealand, North Africa, the Pitcairn Islands, Polynesia, the Rocky Mountains, South America, South Africa, Siberia, the Solomon Islands, the southern United States, and the West Indies. In Redlands, A. K. and A. H. Smiley created a two-hundred-acre garden with "artificial lakes and planted forests" (figure 12.2). "Barren ridges have been changed into flower gardens," explained a writer for *Land of Sunshine* magazine in 1899. "Almost every variety of tree, shrub and flower that flourishes in the semi-tropics is to be found here." More than a thousand species of trees and shrubs from around the world were grown in this private park that the Smileys kept open to the admiring perusal of tourists and townsfolk alike (see, for example, the illustrations by William McClung in folio one).[34]

Celebrations of the world's flora, such gardens also amounted to a "public display of American imperialism." The Columbian exchange—the movement and transplanting of biota among the continents of Europe, Africa, and the Americas following 1492—had been reshaping the world for four hundred years. The exchange of biota between the Americas and Asia and the Pacific was more recent in origin; improved steamship transportation emerged in the 1870s to accelerate this Pacific exchange. A particularly rich traffic in biota opened up between California and Australia, with Californians planting eucalyptus and acacia trees by the thousands. Southern Californians gathered in the plants of the Pacific world and beyond and made them their own. The gardens represented an imperialistic appropriation of the world's flora for the purpose of creating an Edenic aura or other marketable products. Knowledge, a sophisticated system of transportation, and the development of new cultural practices were needed to maintain the artificial gardens of spectacular biodiversity.[35]

Luther Burbank worked with plant materials from all over the world to create new plants for the aesthetic and economic delight of his customers. In his experimental garden in Santa Rosa, the diversity of life could be brought together and recombined. He began offering his hybrids in 1893 in a catalogue entitled *New Creations in Plant Life*. Inside were "new creations, lately produced by scientific combinations of Nature's forces, guided by long, carefully conducted, and very expensive biological study." Burbank expounded, "We are

Figure 12.2. Smiley residence, 1890s. Public domain.

now standing just at the gateway of scientific horticulture . . . only having taken a few steps in the measureless fields which will stretch out as we advance into the golden sunshine of a more complete knowledge of the forces which are to unfold all the graceful forms of garden beauty, and wealth of fruit and flowers, for the comfort and happiness of Earth's teeming millions."[36] His catalog included a number of new varieties: quinces and walnuts, more than thirty berries, roses, lilies, peaches, apricots, plums, and prunes. The pages represented a veritable cornucopia of invention.

Burbank enjoyed great popularity in Southern California (citrus growers tried to recruit him to Southern California), as well as across the nation. He was famous for making bigger and better fruits (such as his giant plums), more beautiful flowers (such as the Shasta daisy and the improved amaryllis), and living oxymorons (such as the white blackberry and the spineless cactus). His name became synonymous with improvement; burbank entered Webster's as a transitive verb meaning "to improve (anything, as a process or institution) by selecting good features and rejecting bad, or by adding good features."[37] Burbank promised to disclose the secrets of nature and give culture infinite power to shape it to match people's desires. Gardening with Burbank became a mixture of magic, science, and millenarian longing. His plants embodied and seemed to prove beyond a shadow of a doubt that Californians had indeed found a way to reinvent nature and thereby recreate Eden.

Grounds for Contention

The dominant effects of these artifactual Edens was to legitimate conquest, produce conditions of economic growth, and serve the interests of the ascendant class. First, the gardens yielded fruits that could be sold to the nation as condensations of nature's goodness. Second, Southern California itself could be sold to tourists and settlers alike as an exotic place of natural abundance imbued with exceptional therapeutic qualities. Finally, wealthy Southern Californians wrote into their gardened landscapes stories about themselves, narratives that proclaimed their status and reassured them that they lived in and contributed to a cultured and cosmopolitan place. In short, Southern California's garden functioned as a type of growth machine.

Yet the meaning of Southern California's gardens cannot be completely captured by Veblenesque analysis, for there were gardeners who worked against the grain. One may argue, along with David Harvey, that "created ecosystems tend to instantiate and reflect . . . the social systems that gave rise to them, though they do not do so in noncontradictory (i.e. *stable*) ways."[38] Gardens also were places from which to challenge both the emphasis on worldly gain and the spatial construction of social inequality. To some extent, gardens served as grounds for contention.

Consider the work of Theodosia Shepard of Ventura. She used the garden as a platform from which to challenge gender-based social restriction. The association of women with gardens was, of course, a key element of the separate spheres ideology—flowers were considered a realm of femininity and therefore appropriate objects of woman's domestic attentions. The gardens of Southern California blurred the boundaries between the domestic and the public spheres to some extent. Yet separate spheres ideology was expressed in how gardens were used, or at least how they were portrayed. Staged photographs of leisure in Charles and Elizabeth Saunders's garden portray Elizabeth sewing, serving tea, or appreciating a work of Indian basketry, while Charles tends to be reading the newspaper or writing correspondence (figure 12.3).

Yet, over the course of the nineteenth century, actual women used their gardens in a variety of ways, and some women, such as Sarah Cooper, used their botanical expertise to move into the public sphere of authorship.[39] Women developed far-flung networks to share seeds, creating a sowing circle that broke neighborhood bounds. Shepard, a successful hybridizer who lived in Ventura, developed such a network and used her work with flowers as a way to enter successfully into the business world. She became a pioneer of floriculture on the West Coast.

Figure 12.3. Charles and Elizabeth Saunders in their garden, undated. Huntington Library, San Marino, California.

Shepard cultivated the feminist implications of her work. In 1883 she gave a speech to the Pomological Society of Los Angeles in which she expressed her views of horticulture, women, and enterprise. Only a few years ago, she said, "woman's sphere was very limited. . . . Men loved to call her the queen of the household, but she was a queen bereft of authority; a queen without subjects. . . . She was a queen mostly in song." Shepard noted, "Only a few years since, the culture of flowers was looked upon as a sentimental gratification indulged in only by women. It was considered essentially feminine to love flowers." After acknowledging the joy that plants bring women in their often isolated homes, she insisted that women could become successful commercial horticulturists: "When any woman recognizes her ability in any line of out-of-door work, and goes about it as if she understood herself, the world is not slow to accord her a right as an individual. . . . Pluck is always considered admirable in man or woman." Floriculture was already becoming a big business, and Shepard envisioned independent women playing an important role in this industry. "All fields are open to you," she said.[40] Here was gardening for a profit, but with every flower sold the patriarchal foundations of Los Angeles's gardens were eroded.

The working class and immigrants found ways to do their own gardening in the interstices of Southern California's agricultural empire (as the Chamber of Commerce called it). Mexican workers living in *colonias* maintained their own vegetable gardens. Chinese, Russian, Italian, and Japanese immigrants developed truck gardens and sold their produce in downtown Los Angeles. Sotaro Endo grew carnations in downtown Los Angeles in the 1890s, and Japanese Americans, growing violets, chrysanthemums, garden plants, and roses, went on to play an important role in the development of flower markets in Los Angeles. These are instances where land not only was not turned into profit for the ascendant class, but where workers were able to use the land to secure for themselves some small piece of the agrarian dream.[41]

Finally, consider Ezra and Jeanne Carr's garden in Pasadena at West Colorado and Orange Grove Boulevard, called Carmelita (little orchard-garden). Like other gardens, Carmelita included an impressive array of exotics: the Bunya-bunya of Australia, China's Tree of heaven, the Blue Palm of Mexico, Nordman's Fir of Greece, the Sago Palm of Java, the Deodor of India and Afghanistan, the Bhutan Pine of the Himalayas. There were forty-six grape vines, nine nut trees, eighteen varieties of deciduous fruit, and nine varieties of citrus. The Auraucarias had originally been collected in Valparaiso, Chile, during George Vancouver's voyage of discovery in the 1790s and were sent back to Britain's Royal Botanic Garden at Kew. John Muir, a close friend of Jeanne

Carr's, said Carmelita was "nothing less than an exhaustive miniature of all the leafy creatures of the globe."[42]

Muir was a lifelong friend of the Carrs, whom he first met while a student at the University of Wisconsin, where Ezra had taught before moving on to the University of California. Jeanne Carr, for all of the exotics that were incorporated into the designed space of Carmelita, did much to spread appreciation for California's native plants. "No effort of the Landscape Gardener's art," she conceded, "can equal the beauty of Nature's wild parks and gardens." Carmelita was run as a semipublic garden, open to the public for enjoyment (eventually much of it was turned over to the city and would become the site of the Norton Simon Museum). Guests included Muir and Helen Hunt Jackson, two eminent figures in the genre of California garden writing. Muir created a literature of the garden for the mountains and Jackson for the valleys of Southern California. Jackson stayed with the Carrs when she was researching *Ramona*, and the story spread that she wrote the novel on these grounds in a vine- and flower-covered cabin. Though the story proved apocryphal, she certainly drew inspiration from Carrs' gardens.[43]

Muir melded Romanticism's valuation of wilderness as sublime with garden imagery, creating poetic portraits of the botanic wonderland of mountain valleys. In defending the doomed Hetch Hetchy Valley, he waxed eloquent about the "gardens, groves and meadows of its flowery park-like floor." Muir insisted that "everybody needs beauty as well as bread, places to play in and pray in, where Nature may heal and cheer and give strength to body and soul." Rejecting an absolute dichotomy between garden and wilderness landscapes, Muir put the gardens of the mountains on a continuum with the "poor folks' window gardens" and the "costly lily gardens of the rich." But Yosemite and Hetch Hetchy were "natural landscape gardens," and Muir sought to preserve them by investing them with all of the moral significance of the Garden of Eden. Using this rhetorical ground to challenge the utilitarian "devotees of ravaging commercialism" who desired to dam Hetch Hetchy, Muir charged that their "arguments are curiously like those of the devil devised for the destruction of the first garden—so much of the very best Eden fruit going to waste, so much of the best Tuolumne water."[44]

While Muir's critique of capitalist exploitation of nature has long been recognized, Jackson used garden rhetoric to make a more historically trenchant critique of the Anglo transformation of landscape in California. This may be surprising, since *Ramona* has most often been reduced to a puff piece creating what Carey McWilliams called the Spanish Fantasy Past. The romance between Ramona and Allessandro, cast as a noble Roussouian Indian, captivated attention, but the garden settings were essential to creating the regional aura in which the plot developed. The gardeners of Southern California were inspired by her portrait of the view from Señora Moreno's veranda: "between the veranda and the river meadows . . . all was garden, orange grove, and almond orchard; the orange grove always green, never without snowy bloom or golden fruit; the garden never without flowers, summer or winter." The languid and colorful beauty of such scenes were by the turn of the century being turned into a regional iconography, another way to promote growth by turning the colorful mission past into a marketable identity. (The rehabilitation of the image of the Californios was probably only possible from a position of secure Anglo ascendancy which coincided with a mood of anti-modern lament for a lost past.)[45]

But Jackson's deeper goal was to undermine the Anglo discourse of progress and improvement: her garden narrative was meant to manifest the violence of deterritorialization. The relationship of both Californios and natives to a pastoral and garden landscape is depicted as deep, profound, and fundamentally healthy. Against this backdrop, the fragmentation of landscape becomes all the more tragic. The tragic theme is dramatized in the flight of Alessandro and Ramona and their experience as refugees. The ancestral land at Temecuela has been usurped by the Americans (Alessandro's very home has been occupied by greedy Americans). They wander, searching all across Southern California for a space of refuge. Finally, they find an Indian community that seems to have evaded the American land regime, and Alessandro puts his hands to the plough. But before the harvest, an American usurps his title. Alessandro (who has the power to expose the essences of people with the names he gives them) says, "That is their name,—a people that steals, and that kills for money."[46]

Finally, Ramona and Alessandro retreat to the mountains of San Jacinto, where they make a last attempt to recreate the garden, planting wheat and vegetables. But the repeated severing of connections to the landscape enforced by American law have taken their toll. Alessandro goes mad. Sometimes, he runs for hours, imagining that the Americans are after him. At other times, he imagines himself back in control of the California landscape, and shepherds vast herds of goats or sheep (though they are not his own). The madness embodies the history of violent dispossession. The deterritorialization of California by Anglos attempting to inscribe a new system of land titles, rights, and uses is at the heart of the story. Historically, this process was legitimated with the notion that Americans were liberating and improving a land that had been hovering too long in languid idleness. "In the hands of an enterprising people," Richard Henry Dana had written in 1840, "what a country this might be."[47]

Ramona worked to unravel the negative stereotypes of native Californians as "diggers," a subhuman people with no real claim to the land. Jackson mobilized an oppositional stereotype: Allessandro as a noble Indian, capable of both living in harmony with nature and working hard to turn nature into a garden. While the history of deterritorialization could not now be reversed, Jackson hoped to create the political will to open up space for native Californians to join in the agrarian republic. In 1883, Jackson had been appointed commissioner of Indian affairs, and, along with Abbott Kinney, made an investigation of the state's Indian peoples and issued a report. (Kinney was also a great garden advocate, promoting citrus culture and Australian eucalyptus and creating the Mediterranean fantasy landscape of Venice.) Though Kinney and Jackson thought it was "humanly speaking, impossible to render [native Californians a] full measure of justice," Jackson hoped that her literary work might aid the cause. Very little was actually accomplished in redressing the territorial dispossession of Indians, despite a growing reform effort in the 1880s and 1890s. Nationally, much reform aimed at turning Indian communities into collections of freeholding yeoman working in the soil.[48]

Another major approach was the development of modern boarding schools with the goal of teaching Indians to assimilate the values and beliefs of the dominant society. Such schools embraced Richard Henry Pratt's motto for the Carlisle Institute: "Kill the Indian and Save the Man." Horatio Rust, who was praised by Pratt for his work, had run such a school in Perris (not too far from Temecuela, where Alessandro's people were uprooted). Rust shared Jackson's sense of outrage (and penchant for writing stereotypically of native Californians). He wrote, "In his simplicity [the California Indian] believed that the Great Spirit . . . had given him the land and water and the air he breathed alike as an inheritance for his use and his children forever. . . . The white man's law took away his land and ordered him off." Rust had also been inspired by European garden schools. In 1901, the Sherman Institute opened as a model school in Riverside, in the heart of the Anglo garden.[49]

But this kind of Indian policy reform, rather than creating a radical questioning of the legitimacy of conquest, could be turned into an emblem celebrating the conquistadors' achievement. Consider how the school is represented in a 1901 issue of *Sunset* magazine. It is depicted as a neatly kept institution of progressive education, with its palm tree border and mission-style buildings. Look at the landscape, *Sunset* invites its readers. Where once was nothing but "sunshine and sagebrush" now gleams "the largest orange-growing district in the world." (The crop was worth 1.5 million dollars.) Where once were Indians living haplessly in sage and desert now are Americans in the making. It is a vision of nature and culture undergoing the most orderly improvement and growth.[50] But Indigo, the girl in Silko's *Gardens in the Dunes*, would have known that the oranges now grown for export hung over a landscape that had once yielded mesquite beans, pinion, acorns, cactus buds, chia, and two hundred other plants useful to people.

The Enclosure of Abundance

Clues to the nature of this new Anglo garden can be gleaned from Rust himself, who was renowned for his horticultural achievements in Pasadena (a German magazine printed a picture of one of Rust's rosebushes under the caption "Ein Rosenbusch in Californien"). But every garden has a serpent, and Rust's carried a baseball bat. In the summer of 1906, Rust petitioned the city council for help. It seems that boys were playing baseball on the street, and "ball playing is not conducive to the care of lawn and ornamental plants." And the boys, retrieving their stray balls, would also pick oranges from his trees, "giving no thought to the mutilated hedge and scattering orange peel on the street." Further, "I have endeavored to improve all my holdings," he complained, "and now I only ask you to protect me and all who use the streets in what seems to be our natural rights." It is tempting to see Rust as simply a killjoy. But he was expressing a widespread belief in what was natural about the garden landscape. The right that seemed so natural to Rust was to make the landscape into private property, a fenced-in organic richness valuable for producing an exportable crop, for augmenting civic pride and land values. This was a thoroughly commodified cornucopia. Such a conception of natural rights did not include usufruct: there are stories of growers rigging guns to their orange trees to discourage would-be poachers.[51]

Along with omnipresent visual signs of abundance, Southern California gardens produced scarcity. Fenced-in, this garden became forbidden. That sense of simultaneous immersion in and exclusion from the landscape of abundance was perhaps best conveyed by Charlie Chaplin in his 1936 film *Modern Times*. The film presents icons of abundance: the traditional one of the garden landscape and the emergent ones of the factory and the department store. The alienation that the Little Tramp experiences in the world of scientific management is remembered by all—his body becomes a cog in the machine. But the Little Tramp and his waterfront companion also spend a wondrous night in the department store. After being expelled from this "land of desire," the two wander into the garden landscape of a typical Los Angeles suburb. Sitting on the curb, the Little Tramp fantasizes about what life would be like in such a garden home. He has only to open the front door, and a cow walks up to deliver fresh milk. Bunches of grapes hang invitingly close, and oranges grow right outside the living room window, ripe for plucking. But the policeman shows up, and the California dream dissolves. And like that, Chaplin exposes the failure nineteenth-century promoters of horticulture, who had envisioned the growth of a democratic idyll in what instead became a deeply commodified place with invidious social distinctions written into the landscape.[52]

The gardens naturalized social inequality and sublimated the facts of conquest, proclaiming instead that the order of Southern California's landscape was more a manifestation of natural evolution than a contested product of social construction. The garden is a symbol of original purity, but the gardens of Southern California cannot be entered innocently. It takes imagination to see these gardens in their true light. Find the postcard-perfect garden. Ask Hieronymus Bosch, who had some experience painting both gardens and oranges, to retouch the image. Only then might we come up with an adequate portrait of the garden of worldly delights.

13

Changing Attitudes toward Animals among Chicanas and Latinas in Los Angeles

UNNA LASSITER AND JENNIFER WOLCH

Tierra natal. This is home, the small towns in the Valley, *los pueblitos* with
chicken pens and goats picketed to mesquite shrubs. *En las colonias* on the
other side of the tracks, junk cars line the front yards of hot pink and lavender-
trimmed houses—Chicano architecture we call it, self-consciously.

Gloria Anzaldúa, *Borderlands/La Frontera: The New Mestiza*

CHICKENS, roosters, rabbits, sheep, and goats, living in tiny backyards
or even on the apartment balcony, are an increasingly common sight
in Los Angeles' dense Latino neighborhoods, especially those with
large shares of immigrants. Latino immigrant residential communities in
Southern California, where zoning regulations were characteristically lax, have
always included animals; Don Normark, for example, provides photographic
evidence of this in his 1949 images of Chavez Ravine, where farm animals such
as goats were common. However, today such animals may be found in dense
apartment communities and inner-ring suburbs with cramped yards.[1]

There are no quantitative data on the distribution of urban animals by
species in Los Angeles (other than licensed dogs). But neighborhood observations and interviews with law enforcement officers, animal services personnel,
and real estate professionals who frequent these neighborhoods together paint
a picture of neighborhoods where large numbers of diverse animals are kept in
yards and patios. Roosters and chickens are especially common and often are
tucked in close to houses and apartments, despite legal separation requirements
that coops maintain specific distances from housing units and neighboring
properties. It is not uncommon to encounter the birds in the street, and in

lower-density areas, larger animals such as sheep, goats, and horses are often encountered in backyards, regardless of zoning.[2]

Many of these creatures, who once inhabited the barnyard, are no longer destined for the chopping block. Rather, they are kept as pets, receiving love and affection from their human families while also serving as embodied links to a rural past in which farm animals were an integral part of the home, the daily routine, and the landscape. Thus in some of the most inhospitable neighborhoods in the Los Angeles region, animals appear to at once reflect the assimilation of immigrants and their first-generation children and serve as a central means to retain cultural identity (see figure 13.1).

It is not surprising that nature-society relationships in general, and attitudes toward animals in particular, are renegotiated when people move from one region of the world to another. How exactly this process occurs, why people hold on to certain beliefs and practices related to animals, but not others, and how these changes serve to remake the local landscape and its meanings are intriguing questions that are not well investigated.

We explored these questions through conversations with low-income Latina immigrants and first-generation Chicanas living in south central Los Angeles.[3] The Latinas were mostly from rural backgrounds, while many of the

Figure 13.1. Llamas and sheep in backyards, 2002. Unna Lassiter.

urban-born Chicanas had relatives in rural Mexico whom they visited regularly. Our conversations highlighted the nature of traditional animal practices common in rural Mexico and Central America, and how, now that they are living in Los Angeles, these women reflect upon such practices and explain them. The discussions also revealed the variety of influences that have affected the women's current ideas about how people should interact with animals, both wild and domestic.

The Latina group was composed mostly of women in their midthirties, who had lived in Los Angeles for at least eight years but had not been born there. Almost none of these women had a high school degree. The Chicanas, a younger group, were either born in Los Angeles or had arrived there as very small children. Some were going to college, while others already had a college degree (see appendix A). About half the women in each group had worked with animals, on family farms for the most part. Our brief demographic survey indicated that all participants had kept pets, especially dogs and cats but also farm animals (see appendix B). The Chicanas, however, had had a greater variety of animals, including birds, small mammals, fish, reptiles, and even insects, as pets.

The women's family and cultural traditions relating to animals and their interactions with both wild and domestic animals in Southern California were at the heart of our conversations with them. Because we consider acculturation as a multigenerational process, we were especially interested in the Latinas' discussion of practices and attitudes before and after arriving in the United States and the first-generation Chicanas' comparisons between their attitudes and those of their elders. Their attitudes toward the practices of others—both other Chicanos/Latinos and people of other racial/ethnic backgrounds—were also a significant focus of our attention. Certain Mexican animal-related practices are disparaged in mainstream American culture, as are those of other groups (especially immigrants), and we wanted to learn about the women's responses to this potential source of racial/ethnic tension.

Our qualitative analysis of the group discussions involved categorizing participants' statements according to the type of human-animal interaction, their knowledge about animals, their perceptions about various sorts of animals and interactions, and their basic attitudes toward nature and animals.[4] Also, we explored the question of why people hold on to certain beliefs and practices and not others and how these changes remake the meaningfulness of animals and the local landscape of human-animal relationships.

The terms barnyard, backyard, and bed have both literal and metaphorical meanings and evoke places in which different attitudes toward animals dominate and serve to shape practice. The barnyard, although often depicted in bucolic images as benign, is in fact a place where animals are slaughtered and their remains processed. The backyard, which we take to encompass the space surrounding the home (front as well as back), embraces what is commonly termed *la yarda*. This is a space that is much closer to the home. This is the domain of pets or domestic animals that are protected from the prospect of slaughter, whose welfare is important to humans, and who are but one step away from the human household. The bed, however, is perhaps the most comfortable, private, and intimate space we inhabit, typically shared only with those considered close kin. The welcoming of certain animals into this private, domestic space, by inviting them to curl up on the bedspread, suggests a reconfiguration of human-animal relations and reevaluation of the human-animal bond.

Latino Los Angeles

Until the 1970s scholars knew little about Mexican urbanization in the United States generally or about Los Angeles specifically. They tended to dismiss barrio life and dehumanize it as marginal, with Mexican Americans being considered a "casual labor force," eager to return to Mexico, and with "no claim to American society."[5] By the late 1970s, Chicano scholars such as Albert Camarillo began to reframe such distorted views by recovering the history of Latinos in the Southwest United States. This study and those that followed took the form of regional historiographies that focused on the history of labor and gender relations. In this fashion they have not only reinscribed the Latino contribution to American life, but, more recently, have also begun to identify a Mexican American transformation of the urban environment.[6]

Ricardo Romo reframed the East Los Angeles barrio as a place that "provided a sense of identity with the homeland and a transition into American society," an "acculturation way station." He described the creation of a new urban culture there, thus challenging the long-standing view that "Sonoratown" or "Little Mexico" in 1930s Los Angeles were simply small versions of Mexican towns. A number of recent autobiographies have also contributed to the understanding of barrios and Latino family relationships in Southern California, the trials of illegal immigrants, and everyday life at a street level.[7]

Early on, Chicano scholars were also influential in redefining acculturation, a process that until then had been seen as dependent on group adjustment, taken to mean Americanization, and based on factors that ranged from perceived cultural compatibility to the ability to speak English. This perspective had critically defined policies, practices, and perceptions, which affected the everyday experience of Latinos in Los Angeles. Mary Helen Ponce, for instance, who describes her childhood in the Pacoima Barrio of the San Fernando Valley in Los Angeles in the 1940 and 1950s, writes, "We lived in two worlds: the secure barrio that comforted and accepted us, and the Other, the institutions such as school that were out to sanitize, Americanize, and de-lice us at least once a year, usually in the spring, when everything hatched, including lice."[8]

In the 1970s Chicano scholars challenged the notion that "successful" acculturation meant Americanization, and by the 1980s they rejected the notion of a single Mexican American experience, instead asserting that widely diverse acculturative experiences are intertwined and coexist simultaneously.[9] They also cast a more positive light on traits immigrants retained from their homeland, extolling the maintenance of these traits as signs of healthy adjustment. Cultural adjustments were increasingly cast as individual negotiations resulting in multipositionality, characterized by the presence of simultaneous, contradictory attitudes.[10]

This process of adjustment and negotiation is expressed in Latino neighborhoods in Los Angeles, most of which were originally built for Anglo residents. Here, the use of public as well as private space is typically personalized to reflect American mainstream ideas as well as Mexican or Central American values and practices, acting to reconfigure the urban landscape. The resulting neighborhood spaces, evocatively described by James T. Rojas, feature murals, graffiti, strolling street vendors, cruising cars, and various props, such as music and store signs, as well as streets lined with personalized yardas boasting fences, ornaments, and lively social interactions of many types.[11]

Only a small body of research, however, has explored how acculturation shapes Latino practices and attitudes toward nature or animals in Latino neighborhoods and communities. John Baas, Alan Ewert, and Deborah Chavez found some differences in participation in nature-related activities (such as biking) between U.S.-born and Mexican immigrants. James Gramann, Myron Floyd, and Regelio Saenz and Sandra Shaull and Gramann highlighted the importance of social activities, especially within the family, in shaping Mexican American appreciation for nature. Floyd and Francis Noe used the New Environmental Paradigm scale to investigate the environmental values of Latino immigrants in South Florida, showing the importance of culture in shaping their thinking about the environment. Barbara Lynch, observing that Latino discourses about the environment were seldom noted, set out to analyze Latino writings about ideal landscapes. She pointed out that "the deepest roots of Latin American environmentalism . . . come from resistance to conquest" and characterized Latino perspectives on nature as more holistic than Anglo views. This conclusion was reinforced by Victor Corral-Verdugo and Luz Armendariz's survey research on Latino environmental values.[12]

Despite these suggestive results, work on Latino immigrant acculturation and nature remains limited and has not been placed within an urban context such as Southern California. Nor has any work been directed specifically at attitudes toward animals. In fact, the research on attitudes toward animals has so far made little progress in illuminating how cultural contexts dynamically shape attitudes, especially how attitudes change as people immigrate and raise children in a new social environment.

Animals in the Barnyard

Attitudes based on the practical and material exploitation of animals as sources of food, clothing, transport, or sport have been historically prevalent and remain so in many communities. Typically referred to as traditional or utilitarian, such attitudes hold that the benefits of animal use for humans take precedence over issues of animal welfare. Utilitarian attitudes are typically associated with people from rural backgrounds who depend on animals for their livelihood.[13] Since many of our focus group respondents had come from poor or rural backgrounds, we expected that the women's attitudes regarding animals would be predominantly utilitarian. Although ideas about conservation and protection of threatened/endangered animals (such as gray whales, sea turtles, and the Mexican jaguar) increasingly shape Mexican public opinion, often movements have been stimulated by international environmental organizations. Thus it was unclear the extent to which more biocentric attitudes would be articulated by our groups.

Both groups of women expressed utilitarian attitudes, attributing them to people from their communities of origin and justifying them on the basis that such views of animals were warranted by dire economic conditions in Mexico. Even pet animals (such as dogs) were described as having little value in rural Mexico, and strays were often seen as pests to be eliminated. The women had lived on farms with barnyards full of chickens, goats, pigs, and cows fed only for slaughter or, in the case of horses, for use as pack animals. Many described an animal's slaughter as a common experience, and the Latinas even explained that the killing of an animal was considered a toughening experience, an education or initiation that was necessary for survival in Mexico. As a woman recounted, economic survival explained the lack of concern for animals in her country of origin: "People back there are more concerned with basic things, like bringing food on the table and employment, stuff like that. These [the rights of animals] are things you don't think about, at least not in those days while I was living there. In our country, the concern is to eat, and if you have to kill an animal . . . well, there might not be any other food."

Freshly caught fish and hunted and trapped wild animals were also part of the family fare in Mexico. This included what might be considered marginal meats from animals such as armadillos, skunks, sea turtles, iguanas, and opossums; their intake indeed suggests that survival was at stake. However, the taste of certain game animals was prized, and one woman even recalled collecting and eating sea turtle eggs, despite knowing that she risked a hefty fine. Several of these women were clearly sorry that their access to fresh meat had diminished since living in the United States. This was in part due to the belief that freshly killed animals provide more energy than refrigerated meat. This concern for meat that is fresh, and thus revitalizing, is exemplified in Mexican butcher shops or *carnicerias*, food trucks and restaurants that are often adorned with colorful murals that depict pigs, horses, longhorn cattle, and chickens in a pasture, along with Mexican symbols such as the Virgin of Guadalupe and stylized Aztec deities (figure 13.2).

The women discussed a range of medicinal uses of animal parts, including remedies against physical ailments such as asthma and scorpion sting and against ailments of the soul, that in Mexico are said to be soothed through the warm blood of a chicken or cow. The persistence of such beliefs was based on the enduring strength of oral tradition. Remedies and family recipes for wellness were passed down through generations by grandparents, aunts and uncles, and sisters of the women with whom we talked. In Los Angeles at least, these

Figure 13.2. Market and butcher shop signage, Long Beach. 2002. Unna Lassiter.

practices are also maintained through more than two hundred *farmacía natur-istas* and *botánicas* from Pacoima to San Pedro. These unlicensed shops offer a panoply of traditional Mexican products at more affordable prices than stan-dard prescription drugs and are the object of police raids whenever someone is hurt by such potions or pills.[14] An assortment of *hierbas* are also grown in neighborhood backyards.

Neither the Latinas nor the Chicanas mentioned the nutritional value of particular animal meats, indicating that more science-based knowledge had not replaced traditional know-how, at least not in everyday practice. Also, several Latinas recalled the 1950s case of the drug thalidomide, and the deformities it caused in babies, and linked this to a more general distrust of Western medicine.

This tragic case was, however, also used to legitimize medical experimenta-tion on animals, so that such errors might never happen again. Almost half of the Latina participants declared their support of medical experimentation, no matter the consequences for animals. Speaking for the other Latina women, Elena volunteered, "I think that we all agree that it's better to experiment on an animal than on a person." The sentiment was widely shared, and Flora con-tinued on the relative value of animals: "It's better to experiment on animals because it's worse to see a child suffer than a dog." And Dolores concurred: "I

Figure 13.3. Attendees of the blessing of the animals, in folkloric costume, 2002. Unna Lassiter.

say that it makes me sad, that they experiment on animals, but yes, it's better than on humans."

At times, tradition itself is a necessity, and as we had expected, both Latinas and Chicanas reported that they continued the Catholic practice of eating fish rather than meat on Fridays in Los Angeles. But several Chicanas explained that family habit dictated the practice rather than religious devotion. As Isabel said, "Yeah, I keep the tradition about eating fish. I don't see anything really weird about this really, that's what my parents taught me. That's cool, it's OK with me."

More telling, perhaps, was the account by a woman of seeking refuge in a church as a little girl while a pig was being slaughtered at home, or another's belief that the killing of a deer by her father in Mexico was a sin. These women reinterpreted their religion to distance themselves from traditional practices. The Catholic ritual of the Blessing of the Animals is widely enacted in Los Angeles and brings out the farm animals that so many Latinos keep as beloved pets, along with parrots, guinea pigs, cats, dogs, and iguanas (figure 13.3).

Another traditional attitude is fear. On several occasions, Latina participants mentioned being disgusted or frightened by the sight of an animal. Some explained such fears on the basis of frightening tales and Mexican *cuentos* (stories) about a crazed black dog and giant sea creatures. In *Borderlands/La Frontera*, Gloria Anzaldúa recalls hearing her grandmother tell her stories "like the one about her getting on top of the roof while down below rabid coyotes were ravaging the place and wanting to get at her." And, "My father told stories about a phantom giant dog that appeared out of nowhere and sped along the side of the pickup no matter how fast he was driving." The women's fear of such dangerous or bizarre creatures was sometimes used to justify their decision not to intervene to help an animal in distress.[15]

Finally there was little evidence of "dominionistic" attitudes toward animals, meaning attitudes that sanctioned human domination of animals for any purpose. Specifically, there was virtually no support among the women for practices that used animals for sport—dogfighting, cockfighting, rodeo, or bullfighting. Certain of these male-dominated activities clearly have economic motivations (for example, cockfighting) and are deeply constitutive of cultural and gendered identities. But the Chicanas especially made a distinction between using animals "to carry things, to move from one place to another, for food . . . but to use as a sport, you just don't do that." In Mexico, these practices are meeting growing protest. Although illegal in the United States, cockfighting takes place in the South and Southwest, with animals being bred for this purpose in Los Angeles' inner-city neighborhoods and suburban backyards.[16]

Animals in the Backyard

The women most often described animals and their relationships with them in humanistic terms. An important focus of concern for the women in both groups had to do with the pain animals feel, specifically domestic animals. The women, especially Latinas, gave vivid descriptions of the slaughter of animals (for food or sports such as cockfighting) and of the cries of animals and the gory remains they had once seen on such a routine basis. As a Latina recounted, "That was something terrible. That penetrated my whole childhood and I'm still suffering nightmares." Another related, "My mother raised many pigs. Because we had seen them since they were born, and because we could tell my father was going to kill this one on that particular day, we'd hurry and go to Church very early or to the garden next door, so that we would not hear the pig screaming for ten or fifteen minutes until it had bled to death. It is a very sad, sad, and ugly experience."

Another woman reiterated, "I saw all that when I was little. That's why, when I watch here on TV how they kill animals here, I think that's nothing compared to how they suffer in our countries."

Contradictions in our respondents' attitudes arose about the question of killing animals for food. While many insisted that they refused to eat animals whose slaughter they had witnessed, they were willing to buy packaged meat in the supermarket. They resolved this contradiction by a conviction that slaughter methods here in the United States, learned about on TV, were far more humane than those used in their personal experience in rural areas of Mexico and Central America. In these places, the grandmother chopped off the favorite chicken's head with a dull knife and the pig screamed and screamed as the household's men cut her throat. As one participant said, "Here I eat [meat] because I don't see [the animal being killed], but over there I don't eat the meat when I've just seen the animal being killed." Most of the Chicanas agreed that they too disliked the killing of food animals, especially if they saw or heard the animal being killed. Women in both groups were relieved to no longer be subjected to this kind of scene, and one added how glad she was that her daughter would never have to witness it. But the women also recognized that they now ate meat with little thought of the suffering of pigs and chickens.

The Latinas discussed the fact that sporting practices such as rodeos and bullfights take place in Mexico and were critical of them on the basis of cruelty and ugliness and because people enjoy themselves at the expense of suffering animals. One of the women defended rodeos when downed animals were quickly slaughtered and used for food, but another powerfully argued against cockfighting—because the roosters receive better care than do children. The

Chicanas expressed disapproval of cockfights, dogfights, and bullfights more strongly than the Latinas, but they also recognized that these practices play a social role for men. They expressed some derision about this, indicating perhaps that they are not impressed by such shows of masculine bravado. In the end, one of them simply said, "I think that people just don't realize that animals feel . . . and that if you hurt them, they hurt."

While several Latinas described being scared by animals in Mexico (on the basis of sensational stories, superstition, or frightening contact), the women had familiarized themselves anew with wild animals in aquariums or televised documentaries in their contemporary Southern California urban context. For instance, one of them recounted, "I had never seen an octopus in real life, only at the movies, where they were crazed animals with long tentacles and who ate people. It made me laugh when I saw how small they really are." By seeing animals in a safe context, this woman at least was led to reflect on her earlier ideas about animals, and to think (erroneously) that animals pose no threat to human safety. The women's attitudes were also profoundly shaped by exposure to the media—especially TV documentaries about human-animal interactions, endangered species, and the environment more generally.[17]

A Chicana admitted that because she had become so used to animals as pets, she had little inkling about what to do if she were to see a wild animal such as a cougar: "We see a big one, what are we going to do with it? You just can't tell it to 'come here' or 'sit down'!" Those who were mothers expressed the importance of teaching their children about animals and the environment. These lessons were perceived as valuable for several reasons: it is good for children to learn about animals, and, since children have fewer interactions with animals here in the United States, this experience has to be provided through other means. Elena, a Latina, explained her understanding of the role of aquariums in this context: "I believe that children must be taught the value of animals. We have to teach them what kind of species there are to eat, and teach them at an early age how to fish and not take things out of the sea that really will not be used. I guess that's why these places [aquariums, zoos] exist, to educate our children little by little. Since our parents could not educate us, we have the opportunity to raise our children with a little more education."

Turning to the subject of their life in Los Angeles, the women clearly articulated the ways their attitudes and practices had changed. Traditional practices of slaughter, witnessed by many of the women we spoke with, were deeply traumatizing and left indelible impressions. Also, many of the uses of animals for sport were seen as cruel and largely indefensible. They fondly recalled farm animals they had loved as children and described how they had come to disparage traditional ways despite understanding their necessity in that time and place. By being able to approach animals with fewer fears (or less guilt), the women with whom we spoke had formed meaningful bonds with animals and become more sympathetic to their needs and more attuned to their pain.

Under the influence of norms operating within mainstream American society, these women have adopted other or new practices, including raising pets. Also, they have had direct or indirect contact with normative American ideas about the proper treatment and rights of animals. Adrian Franklin links the growing human need for and reliance on pets to another, more complex sociopolitical trend: ontological security, a need for order when all else seems a whirlpool of change, whereby people experience "a loss of a sense of the very reality of things and of persons" at their very core.[18] These women may embody this postmodern malaise, living betwixt and between cultures, feeling neither here nor there, and thus revising their everyday practices and identities.

But perhaps most of all, the change toward more humanistic approaches to animals was explained by personal or family experiences and the need to extend good care beyond human members of the family, to family pets and to animals everywhere. Indeed, as Ron Martin suggests, pet keeping may in part replace the farm animals that are an integral part of a traditional Mexican rural household, leading to the not-so-unusual sight of "chicks thriving on corn feeds and taking afternoon naps" in the backyards of South Los Angeles, the East Side, and the San Fernando Valley. This practice has led to concern among some Anglo residents, who wish to ban practices—such as keeping farm animals in suburban neighborhoods—that do not seem to fit into typical urban beautification or community development schemes (figure 13.4).[19]

Animals in Bed

For our Latina and Chicana participants, not only had animals moved from the realm of food and the barnyard into the family's backyard, but some had moved into the more intimate spaces of humans—inside their homes—as the women's attitudes became more moralistic and biocentric. This strong affinity and meaningfulness seemed to be based on a compassion only granted to kin. The Latinas especially had begun keeping more animals as pets since moving to the United States (figure 13.5), a trend reflected in the urban landscape by new pet stores emerging in Latino neighborhoods catering to customers with pets ranging from iguanas and parrots to Chihuahuas and rottweilers and by the popularity of public events such as the Catholic Blessing of the Animals ceremonies that attract mostly Latino pet owners.

Many women in both groups went so far as to let their pet cats and dogs crawl onto the bed and sleep next to them. Such a scene would previously have

Figure 13.4. Farm animals in a suburban Los Angeles neighborhood, 2002. Unna Lassiter.

Figure 13.5. Pet store signage, 2002. Unna Lassiter.

been unthinkable according to many of the women, but now they saw animals as potential companions. They were very critical of people who keep pets in poor conditions, are ignorant of the animal's needs, or hold captive wild animals that the women thought should be running free. They disapproved of those who fail to have their pets vaccinated or who allow them to reproduce at will, and discussed at some length the cost of neutering and spaying pets.

Interestingly, this ethic of care was based on the notion of animal rights. Marina explained that her traditional views had changed when a friend (in the United States) gave her some literature on animal rights and that this had led her to critically rethink the past treatment of animals in her family: "In terms of how they treated animals, I disagree with my grandparents. I mean, they had animals themselves but somehow they disregarded animals as animals as animals [*sic*], with no rights at all. So they would do things to an animal that I would never do to an animal, like throw stones at a dog . . . or kick an animal. . . . It was very easy for them to do that."

According to Suzanne Michel, this sort of ethic or politics of care is often dismissed for its household base, yet it plays an important role in the support of animal-welfare agencies and animal-rights agencies and in the development of political grassroots efforts.[20] For instance, individuals who regularly rescue cats and dogs from animal shelters and oversee their subsequent adoptions are only now becoming recognized by governmental agencies as legitimate partners in solving shelter (and pet) overpopulation. And it was also through an ethic of care, extending from traditional family values in the case of the Latinas, that they reconfigured their relationship to animals after arrival in the United States, a transformation enhanced by the satisfying social context in which these interactions took place or were imagined. It is thus no longer acceptable to kill an animal in the backyard.

The Chicanas' concern for animals was also filtered by their families: not only did they try to carefully choose their role models for shaping their attitudes toward animals, but they astutely explained how some parental attitudes toward animals had to be negotiated. Thus Louisa explained that she and her siblings had secretly plotted to have the cat neutered against their father's will, with help from their mother. Interestingly, the household's women could not bring themselves to make their father's dog undergo the same procedure, because "a dog is a man's best friend," and she explained, "you wouldn't do that to your best friend."

When Rosa, a Chicana, expressed her outrage at her father's lack of willingness to take their sick dog to the vet ("That's the way my father is. As soon as my dog gets sick or something, he just wants to throw it away and says, 'don't bother with the vet, it's not worth it.'"), many in the group concurred that her father's attitude was contemptible. Gaby told this story: "I remember my dad saying something about 'no, don't sleep with your cat, because if you sleep with your cat, he's going to eat your soul.' I've always had cats and I love my cats, they sleep with me. They were in my room, and he was always telling me: 'don't sleep with the cat because he'll eat your soul.' But I did, I love cats."

Neither this young woman's father's admonitions nor the widespread belief that cats steal souls held her back from cuddling with her feline companion.

Similar concerns for the welfare and rights of animals extended to wild animals, and a Latina said, "Animals everywhere are disappearing because we don't take good care of them." The human-animal hierarchy became more muted, and was increasingly tied to a relationship of solidarity and kinship with other earthly creatures. In response to our question about the rescue of wild animals—in this case, starving sea lions whose dying on the local beaches was widely publicized—the Chicanas insisted that we should help animals. Human assistance was obligatory not only because we can do it, but especially because "we are the only ones who can do it." Statements of support for animals were so emphatic among these women that when an older member of the group cautioned them that this might be a costly proposition, she partly recanted due to silent but clear objection: "I mean ideally we should, sure, I mean help them. I don't know. People say it's very costly to build sanctuaries for animals, and they complain how they're feeding animals instead of feeding children. The whole world goes hungry and there's this debate going on. . . . But in an ideal world we should be feeding animals and humans, I guess."

Despite the fact that this speaker was seen as a leader in the Chicana group (she was older and a recognized leader in the community), this was one instance in the discussion when others did not jump on the bandwagon. Uncharacteristically, her words were not echoed by the young women, producing a moment of slight but perceptible unease that led to her partial retraction.

The Latinas focused on the human failure to anticipate a condition (even a natural context such as El Niño) leading to the local mass starvation of sea lions. They underlined again how the ethic of care extends from familiar domestic virtues such as "running a house in good order." Finally, the decision to rescue should note hinge on which kinds of animals are suffering, with nearly all respondents saying that differences do not matter (with one exception made of hyenas, apparently because of their appearance and penchant for carrion). The Chicanas did not favor particular species, but specified that knowledgeable persons should be the ones to provide help.

Many of the women kept companion animals of a wide variety, including farm animals such as chickens and rabbits. They were critical of traditional parents or grandparents who saw such animals as an added burden and something to be disposed of if inconvenient. Such animals had come to be seen as part of the family, to be kept in the backyard or even, if they were lucky, invited onto the bed to be cuddled. Thus, although the women rejected the violence of their rural heritage, embracing more biocentric attitudes and adopting prevailing ideas about human obligations for animal welfare, they nonetheless wanted to live in households with a variety of animals linked in tradition and memory to rural ways of life (figure 13.6). In fact their attitudes were based on an ethic of care that enlarged human families to families of humans and animals, on a surprisingly equal footing, while at the same time remaining true to a Mexican syncretic worldview.[21]

Animals and Cultural Difference

Deeply normalized animal practices can become the basis for racialization, especially in world cities where rural and urban practices make contact and people from diverse origins and cultural relations to nature end up living in proximity. Dianne Walta Hart, for instance, describes how practices, including some animal-related practices, are used to justify intolerance and quotes an

Figure 13.6. A goat is sorely missed, 2002. Unna Lassiter.

African American man at the height of the most recent public debate on ille-gal immigration: "Latinos put twenty to thirty people in a home, [keep] goats, [grow] corn in the front yard, and [hang] their wash on the front fence." We and a colleague found that Filipina immigrants were acutely aware of this racialization process and adopted a stance of cultural relativism to defend their own practices and by extension their own cultural position. We saw this same pattern among the women with whom we spoke, who self-consciously tolerat-ed some cultural practices widely regarded by mainstream American culture as cruel, such as dog eating. Tolerance was extended in particular if newcomers to this country carried out the practice in question.[22]

Several Latinas pointedly argued that by criticizing others, one might run the risk of becoming criticized for the same sort of activities in return: "First you have to understand the culture and where they're coming from. And what is normal and acceptable in their society. They don't know anything else prob-ably, maybe they're newcomers here. I don't know. As an immigrant, I did a lot of stuff that wasn't . . . acceptable, or probably was weird for other people. But that's the way I was, I didn't know any other way to be. Especially here, it's all culture, it's all diverse, culturally diverse. And each culture, not race, each cul-ture, has a different way of being." Many women agreed with this position, and another went on, "It's the same case with Santeria. I mean, as much as I dis-agree with the practice of sacrificing animals, especially the way they do it . . . I mean it's a cultural and religious thing, and if you don't want them doing that, then maybe someone else's not going to want us doing something else. So we have to find an understanding of different ways of being."[23]

Because the women experienced cultural contrasts in practices and atti-tudes with heightened acuity, they were more aware of nature and of animals as social constructs. *Los Angeles Times* columnist Al Martinez recently demon-strated how animal-rights activists normalize certain kinds of behaviors toward animals but can "slip into racism in defense of a position" when they criticize a practice that they find objectionable. He replied by engaging in some racial-ization himself: "I am not inclined to beat, intimidate or barbecue my animals. Canine taquitos are never on my menu. Additionally, I am teaching [my ani-mals] basic English so that they'll be able to communicate with those who seek to empower them."[24]

It was no surprise then that the topic of cultural attitudes should be of con-cern to the women we interviewed as well. Unlike Martinez, several women defended their cultural practices—or those of other marginalized groups—on the basis of cultural survival. They could recount a number of different cultur-al practices that shocked them but which some defended. Flora, a Latina, told a story about an Asian man in Beverly Hills who had been given a puppy by his Anglo neighbor. He proceeded to fatten the dog and then had it slaughtered and served up as a meal—that he offered to his outraged neighbor. While our storyteller was indignant, she added, "He didn't do it with a bad intention. It's his culture. It may look bad, but everybody has their own culture." Silvia argued that dogs are like possessions: "So much trouble for a dog. Wasn't it their dog?" In supporting such practices, the women expressed various shades of utilitarianism and dominionism in defense of cultural identity, despite the close bonds with companion animals they later described and despite an understanding of animals as sentient beings deserving of respect that they gained in the United States.

Although their experience of cultural difference made these women sympathetic to other immigrants whose animal practices ran afoul of dominant U.S. norms, they were firm in their conviction that newcomers had to learn what was and what was not acceptable and soon comply with these standards. Moreover, some sorts of practices—even those associated with their own culture such as horse tripping at rodeos and dogfighting—were seen as simply unacceptable. Several Latinas were critical of people in the United States who fish for the sport of it, know little about the fish they catch, and do not eat them. They were particularly outraged by the fact that children were taught to fish and hunt for sport. They set this up in contrast to their familial experiences, especially in their native country, where these activities are a necessary part of everyday life and where everyone knows what animals can and cannot be eaten.

Contradictory convictions that new immigrants must conform but that American practices are problematic also suggest a creative process of selectively rejecting and accepting both traditional ways and values characteristic of their new setting. This echoes Gloria Anzaldúa, who chose the sacrifice of an animal to represent the point of origin of the transcendental process of acculturation: "La mestiza has gone from being the sacrificial goat to becoming the officiating priestess at the crossroads. . . . I am participating in the creation of yet another culture, a new story to explain the world and our participation in it, a new value system with images and symbols that connect us to each other and to the planet."[25]

A recent exhibit of photographs in Los Angeles illustrated the process of Latino acculturation and celebrated people's everyday efforts to survive and revive their neighborhoods. Not all the images were indicative of immigrant progress; some clearly portrayed the ingrained poverty and hardship of immigrant Latino neighborhood landscapes. Some Latino groups felt that the exhibit portrayed Latinos negatively. An image that provoked particular hostility was that of a dead dog, killed in a dogfight, lying in an alley. Not surprisingly, given the iconic (if contradictory) status of dogs in American society, critics were very quick to point out that this behavior was not condoned in the broader Latino community. But the exhibit also showed pet horses and farm animals tucked into backyards, reflecting how, in Los Angeles, Latino households are customizing the traditional Mexican yarda and incorporating animals into everyday neighborhood life. Thus lively Latino and Chicano perspectives on animals rooted in a distinct border culture are reshaping and reviving the urban landscape and—as the roosters crow—adding new sounds as well.[26]

Our conversations about animals with low-income inner-city Latinas and Chicanas in Los Angeles ranged widely, covering such topics as their interactions with different sorts of animals, knowledge of animal biology and behavior, attitudes toward animals, and normative ideas about human-animal relations. Given the modest economic status of participants and rural origins of many, we expected that the women's attitudes would lean toward utilitarianism and dominionism. Such attitudes were indeed voiced, but in highly specific contexts such as economic necessity. The Latinas expressed clearly, for instance, how in Mexico extreme poverty and concerns for survival precluded the sort of consideration afforded animals in the United States. This situation is changing; in 1995 the first-ever Latin American antibullfight conference was held in Mexico, and the award-winning film *Amores Perros* triggered protests in Mexico over dogfighting and its sociocultural context.[27] But the Latinas did uphold the right of other cultures to retain some practices, either because they had not yet acculturated or because they did not want their own culture to be criticized. Critical physical and cultural human needs thus underpinned the structure of their attitudes.

Putting traditional beliefs about their expendability aside, these women have brought at least some animals from the barnyard into the backyard, or perhaps the front yard and the LA-style yarda—a setting Rodolfo Acuña has described as a Chicano innovation.[28] In the context of a rapidly changing social environment, animals serve as familiar landscape elements, reminding household residents of home or visits to family farms in Mexico, but also encouraging their children to adopt new attitudes toward nature. And at least some animals had received an invitation to come indoors, enjoy more intimate companionship, and share in the life of the family.

Attitudes are transformed through necessity and survival, including cultural survival. They contribute to redefining the landscape, allowing an inner-city neighborhood to become a way station where people enjoy cultural safety but can also try on, or express, different attitudes.[29] This research points to the necessity of considering informal practices, such as human-animal interactions, through which new attitudes might first be expressed and how they come to be inscribed onto the dynamic urban landscape of Los Angeles.

Appendix A: Profile of Focus Group Participants

Chicana participants

Participant	Age	LA residency in years, followed by place of birth if not LA	Educational achievement	Type of animal experience
Isabel	19	19	Some college	Pets
Louisa	23	23	Associate degree	Farm, pets
Lena	19	19 (Mexico)	Some college	Farm, pets, pet store
Carlotta	19	8 (Washington)	Some college	Farm, pets
Rosa	18	18	High school diploma	Farm, pets
Gaby	19	19	Some college	Pets
Marietta	18	18	Some college	Pets

Latina participants

Participant	Age	LA residency in years, followed by place of birth if not LA	Educational achievement	Type of animal experience
Silvia	n.d.	10 (Mexico)	No high school diploma	Farm, pets
Susana	n.d.	10 (Mexico)	No high school diploma	Farm, pets
Flora	30	30	No high school diploma	Farm, pets
Veronica	36	13 (Mexico)	No high school diploma	Farm, pets
Ofelia	38	20 (Mexico)	No high school diploma	Pets
Filipa	39	13 (Mexico)	No high school diploma	Pets
Juliet	42	17 (Mexico)	Some college	Pets
Elena	23	7 (Mexico)	High school diploma	Farm, pets
Dolores	62	33 (Mexico)	No high school diploma	Farm, pets, animal clinic
Marina	35	35 (Guatemala)	Bachelor's degree	Pets

Note: n.d. = no data.

Appendix B: Demographic Questionnaire

Thank you for participating in this discussion on animals. Your opinions are of great help to us. Before we begin, please tell us

Overall, how well do you know the others who are in the room this evening?
      (not at all, somewhat, or very well?)
How old are you?
What is the last school year/grade you completed?
How long have you lived in Los Angeles?
Where were you born?
Are you a member of an animal or animal rights organization?
Have you ever worked with animals?
      (on a farm; in a stable; in a pet store; at a vet; in a park or zoo;
      in a slaughterhouse; elsewhere)
Have you ever owned a pet or raised animals? If so, what kind?
      (a dog; cat; bird; snake; or turtle; other)

Thank you.

Epilogue

The Present as History

ROBERT GOTTLIEB

L os Angeles and the environment. Place those words together and the worst is often assumed. Some would argue that Los Angeles is better characterized as an anti-environment. The litany of environmental problems seems endless. After the passage of the 1970 Clean Air Act, Los Angeles County had more days when air quality standards were exceeded than any other region, until Houston finally began to challenge its supremacy as top air polluter in the late 1990s. Los Angeles residents experience the longest commutes on the most congested freeways. Many Los Angeles neighborhoods along the path of the fifty-three-mile Los Angeles River, in places such as Maywood, South Gate, and Lynwood, confront a graffiti-marked, garbage-strewn concrete channel. "Don't fish, don't swim" signs are posted at the beaches, particularly after the first rains of the season, which locals call the Big Flush. Los Angeles is also reviled as the West's resource imperialist, whose prime water agency has long sought to accommodate regional growth by securing ever more distant water supplies. And Los Angeles is perhaps most identified with its endless sprawl, an ever expanding area that the *Los Angeles Times*, in its headiest booster days, once called "The Great Pacific Littoral."

When I first came to Los Angeles in 1969, I encountered two representations, both issued by an irreverent counterculture group that effectively characterized Los Angeles in these ways. The first had a hip-looking Hollywood type with a shark-tooth necklace standing in front of Los Angeles City Hall, with the caption, "I breathe for taste. I live in Los Angeles, California." The second card had a businessman with a briefcase wading in the Pacific Ocean looking puzzled. This caption read, "Los Angeles? But where is it?"

Over the next three decades that question of how to find and define Los

Angeles as a place, and particularly as an environment, preoccupied me, whether as researcher, teacher, policy person, environmental activist, citizen, or resident. Part of that search seemed straightforward: environmental lessons from Los Angeles appeared transparent. Too much sprawl, too many cars, too much polluted groundwater, too few parks, too much air pollution, too much fast food.

Though Los Angeles is often defined as "placeless," I wonder if those lessons are the only lessons Los Angeles might have to offer about the environment. Perhaps other lessons can be drawn from Los Angeles' rich and fabled environmental history. We may be witnessing a change in environmental discourse as well, where a new kind of urban environmental and community awareness is taking root.

Retreat of the Water Buffaloes

From 1980 through the end of 1987, I served on the board of directors of the Metropolitan Water District (MWD) of Southern California, arguably the largest and most powerful water agency in the country. The MWD had long sought new and increasingly distant sources of water to supply continually increasing numbers of far-flung customers. The MWD had been established in 1928 to secure Colorado River water for thirteen cities in what was then called the coastal plain of Southern California. Today, the MWD has stretched its service area considerably, functioning as a supraregional water importer and wholesaler serving twenty-seven member agencies who provide water for 17 million people in six Southern California counties.

When I joined the fifty-one-member MWD board, I was deeply involved in research about the critical role of water in promoting urban growth agendas, especially the resource-based coalitions that so heavily influenced water policy, and the implications of that policy for urban development. I quickly discovered that the link between water development and urban growth was a widely accepted assumption of water policy. But what astounded me was how deeply embedded the development culture had become at MWD, which, after all, was still a public agency. Board members made little distinction between their public role and the agendas of their private counterparts. This was the very definition of the water industry, the name of this confluence of private interests and public agencies. Joining the board of directors of an agency such as the MWD was like a rite of passage to this exclusive club of water decision makers and private beneficiaries.

Shortly after I joined the board, a referendum was placed on the ballot in California to stop the construction of a major water conveyance facility, the Peripheral Canal. The canal was designed to bring water around the Sacramento Bay Delta in northern California to the big farms on the west side of the Central Valley and over the Tehachapi Mountains into Southern California. I opposed the Peripheral Canal both for environmental reasons and for its stimulus to further sprawl, but was almost always outvoted fifty to one. The board chairman at the time, who represented the city of Burbank, was livid at this opposition; he would constantly refer to the canal as the "final solution" and would suggest that opposition in Southern California was tantamount to heresy. Directors, a number of them thirty- and forty-year veterans of the water industry, would refuse to greet me in the hallway, lowering their heads as they passed by the infidel. At one board meeting, the chairman and another director, a long-time developer, stage-managed an attack on my positions and myself. They called for legal action for what they argued was my intentional refusal to acknowledge, as they saw it, the irrefutable fact that Southern California was in a water crisis. The crisis rhetoric used at the time was quite extraordinary; at one television debate I had with another director, he argued forcefully and in all seriousness that Southern Californians might have to drink water from toilet bowls if somehow the anti–Peripheral Canal referendum were to pass.

By election day the Southern California water industry had gathered support for its position from the media, elected officials, the developers, and literally everyone else who constituted a who's who of the Southern California business and political leadership. Yet, amazingly, 40 percent of Southern Californians still voted against the canal. This, along with extraordinary majorities of 90 percent or more in northern California, sent the Peripheral Canal down to defeat.

The Peripheral Canal election proved to be a turning point for the water industry. During the next two decades, water policy reached an impasse. The water industry belief in imported water—the idea that new sources could always be located to support continued urban expansion and an export-oriented industrial agriculture—was in serious retreat though not fully laid to rest. Nevertheless, it had slowly dawned on some water industry participants that a new water discourse was emerging and that imported-water advocates were increasingly seen as "water buffaloes" rather than respected leaders.

By the new century, some important changes had taken root. The MWD had new leadership, including a Latino general manager and his top assistant, another Latino, who promoted the view that the MWD was also about community partnerships and environmental justice. But this had not yet become a revolution; the MWD also found itself in the difficult and not-yet-resolved dilemma of seeking to hold on to some of its long-held goals for water and growth while recognizing that the language and strategies of water had fundamentally changed. Instead of talking about imported water, the MWD focused on stretching existing supplies and, most notably, sought new supplies through water exchanges and trade-offs. No longer able to count on an expanding water supply pie, the MWD made reallocation rather than new allocations the order of the day. In some ways, this represented a tactical adjustment rather than a strategic shift: water markets could still represent a new source of supply and thus ensure that more water allowed for new growth.

However, the water industry also became subject to other demands, including a growing concern about water quality. During the 1980s and 1990s, when fears about water quality intensified dramatically with reports about contaminated groundwater wells and the toxicity of disinfection by-products, the water industry strongly resisted efforts to impose increased regulation. But a few water industry figures, including those at the MWD, began to recognize that water quality issues required different kinds of approaches, which looked at the causes of water quality degradation and ways to treat the water to end exclusive reliance on a chlorine-based system. For much of the twentieth century, the water agency focus on water quality matters had been limited to nagging concerns about taste and odor. Now public health considerations were forcing not only a reevaluation of treatment methods but an attempt to address the source of the contamination as well.

In that light, a new language of watershed management also began to force its way into the deliberations of the water industry. Water officials reluctantly came to the conclusion that watershed issues inevitably had both water quality and water supply implications. In Los Angeles, the interest in watershed management became a focus for the MWD, partly because of legislative requirements that obliged the agency to take a role in the watershed issues associated with the Los Angeles River. While the MWD was rather slow to enter the debates about how a watershed approach actually changed the dynamics of water policy, a coalition of community and environmental groups emerged in the 1990s to promote a vision of watershed restoration and community renewal. As a consequence, a very different kind of debate emerged about water policy that took as its starting point how to meet community and watershed needs rather than the assumption about growth and development and securing distant imported supplies that had so long dominated the discourse about water policy. Though the jury is still out concerning outcomes, the terrain has clearly shifted.

Welcome to the Foodshed

Food issues provide a second illustration about a changing environmental awareness in Los Angeles. The relevance of food to this shift might at first seem rather obscure. The Los Angeles region, after all, is the home of the first fast-food drive-in. Los Angeles is also the home of giant doughnut signs and Golden Arches in every neighborhood. It has a large food-processing sector, and its retail sector often takes the lead in identifying emerging industry trends, such as the abandonment of inner-city store locations in favor of suburban and exurban sites, as well as the rapid regional and even national consolidation of chains. Through the 1980s and 1990s, Los Angeles also experienced a number of food-insecurity indicators, such as the growing number of people who became dependent on food banks and food pantries as a source of food, the lack of access to fresh and affordable food, and the increase in obesity and diet-related concerns. One small example of this trend was recently traced in a food-mapping exercise undertaken by a community organization in south central Los Angeles. The exercise revealed that in a two-square-mile area in one inner-city neighborhood there were fifty-three restaurants; fifty-two of these were fast-food outlets, and only one was a sit-down restaurant. Other findings pointed to the lack of quality in food markets in the area.[1]

The search for an environmental ethic of place, urban or otherwise, figures prominently in analyzing food system issues. How and where food is grown; how and where it is processed and manufactured, packaged and shipped; where and how it is sold or made available; where people eat and what they eat all constitute a food system. The dominant food system that has emerged in the past three or four decades is best characterized as a global food system, one that has increasingly reduced and eventually eliminated any connection to place. In the process, a food-growing, food-making, and food-consuming experience has been created that is the same everywhere, anyplace, anytime. It is a food system that has horrendous environmental consequences, including the way food is grown, the loss of biodiversity and crop and seed diversity, the occupational hazards in the way food is processed, and the use of hazardous chemicals through each of its stages. It is a food system that has significant public health implications. These stem from problems of access to food as well as the quality of the food we eat. What is offered in those fifty-two south central Los Angeles restaurants? It is a food system that is socially and economically unjust. Small family farmers, including those who ring the Los Angeles basin, are losing their livelihood and their vocation in the face of food system restructuring. The food-processing workforce faces declining wages and eroding working conditions. The fast-food industry has been at the forefront in creating a low-wage workforce. This new food system has exacerbated the problem of lack of food access in low-income communities, where food costs more even though it is not as fresh or healthy or culturally appropriate as elsewhere.

While Los Angeles does not represent a headquarters city for the global food system—in fact, one could argue that this dispersed, globalized system of production and distribution has eliminated any connection to place—food issues in Los Angeles do reflect various aspects of that system. However, groundbreaking food initiatives in Los Angeles have helped sustain the development of an alternative community food system. These initiatives in turn have reinforced and extended the sense of place that has emerged in Los Angeles among various groups and constituencies.

As opposed to a globalized system whose dominant metaphors are distance and durability, the metaphors for a community food system, as sociologist Harriet Friedmann has argued, can be defined as seasonality and locality.[2] The distances between where food is grown and where it is consumed have grown exponentially in the past three or four decades as food growing, production, and distribution have become globally dispersed. At the same time, the durability of products has been a result of the increased processing that occurs (such as a potato transformed into a chemically processed potato chip or a cryogenically frozen french fry). Locality and seasonality, on the other hand, signify a direct link between local or regional producers and local consumers, who come to appreciate the source of the food, the potential diversity of food crops and diets, the reduced distance between where food is produced and where it is consumed, and the social capital associated with farming as a local or regional activity.

Los Angeles, like other cities, has been the site for an increasing number of important community food system initiatives, such as neighborhood farmers' markets, community and school gardens, and even modest attempts to create new urban farms. Some initiatives, such as community-supported agriculture, seek to establish a new community of interests between farmer and consumer while also providing modest protection for a small farmer against the economic stresses of a concentrated land and food-production system. Organizations such as California's Community Alliance for Family Farmers speak of a new food ethic, both for farmers, who can develop a land ethic and a connection to farming as vocation, and for consumers, or "eaters," who establish a different connection to the source of their food as well as its quality and variation.

In Los Angeles, this new kind of food ethic and community food system approach has emerged in some interesting and exciting ways. One compelling example involves the development of a farm-to-school model first implemented as a farmers' market fruit and salad bar at an elementary school in Santa Monica, which used the farmers' market as a venue for establishing the direct farm-to-cafeteria link. Quality, a core food-ethic value, has been key to the farm-to-school program. Not only is the produce made available in such a program fresh, but its taste and variety become part of providing a very different

kind of food experience. At several schools that have a salad bar and school garden program, produce harvested from the garden is displayed. This has also
encouraged students to try things they have never tasted before. Teachers and
staff can purchase a salad bar meal as well (and many have). Parents have even
asked for permission to buy a salad bar lunch and eat with their children. At
the same time, knowledge about where the food comes from—a sense of place
related to a connection to the food—is further extended through farm and
farmers' market tours, with a few teachers seeking to integrate the food experience into their science and nutrition curriculum. The program's success can
then be measured not just in the tremendous participation and the improved
nutrition for the children but in how the program has changed the nature of
the food experience. And it helps establish, as have other community food initiatives, a new food consciousness and a reawakened environmental ethic of
place.

Today in Los Angeles, with its enormous diversity, where we are more likely to identify the differences rather than the sameness in neighborhoods and
cultures, we can find an emerging environmental ethic of place, if not at the
heart of Los Angeles' identity, at least at its margins. There are now advocates
for building community, remaking watersheds, reducing the distance between
food grown and food consumed, and reinventing nature in the heart of the city.
Asking a different set of questions and seeking to identify alternative lessons
can help shed light on why Los Angeles has for so long been considered an anti-
environment and suggest how a new environmental discourse—and sense of
place—might be realized.[3]

Notes

Introduction: The Metropolitan Nature of Los Angeles

1. William Cronon, *Nature's Metropolis: Chicago and the Great West* (New York: Norton, 1991); Ted Steinberg, *Down to Earth: Nature's Role in American History* (New York: Oxford University Press, 2002); Donald Worster, *Nature's Economy: A History of Ecological Ideas* (New York: Cambridge University Press, 1985; repr. 1994); John Richards, *The Unending Frontier: An Environmental History of the Early Modern Period* (Berkeley: University of California Press, 2003).

2. Mike Davis, *Ecology of Fear: Los Angeles and the Imagination of Disaster* (New York: Metropolitan Books, 1998); Robert Dawson and Grey Brechin, *Farewell, Promised Land: Waking from the California Dream* (Berkeley: University of California Press, 1999); David Stradling, *Smokestacks and Progressives: Environmentalists, Engineers, and Air Quality in America, 1881–1951* (Baltimore: Johns Hopkins University Press, 1999); Andrew Hurley, ed., *Common Fields: An Environmental History of St. Louis* (St. Louis: Missouri Historical Society Press, 1997).

3. Samuel P. Hays, *Explorations in Environmental History* (Pittsburgh: University of Pittsburgh Press, 1998); Joel Tarr, *The Search for the Ultimate Sink: Urban Pollution in Historical Perspective* (Akron, OH: University of Akron Press, 1996); David Naguib Pellow, *Garbage Wars: The Struggle for Environmental Justice in Chicago* (Cambridge, MA: MIT Press, 2002); Laura Pulido, *Environmentalism and Economic Justice: Two Chicano Struggles in the Southwest* (Tucson: University of Arizona Press, 1996); Andrew Hurley, *Environmental Inequalities: Class, Race, and Industrial Pollution in Gary, Indiana, 1945–1980* (Chapel Hill: University of North Carolina Press, 1995).

4. Cronon, *Nature's Metropolis*; Ari Kelman, *A River and Its City: The Nature of Landscape in New Orleans* (Berkeley: University of California Press, 2003); Karl Haglund, *Inventing the Charles River* (Cambridge, MA: MIT Press, 2002); Matthew Gandy, *Concrete and Clay: Reworking Nature in New York City* (Cambridge, MA: MIT Press, 2002); Matthew Klingle, *Urban by Nature: Seattle and the Making of the American Environmental Metropolis* (forthcoming).

5. William Moore's diaries are in the Solano-Reeve Collection, Huntington Library, San Marino, CA.

6. Elwood Mead, "The Agricultural Situation in California," in *Report of Irrigation Investigations in California*, Bulletin no. 100, United States Office of Experiment Stations (Washington DC: Government Printing Office, 1901), 26. For a similar assessment from the nineteenth century, see John S. Hittell, *The Resources of California: Comprising Agriculture, Mining, Geography, Climate &c, and the Past and Future Development of the State* (New York: A. Roman, 1869); for the 1920s, see Chamber of Commerce publications such as the series *Los Angeles: Center of an Agricultural Empire*.

7. Frank Meline, *Los Angeles: Metropolis of the West* (Los Angeles: Frank Meline, 1929), 14. See also George Baker, "Urgent Need for Park Felt on the East Side," *CMD Magazine*, August 1927.

8. William Fulton, *Guide to California Planning* (Point Arena, CA: Solano Press Books, 1991).

9. Dana W. Bartlett, *The Better City: A Sociological Study of a Modern City* (Los Angeles: Neuner, 1907), 191.

10. *Parks, Playgrounds and Beaches for the Los Angeles Region: A Report Submitted to the Citizens' Committee on Parks, Playgrounds and Beaches* (Los Angeles: Citizens' Committee on Parks, Playgrounds and Beaches, 1930).

11. Greg Hise and William Deverell, *Eden by Design: The 1930 Olmsted-Bartholomew Plan for the Los Angeles Region* (Berkeley: University of California Press, 2000).

12. Los Angeles Area Chamber of Commerce (LAACC), *Stenographer's Notes, 1922* (December 14) in the LAACC Collection, University of Southern California, Department of Special Collections. For an interpretation of this development type, see Greg Hise, "'Nature's Workshop': Industry and Urban Expansion in Southern California, 1900–1950," *Journal of Historical Geography* 27, no. 1 (2001): 74–92; essays by Mike Davis and Becky M. Nicolaides in *Metropolis in the Making: Los Angeles in the 1920s*, ed. Tom Sitton and William Deverell (Berkeley: University of California Press, 2001).

13. Charles Mulford Robinson, *The City Beautiful: Report of the Municipal Art Commission for the City of Los Angeles* (Los Angeles, 1909); Community Redevelopment Agency, *Downtown Strategic Plan, Los Angeles* (Los Angeles, 1993).

14. Michael Leccese and Kathleen McCormick, eds., *Charter of the New Urbanism* (New York: McGraw-Hill, 2000).

15. "Hahn Steps Up Efforts to Block Landfill's Expansion into L.A.," *Los Angeles Times*, March 13, 2003.

16. For Los Angeles, see the projects and reports TreePeople, http://www.treepeople.org/, has sponsored, especially the Rethinking Our Cities initiative; the University of Southern California Center for Sustainable Cities studies assessing access to and distribution of park and recreation space in the county, http://www.usc.edu/dept/geography/ESPE/; and ongoing efforts to recast the region's watersheds as urban amenities, most notably the work of Friends of the Los Angeles River http://www.folar.org/.

Southern California, 1900

1. *Art Work on Southern California*, text signed in facsimile by Lou V. Chapin (San Francisco: California Photogravure, 1900).

Chapter 1: Political Ecology of Prehistoric Los Angeles

1. See, for example, John L. Bean and Charles R. Smith, "Gabrielino," in *Handbook of North American Indians*, ed. William C. Sturdevant (Washington DC: Smithsonian Institution, 1978), 8:538–49; Bernice E. Johnston, *California's Gabrielino Indians*. Publications of the Frederick Webb Hodge Anniversary Publication Fund 8 (Los Angeles: Southwest Museum, 1962); Alfred L. Kroeber, *Handbook of the Indians of California* (originally published as Bulletin No. 78 of the Bureau of American Ethnology, Washington DC: Smithsonian Institution, 1925; repr., New York: Dover Books, 1976), citations are to the Dover edition; William McCawley, *The First Angelinos, The Gabrielino Indians of Los Angeles* (Banning, CA: Malki Museum/Ballena Press Cooperative, 1996).

2. McCawley, *First Angelinos*.

3. Kroeber, *Handbook*.

4. Kroeber, Alfred L., *Anthropology* (New York: Harcourt-Brace, 1948), 811.

5. Edwin F. Walker, *Five Prehistoric Sites in Los Angeles County, California*. Publications of the Fredrick Webb Hodge Anniversary Publication Fund 4 (Los Angeles: Southwest Museum, 1951), 2.

6. Kroeber, *Handbook*, 551.

7. John J. Rawls, *Indians of California* (Norman: University of Oklahoma Press, 1984), 54.

8. Walker, *Five Prehistoric Sites*, 2.

9. Richard B. Lee and Irven DeVore, eds., *Man the Hunter* (Chicago: Aldine, 1968); Robert L. Kelly, *The Foraging Spectrum: Diversity in Hunter-Gatherer Lifeways* (Washington DC: Smithsonian Institution, 1995).

10. Robert L. Bettinger, *Hunter-Gatherers, Archaeological and Evolutionary Theory* (New York: Plenum, 1991), 48.

11. Lowell J. Bean and Harry Lawton, "Some Explanations of the Rise of Cultural Complexity in Native California with Comments on Proto-Agriculture and Agriculture," in *Native Californians: A Theoretical Perspective*, ed. Lowell J. Bean and Thomas C. Blackburn (Ramona, CA: Ballena, 1976): 19–48; esp. 46.

12. Bean and Lawton, "Some Explanations." See also Chester D. King, "Chumash Inter-village Economic Exchange," in Bean and Blackburn, *Native Californians*, 289–318; Chester D. King, *Evolution of Chumash Society: A Comparative Study of Artifacts Used for Social System Maintenance in the Santa Barbara Channel Region Before A.D. 1804* (New York: Garland, 1990).

13. Brian M. Fagan, *Ancient North America*, 2nd ed. (New York: Thames and Hudson, 1995).

14. McCawley, *First Angelinos*.

15. Brian D. Haley, and Larry R. Wilcoxon, "Anthropology and the Making of Chumash Tradition, *Current Anthropology* 38, no. 5 (1997): 761–94.

16. Thomas C. Blackburn and Kat Anderson, *Before the Wilderness: Environmental Management by Native Californians* (Menlo Park, CA: Ballena, 1993).

17. Chester D. King, "Prehistoric Native American Cultural Sites in the Santa Monica Mountains." (report prepared for the Santa Monica Mountains and Seashore Foundation, and National Park Service, Western Region, 1994; on file, Santa Monica Mountains National Recreation Area).

18. Roy H. Pearce, *Savagism and Civilization* (Berkeley: University of California Press, 1989).

19. Mark E. Basgall, "Resource Intensification Among Hunter-Gatherers: Acorn Economies in Prehistoric California," *Research in Economic Anthropology* 9 (1987): 21–52; see also Jack M. Broughton, "Declines in Mammalian Foraging Efficiency during the Late Holocene, San Francisco Bay, California," *Journal of Anthropological Archaeology* 13 (1994): 371–401; Jack M. Broughton, "Late Holocene Resource Intensification in the Sacramento Valley, California: The Vertebrate Evidence," *Journal of Archaeological Science* 21 (1994): 501–14; Jack M. Broughton, "Widening Diet Breadth, Declining Foraging Efficiency, and Prehistoric Harvest Pressure: Ichthyofaunal Evidence from the Emeryville Shellmound, California," *Antiquity* 71 (1997): 845–62; Jack M. Broughton, "Resource Depression and Intensification During the Late Holocene, San Francisco Bay," *Anthropological Records* 32 University of California Publications (Berkeley, CA, 1999); Jack M. Broughton and Donald K. Grayson, "Diet

Breadth, Adaptive Change, and the White Mountains Fauna," *Journal of Archaeological Science* 20 (1993): 331–36; Jack M. Broughton and James F. O'Connell, "On Evolutionary Ecology, Selectionist Archaeology, and Behavioral Archaeology," *American Antiquity* 64 (1999): 153–65; L. Mark Raab, "Optimal Foraging Analysis of Prehistoric Shellfish Collecting on San Clemente Island, California," *Journal of Ethnobiology* 12 (1992): 63–80; L. Mark Raab and Daniel O. Larson, "The Medieval Climatic Anomaly and Punctuated Cultural Evolution in Coastal Southern California," *American Antiquity* 62 (1997): 319–36; L. Mark Raab, Judith F. Porcasi, Katherine Bradford, and Andrew Yatsko, "Debating Cultural Evolution: Regional Implication of Fishing Intensification at Eel Point, San Clemente Island," *Pacific Coast Archaeological Society Quarterly* 31 (1995): 3–27.

20. L. Mark Raab, "Debating Southern California Coastal Prehistory: Political Economy vs. Resource Intensification," *Journal of California and Great Basin Anthropology* 18 (1996): 64–80.

21. Mark E. Basgall, "Resource Intensification Among Hunter-Gatherers: Acorn Economies in Prehistoric California," *Research in Economic Anthropology* 9 (1987): 21–52.

22. Eric Wohlgemuth, "Resource Intensification in Prehistoric Centeral California: Evidence from Archaeobotanical Data," *Journal of California and Great Basin Anthropology* 18 (1996): 81–103. See also, for instance, Brian F. Byrd and Seetha N. Reddy, "Late Holocene Adaptations along the Northern San Diego Coast: New Perspectives on Old Paradigms," in *Catalysts to Complexity, Late Holocene Societies of the California Coast*, ed. Jon M. Erlandson and Terry L. Jones (University of California, Los Angeles, 2002), 6:41–62.

23. Broughton, "Resource Depression"; Broughton and O'Connell, "Evolutionary Ecology."

24. Charles E. Kay, "Afterword: False Gods, Ecological Myths and Biological Reality," in *Wilderness and Political Ecology*, ed. Charles E. Kay and Randy T. Simmons (Salt Lake City: University of Utah Press, 2002), 238–61; on resource availability, see Broughton, "Widening Diet Breadth"; Broughton, "Resource Depression."

25. William Preston, "Serpent in Eden: Dispersal of Foreign Diseases Into Pre-Mission California, *Journal of California and Great Basin Anthropology* 18 (1996): 2–37.

26. Patricia M. Lambert, "Health in Prehistoric Populations of the Santa Barbara Channel Islands," *American Antiquity* 58 (1993): 509–22; Patricia M. Lambert and Phillip L. Walker, "Physical Anthropological Evidence for the Evolution of Social Complexity in Coastal Southern California," *Antiquity* 65 (1991): 963–73; Phillip L. Walker, "Porotic Hyperostosis in a Marine-Dependent California Indian Population," *American Journal of Physical Anthropology* 69 (1986): 345–54; Phillip L. Walker, "Cranial Injuries as Evidence of Violence in Prehistoric Southern California," *American Journal of Physical Anthropology* 80 (1989): 313–23; Phillip L. Walker, "The Effects of European Contact on the Health of Alta California Indians," in *Columbian Consequences*, ed. D. H. Thomas, Archaeological and Historical Perspectives on the Spanish Borderlands West (Washington DC: Smithsonian Institution Press, 1989): 1:349–64; Phillip L. Walker and Patricia M. Lambert, "Skeletal Evidence for Stress During a Period of Cultural Change in Prehistoric California," *Journal of Paleopathology*, Monographic Publication no. 1, ed. L. Capasso (Chieti, Italy: Marino Solfanelli, 1989), 207–12.

27. On the skeletal data, see L. Mark Raab, "Debating Southern California Coastal Prehistory." Lambert, "Health in Prehistoric Populations," 517.

28. Jonathon T. Overpeck, "Warm Climate Surprises," *Science* 271 (1996): 1820–21.

29. Terry L. Jones, Gary M. Brown, L. Mark Raab, Janet L. McVickar, William G. Spaulding, Douglas J. Kennett, Andrew York, and Phillip L. Walker, "Environmental Imperatives Reconsidered: Demographic Crises in Western North America during the Medieval Cli-

matic Anomaly," *Current Anthropology* 40 (April 1999): 137–70; Raab and Larson, "Medieval Climatic Anomaly."

30. Raab and Larson, "Medieval Climatic Anomaly."

Chapter 2: The Los Angeles Prairie

1. See, for example, Sterling C. Keeley, ed., *The California Chaparral: Paradigms Reexamined*, Natural History Museum of Los Angeles County Science Series no. 34 (Los Angeles, 1989); John F. O'Leary, "Californian Coastal Sage Scrub: General Characteristics and Considerations for Biological Conservation," in *Endangered Plant Communities of Southern California*, Southern California Botanists Special Publication no. 3, ed. Allan A. Schoenherr (Claremont, CA, 1990): 24–41; Richard A. Minnich and Raymond J. Dezzani, "Historical Decline of Coastal Sage Scrub in the Riverside-Perris Plain, California," *Western Birds* 29 (1998): 366–85; C. M. Thomas and S. D. Davis, "Recovery Patterns of Three Chaparral Shrub Species After Wildfire," *Oecologia* 80 (1989): 309–20; Jon E. Keeley and C. J. Fotheringham, "Trace Gas Emissions and Smoke-induced Seed Germination," *Science* 276 (1997): 1248–50; Kevin Crooks and Michael E. Soulé, "Mesopredator Release and Avifaunal Extinctions in a Fragmented System," *Nature* 400 (1999): 563–66; Jon E. Keeley, C. J. Fotheringham, and Marco Morais, "Reexamining Fire Suppression Impacts on Brushland Fire Regimes," *Science* 284 (1999): 1829–83.

2. Peter H. Raven and Daniel I. Axelrod, *Origin and Relationships of the California Flora* (Berkeley: University of California Press, 1978); Richard M. Cowling, Philip W. Rundel, Byron B. Lamont, Mary Kalin Arroyo, and Margarita Arianoutsou, "Plant Diversity in Mediterranean-Climate Regions," *Trends in Ecology and Evolution* 11 (1996): 362–66; Peter R. Dallman, *Plant Life in the World's Mediterranean Climates* (Berkeley: University of California Press, 1998).

3. R. C. Rossiter, "Ecology of the Mediterranean Annual-Type Pasture," *Advances in Agronomy* 18 (1961): 1–56; Louise E. Jackson, "Ecological Origins of California's Mediterranean Grasses," *Journal of Biogeography* 12 (1985): 349–61; Mark A. Blumler, "Invasion and Transformation of California's Valley Grassland, a Mediterranean Analogue Ecosystem," in *Ecological Relations in Historical Times: Human Impact and Adaptation*, ed. Robin A. Butlin and Neil Roberts (Oxford: Blackwell, 1995), 308–32.

4. On what the Spanish found, see Peter H. Raven, "The California Flora," in *Terrestrial Vegetation of California*, California Native Plant Society Special Publication no. 9, ed. Michael G. Barbour and Jack Major (Sacramento, CA, 1977), 109–37; Raven and Axelrod, *Origin and Relationships*. California's prairies are also frequently referred to as grasslands. However, the vast majority of grass species in these grasslands are recent invaders from the Mediterranean region. Forbs and wildflowers, rather than grasses, constituted the majority of native species in this ecosystem at the time of European settlement. Therefore, the term prairie is a preferred descriptor; see Paula M. Schiffman, "Mammal Burrowing, Erratic Rainfall and the Annual Lifestyle in the California Prairie: Is it Time for a Paradigm Shift?" in *2nd Interface Between Ecology and Land Development in California*, U.S. Geological Survey Open-File Report 00-62, ed. Jon E. Keeley, Melanie Baer-Keeley, and C. J. Fotherinham (Sacramento, CA, 2000), 153–60.

5. Ted L. Hanes, "California Chaparral," 417–69, Harold A. Mooney, "Southern Coastal Scrub," 471–89, James R. Griffin, "Oak Woodland," 383–415, all in Barbour and Major, *Terrestrial Vegetation*; Ronald D. Quinn, "The Status of Walnut Forests and Woodlands (*Juglans californica*) in Southern California," in Schoenherr, *Endangered Plant Communities*, 42–54,

Peter A. Bowler, "Riparian Woodland: An Endangered Habitat in Southern California," 80–97, both in Schoenherr, *Endangered Plant Communities*; Allan A. Schoenherr, *A Natural History of California* (Berkeley: University of California Press, 1992); Blake Gumprecht, *The Los Angeles River* (Baltimore: Johns Hopkins University Press, 1999).

6. Norman Myers, Russell A. Mittermeier, Cristina G. Mittermeier, Gustavo A. B. da Fonseca, and Jennifer Kent, "Biodiversity Hotspots for Conservation Priorities," *Nature* 403 (2000): 853–58.

7. Alfred. L. Kroeber, *Handbook of the Indians of California* (originally published as Bulletin No. 78 of the Bureau of American Ethnology, Washington DC: Smithsonian Institution, 1925; repr. New York: Dover, 1976); William McCawley, *The First Angelinos: The Gabrielino Indians of Los Angeles* (Banning, CA: Malki Museum/Ballena Press Cooperative, 1996); John R. Johnson, "The Indians of Mission San Fernando," in *Mission San Fernando, Rey De España, 1797–1997*, ed. Doyce B. Nunis Jr. (Los Angeles: Historical Society of Southern California, 1997), 249–90; M. Kat Anderson, Michael G. Barbour, and Valerie Wentworth, "A World of Balance and Plenty," 12–47, William Preston, "Serpent in the Garden: Environmental Change in Colonial California," 260–98, both in *Contested Eden: California Before the Gold Rush*, ed. Ramón A. Gutiérrez and Richard J. Orsi (Berkeley: University of California Press, 1998).

8. Anderson, Barbour, and Wentworth, "World of Balance"; Preston, "Serpent in the Garden"; Roderick Nash, *Wilderness and the American Mind*, 3rd ed. (New Haven, CT: Yale University Press, 1982); Arturo Gómez-Pompa and Andrea Kaus, "Taming the Wilderness Myth," *Bioscience* 42 (1992): 271–79; Thomas C. Blackburn and Kat Anderson, eds., *Before The Wilderness: Environmental Management by Native Californians* (Menlo Park, CA: Ballena, 1993); Thomas R. Vale, "The Myth of the Humanized Landscape: An Example from Yosemite National Park," *Natural Areas Journal* 18 (1998): 231–36; Dave Foreman, "The Pristine Myths," *Wild Earth* 11 (2001): 1–5; William L. Preston, "Portents of Plague from California's Protohistoric Period," *Ethnohistory* 49 (2002): 69–121; Thomas R. Vale, "The Pre-European Landscape of the United States: Pristine or Humanized?" in *Fire, Native Peoples, and the Natural Landscape*, ed. Thomas R. Vale (Covelo, CA: Island Press, 2002), 1–39.

9. Herbert Eugene Bolton, ed. and trans., *Anza's California Expeditions*, Font's Complete Diary of the Second Anza Expedition, vol. 4 (Berkeley: Regents of the University of California, 1930, reissued New York: Russell and Russell, 1966); Herbert Ingram Priestley, trans., *A Historical, Political, and Natural Description of California by Pedro Fages, Soldier of Spain* (Berkeley: University of California Press, 1937), antelopes mentioned on p. 22.

10. John A. Byers, *American Pronghorn* (Chicago: University of Chicago Press, 1997); Bolton, *Anza's California Expeditions*, 247.

11. Priestley, *Pedro Fages*, 12.

12. S. B. Dakin, *A Scotch Paisano: Hugo Reid's Life in California 1832–1852, Derived From His Correspondence* (Berkeley: University of California Press, 1939), 4; M. H. Newmark and M. R. Newmark, eds., *Sixty Years in Southern California, 1853–1913, Containing the Reminiscences of Harris Newmark* (1916; repr. Los Angeles: Zeitlin and Ver Brugge, 1970), 24, 215–16. From his use of the word *tausan* in other contexts, it is clear that the Hungarian-born Xántus misspelled and mispronounced *thousand*. Ann Zwinger, *John Xántus: The Fort Tejon Letters 1857–1859* (Tucson: University of Arizona Press, 1986), 9; Francis P. Farquhar, ed., *Up and Down California in 1860–1864: The Journal of William H. Brewer, Professor of Agriculture in the Sheffield Scientific School from 1864–1903* (Berkeley: University of California Press, 1966): 21.

13. Tracy I. Storer and Lloyd P. Tevis Jr., *California Grizzly* (Berkeley: University of California Press, 1955; reissued 1996). Black bears are not native to Southern California. Ironically, just a few years after the extirpation of the grizzly, black bears were introduced to the San

Gabriel and San Bernardino Mountains from the Sierra Nevada; see A. E. Burghduff, "Black Bears Released in Southern California," *California Fish and Game* 21 (1935): 83–84.

14. Farquhar, *William H. Brewer*, 47; Zwinger, *John Xántus*, 8–9. In an endnote on page 18, Zwinger mistakenly suggests that the bears that Xántus referred to on June 5, 1857, were black bears rather than grizzly bears.

15. Storer and Tevis, *California Grizzly*, 56, 61; on burrowing mammals and plants species, see Schiffman, "Mammal Burrowing."

16. Aldo Leopold, *A Sand County Almanac* (Oxford: Oxford University Press, 1949, repr. New York: Ballentine Books, 1982), 278; Susan E. Tardiff and Jack A. Stanford, "Grizzly Bear Digging: Effects on Subalpine Meadow Plants in Relation to Mineral Nitrogen Availability," *Ecology* 70 (1998): 2219–28; Charles J. Krebs, *Ecology*, 5th ed. (San Francisco: Cummings, 2001), 471–74.

17. Priestley, *Pedro Fages*, 12, 22; Bolton, *Anza's California Expeditions*, 247; Farquhar, *William H. Brewer*, 47. The relatively small wingspan suggests that this eagle was a juvenile. Or, perhaps, it was actually another native raptor such as a ferruginous hawk, rough-legged hawk, or northern harrier—all of which are large impressive birds but smaller than adult eagles.

18. Bolton, *Anza's California Expeditions*, 173, 187; on the plant species, see LeRoy Abrams, *Flora of Los Angeles and Vicinity* (Lancaster, PA: New Era, 1917).

19. Priestley, *Pedro Fages*, 16. Although Fages's descriptions of Southern California's prairie species composition were unspecific, his diary did include mention of the identities of many chaparral and riparian woodland shrubs and trees. Elliott Coues, ed. and trans., *On the Trail of a Spanish Pioneer: The Diary and Itinerary of Francisco Garces in His Travels Through Sonora, Arizona and California 1775–1776* (New York: Francis P. Harper, 1900), 1:242, 267; Edwin Bryant, *What I Saw in California* (New York: Appleton, 1848; repr. Lincoln: University of Nebraska Press, 1985), 391; Farquhar, *William H. Brewer*, 45, 47.

20. Bryant, *What I Saw*, 448–49.

21. Abrams, *Flora*; Lyndon Wester, "Composition of Native Grasslands in the San Joaquin Valley, California," *Madroño* 28 (1981): 231–41; Anderson, Barbour, and Wentworth, "World of Balance"; Earl W. Lathrop and Robert F. Thorne, *A Flora of the Santa Rosa Plateau, Southern California*, Southern California Botanists Special Publication no. 1 (Claremont, CA, 1985); George Butterworth and Ann Chadwick, *Checklist of Plants of Carrizo Plain Natural Area* (Bakersfield, CA: U.S. Department of Interior Bureau of Land Management, 1995).

22. Bolton, *Anza's California Expeditions*, 244; Abrams, *Flora*.

23. T. W. Mulroy and P. W. Rundel, "Annual Plants: Adaptations to Desert Environments," *BioScience* 27 (1977): 109–14; Kevin J. Rice, "Impacts of Seed Banks on Grassland Community Structure and Population Dynamics," in *Ecology of Soil Seed Banks*, ed. Mary Allessio Leck, V. Thomas Parker, and Robert L. Simpson (New York: Academic, 1989), 211–30; Schiffman, "Mammal Burrowing." Since 1877, when continuous monitoring of rainfall began in the Los Angeles civic center, seasonal (July 1–June 30) rainfall amounts have varied from 4.42 inches in 2001–2002 to 38 inches in 1883–1884; see *Los Angeles Times*, July 5, 2002. Year-to-year variability of this magnitude would have also characterized the presettlement era.

24. G. Ledyard Stebbins, "Colonizing Species of the Native California Flora," in *The Genetics of Colonizing Species: Proceedings of the First International Union of Biological Sciences Symposia on General Biology*, ed. H. G. Baker and G. Ledyard Stebbins (New York: Academic, 1965), 173–95; Raven and Axelrod, *Origin and Relationships*; J. P. Grime, "Evidence of the Existence of Three Primary Strategies in Plants and Its Relevance to Ecological and Evolutionary Theory," *American Naturalist* 111 (1979): 1169–94; Schiffman, "Mammal Burrowing."

25. Lowell John Bean and Harry W. Lawton, "Some Explanations for the Rise of Cultural Complexity in Native California with Comments on Proto-Agriculture and Agriculture," 27–54, Jan Timbrook, John R. Johnson, and David D. Earle, "Vegetation Burning by the Chumash," 117–49, Kat Anderson, "Native Californians as Ancient and Contemporary Cultivators," 151–74, all in Blackburn and Anderson, Before The Wilderness; McCawley, First Angelinos; Anderson, Barbour, and Wentworth, "World of Balance"; Preston, "Serpent in the Garden, 260–98; M. Kat Anderson and David L. Rowney, "California Geophytes: Ecology, Ethnobotany, and Conservation," Fremontia 26, no. 1 (1998):12–18; Anderson, Barbour, and Wentworth, "World of Balance"; Jacob Bendix, "Pre-European Fire in California Chaparral," in Vale, Fire, 269–93; Jon E. Keeley, "Native American Impacts on Fire Regimes of the California Coastal Ranges," Journal of Biogeography 29 (2002): 303–20.

26. Preston, "Serpent in the Garden"; Preston, "Portents of Plague."

27. Vale, "Myth of the Humanized Landscape"; Foreman, "Pristine Myths."

28. Robert Glass Cleland, The Cattle on a Thousand Hills: Southern California 1850–80 (San Marino, CA: Huntington Library, 1941), on cattle 15, 21, on sheep and hogs, 22; Bryant, What I Saw, 391; Manley quote in Dane Coolidge, California Cowboys (New York: Dutton, 1939; repr. Tucson: University of Arizona Press, 1989), 35; Farquhar, William H. Brewer, 20, 44.

29. Cleland, Cattle, 126, 131; Anthony Joern, "Insect Herbivory in the Transition to California Annual Grasslands: Did Grasshoppers Deliver the Coup de Grass?" in Grassland Structure and Function: California Annual Grassland, ed. L. F. Heunneke and H. A. Mooney (Dordrecht, Netherlands: Kluwer Academic, 1989), 117–34; Charles L. Hogue, Insects of the Los Angeles Basin (Los Angeles: Natural History Museum of Los Angeles County, 1993), 70.

30. Joern, "Insect Herbivory"; Frederic Wagner, "Grazers, Past and Present," in Heunneke and Mooney, Grassland, 151–62; William S. Longland, "Risk of Predation and Food Consumption by Black-tailed Jack Rabbits," Journal of Range Management 44 (1991): 447–50; Mark A. Blumler, "Some Myths About California Grasslands and Grazers," Fremontia 20 (1992): 22–27; Elizabeth L. Painter, "Threats to the California Flora: Ungulate Grazers and Browsers," Madroño 42 (1995): 180–88; Byers, American Pronghorn; Han Olff and Mark E. Ritchie, "Effects of Herbivores on Grassland Plant Diversity, Trends in Ecology and Evolution 13 (1998): 261–65.

31. On plant damage, see Wagner, "Grazers, Past and Present"; Painter, "Threats to the California Flora"; Stanley W. Trimble and Alexandra C. Mendel, "The Cow as a Geomorphic Agent—A Critical Review," Geomorphology 13 (1995): 233–53; Coolidge, California Cowboys, 35; on the 1860s climatic changes, see Cleland, Cattle, 126–37; L. T. Burcham, "Cattle and Range Forage in California: 1770–1880," Agricultural History 35 (1961): 140–49.

32. Cleland, Cattle, 57; Herbert G. Baker, "Patterns of Plant Invasion in North America," in Ecology of Biological Invasions of North America and Hawaii, ed. H. A. Mooney and J. A. Drake (New York: Springer, 1986); Harold F. Heady, "Valley Grassland," in Barbour and Major, Terrestrial Vegetation, 491–514; Jonathan D. Sauer, Plant Migration (Berkeley: University of California Press, 1988), 82–84; Jon E. Keeley, "The California Valley Grassland," in Schoenherr, Endangered Plant Communities, 2–23; H. F. Heady, J. W. Bartolome, M. D. Pitt, G. D. Savelle, and M. C. Stroud, "California Prairie," in Natural Grasslands, ed. R. T. Coupland (Amsterdam: Elsevier, 1992), 313–35; John L. Harper, "Establishment, Aggression, and Cohabitation in Weedy Species," in Baker and Stebbins, Genetics of Colonizing Species, 243–68; Sauer, Plant Migration, 83.

33. G. W. Hendry, "The Adobe Brick as a Historical Source," Agricultural History 5 (1931): 110–27; Sauer, Plant Migration, 83; Timothy P. Spira and Lisa K. Wagner, "Viability of Seeds Up to 211 Years Old Extracted From Adobe Brick Buildings of California and Northern Mex-

ico," *American Journal of Botany* 70 (1983): 303–07; Scott Mensing and Roger Byrne, "Invasion of Mediterranean Weeds into California Before 1769," *Fremontia* 27, no. 3 (1999): 6–9.

34. Jackson, "Ecological Origins"; Richard N. Mack, "Temperate Grasslands Vulnerable to Plant Invasions: Characteristics and Consequences," in *Biological Invasions: A Global Perspective*, ed. J. A. Drake, H. A. Mooney, F. di Castri, R. H. Groves, F. J. Kruger, M. Rejmanek, and M. Williamson (New York: Wiley, 1989); Heady et al., "California Prairie"; Juan E. Malo and Francisco Suarez, "Establishment of Pasture Species on Cattle Dung: The Role of Endozoochorous Seeds," *Journal of Vegetation Science* 6 (1995): 169–74; Juan E. Malo and Francisco Suarez, "Herbivorous Mammals as Seed Dispersers in a Mediteranean Dehesa," *Oecologia* 104 (1995): 246–55.

35. Paula M. Schiffman, "Promotion of Exotic Weed Establishment by Endangered Giant Kangaroo Rats (*Dipodomys ingens*) in a California Grassland," *Biodiversity and Conservation* 3 (1994): 524–37; N. G. Seligman, "Management of Mediterranean Grasslands," in *The Ecology and Management of Grazing Systems*, ed. J. Hodgson and A. W. Illius (Oxfordshire, UK: CAB International, 1996), 359–91; Daniel Zohary and Maria Hopf, *Domestication of Plants in the Old World*, 3rd ed. (Oxford: Oxford University Press, 2000), 78–82; Schiffman, "Mammal Burrowing"; Mark S. Minton and Richard N. Mack, "Dampening Environmental Stochasticity Among Immigrant Plants: the Role of Cultivation," in *Official Meeting Program: The Ecological Society of America 86th Annual Meeting* (Washington DC: 2001), 160.

36. On early settler perceptions, see Dick Harrison, "The Visual Quality of the Natural Environment in Prairie Fiction," in *Environmental Aesthetics: Essays and Interpretation*, University of Victoria Western Geographical Series, ed. Barry Sadler and Allen Carlson (Victoria, British Columbia: 1982), 20:143–57. On modern research in this area, see, for example, Rossiter, "Ecology of the Mediterranean"; Wester, "Composition of Native Grasslands"; Jackson, "Ecological Origins"; Huenneke and Mooney, *Grassland Structure and Function*; Mack, "Temperate Grasslands"; Keeley, "California Valley Grassland"; Carla M. D'Antonio and Peter M. Vitousek, "Biological Invasions by Exotic Grasses, the Grass/Fire Cycle, and Global Change," *Annual Review of Ecology and Systematics* 23 (1992): 63–87; Jason G. Hamilton, "Changing Perceptions of Pre-European Grasslands in California," *Madroño* 44 (1997): 311–33.

Chapter 3: Ranchos and the Politics of Land Claims

1. The general historical literature on the California Land Act is large; see R. H. Avina, "Spanish and Mexican Land Grants in California" (master's thesis, University of California, 1932); H. H. Bancroft, *History of California* (San Francisco: History Company, 1874–1890); Robert Glass Cleland, *The Cattle on a Thousand Hills: Southern California, 1850–80* (San Marino, CA: Huntington Library, 1941); R. G. Cowan, *Ranchos of California: A List of Spanish Concessions 1775–1822 and Mexican Grants 1822–1846* (Los Angeles: Historical Society of Southern California, 1977); Paul W. Gates, *Land and Law in California* (Ames: Iowa State University Press, 1991); T. H. Hittell, *History of California* (San Francisco: N. J. Stone, 1898); L. Pitt, *The Decline of the Californios: A Social History of the Spanish-Speaking Californians, 1846–1890* (Berkeley, University of California Press, 1966); W. W. Robinson, *Land in California* (Berkeley: University of California Press, 1948). While a number of these sources provide some partial summary statistics on what happened to grants, usually in a couple of sentences or a footnote, it is very difficult to get any general perspective on what happened.

2. Unless otherwise noted, the remainder of this section draws on Bancroft, *History*; Gates, *Land and Law*; H. W. Halleck, *Report*, House Ex. Doc., 31st Cong., 2d sess., 1850, 5, no. 17, serial 573; W. C. Jones, *Report of the Secretary of the Interior*, Senate Ex. Doc., 31st Cong., 2d sess., 1850, 3, no. 18, serial 589.

3. See, generally, W. W. Robinson, *Land in California* (Berkeley, University of California Press, 1948); Rose H. Aviña, *Spanish and Mexican Land Grants in California* (San Francisco: R and E Research Associates, 1973).

4. Gates, *Land and Law*, 4.

5. *U.S. Statutes at Large*, vol. 9, 631 ff. Specifically excluded, however, was "any town lot, farm lot, or pasture lot." Each town was to submit a single claim for the land within its boundaries. The term claimant refers to the individual that filed the claim. Because of inheritance, sale, or transfer, this person might not be the original grantee. If an owner failed to submit a claim, the land would revert to the public domain. In deciding cases, the act directed that the commission and the courts "shall be governed by the treaty of Guadaloupe Hidalgo, the law of nations, the laws, usages, and customs of the government from which the claim is derived, the principles of equity, and the decisions of the Supreme Court of the United States, so far as they are applicable."

6. Grants refer to all claims submitted under the California Land Act. Almost all grants ever made are believed to have been submitted under the act. Grants that were ultimately patented under the California Land Act were assigned to modern counties based on the location of the majority of the acreage of the grant. So, for instance, a grant where 90 percent of the acreage was located in Los Angeles County and 10 percent of the acreage was located in Orange County would be listed as located in Los Angeles County. Grants that were not patented were assigned to counties based on the best available information about location. Any demarcation of the Los Angeles area is to some degree arbitrary, but most ranchos to the south of these counties were closer to San Diego and most to the north were closer to Santa Barbara. There is almost no indication either at the time or after the fact that substantial numbers of grants were not submitted, either in protest or for other reasons. Indeed, only thirty-one late claims were submitted, suggesting that virtually all grants were submitted before the official deadline. (Bowing to lobbying, Congress ultimately allowed these thirty-one to be considered, despite their late submission.)

7. The grants and land commission numbers are San Pedro (LC 398), Ballona (LC 369), Jurupa (LC 361), Valle (LC 231), Los Alamos (LC 498).

8. Gates, *Land and Law*, 29.

9. On the lawyers' fee, see Gates, *Land and Law*, 17–18; T. O. Larkin, *The Larkin Papers: Personal, Business, and Official Correspondence of Thomas Oliver Larkin* (Berkeley: University of California, 1951–1968), 10:22–23; Adolphus Carter Whitcomb and Thomas Oliver Larkin, Agreement, September 29, 1852. On other expenses, see, for example, R. C. Gillingham, *The Rancho San Pedro : The Story of the Famous Rancho in Los Angeles County and of Its Owners the Dominguez Family* (Los Angeles: Museum Reproductions, 1983), 200.

10. He also alleges that 10 percent of the landowners were reduced to bankruptcy. Cleland, *Cattle*, 41, citing Hittell, *History*.

11. Unlike partition suits, patents were commonly issued in the names of the original grantees, even if the grantee no longer owned the land.

12. On squatters, the ranch diary Henry Dalton kept between 1867 and 1875 "tells an eloquent story of confrontations, injunctions, broken dams, stopped up ditches, arrests, and threats." S. G. Jackson, *A British Ranchero in Old California: The Life and Times of Henry Dalton and the Rancho Azusa* (Glendale, CA: Arthur H. Clark and Azusa Pacific College, 1977), 205. Dalton's case was a bit difficult to interpret, however, because he was fighting squatters primarily on land that was never confirmed. On Mission San Gabriel, see *Los Angeles Star*, June 23, 1855. On Jurupa and San Bernardino, see Gates, *Land and Law*, 308; Robinson, *Land in California*, 127; G. W. Beattie and H. P. Beattie, *Heritage of the Valley; San Bernardino's First*

Century (Pasadena, CA, San Pasqual Press, 1939), 245, 263–64. On Mission San Buenaventura and Sespe, see Gates, *Land and Law*, 203; Robinson, *Land in California*, 127; and K. Clay and W. Troesken, "Squatting and the Settlement of the United States: New Evidence from Post-Gold Rush California," *Advances in Agricultural Economic History* 1 (2000): 207–34.

13. Cleland, *Cattle*, 115–21, 135–36.

14. On grant provisions, see W. Colton, *Three Years in California [1846–1849]* (New York: A. S. Barnes, 1850), 359; Bancroft, *History*, 6:532. On the sketches, see Halleck, *Report*, 122.

15. For the congressional discussion, see the *Congressional Globe*, September 27, 1850; January 2–3, 8–9, 27–31, 1851; February 4–5, 1851. The costs of confirming invalid claims clearly concerned the Senate. Senator Gwin of California argued against confirmation, because "a principle like this would have a tendency to open the flood-gates of iniquity and inundate the whole country with spurious and fictitious claims." He went on to cite government losses of more than 10 million dollars in Louisiana due to the confirmation of fraudulent claims and the potential for even more severe problems in California. W. Gwin, "Speech of Mr. Gwin, of California, in reply to Mr. Benton. Senate, Thursday, January 2, 1851," 93–97, Huntington Library, San Marino, CA.

16. For instance, claimants in Missouri had had numerous opportunities for their cases to be heard and reheard as a result of lobbying by their politicians in Washington. Thomas Benton, "Land Titles in New Mexico and California," *Congressional Globe*, January 15, 1849, 257.

17. Gates, *Land and Law*, 27–28.

18. John M. Berrien, "Land Titles in California," *Congressional Globe*, February 4, 1851, 426.

19. On the surveyor general, see M. Ebright, *Land Grants and Lawsuits in Northern New Mexico* (Albuquerque: University of New Mexico Press, 1994), 39, 40. See also See R. W. Bradfute, *The Court of Private Land Claims: The Adjudication of Spanish and Mexican Land Grant Titles, 1891–1904* (Albuquerque: University of New Mexico Press, 1975).

Chapter 4: Pollution and Public Policy at the Turn of the Twentieth Century

1. *Los Angeles Express*, April 20, 1907. J. W. Eddy was the owner of Angel's Flight and was associated with Henry Huntington's power company.

2. U.S. Bureau of the Census, *Thirteenth Census of the United States: 1910*, vol. 1, *Population* (Washington DC: Government Printing Office, 1912), 180, vol. 9, *Manufactures*, 94; Louis Perry and Richard Perry, *A History of the Los Angeles Labor Movement, 1911–1941* (Berkeley: University of California Press, 1963), 5; *Los Angeles Express*, November 22, 1905, February 7, May 12, 16, 25, June 6, October 3, 1906.

3. This social profile of Los Angeles reflects studies of the 1900 and 1910 United States manuscript census. In collecting this data, blue-collar workers were considered to be either unskilled manual workers (typically listed as laborers in the census) or skilled manual workers (including a broad range of occupations, such as carpenters, bricklayers, locomotive engineers, etc.). People in certain occupations, such as street peddlers and retail clerks, probably were more working class in orientation than middle class, but in this case they are considered white collar, respectively placed in the categories of proprietor or clerical. Because of this, these studies tend to underestimate the total working-class population of the city. These studies were also originally conducted in relationship to an examination of working-class voting behavior, and noncitizens and women are excluded. Since noncitizen immigrants tended to be disproportionately blue collar, this bias again leads to an underestimation of the working-class population, particularly in wards such as the Seventh and Eighth where there were significant foreign-born populations.

4. Grace Stimson, *Rise of the Labor Movement in Los Angeles* (Berkeley: University of California Press, 1955), 200–1, 318–20.

5. Charles Lockwood, "In the Los Angeles Oil Boom, Derricks Sprouted Like Trees," *Smithsonian,* October 1980, 190, 191; Merry Ovnick, *Los Angeles: The End of the Rainbow* (Los Angeles: Balcony, 1994), 105–6, 147; Leonard and Dale Pitt, *Los Angeles From A to Z: An Encyclopedia of the City and County* (Berkeley: University of California Press, 1997), 364–65.

6. Lockwood, "Oil Boom," 196. Marshall Stimson, a leader in the progressive reform movement, reflected back on the devastation caused by oil production in 1944, when the city proposed easing restrictions on drilling. Marshall Stimson to Ed Ainsworth, editor of the *Los Angeles Times*, February 9, 1944, Marshall Stimson Collection, Huntington Library, San Marino, CA, box 1. Mayor Snyder quoted in Lockwood, "Oil Boom," 197–98.

7. *Los Angeles Times*, May 15, 1901; *Los Angeles Express*, April 20, May 3, 11, 16, 17, 1901, January 30, 1902, September 5, 9, 13, October 20, 25, 27, 31, 1905. Los Angeles City Council, *Minutes*, 73:354–55. It is also unclear how successful the oil supervisor really was in checking the problem of runoff. In an incident in 1907, for instance, petroleum draining from the city oil fields flooded Echo Park Lake, which caught fire and burned for three days. Lockwood, "Oil Boom," 198.

8. On the by-products, see Corey L. J. Fischer, Robert D. Schmitter, and Eliesh O'Neil Lane, "Manufactured Gas Plants: The Environmental Legacy," Hazardous Substance Research Centers, http://www.hsrc.org/hsrc/html/tosc/sswtosc/mgp.html#oil, November 1999. This is an ecological problem that persistently haunts the city. Recent excavations in Southern California have uncovered vast pits of this material, left over from early operations, that still pose an environmental hazard. *Los Angeles Times*, October 19, 1995. The quote is from *Los Angeles Times*, January 17, 1904.

9. *Los Angeles Express*, September 11, 14, 15, 1903; *Los Angeles Record*, January 19, 1907, January 16, 17, 1908.

10. *Los Angeles Times*, November 9, 1901.

11. *Los Angeles Express*, August 21, September 6, October 18, 19, 21, 25, November 8, 15, 22, 1901; *Los Angeles Times*, September 26, October 1, November 8, 9, 16, 17, 22, 23, 1901; *Los Angeles Record*, November 15, 16, 22, 1901.

12. *Los Angeles Express*, November 26, 1901; *Los Angeles Times*, November 23, 1901.

13. *Los Angeles Express*, November 30, December 4, 1901, February 20, March 4, 6, 14, July 28, 1902; *Los Angeles Times*, November 26, 27, 1901, February 21, 26, March 5, 9, 16, April 13, 1902; *Los Angeles Record*, November 28, 1901, February 14, 19–21, 24, 27, 28, March 3–5, 7, 10, 11, 17–19, April 4, 9, October 21, 1902; Los Angeles City Council, *Minutes*, 61:555, 603–5, 652, 659; 62:254.

14. *Los Angeles Express*, October 14, November 26, 1901; *Los Angeles Times*, November 17, 1901.

15. *Los Angeles Times*, April 12, June 23, 26, 28, 1904; *Los Angeles Record*, July 16, 26–27, 1904; Los Angeles City Council, *Minutes*, 69:77–78.

16. *Los Angeles Times*, May 25, June 14, 18, 23, 1904; Los Angeles City Council, *Minutes*, 69:242, 351.

17. *Los Angeles Record*, July 26, 1904.

18. *Los Angeles Times*, June 28, 1904; Los Angeles City Council, *Minutes*, 69:284, 290, 323, 345–46.

19. *Los Angeles Record*, July 30, August 2, 1904.

20. *Los Angeles Times*, July 18, 27, 1904.

21. *Los Angeles Record*, August 15, 1904; *Los Angeles Times*, August 16, 1904.

22. On the initiative campaign, see *Los Angeles Times*, August 16, 23; on the counterpetition, see *Los Angeles Times*, July 18, 1904.

23. *Los Angeles Express*, August 16, 1904; *Los Angeles Examiner*, December 4, 1904; Los Angeles City Council, *Minutes*, 69:383, 390, 415.

24. Los Angeles City, *Records of Election Returns* (December 5, 1904, to December 9, 1920), 1:10–12; *Los Angeles Express*, August 15, 1904.

25. *Los Angeles Express*, April 8, October 7, 1905; *Los Angeles Times*, April 30, 1905.

26. *Los Angeles Record*, May 13, June 29, 1905; *Los Angeles Times*, April 30, May 7, 1905.

27. *Los Angeles Times*, March 26, 1905, May 16, 1906.

28. *Los Angeles Examiner*, December 1, 1906; *Los Angeles Express*, October 7, 1905, October 20, 1909; *Los Angeles Record*, September 22, 1902, March 25, 1905, June 2, 1905, July 28, November 2, 1906; *Los Angeles Times*, October 8, 1905.

29. *Los Angeles Times*, February 3, 14, 17, April 8, 28, May 18, June 22, August 4, 1905; *Los Angeles Record*, June 22, August 2, 1905; *Los Angeles Express*, August 23, 24, September 1, 1905; Los Angeles City Council, *Minutes*, 70:478–79.

30. *Los Angeles Express*, March 17, 20, 21, September 18, 1905; *Los Angeles Record*, March 20, 21, May 10, 17, 19, 1905; *Los Angeles Times*, March 14, 17, 1905. Los Angeles City Council, *Minutes*, 70:167, 227–28, 407–8, 419, 422, 478–79. Fred L. Baker, the owner of the firm, also served as a close adviser to the mayor and was appointed by him to the water board at the beginning of his term. Ultimately, their relationship faltered, and McAleer resigned his salaried position as a superintendent of the Baker Iron Works. The *Express* of September 18, 1905, attributed this break to political fallout from the garbage scandal.

31. *Los Angeles Times*, May 18, June 8, 10, August 24, September 1, 1905; *Los Angeles Record*, May 18, September 7, 11, 16, October 4, 17, December 11, 1905, January 10, February 13, 1906; *Los Angeles Express*, August 24, September 1, 1905, January 13, 20, 26, March 19, 26, April 1, 1906; Los Angeles City Council, *Minutes*, 73:392.

32. *Los Angeles Times*, July 7, 1907. A similar editorial appeared in the *Times* on March 31, 1907.

33. *Los Angeles Times*, September 21, 1907; Los Angeles City Council, *Minutes*, 74:161.

34. *Los Angeles Times*, February 11, March 29, 31, July 7, September 21, October 13, 22, 1907, January 21, 1908; *Los Angeles Express*, March 30, August 21, September 27, October 12, November 23, 1907; *Los Angeles Record*, February 14, April 25, May 16, July 13, 1907; Los Angeles City Council, *Minutes*, 74:104, 273, 427, 461.

35. *Los Angeles Record*, February 28, 1908; *Los Angeles Times*, July 20, August 4, 1909; Los Angeles City Council, *Minutes*, 75:261, 285, 360, 403, 493, 330, 574; 76:299, 384, 441–42; 78:532–33

36. *Los Angeles Times*, August 27, 1908. See also *Los Angeles Times*, July 16, 1908.

37. *Los Angeles Times*, January 21, 1908; *Los Angeles Express*, February 14, 1908.

38. *Los Angeles Times*, August 4, 8, 11, 12, 24, 25, October 6, 8, 1909; quotation is from August 25.

39. *Los Angeles Express*, October 16, 1909; *Los Angeles Times*, October 8, November 12, 1909, June 26, July 8, 10, 1910.

40. *Los Angeles Times*, December 8, 21, 1910, January 11, March 8, 16, May 16, 1911; *Los Angeles Express*, March 8, 11, 13, 15, June 3, 7, 1911; Los Angeles City Council, *Minutes*, 83:225–26, 325–26, 329; 84:46–52, 541; 85:1–2.

Chapter 5: Beaches versus Oil in Greater Los Angeles

1. California Department of Conservation, *1997 Annual Report of the State Oil & Gas Supervisor*, 55, 56, 57, 61.

2. *Hollister v. Kingsbury*, California Court of Appeals, February 2, 1933, 129 Cal. A 420, 423. For criticism of Kingsbury's change of course, see Howard Kegley, "Wells Reveal State Loss," *Los Angeles Times*, February 26, 1928; "Oil Drilling on Tidelands Up In Court: Several Cases Reach High Tribunal; Ventura Case Is Test," *San Francisco Chronicle*, December 7, 1927; "Oil Rush May Ruin Beaches," *San Francisco Chronicle*, September 27, 1928. See *J. R. Kelley v. W. S. Kingsbury*, Supreme Court of California, July 18, 1930, 210 Cal. 37, which upheld Kingsbury's discretion to define the boundaries of the Ellwood field and thus reject petitioner's permit application, and its companion case, *T. G. Kennedy v. W. S. Kingsbury*, Supreme Court of California, July 18, 1930, 210 Cal. 667; J. R. Kelley, "Petition for Writ of Mandate: *J. R. Kelley v. W. S. Kingsbury*, Surveyor-General State of California, Ex-Officio Register of the State Land Office," January 28, 1930, State Lands Commission—Correspondence 1930, CSA (hereafter CSA). The California Court of Appeals upheld Kingsbury's broad definition of the Ellwood field in *Leo I. Farry v. Lyman King*, Director of Finance, California Court of Appeals, January 22, 1932, 120 Cal. A 118. See also "Writ Refused in Tideland Oil Case," *San Francisco Chronicle*, February 17, 1929, concerning oil and gas on state-owned tidelands inside Huntington Beach city limits.

3. Kegley, "State Loss"; "Favor Drilling Tidelands," *Los Angeles Times*, February 27, 1928.

4. "Oil Rush May Ruin Beaches," *San Francisco Chronicle*, September 27, 1928.

5. "Webb Scores Oil Drilling In Tideland: Attorney Declares State Has Full Control Over Ocean Beaches," *San Francisco Chronicle*, January 24, 1928.

6. U. S. Webb, "Brief of Respondent in *Boone v. Kingsbury*," January 1928, Supreme Court of California Records, Box WPA 24291-24311, Folder WPA 24310: *Boone v. Kingsbury*, S. F. No. 12707, CSA, 38, 43, 59, 70–71.

7. Secretary of the interior Ray Lyman Wilbur simultaneously claimed discretion to refuse permits for federal oil lands under the 1920 mineral-leasing law, a position ultimately upheld by the U.S. Supreme Court. See chapter 2, note 74.

8. *Boone v. Kingsbury*, Supreme Court of California, December 31, 1928, 206 Cal. 148, 165, 181–82.

9. "Tidelands Oil Hunt Approved," *San Francisco Chronicle*, January 1, 1929; "Oil Well on Island of Steel," *Los Angeles Times*, November 14, 1932; "Oil Drill Threat for Beaches Seen in Court Ruling," *San Francisco Examiner*, January 6, 1929; "Tideland Oil Decision Hit by Justice: Judge Shenk Dissents in Permit Granted Drilling Firm," *San Francisco Chronicle*, January 6, 1929; "U.S. Will Rule on Oil Permits: State Surveyor-General to Carry Tideland Case to Supreme Court," *San Francisco Chronicle*, April 5, 1929. The U.S. Supreme Court dismissed Kingsbury's federal appeal for "want of a substantial federal question." *Workman v. Boone*, Supreme Court of the United States, October 28, 1929, 280 U.S. 517.

10. "Oil Prospecting Pleas Rejected," *Los Angeles Times*, December 23, 1929; "Oil Production Curb Discussed," *Los Angeles Times*, December 23, 1929; "Decision on Oil Drilling Requested," *Los Angeles Times*, March 7, 1930.

11. "Quick Curb Asked Against Tideland Oil Prospectors," *San Francisco Examiner*, January 11, 1929; "Senate Passes Tideland Bill," *San Francisco Chronicle*, January 18, 1929; "Young Signs Tideland Bill," *San Francisco Examiner*, January 18, 1929; "Curb on Beach Drilling Urged," *San Francisco Examiner*, January 9, 1929; "Bill Will Save State Beaches: Governor Signs Measure Banning Drilling; Natural Gas Waste Stopped," *San Francisco Chronicle*, May 29, 1929.

12. *Hollister v. Kingsbury*, 429.

13. The description of the Ellwood field is in "Tidelands Promise to Become Big Oil Field," *San Francisco Chronicle*, August 17, 1929. For the drilling race, see "Gas Spouting Oil Well Still Balks Control," *San Francisco Chronicle*, August 9, 1929; "Drillers Race to Strike Oil on Tidelands," *San Francisco Chronicle*, September 6, 1929; "Third Well Planned at Santa Barbara," *San Francisco Chronicle*, October 8, 1929; "Santa Barbara Oil Area Being Fully Tested," *San Francisco Chronicle*, October 21, 1929; "Pacific Western Brings in Well," *San Francisco Chronicle*, November 19, 1929; "Wildcat Well Comes in 'Barefoot'; Proves Up New Santa Barbara Field," *San Francisco Chronicle*, November 28, 1929.

14. Howard Kegley, "Ocean Oil Wells Bonanza," *Los Angeles Times*, April 14, 1930. See also "Tideland Development Ellwood Field Promises to Become Great Producer," *San Francisco Chronicle*, February 16, 1930; "Barnsdall Oil Hits Producer In Ocean Bed," *San Francisco Chronicle*, September 6, 1930. On the Barnsdall curtailment, see "Barnsdall Oil Hits Producer."

15. "Survey Begun on Beach Uses: Oil Drilling and Industrial Exploitation Studied," *Los Angeles Times*, July 19, 1930; "Meeting Will Launch Battle Against Leasing," *Los Angeles Times*, July 20, 1930; "Court Blocks Beach Drilling," *Los Angeles Times*, July 20, 1930; "Webb Blocks L. A. Tide Land Leasing," *San Francisco Chronicle*, August 22, 1930.

16. On the lawsuit, see *Lewis Stone v. City of Los Angeles*, California Court of Appeals, 114 Cal. A 192, May 18, 1931; "City Plea Lost On Oil Leasing," *Los Angeles Times*, July 19, 1931. On oil revenue, see "Beaches and Oil," *Los Angeles Times*, October 9, 1930.

17. For typical contractual arrangements that stipulated competitive production, see *A. T. Jergins Trust v. Commissioner of Internal Revenue*, Docket No. 29940, United States Board of Tax Appeals, March 5, 1931, 22 B.T.A. 551, 553–54; "Banning Lease with T. F. Gessel," August 29, 1930, Banning Collection, box 20, folder 2, Huntington Library, San Marino, CA, 11; "Banning Lease with Superior Oil Company," 1925, Banning Collection, box 20, folder 2, Huntington Library, San Marino, CA; "Oil Conservation Program Gets First Results From Price Cut in Signal Hill," *San Francisco Chronicle*, October 23, 1929. On well spacing, see John Ise, *United States Oil Policy* (New Haven, CT: Yale University Press, 1926), esp. chap. 12; Jules Tygiel, *The Great Los Angeles Swindle: Oil, Stocks, and Scandal During the Roaring Twenties* (New York: Oxford University Press, 1994). On depletion of the Huntington Beach field, see Ise, *Oil Policy*, 211, 216, 108.

18. "State Wins—If It Loses," *Los Angeles Times*, June 30, 1928; "State Victor in Beach Fight," *Los Angeles Times*, July 3, 1928.

19. "Our Huntington Beach Retaining Wall," *Standard Oil Bulletin*, February 1927, 10.

20. "Court Forbids Ocean Drilling," *Los Angeles Times*, February 10, 1930; *Arthur Carr v. W. S. Kingsbury*, California Court of Appeals, January 16, 1931, 111 Cal. A 165, 169. See also *Thomas A. Joyner v. W. S. Kingsbury*, California Court of Appeals, February 16, 1929, 97 Cal. A 17; *Roy Maggart v. W. S. Kingsbury*, California Court of Appeals, January 16, 1931, 111 Cal. A 765; *C. C. Cummings v. W. S. Kingsbury*, California Court of Appeals, January 16, 1931, 111 Cal. A 763; *Feisthamel v. W. S. Kingsbury*, California Court of Appeals, January 16, 1931, 111 Cal. A 762; *Thomas A. Joyner v. W. S. Kingsbury*, California Court of Appeals, January 16, 1931, 111 Cal. A 764; "Supreme Court Upholds State Oil Land Law," *San Francisco Chronicle*, October 20, 1931; "Oil Well Zone Review Denied," *Los Angeles Times*, October 20, 1931.

21. "Groups Appeal to Rolph," *Los Angeles Times*, May 27, 1931; "Supervisors Ask Rolph to Veto Tidelands Bill," *Los Angeles Times*, June 2, 1931; "Governor, Senator Speak: Two Officials Side with Santa Barbara Against Oil Drilling on Beaches," *Los Angeles Times*, May 11, 1931.

22. On Standard Oil lobbying, see Eustace Cullinan to William A. Smith, May 22, 1931,

Gerald T. White History Project, Chevron-Texaco Archives, Dublin, CA (hereafter GTWHP), carton 0155071, folder government relations; James E. Degnan to Felix T. Smith, January 27, 1931, GTWHP, carton 0155081, folder Producing—Huntington Beach. On Hearst, see "The Tide Lands At Huntington Beach," *Newport News*, May 28, 1931. The Rolph quote is in "Tidelands Oil Bill Vetoed," *Los Angeles Times*, June 18, 1931. On the June 19 drama, see Felix T. Smith to Oscar Lawler, June 27, 1931, GTWHP, carton 0155081, folder producing—Huntington Beach; Oscar Lawler to Vincent Butler, July 7, 1931, GTWHP, carton 0155081, folder producing—Huntington Beach.

23. Elson G. Conrad and L. W. Blodget, "Argument Against Preventing Leasing of State-Owned Tide or Beach Lands for Mineral and Oil Production Referendum Measure," in Secretary of State, "Referendum Measures, with Arguments Respecting the Same" (Sacramento: California State Printing Office, May 3, 1932), 5–6.

24. "Tidelands Oil Battle Opens," *Los Angeles Times*, May 17, 1932; *Roy Maggart v. W. S. Kingsbury*, California Court of Appeals, January 16, 1931, 111 Cal. A 765; Porter Flint, "Oil News," *Los Angeles Times*, September 11, 1932. After the electorate rejected the November 1932 proposition, the Pacific Exploration Company's lease option expired (because it was unable to carry out the drilling terms). In July 1933, the Huntington Beach City Council, meeting in secret session, negotiated a new lease with the Southwest Exploration Oil Company, affiliated with the prominent Hancock Oil Company. Most likely, the city council switched lessees hoping that Hancock would have more political clout and successfully push through legislation in 1934 allocating oil rights to the city. "Renewal of Tidelands Oil Battle Looms as Huntington Beach Grants Lease," *Los Angeles Times*, July 9, 1933.

25. *Arthur Carr v. W. S. Kingsbury*, California Court of Appeals, January 16, 1931, 111 Cal. A 165, 169; "Drilling Lease Made By City," *Los Angeles Times*, August 13, 1932; "Friendly Suit Filed to Test Lease Validity," *Los Angeles Times*, August 18, 1932; "Battle on Oil Will Be Bitter," *Los Angeles Times*, December 12, 1932; "Six City Streets Leased for Oil Drilling by Huntington Beach City Council," *Los Angeles Times*, May 27, 1933; Porter Flint, "Oil News," *Los Angeles Times*, June 1, 1933.

26. "Drilling Lease Made By City," *Los Angeles Times*, August 13, 1932; "Oil Lease Injunction Explained," *Los Angeles Times*, November 4, 1932; "Tidelands Oil Battle Opens," *Los Angeles Times*, May 17, 1932. For a related discussion of local struggles for control over oil and gas development, see Paul Sabin, "Voices from the Hydrocarbon Frontier: Canada's Mackenzie Valley Pipeline Inquiry (1974–1977)," *Environmental History Review* 19 (Spring 1995): 17–48; Paul Sabin, "Searching for Middle Ground: Native Communities and Oil Extraction in the Northern and Central Ecuadorian Amazon, 1967–1993," *Environmental History* 3 (April 1998): 144–68.

27. C. G. Ward, chairman, Civic Betterment Committee, Huntington Beach Chamber of Commerce, and Willis H. Warner, secretary and treasurer, Beach Protective Association, Huntington Beach, California, "Argument Against Initiative Proposition No. 11," in Secretary of State, "Proposed Amendments to Constitution and Proposed Statutes, with arguments respecting the same," November 10, 1932; "Oil Drilling Move Opposed," *Los Angeles Times*, October 14, 1932.

28. On the governor, see "Beach Oil Fight Pushed," *Los Angeles Times*, September 27, 1932; "Rolph Raps Beach Oil Proposal," *Los Angeles Times*, November 6, 1932; "Rolph Orders Oil Drill Quiz," *Los Angeles Times*, October 29, 1932; "Realtors Battle Move to Drill on Tidelands: Beaches Belong to People Must Not Be Ruined, Rolph Asserts," *San Francisco Chronicle*, October 9, 1932. On the mayor and board positions, see L. A. Barrett, "Joint Report of Mineral Resources Section and Forestry Section," *Transactions of the Commonwealth Club* 27,

no. 5 (September 27, 1932); "Rossi in Save Beaches Move: Mayor Works Against Oil Proposal," *San Francisco Chronicle*, October 14, 1932.

29. Ward and Warner, "Argument Against Initiative Proposition No. 11"; "Vote on State Propositions," *Los Angeles Times*, November 11, 1932.

30. For further political efforts, see "Tidelands Oil Wells Approved," *Los Angeles Times*, July 19, 1933; "Huntington Beach Oil Leasing Wins In Assembly," *Los Angeles Times*, July 22, 1933; "Beach Oil Drilling," *Los Angeles Times*, July 25, 1933.

31. Howard Kegley, "Oil News," *Los Angeles Times*, August 12, 1931; Howard Kegley, "Oil News," *Los Angeles Times*, October 14, 1931; Howard Kegley, "Oil News," *Los Angeles Times*, June 6, 1932; R. E. Allen to members, Central Proration Committee, January 30, 1933, Lloyd Collection, box LCL 8(1), folder Central Proration Committee and Planning and Coordination Committee, letters, and so on, Huntington Library, San Marino, CA; Howard Kegley, "Oil News," *Los Angeles Times*, July 11, 1933; Affidavit of C. M. Potter, January 2, 1934, *People of the State of California v. Termo Oil Company*, case no. 31452 in Orange County Courthouse; Howard Kegley, "Oil News," *Los Angeles Times*, August 9, 1933; "Six City Streets Leased for Oil Drilling by Huntington Beach City Council," *Los Angeles Times*, May 27, 1933.

32. Arthur Alexander, "Supplemental Expense Account," November 1, 1934, Finance—State Lands—Los Angeles, CSA; Affidavit of Arthur H. Alexander, October 25, 1933, in *People of the State of California v. H. John Eastman, Ltd.*, case no. 31452, Orange County Superior Court; Affidavit of C. M. Potter, January 2, 1934, *People of the State of California v. Termo Oil Company*, case no. 31452, Orange County Superior Court.

33. "Huge State Oil Loss in Beach Field Rumored: Official Reported Perturbed Over Talk of Pilfering," *San Francisco Chronicle*, September 6, 1933; "State to Restrain Illegal Oil Practice," *San Francisco Chronicle*, September 14, 1933. See also "Huntington Beach Oil Leasing Wins In Assembly," *Los Angeles Times*, July 22, 1933.

34. "Gas Tax Raid Proposed as Budget Aid," *San Francisco Chronicle*, December 24, 1932; R. W. Jimerson, "State Legislators Extend Battle Against Income Tax: Vandegrift Warning Points Out Perils to California," *San Francisco Examiner*, July 10, 1933; "Vandegrift Estate Goes to Widow, Children, Father," *Sacramento Bee*, December 23, 1949; "Vandegrift, Legislative Auditor, Dies," *Sacramento Bee*, December 17, 1949.

35. On Vandegrift's threat to prosecute, see "State Will Press Fight in Oil Row," *Los Angeles Times*, September 29, 1933; "State to Press Oil Well Suits," *Los Angeles Times*, September 20, 1933. On his instructions to Daugherty, see "State Finance Head in Oil Row," *Los Angeles Times*, October 19, 1933; "Dock Approved by Vandegrift," *Los Angeles Times*, February 4, 1934. The quotes on litigation are in "Tidelands Row Aired," *Los Angeles Times*, November 2, 1933.

36. Anonymous to Culbert L. Olson, July 9, 1935, Culbert L. Olson Papers, MSS C-B 442, box 3, Bancroft Library, University of California, Berkeley; for details on Jefferson, see, H. R. Philbrick, *Legislative Investigative Report* (Sacramento: Edwin N. Atherton, 1938), sec. 4, 42, sec. 2, 18.

37. "State Revenue Increase Seen," *Los Angeles Times*, January 2, 1934; "Governor Is Due to Hold Hearing on Tideland Oil," *Sacramento Bee*, July 10, 1935.

38. U. S. Webb to Dudley D. Sales, C. R. Smith, William H. Cree, October 3, 1933, in the complaint of Utt in *James B. Utt v. Rolland A. Vandegrift*, Sacramento Superior Court, December 9, 1933, case no. 49963. See also *Hollister v. Kingsbury* (reversing Glenn's order that Kingsbury grant a prospecting permit to Hollister).

39. Floyd J. Healey, "Oil Royalties Plan Drawn Up," *Los Angeles Times*, December 8, 1933; "Restrainment of State Oil Suits Sought: Beach City Asserts Action Interfering with Valuations," *San Francisco Chronicle*, January 5, 1934. The Department of Finance won a court judg-

ment against the Termo Oil Company, but then settled for royalties under an easement. *People of the State of California v. Termo Oil Company*, Orange County Superior Court, case 31452, "Judgment and Decree," August 8, 1938. On Vandegrift's threats, see "Beach Oil Pool Heads Warned," *San Francisco Chronicle*, March 24, 1934; "Vandegrift Will Submit Leases to Legislature," *Los Angeles Times*, February 24, 1934.

40. The city's position is given in "Restrainment of State Oil Suits Sought: Beach City Asserts Action Interfering with Valuations," *San Francisco Chronicle*, January 5, 1934. On the concerns about Standard Oil, see George Bush and Lewis Blodget, "Reply Memorandum on Behalf of Certain Defendant Property Owners," April 1934, Olson Papers, box 3, Bancroft Library, University of California, Berkeley, from the case *State of California v. Milroy Oil Co.*, *Pacific Electric Railway Company v. Milroy Oil Co.*, Orange County Superior Court, 4–5.

41. "State Demands $400,000 from Oil Operators: Suits Filed in Attempt to Shut Down Beach Producers," *San Francisco Chronicle*, January 31, 1934; "State's Share on Oil Set High," *Los Angeles Times*, January 24, 1934; "Beach City Accuses State in Oil Scheme: Municipality Says Group Promised Leniency to Large Firms," *San Francisco Chronicle*, February 4, 1934.

42. On Shadle's estimate, see "Tide Lands Oil Row Settled," *San Francisco Chronicle*, December 16, 1934. For the later calculation, see "Production Data Huntington Beach Field," October–November 1936, Olson Papers, box 3, Bancroft Library, University of California, Berkeley.

43. "New Director Opens Probe of Oil Royalties: State Officials, Standard Oil Alleged Plot Under Investigation," *San Francisco Chronicle*, February 6, 1934; California Legislature, Special Committee on the Abstraction of Oil and Gas from Tidelands of the State of California, *In the Matter of the Investigation by a Special Committee of the Senate of the State of California of the Abstraction of Oil and Gas from the Tidelands of the State of California: Reporter's Transcript of the Proceedings* (Sacramento: California State Printing Office, 1935–1937), July 9, 1935, and July 10, 1935, 8–15 (hereafter Olson Committee, *Proceedings*).

44. R. E. Allen to members, Central Proration Committee, August 14, 1933, Lloyd Collection, box LCL 8(1), folder Central Proration Committee and Planning and Coordination Committee, letters, and so on, Huntington Library, San Marino, CA; see also Emil Kluth to Ralph B. Lloyd, October 26, 1933, Lloyd Collection, box LCL 8 (1), folder Central Proration Committee, Huntington Library, San Marino, CA.

45. *Union Oil Company of California v. Reconstruction Oil Company*, California Court of Appeals, April 2, 1937, 20 Cal. A 2d 170; *Union Oil Company of California v. Mutual Oil Company*, California Court of Appeals, March 3, 1937, 19 Cal. A 2d 409; *Union Oil Company of California v. Mutual Oil Company*, Court of Appeals of California, June 30, 1937, 21 Cal. A 2d 620; *Pacific Western Oil Co. v. Bern Oil Company, Ltd.*, Supreme Court of California, March 3, 1939, 13 Cal. 2d. 60; *People v. Bert Brunwin*, California Court of Appeals, November 19, 1934, 2 Cal. A 2d 287; *Bern Oil Co. v. Superior Court*, February 27, 1935, 5 Cal. A (2d) 21; *Pacific Western Oil Co. v. Bern Oil Company, Ltd.*, Supreme Court of California, March 3, 1939, 13 Cal. 2d. 60.

46. Nathan Newby to Culbert L. Olson, April 22, 1937, Olson Papers, box 3, Bancroft Library, University of California, Berkeley; "Beach Oil Pool Heads Warned," *San Francisco Chronicle*, March 24, 1934; "State Demands $400,000 from Oil Operators: Suits Filed in Attempt to Shut Down Beach Producers," *San Francisco Chronicle*, January 31, 1934; "State Files New Claim in Oil Dispute: Damages of $500,000 Sought from Calif. Producers," *San Francisco Chronicle*, February 1, 1934.

47. Ralph Lloyd to Harold Ickes, September 18, 1933, Lloyd Collection, box LCL 8 (1), folder Central Proration Committee and Planning and Coordination Committee, letters, and

so on, Huntington Library, San Marino, CA. In January 1934, Orange County assemblyman Craig asked Vandegrift to allow one hundred additional property owners in Huntington Beach to drill into the state pool on a royalty basis, but Vandegrift refused, declaring the Huntington Beach field overdrilled. "State's Share on Oil Set High," *Los Angeles Times*, January 24, 1934.

Chapter 6: Who Killed the Los Angeles River?

1. Upper Los Angeles River Area Watermaster, *Watermaster Service in the Upper Los Angeles River Area, Los Angeles County: 1992–93 Water Year* (Los Angeles, 1994), app. C; U.S. Army Corps of Engineers, *Operation and Maintenance Manual, Los Angeles County Drainage Area Project, California* (Los Angeles, 1975).

2. Friends of the Los Angeles River, *The LACDA Public Response Guide: A Guide Toward Informed Flood Control Decisions* (Los Angeles, 1994); Tom Hayden and Lewis MacAdams, "Flood Control by Riparian Rape," *The Los Angeles Times*, November 3, 1997; Mike Davis, *Ecology of Fear: Los Angeles and the Imagination of Disaster* (New York: Metropolitan Books/Henry Holt, 1998), 67–72; U.S. Army Corps of Engineers, *Operation and Maintenance Manual*; U.S. Army Corps of Engineers, *Annual Report* (Washington DC, 1960), 1522, 1546–47.

3. National Climatic Data Center, *Comparative Climatic Data for the United States Through 1992* (Asheville, NC, 1993), 89; Gordon R. Miller, "Los Angeles and the Owens River Aqueduct" (PhD diss., Claremont Graduate School, 1977), 28; Allen W. Weltz, *The Gabrielino Indians at the Time of the Portola Expedition*, map (Los Angeles: Southwest Museum, 1962); Felipe de Neve, "Translation of Portion of Order of Governor Felipe de Neve for Founding of Los Angeles," *Annual Publications, Historical Society of Southern California* 15, part 2 (1933): 154.

4. Irving McKee, "The Beginnings of California Winegrowing," *Quarterly, Historical Society of Southern California* 30, no. 1 (1948): 50–71; Cleve E. Kindall, "Southern Vineyards: The Economic Significance of the Wine Industry in the Development of Los Angeles, 1831–1870," *Historical Society of Southern California Quarterly* 41, no. 1 (1959): 26–37; Iris Higbie Wilson, *William Wolfskill, 1798–1866, Frontier Trapper to California Ranchero* (Glendale, CA: Arthur H. Clark, 1965), 176; H. D. Barrows, "Water for Domestic Purposes Versus Water for Irrigation," *Annual Publications, Historical Society of Southern California* 8 (1911): 208–9.

5. William Mulholland, "A Brief Historical Sketch of the Growth of the Los Angeles City Water Department," *Public Service*, June 1920; Thomas Brooks, *Notes on Los Angeles Water Supply* (Los Angeles: Bureau of Water Works and Supply, 1938); Los Angeles City Water Co. advertisement in Southern California Bureau of Information, *Southern California: An Authentic Description of Its Natural Features, Resources, and Prospects* (Los Angeles: Bureau of Information, 1892), 79.

6. William Hamilton Hall, *Irrigation in California [Southern]: The Field, Water-Supply, and Works, Organization and Operation in San Diego, San Bernardino, and Los Angeles Counties* (Sacramento: State Engineer of California, 1888), 544–45, 557; "Report of Water Overseer," December 3, 1894, June 21, 1897, Los Angeles City Archives; "Report of the Water Overseer, 1899," Los Angeles City Archives; Fred Eaton, "Annual Report of the Mayor, 1900," Los Angeles City Archives; Edward M. Boggs, "A Study of Water Rights on the Los Angeles River, California," in *Report of Irrigation Investigations in California*, U.S. Department of Agriculture Office of Experiment Stations Bulletin 100 (Washington DC: Government Printing Office, 1901), 345; Los Angeles City Council, *Minutes*, April 11, 1900.

7. Los Angeles Board of Public Service Commissioners (hereafter LABPSC), *Complete*

Report on the Construction of the Los Angeles Aqueduct (Los Angeles, 1916), 35; Los Angeles Board of Water Commissioners (hereafter LABWC), *Annual Report* (Los Angeles, 1902); Brooks, *Notes*; Los Angeles Directory Co., *Los Angeles City Directory* (Los Angeles, 1902); "Mountain Supply," *Los Angeles Record*, February 28, 1898.

8. LABWC, *Annual Report*, 1910, 11–14; Brooks, *Notes*; Los Angeles County Board of Engineers, Flood Control (hereafter LACBEFC), *Report of the Board of Engineers, Flood Control to the Board of Supervisors, Los Angeles County, California* (Los Angeles, 1915), 127–28.

9. Los Angeles Directory Co., *City Directory*, 1913; Los Angeles Department of Water and Power, *Data on Available Water Supply and Future Requirements of the City of Los Angeles and the Metropolitan Area* (Los Angeles, 1928), 44; Mulholland, "Historical Sketch"; Brooks, *Notes*; LABWC, *Annual Report* (1906), 15; LABWC, *Annual Report* (1910), 10; Harry Carr, *Los Angeles: City of Dreams* (New York: D. Appleton-Century, 1935), 145; G. Wharton James, *Picturesque Southern California* (Pasadena, CA: G. Wharton James, 1898), 29.

10. LABPSC, *Annual Report* (1916), 11; LABPSC, *Annual Report* (1917), 10–11; LABPSC, *Annual Report* (1918), 12; LABPSC, *Annual Report* (1920), 17; LABPSC, *Annual Report* (1921–1925); LABPSC, *Annual Report* (1930), 10–11.

11. Charles D. Warner, *Our Italy* (New York: Harper, 1891); Jimmie Rodgers, "Blue Yodel No. 4 (California Blues)," on *Never No Mo' Blues: Jimmie Rodgers Memorial Album* (RCA Records LP AHM1-1232).

12. Meg Perry, "A Historical Analysis of Land Use Transitions Occurring in the Los Angeles River/Alameda Street Sector of Downtown Los Angeles" (master's thesis, California State University, Los Angeles, 1995), 41.

13. Charles J. Fisher, "The Influence of the Railroad on Industrial Development in Los Angeles," in *Cruising Industrial Los Angeles* (Los Angeles: Los Angeles Conservancy, 1997), 8–9; Boyle Workman, *The City That Grew* (Los Angeles: Southland, 1935), 231; Robert M. Fogelson, *The Fragmented Metropolis: Los Angeles, 1850–1930* (Cambridge, MA: Harvard University Press, 1967), 138–39; Perry, "Historical Analysis," 65–66, 88–89; Harris Newmark, *Sixty Years in Southern California, 1853–1913* (New York: Knickerbocker, 1916), 601.

14. Pro Bono Publica, "A Wholesale Misdemeanor," *Los Angeles Times*, December 6, 1887; "The Sewer Problem—What Should Be Done," *Los Angeles Times*, July 25, 1889.

15. Fogelson, *Fragmented Metropolis*, 33–34; Los Angeles City Council, *Minutes*, August 12, 1896, September 21, 1903; T. F. Osborn to Los Angeles City Council, November 23, 1904, Los Angeles City Council Petitions 1904, Communication 1347, Los Angeles City Archives.

16. "They Build Nests in the River Bed," *Los Angeles Times*, January 6, 1901; Los Angeles City Council, *Minutes*, December 12, 1903; Los Angeles City Ordinance 21780 (New Series), January 31, 1911; Woody Guthrie, "Los Angeles New Year's Flood," on disc 3 of *Library of Congress Recordings* (Rounder Records CD 1041/2/3).

17. Los Angeles City Council, *Minutes*, April 27, 1896, November 11, 1901, August 3, 1903, November 18, 1907.

18. Los Angeles City Council, *Minutes*, February 13, 1912 (quote from parks commissioner); James W. Reagan to Los Angeles City Council, October 7, 1920, Los Angeles City Council Petitions 1920, Communication 2606, Los Angeles City Archives; Los Angeles Board of Public Works to Los Angeles City Council, October 18, 1920, Los Angeles City Council Petitions 1920, Communication 2606, Los Angeles City Archives; Los Angeles City Council, Resolution, October 20, 1925, Los Angeles City Council Petitions 1925, Communication 6420, Los Angeles City Archives.

19. Dana W. Bartlett, *The Better City: A Sociological Study of the Modern City* (Los Ange-

les: Neuner, 1907), 32–33; Charles Mulford Robinson, *The City Beautiful. Report of the Municipal Art Commission for the City of Los Angeles* (Los Angeles: William J. Porter, 1909), 2–3.

20. *From Pueblo to City, 1849–1910* (Los Angeles: LeBerthon, 1910), 66; Los Angeles City Council, *Minutes*, February 13, 1912.

21. U.S. Engineer Office, *Los Angeles County Drainage Area Flood Control* (Los Angeles, 1939), 1, 9; U.S. Congress, House, *Survey Report for Los Angeles River Watershed*, 77th Cong., 1st sess., 1941, H. Doc. 426, Serial 10599, 18; Richard E. Bigger, *Flood Control in Metropolitan Los Angeles*, University of California Publications in Political Science (Berkeley: University of California Press, 1959), 6:2; LACBEFC, *Report of the Board of Engineers*, 205; James W. Reagan, comp., "A Report on Floods, River Phenomena and Rainfall in the Los Angeles Region, California," 1914–1915 (University Research Library, University of California, Los Angeles, typescript), 9, 25, 43, 96; Don Jose del Carmen Lugo, "Life of a Rancher," trans. Thomas Savage, *Quarterly, Historical Society of Southern California* 32, no. 3 (September 1950): 190–91.

22. J. M. Guinn, "Exceptional Years: A History of California Floods and Drought," *Publications of the Historical Society of Southern California* 1, pt. 5 (1890): 33; "Old Map Showing Zanja System," zanjas superimposed on H. J. Stevenson's 1876 "Map of the City of Los Angeles, California," photocopy, Los Angeles Department of Water and Power Library; *Los Angeles Star*, January 25, 1862.

23. Newmark, *Sixty Years in Southern California*, 401; Perry, "Historical Analysis," 33; "Old Map Showing Zanja System"; H. J. Stevenson, "Map of the City of Los Angeles California" (Los Angeles, 1884); Workman, *City That Grew*, 151, 182–83.

24. J. J. Warner, "A Warning," *Los Angeles Times*, July 30, 1882; J. J. Warner, letter to the editor, *Los Angeles Times*, August 6, 1882.

25. Southern California Directory Co., *Los Angeles City and County Directory for 1881–2* (Los Angeles, 1881); Alfred Moore, letter to the editor, *Los Angeles Times*, August 2, 1882; "The Sufferers," *Los Angeles Times*, February 18, 1884, extra edition, 2:45 p.m.; "The Last Flood," *Los Angeles Times*, January 20, 1886; Los Angeles Directory Co., *Maxwell's Los Angeles City Directory and Gazetteer of Southern California* (Los Angeles, 1894).

26. U.S. Bureau of the Census, *Twelfth Census of the United States, Taken in the Year 1900, Population, Part 1* (Washington DC: Government Printing Office, 1901); U.S. Bureau of the Census, *Thirteenth Census of the United States, Taken in the Year 1910*, vol. 1, *Population* (Washington DC: Government Printing Office, 1913); U.S. Bureau of the Census, *Fourteenth Census of the United States, Taken in the Year 1920*, vol. 1, *Population* (Washington DC: Government Printing Office, 1921); Howard J. Nelson, *The Los Angeles Metropolis* (Dubuque, IA: Kendall/Hunt, 1983), 267; Leonard Pitt and Dale Pitt, *Los Angeles A to Z: An Encyclopedia of the City and County* (Berkeley: University of California Press, 1997), 175; E. Caswell Perry, *Burbank: An Illustrated History* (Northridge, CA: Windsor, 1987), 37; Félix Violé, "Map of Los Angeles and Surroundings," History Department, Los Angeles Public Library, 1916; Central Manufacturing District, Inc., *Central Manufacturing District and Los Angeles Junction Railway, Los Angeles, California, Showing Rail and Harbor Connections, Traffic Roads, Residential and Industrial Areas*, map (Los Angeles, 1932).

27. Ralph B. Wertheimer, *Flood Plain Zoning: Possibilities and Legality With Special Reference to Los Angeles County, California* (Sacramento: California State Planning Board, 1942), 2; LACBEFC, *Report of the Board of Engineers*, 225; Los Angeles County Regional Planning Commission, "Land Use Survey, County of Los Angeles," 16 vols. (San Marino, CA: Huntington Library, 1939); Los Angeles Department of City Planning, "Land Use Survey, City of Los Angeles," 10 vols. (San Marino, CA: Huntington Library, 1939).

28. The content of hundreds of interviews conducted by county flood-control officials after the flood of 1914, along with testimony given at a public hearing held by federal government flood-control engineers in 1936, suggests that residents had little concern for the natural character of the region's rivers and streams. Most opposition to flood-control efforts was based on differences in opinion about the best method for reducing the flood risk and the most equitable means for financing the work. Aesthetics do not seem to have been an issue. Harold E. Hedger, chief engineer of the flood control district until 1959, later commented that the only environmental concern considered in flood-control planning was whether stream channels should be left open or covered completely like sewers. See Reagan, "Report on Floods"; U.S. Army Corps of Engineers, Los Angeles District, "Transcript of Hearing and Exhibits to Accompany Preliminary Examination Report, Flood Control, Los Angeles and San Gabriel Rivers and Their Tributaries, California," March 31, 1936, (Water Resources Center Archives, University of California, Berkeley, typescript); Stanley R. Steenbock, "And Keep Your Honors Safe . . .: A Brief Overview and Affectionate Farewell to the Los Angeles County Flood Control District, 1915–1985," (Alhambra, CA: Los Angeles County Department of Public Works Technical Library, typescript, 1985), 40.

Chapter 7: Flood Control Engineering in the Urban Ecosystem

The author thanks Mary Coomes, William Deverell, Glen Gendzel, Greg Hise, Kathy Kolnick, and Phoebe Kropp for their insights and editing assistance.

1. National Research Council, Committee on Natural Disasters, and Environmental Quality Laboratory, California Institute of Technology, *Storms, Floods, and Debris Flows in Southern California and Arizona, 1978 and 1980: Overview and Summary of a Symposium, September 17–18, 1980* (Washington DC: National Academy Press, 1982), 11. There is some dispute about how the debris got there. Flood-control officials maintained that the water nearly overflowed the levees, leaving the debris behind as evidence. A few Long Beach residents, however, claimed that waves well below the levees could have tossed it there; Friends of the Los Angeles River (hereafter FoLAR), "Proposed Flood Control Strategy for the Los Angeles and San Gabriel River Systems," appendix (Los Angeles Public Library, hereafter LAPL, 1995); D. J. Waldie, "The Myth of the L.A. River," *Buzz*, April 1996, 84.

2. I borrow this term from the geographer Kenneth Hewitt, who uses it to describe disaster-management systems that give "precedence in support and prestige to bureaucratically organised institutions, centrally controlled and staffed by or allocating funds to specialised professionals." He suggests that technocracies both support and are supported by a paradigm that conceives natural disasters to be extraordinary disruptions to otherwise stable and predictable societal systems. After defining disasters in this way, society "can then focus daunting technical equipment and expertise upon tasks technocracy understands: forecasting physical conditions; ever more complete containment of natural processes; educating government and the public; devising general, centrally controlled systems to protect those at risk; to zone 'high hazard' areas; redesigning installations; and if all else fails, organising relief on a grand scale." Kenneth Hewitt, "The Idea of Calamity in a Technocratic Age," in *Interpretations of Calamity from the Viewpoint of Human Ecology*, ed. Kenneth Hewitt (Boston: Allen & Unwin, 1983), 8, 16, 19, 20.

3. Theodore Osmundson, "How to Control the Flood Controllers," *Cry California*, Summer 1970, 33; the engineer's quote is in Judith Coburn, "Whose River Is It, Anyway?" *Los Angeles Times Magazine*, November 20, 1994, 52–54.

4. Robert H. Wiebe, *The Search for Order, 1877–1920* (New York: Hill and Wang, 1967); Samuel P. Hays, *Conservation and the Gospel of Efficiency: The Progressive Conservation*

Movement, 1890–1920 (Cambridge, MA: Harvard University Press, 1959; repr., New York: Atheneum: 1969).

5. Los Angeles County Flood Control Association, "Minutes of Convention," July 1, 1914, Old Document Files 4834F, Executive Office of the Los Angeles County Board of Supervisors (hereafter LACBS), Los Angeles. On the proposal, see Los Angeles County Board of Engineers, Flood Control (hereafter LACBEFC), by Frank Olmsted, Los Angeles, to Los Angeles County Board of Supervisors, Los Angeles, August 3, 1914, Old Document Files 4838F, LACBS; LACBEFC, Los Angeles, to Los Angeles County Board of Supervisors, Los Angeles, September 19, 1914, Old Document Files 4850F, LACBS; "Notes for River Control," n.d., Old Document Files 4857F, LACBS; LACBEFC, *Reports of the Board of Engineers Flood Control to the Board of Supervisors Los Angeles County California* (Los Angeles, 1915), 5–11, the engineer's quote is on p. 31.

6. Technically, the flood-control district was a separate entity from the county. This was important because county bond elections required a two-thirds majority approval from the electorate, whereas special districts such as the LACFCD could get bonds approved with a simple majority. In practice, however, the district was essentially a county agency. Its boundaries coincided with the urbanized portion of the county, its executive body was the County Board of Supervisors, and its legal and administrative staffs were also made up of county officials. Eventually the district merged with the county government.

7. "An Act to Create a Flood Control District . . .," *Cal Stats*, 1915, chap. 755.

8. California State Planning Board, "Flood-Plain Zoning: Possibilities and Legality with Special Reference to Los Angeles County, California," by Ralph B. Wertheimer, June 1942, Water Resources Center Archives (hereafter WRCA).

9. "Why Build in Flood Control Channels?" *Municipal League Bulletin*, April 1938, 4; *Parks, Playgrounds and Beaches for the Los Angeles Region: A Report Submitted to the Citizens' Committee on Parks, Playgrounds and Beaches* (Los Angeles: Citizens' Committee on Parks, Playgrounds and Beaches, 1930); Charles W. Eliot and Donald F. Griffin, *Waterlines: Key to Development of Metropolitan Los Angeles* (Los Angeles: Haynes Foundation, 1946); Planning Board, "Flood-Plain Zoning," 10–18. Various forms of flood-hazard zoning were in also effect in the 1930s in cities in New Hampshire, Ohio, and Wisconsin; Planning Board, "Flood-Plain Zoning," 1.

10. On the LACFCD officials' comments, see N. B. Hodgkinson to Paul Baumann, October 27, 1937; Hodgkinson to Baumann, November 30, 1937; Finley B. Laverty to Baumann, October 28, 1937; each letter is housed at the Los Angeles County Department of Public Works Technical Library (hereafter LACDPWTL), Alhambra, CA. On the engineers, see James G. Jobes, "Lessons from Major Disasters" (address to the University of Southern California Institute of Government, June 15, 1939, Public Affairs Office of the Los Angeles District of the Army Corps of Engineers (hereafter PAO), Los Angeles); Anthony F. Turhollow, *A History of the Los Angeles District, U.S. Army Corps of Engineers* (Los Angeles: U.S. Army Engineer District, 1975), 229.

11. *Parks, Playgrounds and Beaches*; Greg Hise and William Deverell, *Eden by Design: The 1930 Olmsted-Bartholomew Plan for the Los Angeles Region* (Berkeley: University of California Press, 2000), 32–46.

12. On the early initiatives, see Marc A. Weiss, *The Rise of the Community Builders: The American Real Estate Industry and Urban Land Planning* (New York: Columbia University Press, 1987), see esp. chap. 4. On the chamber of commerce position, see Los Angeles Chamber of Commerce, "Stenographer's Reports," April 2, 1936, 8–10, box 21, Los Angeles Area Chamber of Commerce Collection, Regional History Center, University of Southern Cali-

fornia (hereafter LAACC), Los Angeles. For additional examples of the chamber hesitating to endorse one aspect or other of federal flood control out of fear of supporting federal interference, see Los Angeles Chamber of Commerce, "Stenographer's Reports," February 2, 1939, 10–12, box 28; April 25, 1940, 1, box 28, February 26, 1942, 2–4, box 28, June 29, 1944, 3–6, box 28, LAACC. Nor did the U.S. Department of Agriculture think zoning was a practical possibility. It devoted only three paragraphs to the subject on the last page of a sixty-seven-page *Survey Report* in 1941 and concluded that "it would be very difficult to bring sufficient pressure to bear to initiate zoning regulations"; U.S. Department of Agriculture, *Survey Report for the Los Angeles River Watershed* (Washington DC: Government Printing Office, 1941), 67, PAO. On the chamber's position in the latter 1920s and 1930s, see Los Angeles Chamber of Commerce, "Stenographer's Reports," 1925–1937, boxes 10–28, LAACC. The book on a master plan is George W. Robbins and L. Deming Tilton, eds., *Los Angeles: Preface to a Master Plan* (Los Angeles: Pacific Southwest Academy, 1941), 87–89 and chap. 13.

13. C. H. Howell to John Anson Ford, April 12, 1938, LACDPWTL; Los Angeles Chamber of Commerce, "Stenographer's Reports," March 26, 1936, 4–9, box 21, LAACC.

14. Thomas Ford to John Anson Ford, March 29, 1936, box 71, John Anson Ford Collection (hereafter JAF), Huntington Library, San Marino, CA; Los Angeles Chamber of Commerce, "Stenographer's Reports," March 26, 1936, 4–9, box 21, LAACC; Municipal League of Los Angeles to Board of Engineers for Rivers and Harbours, Washington DC, December 11, 1939, box 10, JAF.

15. Donald M. Baker to John Anson Ford, Los Angeles, December 13, 1934, box 10, JAF; Donald M. Baker, "Discussion," in E. Courtlandt Eaton, "Flood and Erosion Control Problems and Their Solution," *Transactions of the American Society of Civil Engineers* 101 (1936): 1356–59.

16. Eaton, "Flood and Erosion," 1362.

17. On the storm, see Richard Bigger, *Flood Control in Metropolitan Los Angeles* (Berkeley: University of California Press, 1959), 3. On the aftermath, see Turhollow, *History*, 158; "Mopping Up," *Los Angeles Times*, March 4, 1938; "Southland Starts Rebuilding," *Los Angeles Times*, March 5, 1938; Harold H. Story, "Memoirs of Harold H. Story," 1967, 794, transcript, University of California, Los Angeles, Oral History Program, Special Collections Library (containing Shaw quote).

18. Department of the Interior, U.S. Geological Survey, *Urban Sprawl and Flooding in Southern California: Water in the Urban Environment*, by S. E. Rantz, circular, U.S. Geological Survey, 601-B (Washington DC: U.S. Department of the Interior, 1970), B4. The Dillard quote is in "L.A. Dams Prevented Disaster," *Los Angeles Herald-Examiner*, November 28, 1965.

19. Los Angeles Chamber of Commerce, "Stenographer's Reports," September 15, 1938, 2, box 21, LAACC.

20. For local attitudes, see Los Angeles Chamber of Commerce, "Stenographer's Reports," 27 February 1941, 8, box 28, LAACC; Los Angeles Chamber of Commerce, "Annual Report: Conservation Department of Los Angeles Chamber of Commerce," 1941, box 65, LAACC; U.S. Department of Agriculture, *Survey Report*, iii; Warren T. Hannum, "Flood Control in Southern California in Relation to National Defense" (address to the National Resources Planning Board, Los Angeles, March 1, 1941, 4, PAO). The quote on LACDA quote is in Floyd Suter Bixby, "Drainage Doctors: Modern Construction Efficiency in Los Angeles Flood Control Program," *Constructor*, May 1941, 27. See also Los Angeles County Flood Control District, *Annual Report*, 1942, 47–54.

21. The defense concerns are expressed in Myrl Ott, Long Beach, to District Engineer, Los Angeles, December 7, 1946; D. E. Root, Long Beach, to District Engineer, Los Angeles,

December 5, 1946. Originals of both letters can be found in United States Army Corps of Engineers, Los Angeles District (hereafter LAD), "Restudy of Whittier Narrows Project and Alternative Plans for Flood Control," by R. C. Hunter, December 1946, appendix 5, part 3, LACDPWTL. On the official position, see, for example, LAD, "Restudy," in which the army corps cast the flood-control district as the agency "responsible by law for the safety and welfare of the people," and as "legally responsible representatives of local interests" (pp. 23, 28). Meanwhile, it described the opponents of the Whittier Narrows project as "a relatively small local unofficial group" (p. 28); see also Bigger, *Flood Control*, 141, the political warfare quote is on p. 115.

22. LAD, "Project Summary and Historical Sketch Whittier Narrows Flood-Control Basin Near El Monte, California," February 28, 1945, U.S. Army Corps of Engineers, Civil Work Projects, box 451, RG 77, National Archives Pacific Region (hereafter NAPR); LAD, "Restudy"; LAD, "Analysis of Design: Whittier Narrows Flood Control Basin," January 1950, LACDPWTL.

23. L. L. Wise, "Is Los Angeles Ready for a Flood?" *Engineering News-Record*, May 17, 1956, 50. The three 1950s storms combined to do about 13 million dollars of damage. Engineers estimated that without flood-control works, the damages would have totaled another 75 million dollars, still somewhat below the destruction done in 1938, when, adjusting for 1950s dollars, damages totaled 90 million dollars. For damage statistics regarding these floods, see LAD "Report on Flood Damage in Southern California from Flood of 15–18 January 1952," February 12, 1952, U.S. Army Corps of Engineers, General Administration Files, box 180, RG 77, NAPR; LACFCD, "Floods of January 15–18, 1952," WRCA, University of California, Berkeley; LAD, "Report on Flood Damage in Southern California From Floods of January 1954," February 12, 1954, U.S. Army Corps of Engineers, General Administration Files, box 181, RG 77, NAPR; C. H. Chorpening to Thomas H. Kuchel, Washington DC, February 9, 1954, U.S. Army Corps of Engineers, General Administration Files, box 180, RG 77, NAPR; LAD, "Report on Storm and Flood of 25–27 January 1956 in Southern California," March 2, 1956, U.S. Army Corps of Engineers, General Administration Files, box 181, RG 77, NAPR.

24. LAD, "Report on Flood Damage," 1952, 7, NAPR; LAD, "Preliminary Report on Recent Forest Fires and Flood Damage, Los Angeles and San Bernardino Counties, California," February 4, 1954, 3, U.S. Army Corps of Engineers, General Administration Files, box 180, RG 77, NAPR; LAD, "Report on Flood Damage," 1954, 14, NAPR.

25. LAD, "Appendix D: Report on Floods of January and February 1969 in Los Angeles County," December 1969, D74, LACDPWTL; U.S. Geological Survey, *Urban Sprawl*, B8–B9, the quote is from the Foreword. For similarly optimistic assessments of the storm, see LACFCD, "Summary Report," 1969, 33, 45, LACDPWTL. For similarly optimistic assessments of the storm, see LACFCD, "Summary Report," 1969, 33, 45, LACDPWTL. The brochure is LAD, "LACDA Update," September 1987, 1, PAO.

26. J. Daniel Davis, "Rare and Unusual Postfire Flood Events Experienced in Los Angeles County During 1978 and 1980," in *Storms, Floods, and Debris Flows in Southern California and Arizona, 1978 and 1980: Proceedings of a Symposium, September 17–18, 1980*, sponsored by National Research Council, Committee on Natural Disasters, and Environmental Quality Laboratory, California Institute of Technology (Washington DC: National Academy Press, 1982), 244; Gerard Shuirman and James E. Slosson, *Forensic Engineering: Environmental Case Histories for Civil Engineers and Geologists* (San Diego: Academic, 1992), 189.

27. Engineers noticed this problem as early as 1915, and it has accelerated since then. "Research Los Angeles County Flood Control," interviews with Los Angeles County residents, compiled by James W. Reagan, 1914–1915, 55, LACDPWTL; Board of Engineers,

Reports (1915), 174; LACFCD, *Report of J. W. Reagan Engineer Los Angeles County Flood Control District upon the Control of Flood Waters in this District by Correction of Rivers, Diversion and Care of Washes, Building of Dikes and Dams, Protecting Public Highways, Private Property and Los Angeles and Long Beach Harbors* (Los Angeles, 1917), 27–28; LACFCD, "Comprehensive Plan: Preliminary Outline of Ultimate Plan," September 10, 1930, 6, LACDPWTL; U.S. Geological Survey, *Urban Sprawl,* B10; FoLAR, "Proposed Flood Control Strategy," 8.

28. Eric Malnic and Henry Chu, "L.A. Region Faces Major Flood Risk, U.S. Warns," *Los Angeles Times,* October 25, 1997, World Wide Web edition, <http://www.latimes.com>.

29. The flip-bucket quote is in John M. Tettemer, "Closing Comments on Debris and Sediment," in *Storms, Floods, and Debris Flows.* For accounts of the debris flows, see Davis, "Rare and Unusual"; John M. Tettemer, "Sediment Flow Hazards: Special Hydrologic Events," in *Storms, Floods, and Debris Flows.* The 1978 debris flows are the focus of John McPhee's essay, "Los Angeles Against the Mountains," reprinted in this volume as chapter 10.

30. Hal K. Rothman, *The Greening of a Nation?: Environmentalism in the United States since 1945* (Fort Worth, TX: Harcourt Brace, 1998); John Opie, *Nature's Nation: An Environmental History of the United States* (Fort Worth, TX: Harcourt Brace, 1998); Samuel P. Hays, *Beauty, Health, and Permanence: Environmental Politics in the United Sates, 1955–1985* (New York: Cambridge University Press, 1987).

31. Lewis MacAdams, "Restoring the Los Angeles River: A Forty-Year Art Project," *Whole Earth Review,* Spring 1995, 63–67; Coburn, "Whose River"; Los Angeles County Department of Public Works, Department of Parks and Recreation, and Department of Regional Planning, "Los Angeles River Master Plan," June 1996, LAPL; FoLAR, "Proposed Flood Control Strategy"; Blake Gumprecht, *The Los Angeles River: Its Life, Death, and Possible Re-Birth* (Baltimore: Johns Hopkins University Press, 1999).

32. Winston W. Crouch and Beatrice Dinerman, *Southern California Metropolis: A Study in Development of Government for a Metropolitan Area* (Bekeley: University of California Press, 1963), 217–19. The quote on the construction materials is in J. David Rogers, Pleasant Hill, CA, letter to author, September 2, 1998. Rogers teaches engineering at the University of California, Berkeley, and heads Geolith Consultants, a geotechnical engineering consulting firm. The official report acknowledged that some of the construction materials were substandard. Although it maintained that this did not affect the failure, the report acknowledged that the defective materials could have led to failure in a greater flow; Joe Sciandrone et al., "Levee Failure and Distress, San Jacinto River Levee and Bautista Creek Channel, Riverside County, Santa Ana River Basin, California," in *Storms, Floods, and Debris Flows.*

33. National Research Council, *Overview and Summary,* 18.

Chapter 8: Private Sector Planning for the Environment

1. For just a few examples of private organizations involved in urban planning, see Mel Scott, *American City Planning Since 1890* (Berkeley: University of California Press, 1969), 101, 199–210, 397, 436; William C. Johnson, *The Politics of Urban Planning* (New York: Paragon, 1989).

2. Robert M. Fogelson, *The Fragmented Metropolis: Los Angeles, 1850–1930* (Cambridge, MA: Harvard University Press, 1967), 247–72; Scott L. Bottles, *Los Angeles and the Automobile: The Making of a Modern City* (Berkeley: University of California Press, 1987), 102–28; Greg Hise and William Deverell, *Eden By Design: The 1930 Olmsted-Bartholomew Plan for the Los Angeles Region* (Berkeley: University of California Press, 2000), 1–56.

3. Tom Sitton, *The Haynes Foundation and Urban Reform Philanthropy in Los Angeles: A*

History of the John Randolph Haynes and Dora Haynes Foundation (Los Angeles: Historical Society of Southern California, 1999), chap. 2 and 3. For a biography of John R. Haynes, see Tom Sitton, *John Randolph Haynes: California Progressive* (Stanford, CA: Stanford University Press, 1992).

4. John Collier to Harold Von Schmidt, January 3, 1936, copy in Haynes Foundation Addendum to the John Randolph Haynes Papers, Department of Special Collections, University of California, Los Angeles (hereafter Haynes Papers); Sitton, *Haynes Foundation*, 71–77.

5. Fogelson, *Fragmented Metropolis*, 247–72; Scott, *American City Planning*, 204–10, 378; Judith N. Jamison, *Regional Planning*, vol. 3, *Metropolitan Los Angeles: A Study in Integration*, ed. Edwin Cottrell (Los Angeles: Haynes Foundation, 1953), 6–16, 61; Martin J. Schiesl, "City Planning and the Federal Government in World War II: The Los Angeles Experience," *California History* 59 (Summer 1980): 127; Mike Davis, "How Eden Lost Its Garden," *The City: Los Angeles and Urban Theory at the End of the Twentieth Century*, ed. Allen J. Scott and Edward W. Soja (Berkeley: University of California Press, 1996), 162–64; Greg Hise, *Magnetic Los Angeles: Planning the Twentieth-Century Metropolis* (Baltimore: Johns Hopkins University Press, 1997).

6. G. Gordon Whitnall, memorandum to Dr. Remsen D. Bird and William Schuchardt, January 24, 1939, City Planning Commission boxes, Remsen D. Bird Papers, Special Collections, Occidental College (hereafter Bird Papers); Sitton, *John Randolph Haynes*, passim.

7. David C. Hammack, "Russell Sage Foundation," in Harold M. Keele and Joseph C. Kiger, eds., *Foundations* (Westport, CT: Greenwood, 1984), 373–80, quote on p. 375; Shelby M. Harrison and F. Emerson Andrews, *American Foundations for Social Welfare* (New York: Russell Sage Foundation, 1946), 188, 193. On the Russell Sage Foundation project in New York, see John M. Glenn, Lillian Brandt, and F. Emerson Andrews, *Russell Sage Foundation, 1907–1946*, 2 vols. (New York: Russell Sage Foundation, 1947), 2:438–51; David C. Hammack and Stanton Wheeler, *Social Science in the Making: Essays on the Russell Sage Foundation, 1907-1972* (New York: Russell Sage Foundation, 1994), 35–79. On the Buhl Foundation, see Roy Lubove, *Twentieth-Century Pittsburgh: Government, Business and Environmental Change* (New York: Wiley, 1969), 59–86.

8. *Christian Science Monitor*, February 10, 1945, *Los Angeles Times*, March 17, 1939; undated press release (ca. January 1939), Bird Papers. On Frank Shaw's administration, see Tom Sitton, "Urban Reform and Politics in New Deal Los Angeles: The Recall of Mayor Frank Shaw" (PhD diss., University of California, Riverside, 1983).

9. Pacific Southwest Academy file, box 161, Haynes Papers; *Los Angeles Times*, March 17, 1939; Remson D. Bird to John Parke Young, January 30, 1939, Remson D. Bird to Fred Mowder, March 23, 1939, Remson D. Bird to Fletcher Bowron, January 27, 1940, City Planning Commission boxes, Bird Papers.

10. L. Deming Tilton biography notes and copy of Remson D. Bird to L. Deming Tilton, July 7, 1939, grant file 3001a, box 16, Haynes Foundation Office files, Los Angeles (hereafter Haynes Foundation). Tilton also worked half time as a consultant for the National Resources Planning Board and other agencies.

11. Tilton, "Progress Report," September 9, 1939, Los Angeles Planning Project Report file, box 16, Haynes Foundation; "Program of Planning Conference of the County of Los Angeles on Conservation," June 9–10, 1939, City Planning Commission boxes, Bird Papers.

12. Helen Riter to L. Deming Tilton, August 28, 1941, grant file 3001a, box 16, Haynes Foundation; Los Angeles Chamber of Commerce entries in index for city council minutes, Los Angeles City Records Center.

13. L. Deming Tilton memorandum to Board of Trustees, July 13, 1939, grant file 3001, box 16, Haynes Foundation; George W. Robbins and L. Deming Tilton, eds., *Los Angeles: Preface to a Master Plan* (Los Angeles: Pacific Southwest Academy, 1941).

14. William Anderson, review of *Los Angeles: Preface to a Master Plan*, *American Political Science Review* 35 (June 1941): 562–64; Robert E. Alexander, "Architecture, Planning, and Social Responsibility," (University of California, Los Angeles, Oral History Project, 1989), 1:171–72; "Seven Decades of Planning and Development in the Los Angeles Region: Milton Breivogel" (University of California, Los Angeles, Oral History Project, 1989), 69–71; Schiesl, "City Planning," 126–43.

15. *Hollywood Citizen-News*, March 28, 1940; 1939 charter revision files, boxes 107 and 108, Haynes Papers; charter revision file, box 16, Haynes Foundation.

16. Tilton, "Progress Report, September 21, 1940," Los Angeles Planning Project Report file, box 16, and President's Report in Board of Trustees Minutes, September 21, 1940, Haynes Foundation.

17. Mel Scott, *Cities Are For People: The Los Angeles Region Plans For Living* (Los Angeles: Pacific Southwest Academy, 1942); Museum Scrapbooks, 1941–1942, Research Library, Natural History Museum of Los Angeles County.

18. Board of Trustees Minutes, December 15, 1941, February 7, 28, 1942, Haynes Foundation.

19. "Los Angeles Metropolitan Area Studies Project Annual Report, September 1, 1943," grant file 3002, box 17, grant file 2015, box 4, Haynes Foundation; Earl Hanson and Paul Beckett, *Los Angeles: Its People and Its Homes* (Los Angeles: Haynes Foundation, 1944).

20. Board of Trustees Minutes, October 23, November 13, 1943, Charles G. Haines to Charles W. Eliot II, October 8, 1943, grant file 3006, box 17, Haynes Foundation; Marion Clawson, *New Deal Planning: The National Resources Planning Board* (Baltimore: Johns Hopkins University Press, 1981), esp. 64–65.

21. Charles W. Eliot, *Citizen Support for Los Angeles Development* (Los Angeles: Haynes Foundation, 1945). The pamphlet series is listed at the end of most Haynes Foundation publications of the early 1950s.

22. Sitton, *Haynes Foundation*, 111–14.

23. Ibid.

24. *Los Angeles Times*, November 1, 1943; *Los Angeles Daily News*, December 16, 1943; Davis, "How Eden Lost," 166.

25. Grant file 3009, box 21, Haynes Foundation; Donald F. Griffin, *Plans and Actions for Development of the Los Angeles Metropolitan Coastline* (Los Angeles: Haynes Foundation, 1944).

26. Grant file 3006, box 17, Haynes Foundation; Los Angeles County, Citizens Committee on Parks, Beaches, and Recreational Facilities, *Parks, Beaches, and Recreational Facilities for Los Angeles County: Report* (Los Angeles: Haynes Foundation, 1945). On the Olmsted-Bartholomew plan, see Hise and Deverell, *Eden By Design*.

27. Grant file 3011, box 21, Haynes Foundation; Charles W. Eliot, *Waterlines—Key to Development of Metropolitan Los Angeles* (Los Angeles: Haynes Foundation, 1946).

28. Grant file 3016, box 22, Haynes Foundation; Sitton, *Haynes Foundation*, 114–15.

29. Sitton, *Haynes Foundation*, 117–23; Jamison, *Regional Planning*, 62–64.

30. Grant file 3008b, boxes 19 and 20, Haynes Foundation. The volumes in this series (all published by the Haynes Foundation in Los Angeles) are Edwin A. Cottrell and Helen L. Jones, *Characteristics of the Metropolis* (1952); Richard Bigger and James D. Kitchen, *How the Cities Grew* (1952); Judith N. Jamison, *Regional Planning* (1953); Robert F. Wilcox, *Law Enforcement* (1952); Winston W. Crouch, Wendell Maccoby, Margaret G. Morden, and

Richard Bigger, *Sanitation and Health* (1952); James K. Trump, Morton Kroll, and James R. Donoghue, *Fire Protection* (1952); Robert F. Wilcox, *Highways* (1953); Vincent Ostrom, *Water Supply* (1953); Ellis McCune, *Recreation and Parks* (1954); Helen L. Jones, *Personnel Management* (1952); Paul Beckett, Morris Plotkin, and George Pollak, *Governmental Purchasing* (1952); Helen L. Jones, *Schools* (1952); Helen L. Jones, *Libraries* (1953); Winston Crouch, John E. Swanson, Richard Bigger, and James A. Algie, *Finance and Taxation* (1954); Winston W. Crouch, *Intergovernmental Relations* (1954); Edwin A. Cottrell and Helen L. Jones, *The Metropolis: Is Integration Possible?* (1955). The Watkins quote is in Cottrell and Jones, vi.

31. Ralph Beals to Anne M. Mumford, September 10, 1949, Francis H. Lindley to Anne M. Mumford, February 15, 1950, and other correspondence in grant file 2029, box 26, Haynes Foundation.

32. Alexander, "Architecture," 1:229–30, 2:548–49; Robert E. Alexander and Drayton S. Bryant, *Rebuilding A City* (Los Angeles: Haynes Foundation, 1950).

33. *Los Angeles Times*, December 28, 1951; Robert Gottlieb and Irene Wolt, *Thinking Big: The Story of the Los Angeles Times, Its Publishers, and Their Influence on Southern California* (New York: G. P. Putnam's Sons, 1977), 259–65; Don Parson, "This Modern Marvel: Bunker Hill, Chavez Ravine, and the Politics of Modernism in Los Angeles," *Southern California Quarterly* 75 (Fall/Winter 1993): 333–50.

34. Sitton, *Haynes Foundation*, 137–72; Mark I. Gelfand, *A Nation of Cities: The Federal Government and Urban America, 1933–1965* (New York: Oxford University Press, 1975), 282–84.

35. Sitton, *Haynes Foundation*, 180–86, 193–97. The Haynes Foundation symposium "A Sustainable Future? Environmental Patterns and the Los Angeles Past" was held at the California Institute of Technology, September 20–21, 2003.

36. Margaret FitzSimmons and Robert Gottlieb, "Bounding and Binding Metropolitan Space: The Ambiguous Politics of Nature in Los Angeles," in Scott and Soja, *The City*, 197; James T. Lemon, *Liberal Dreams and Nature's Limits: Great Cities of North America Since 1600* (New York: Oxford University Press, 1996), 214, 236. See also Robert Fishman, *Bourgeois Utopias: The Rise and Fall of Suburbia* (New York: Basic Books, 1987), 155–81; Mike Davis, *City of Quartz: Excavating the Future in Los Angeles* (London: Verso, 1990), esp. 153–219; Mike Davis, *Ecology of Fear: Los Angeles and the Imagination of Disaster* (New York: Metropolitan Books, 1998); Roger Keil, *Los Angeles: Globalization, Urbanization and Social Struggles* (Chichester, England: Wiley, 1998).

Chapter 9: Zoning and Environmental Inequity in the Industrial East Side

1. City of Commerce Ordinance no. 527, 1998.

2. Christopher G. Boone and Ali Modarres, "Creating a Toxic Neighborhood in Los Angeles County: A Historical Examination of Environmental Inequity," *Urban Affairs Review* 35, no. 2 (1999): 163–87. The Geiger Company began manufacturing DDT in the early 1960s. Its plant closed before the Toxic Release Inventory data were first collected in 1987. In May 1995, unidentified fumes from the Westelectric Casting Company sent eight students from a nearby school to the hospital, and forty-five children had to be treated at the scene. *Commerce Comet*, May 25, 1995.

3. Gary J. Miller, *Cities by Contract: The Politics of Municipal Incorporation* (Cambridge, MA: MIT Press, 1981).

4. The Emergency Planning & Community Right-To-Know Act of 1986 gave the EPA the authority to collect the information and compile the Toxic Release Inventory database. The act was largely a response to the Union Carbide disaster in Bhopal, India, that killed thousands in 1984. Information on the Toxic Release Inventory and the database can be found

on-line at http://www.epa.gov/enviro/html/qmr.html#toxic. The studies of environmental inequity are Leonetta Burke, "Race and Environmental Equity: A Geographical Analysis in Los Angeles," *Geo Info Systems* 3, no. 9 (1993): 44–50; Tom J. Boer, Manuel Pastor, James L. Sadd, and Lori Snyder, "Is There Environmental Racism? The Demographics of Hazardous Waste in Los Angeles County," *Social Science Quarterly* 78, no. 4 (1997): 793–810; Boone and Modarres, "Toxic Neighborhood"; Laura Pulido, Steve Sidawi and R. O. Vos, "An Archaeology of Environmental Racism in Los Angeles" *Urban Geography* 17, no. 5 (1996): 419–39.

5. United Church of Christ, *Toxic Wastes and Race in the United States: A National Report on the Racial and Socio-Economic Characteristics of Communities with Hazardous Waste Sites* (New York: Commission for Racial Justice, United Church of Christ, 1987).

6. On the historical method of investigating environmental inequity, see, for example, Vicki Been, "Locally Undesirable Land Uses in Minority Neighborhoods: Disproportionate Siting or Market Dynamics?" *Yale Law Journal* 103 (1994): 1383–422. On the reasons minorities live in these areas, see L. Downey, "Environmental Justice: Is Race or Income a Better Predictor?" *Social Science Quarterly* 79, no. 4 (1998): 766–78; Laura Pulido, "Introduction: Environmental Racism," *Urban Geography* 17, no. 5 (1996): 377–79; Steve Sidawi, "Planning Environmental Racism: The Construction of an Industrial Suburban Ideal in Los Angeles County in the Early Twentieth Century" *Historical Geography* 25 (1997): 83–99.

7. Marc A. Weiss, *The Rise of the Community Builders: The American Real Estate Industry and Urban Land Planning* (New York: Columbia University Press, 1987).

8. Los Angeles County Regional Planning Commission, *Third Annual Report of the Zoning Section, 1928*, Hall of Records, Los Angeles, January 1929, Huntington Park County Library R352.96, 3

9. *Ibid*, 10, emphasis in original.

10. *Ibid*., 10; Los Angeles County Regional Planning Commission, *Guide to Los Angeles County Zoning Ordinance*, 1929, 22, emphasis in original.

11. Los Angeles Chamber of Commerce Industrial Department, *Facts About Industrial Los Angeles: Nature's Workshop*, Regional History Center, Special Collections, University of Southern California, Los Angeles Chamber of Commerce Collection [hereafter LACC], box 53, 1924; Mike Davis, *City of Quartz: Excavating the Future in Los Angeles* (New York: Vintage, 1992).

12. On the benefits of zoning to industry, see Los Angeles County Regional Planning Commission, *Seventh Annual Report, Zoning Section, 1932*, LACC, box 66. On the development of of mixed-use areas, Greg Hise, *Magnetic Los Angeles: Planning the Twentieth-Century Metropolis* (Baltimore: Johns Hopkins University Press, 1997).

13. Los Angeles County Regional Planning Commission, *Zoning Ordinance*, 12–13.

14. On the agricultural past of the area, see Charles Elliott, *City of Commerce: An Enterprising Heritage* (Los Angeles: Hacienda Gateway, 1991). See Boone and Modarres, "Toxic Neighborhood," for a photomosaic of the Commerce region in 1938.

15. Central Manufacturing District of Los Angeles, *"Junction Railway Service": A Book of Descriptive Text, Photographs and Testimonial Letters about the Central Manufacturing District of Los Angeles—"The Great Western Market,"* LACC, box 53, 1923. The present distribution of Toxic Release Inventory sites shows a strong spatial correlation with railroads, reflecting the accessibility needs of industry and zoning ordinances that encouraged the location of manufacturing close to railroad lines. See Boone and Modarres, "Toxic Neighborhood," 177.

16. Los Angeles County Regional Planning Commission, *Third Annual Report of the Zoning Section, 1928*, Hall of Records, Los Angeles, January 1929, Huntington Park County Library R352.96.

17. For the location study, see Los Angeles Chamber of Commerce Industrial Department and Board of Supervisors of Los Angeles County, *Survey of 118 Plant Locations in Los Angeles County*, LACC, box 53, 1954. On the firms' concerns, see Los Angeles County Regional Planning Commission, *Industrial Land Requirements in Los Angeles County* (Los Angeles, 1967).

18. Los Angeles County Regional Planning Commission, *First Annual Report of the Zoning Division of the Regional Planning Commission, County of Los Angeles, 1926*, Huntington Park Branch County Library, R352.96.

19. Los Angeles County Regional Planning Commission, *Fifth Annual Report of the Zoning Section, 1930*, LACC, box 66, 1931. Minutes from the public meeting would be a good source to gauge public response to the proposed zoning ordinance, but the records have been destroyed or lost. Neither the Los Angeles Regional Planning Department nor the Board of Supervisors has records of the meetings.

20. Robert M. Fogelson, *The Fragmented Metropolis: Los Angeles 1850–1930* (1967; repr., Berkeley: University of California Press, 1993).

21. On job growth between 1920 and 1940, see Edward W. Soja and Allen J. Scott, "Introduction to Los Angeles: City and Region," in *The City: Los Angeles and Urban Theory at the End of the Twentieth Century*, ed. Allen J. Scott and Edward W. Soja (Berkeley: University of California Press, 1996), 1–21. On postwar suburbanization, see Greg Hise, *Magnetic Los Angeles*.

22. Christopher G. Boone, "Real Estate Promotion and the Shaping of Los Angeles," *Cities* 15, no. 3 (1998): 155–63; G. S. Dumke, *The Boom of the 1880s in Southern California* (San Marino, CA: Huntington Library, 1944); Martin Wachs, "The Evolution of Transportation Policy in Los Angeles: Images of Past Policies and Future Prospects," in Scott and Soja, *The City*, 106–59.

23. Although the area under consideration contained few residents, surrounding communities, such as east Los Angeles, were already settled with large Latino (especially Mexican and Chicano) populations. See Adolfo F. Acuña, *A Community Under Siege: A Chronicle of Chicanos East of the Los Angeles River, 1945–1975* (Chicano Studies Research Center Publications, University of California, Los Angeles, 1984); Ricardo Romo, A. J. Rios-Bustamente, and P. Castillo, *An Illustrated History of Mexican Los Angeles, 1781–1985* (Chicano Studies Research Center Publications, University of California, Los Angeles, 1986).

24. Los Angeles Chamber of Commerce Industrial Department, *Special Report to General Motors Corporation: General Industrial Data, Los Angeles District, June 25, 1929*, LACC, box 53, 1929, 10.

Chapter 10: Los Angeles Against the Mountains

This chapter consists of excerpts from "Los Angeles Against the Mountains" from *The Control of Nature* by John McPhee. Copyright ©1989 John McPhee. Reprinted by permission of Farrar, Straus and Giroux, LLC. Ornamented line spaces represent elisions made by the volume editors for this book.

Transitions in Southern California Landscape Photography, 1900–1940

1. For an incisive discussion of these issues, see Sarah Greenough's essay, "Of Charming Glens, Graceful Glades and Frowning Cliffs: The Economic Incentives, Social Inducements, and Aesthetic Issues of American Pictorial Photography, 1880–1902," in *Photography in Nineteenth-Century America*, ed. Martha Sandweiss (Fort Worth, TX: Amon Carter Museum/Harry Abrams, 1991), 258–81.

2. Norman Klein, *The History of Forgetting: Los Angeles and the Erasure of Memory* (London: Verso, 1997), 9–13.

3. For a more specific reference to Southern California as an ideal climate for the nurturing of Anglo-American culture, see Charles Dudley Warner, "Race and Climate," *Land of Sunshine* January 1896, 103.

4. *Art Work on Southern California* , text signed in facsimile by Lou V. Chapin (San Francisco: California Photogravure, 1900).

5. Charles Dwight Willard, "The New Editor," *Land of Sunshine* 2, no.2 (1894): 12.

6. For a discussion of this term in the context of Japanese American photography, see Sigismund Blumann, "Our Japanese Brother Artists," *Camera Craft* 32, no.3 (1925): 10.

7. A host of photographic compositions initially explored in the early twentieth century by amateur fine-art photographers were completely absorbed into the canon of booster iconography by 1910. These include images of a robed priest framed against a fragment of crumbling mission architecture, Mexican laborers resting in the shade of a pepper tree, and ample quantities of fruit and flowers artfully arranged in living rooms and on dining room tables, to name only a few.

8. Will Connell, *The Missions of California* (New York: Hastings House, 1941).

9. Edward Weston and Charis Wilson, *Seeing California with Edward Weston* (n.p.: Westways/Automobile Club of California, 1939), 6.

10. Edward Weston to Merle Armitage, October 28, 1946. Merle Armitage Archive, Harry Ransom Humanities Research Center, Austin, TX.

11. Quoted in L. Thomas Frye and Therese Heyman, *Peacetime, Wartime & Hollywood: Photographs of Peter Stackpole* (Oakland, CA: Oakland Museum, 1992), 35.

Chapter 11: Thirteen Ways of Seeing Nature in LA

1. LA here means not just the political entity that is the City of Los Angeles, but the huge chunk of the Greater Los Angeles area that is Los Angeles County. On the Los Angeles River, see Jennifer Price, "Paradise Reclaimed: A Field Guide to the L.A. River," *L.A. Weekly*, August 10–16, 2001; Blake Gumprecht, *The Los Angeles River: Its Life, Death, and Possible Rebirth* (Baltimore: Johns Hopkins University Press, 1999); Jared Orsi, *Hazardous Metropolis: Flooding and Urban Ecology in Los Angeles* (Berkeley: University of California Press, 2004); Patt Morrison, *Rio L.A.: Tales from the Los Angeles River* (Santa Monica, CA: Angel City, 2001).

2. Michael Sorkin, "Exploring Los Angeles," in *California Counterpoint: New West Coast Architecture* (New York: Rizzoli, 1982), 8. A new anthology of LA literature, which has quickly become the standard, is David L. Ulin, ed., *Writing Los Angeles: A Literary Anthology* (New York: Library of America, 2002). See also David M. Fine, *Imagining Los Angeles: A City in Fiction* (Albuquerque: University of New Mexico Press, 2000).

3. A trenchant critique of nature writing is Richard White, "The Natures of Nature Writing," *Raritan* 22 (Fall 2002), 145–61.

4. Raymond Chandler, "Red Wind"; the story appeared originally in *Dime Detective* in 1938, and is reprinted in Ulin, *Writing Los Angeles*, 170–217 (quote is in opening paragraph).

5. Critiques of this definition of nature include William Cronon, ed., *Uncommon Ground: Toward Reinventing Nature* (New York: Norton, 1995), and especially Cronon's essay "The Trouble with Wilderness; or, Getting Back to the Wrong Nature," 69–90; Andrew Ross, *The Chicago Gangster Theory of Life: Nature's Debt to Society* (London: Verso, 1994); Jennifer Price, *Flight Maps: Adventures with Nature in Modern America* (New York: Basic Books, 1999); Michael Pollan, *Second Nature: A Gardener's Education* (New York: Atlantic Monthly Press,

1991); Bruce Braun and Noel Castree, eds., *Remaking Reality: Nature at the Millennium* (London: Routledge, 1998).

6. Bill McKibben, *The End of Nature* (New York: Random House, 1989). The piece originally appeared with a big splash in the *New Yorker*.

7. Well-known anthologies of nature writing include Robert Finch and John Elder, eds., *Nature Writing: The Tradition in English* (New York: Norton, 2002); Richard Mabey, ed., *The Oxford Book of Nature Writing* (New York: Oxford University Press, 1995). A rare collection of urban writing is Terrell F. Dixon, ed., *City Wilds: Essays and Stories about Urban Nature* (Athens: University of Georgia Press, 2002); for a lovely set of LA essays, see David Wicinas, *Sagebrush and Cappuccino: Confessions of an L.A. Naturalist* (San Francisco: Sierra Club Books, 1995).

8. My own favorite countermodels include Leah Hager Cohen, *Glass, Paper, Beans: Revelations on the Nature and Value of Ordinary Things* (New York: Doubleday, 1997); Pollan, *Second Nature*; Robert Sullivan, *The Meadowlands: Wilderness Adventures at the Edge of a City* (New York: Scribner, 1998); John McPhee, "Los Angeles Against the Mountains," in *The Control of Nature* (New York: Farrar, Straus and Giroux, 1989, excerpted and reprinted as chap. 10 of this volume). And likely no account of urban nature is more fun than Mark Dion and Alexis Rockman, *Concrete Jungle* (New York: Juno Books, 1996).

9. For excellent histories of cities as places we use and manage nature, see William Cronon, *Nature's Metropolis: Chicago and the Great West* (New York: Norton, 1991); Matthew Gandy, *Concrete and Clay: Reworking Nature in New York City* (Cambridge, MA: MIT Press, 2002); Orsi, *Hazardous Metropolis*; Ari Kelman, *A River and Its City: The Nature of Landscape in New Orleans* (Berkeley: University of California Press, 2003). Works from an urban-design perspective include Anne Whiston Spirn, *The Granite Garden: Urban Nature and Human Design* (New York: Basic Books, 1984); Michael Hough, *Cities and Natural Process* (London: Routledge, 1995). I have learned much about the sustainable-cities approach from geographer Jennifer Wolch: see Wolch et al., "Urban Nature and the Nature of Urbanism," in *From Chicago to L.A.: Making Sense of Urban Theory*, ed. Michael J. Dear (Thousand Oaks, CA: Sage, 2002), 367–402; Politics and Economics panel, "A Sustainable Future? Environmental Patterns and the Los Angeles Past," conference, California Institute of Technology, September 20, 2003. On sustainable cities, see also, for example, David Satterthwaite, ed., *The Earthscan Reader in Sustainable Cities* (London: Earthscan, 1999); Kent E. Portney, *Taking Sustainable Cities Seriously: Economic Development, the Environment, and Quality of Life in American Cities* (Cambridge, MA: MIT Press, 2003). For an environmental science perspective, see, for example, Gretchen C. Daily, ed., *Nature's Services: Societal Dependence on Natural Ecosystems* (Washington DC: Island Press, 1997). On LA in particular, I have found especially helpful Wolch, "Urban Nature"; TreePeople's T.R.E.E.S. project, http://www.treepeople.org/trees; Robert Gottlieb, *Environmentalism Unbound: Exploring New Pathways for Change* (Cambridge, MA: MIT Press, 2001); Southern California Studies Center and Brookings Center on Urban and Metropolitan Policy, *Sprawl Hits the Wall: Confronting the Realities of Metropolitan Los Angeles* (Los Angeles: Southern California Studies Center, University of Southern California, 2001).

10. On the social geography of air in LA, see Laura Pulido et al., "An Archaeology of Environmental Racism in Los Angeles," *Urban Geography* 17 (July 1–August 15, 1996): 419–39; Gary Polakovic, "Latinos, Poor Live Closer to Sources of Air Pollution," *Los Angeles Times*, October 18, 2001; Shipra Bonsal and Sam Davis, *Holding Our Breath: Environmental Injustice Exposed in Southeast Los Angeles* (Los Angeles: Communities for a Better Environment, 1998). On environmental justice in LA generally, see Gottlieb, *Environmentalism Unbound*; Laura

Pulido, "Rethinking Environmental Racism: White Privilege and Urban Development in Southern California," *Annals of the Association of American Geographers* 90 (2000): 12–40. Overviews of the broader environmental justice movement include Daniel Faber, ed., *The Struggle for Ecological Democracy: Environmental Justice Movements in the United States* (New York: Guilford, 1998); Richard Hofrichter, ed., *Reclaiming the Environmental Debate: The Politics of Health in a Toxic Culture* (Cambridge, MA: MIT Press, 2000); Richard Hofrichter, ed., *Toxic Struggles: The Theory and Practice of Environmental Justice* (Salt Lake City: University of Utah Press, 2002).

11. George Ramos, "Couple in Silver Lake Outraged at Coyotes," *Los Angeles Times*, September 22, 2002.

12. For example, Elizabeth Johns, "Spelling's House No Love Boat," *E! News*, E! Channel, March 26, 1997.

13. In Carey McWilliams, *Southern California: An Island on the Land* (Santa Barbara, CA: Peregrine Smith, 1973), 6.

14. At the time, LA's road not taken was a regional plan, commissioned by the Chamber of Commerce but then buried, that would have managed the river as central to watershed functions and to the design of a parks network. Greg Hise and William Deverell, *Eden by Design: The 1930 Olmsted-Bartholomew Plan for the Los Angeles Region* (Berkeley: University of California Press, 2000).

15. Los Angeles County, http://lacounty.info/; U.S. Census Bureau, http://eire.census .gov; "Harbor, Los Angeles, Since 1900," in Leonard Pitt and Dale Pitt, *Los Angeles A to Z: An Encyclopedia of the City and County* (Berkeley: University of California Press, 1997), 190.

16. On LA generally, and on the themes of mythmaking, socioeconomics, and disconnection and erasure, I have been influenced particularly by Mike Davis, *City of Quartz: Excavating the Future in Los Angeles* (London: Verso, 1990); McWilliams, *Southern California*; Allen J. Scott and Edward W. Soja, eds., *The City: Los Angeles and Urban Theory at the End of the Twentieth Century* (Berkeley: University of California Press, 1996); Dear, *Chicago to L.A.*; David Reid, ed., *Sex, Death and God in L.A.* (New York: Pantheon Books, 1992); Ulin, *Writing Los Angeles*; Joan Didion, *Slouching Towards Bethlehem* (ca. 1968; repr., New York: Noonday, 1990), 219–20; Robert M. Fogelson, *The Fragmented Metropolis: Los Angeles, 1850–1930* (Berkeley: University of California Press, 1967); William Fulton, *The Reluctant Metropolis: The Politics of Urban Growth in Los Angeles* (Point Arena, CA: Solano Press Books, 1997); Dolores Hayden, *The Power of Place: Urban Landscapes as Public History* (Cambridge, MA: MIT Press, 1995); Harold Meyerson's regular pieces on LA politics in the *L.A. Weekly*.

17. Charlie LeDuff, "Los Angeles Can't Cope as Rain Finally Arrives," *New York Times*, November 9, 2002; Lisa Schwarzbaum, review of *Matchstick Men*, *Entertainment Weekly*, September 19, 2003, 63.

18. Claude Levi-Strauss, *Totemism*, trans. Rodney Needham (Boston: Beacon, 1963).

19. Michael T. Jarvis, "Edifice Complex," *Los Angeles Times*, January 4, 2004; Ken Tucker, "The Lady Bunch," *Entertainment Weekly*, January 23–30, 2004; David L. Ulin, "Californians Should Be Aware of Their Faults," *Los Angeles Times*, January 16, 2004.

20. For the philanthropy ranking, see Kit Rachlis, "The Patron Class," *Los Angeles*, June 2003, 6.

21. On air pollution and regulation, see, for example, Daniel A. Mazmanian, "Los Angeles' Transition from Command-and-Control to Market-Based Clean Air Policy Strategies and Implementation," in *Toward Sustainable Communities: Transition and Transformations in Environmental Policy*, ed. Daniel A. Mazmanian and Michael E. Kraft (Cambridge, MA: MIT Press, 1999), 77–112; Gary Polakovic, "There's Hope in the Air," *Los Angeles Times*, January 14,

2001. On beach closures and the Natural Resources Defense Council, see Seema Mehta, "Southland Is U.S. Leader in Beach Closures," *Los Angeles Times*, July 25, 2002. On the lawsuit, see Betsy Streisand, "A New Day at the Beach," *U.S. News & World Report*, February 1, 1999, 33; Price, "Paradise Reclaimed."

22. On park space, see Jennifer Wolch et al., "Parks and Park Funding in Los Angeles: An Equity Mapping Analysis," report, Sustainable Cities Program, University of Southern California, 2002; Robert García et al., "The Heritage Parkway in the Heart of Los Angeles," 8th International Urban Parks Conference, New York City, 21–25 June 2003. On policy makers, see, as a major example, "AQMD Board Adopts Environmental Justice Initiatives," *South Coast Air Quality Management District News*, October 10, 1997 (http://www.aqmd.gov/news1/Archives/envjust1.html); for a recent major state victory, see "Recommendations of the California Environmental Protection Agency (Cal/EPA) Advisory Committee on Environmental Justice to the Cal/EPA Interagency Working Group on Environmental Justice," final report, September 30, 2003 (http://www.calepa.ca.gov/EnvJustice/Documents/2003/FinalReport.pdf).

23. Judith Lewis, "Interesting Times," in *Another City: Writing from Los Angeles*, ed. David L. Ulin (San Francisco: City Lights, 2001), 10.

24. See, for example, García et al, "Heritage Parkway."

25. Didion, *Slouching*, 219–20.

26. *Time*, April 19, 1993.

Chapter 12: A Garden of Worldly Delights

1. For information on the Sherman Institute and the larger context of the Indian boarding schools, see David Wallace Adams, *Education for Extinction: American Indians and the Boarding School Experience, 1875–1928* (Lawrence: University Press of Kansas, 1995). Horatio Rust, "Report on the Condition of Mission Indians," October 1892, manuscript, box 9, Horatio Rust Papers, Huntington Research Library, San Marino, California. See also Jane Apostal, "Horatio Nelson Rust: Abolitionist, Archeologist, Indian Agent," *California History* 58 (Winter 1979–80): 304–15. For Rust's recommendations for Indian children, see Horatio Rust to James McLaughlin, November 20, 1900, box 12, Rust Papers, Huntington Library Manuscripts, San Marino, CA (hereafter Rust Papers).

2. Leslie Marmon Silko, *Gardens in the Dunes* (New York: Simon and Schuster, 1999).

3. On the birth of the Washington Navel, see Leon Batchelor and Herbert Webber, eds., *The Citrus Industry* (Berkeley: University of California Press, 1943), 1:531. Shamel's quote is in *California Citrograph*, December 1913, 42.

4. On the relationship between fiction and history and the role of fables in environmental writing, see William Cronon, "A Place for Stories: Nature, History, and Narrative," *Journal of American History* 78 (March 1992): 1347–76. The magic Silko writes of is of course a function of economic, not magical, transformations. See William Cronon, *Nature's Metropolis: Chicago and the Great West* (New York: Norton, 1991), esp. 97–147.

5. The most comprehensive source on California boosterism is Richard Orsi, "Selling the Golden State: A Study of Boosterism in Nineteenth-Century California," (PhD diss., University of Wisconsin, Madison, 1973). The garden imagery and ideals are best explored in Kevin Starr, *Inventing the Dream: California Through the Progressive Era* (New York: Oxford University Press, 1985), esp. 128–75. See also Robert Fogelson, *The Fragmented Metropolis: Los Angeles, 1850–1930* (1967; repr., Berkeley: University of California Press, 1993), esp. 63–84; Kevin Starr, *Americans and the California Dream, 1850–1915* (New York: Oxford University Press, 1973); Kevin Starr, *Material Dreams: California Through the 1920's* (New York: Oxford

University Press, 1990); William Deverell and Douglas Flamming, "Race, Rhetoric, and Regional Identity: Boosting Los Angeles, 1880–1930," in *Power and Place in the North American West*, ed. Richard White and John Findlay (Seattle: University of Washington Press, 1999), 117–43.

6. The phrase is used in a typical example: F. Llewellyn, "Pomona," *Out West*, June 1903, 412.

7. See John Logan and Harvey Molotch, *Urban Fortunes: The Political Economy of Place* (Berkeley: University of California Press, 1987).

8. Charles Francis Saunders, *Finding the Worth While in California* (New York: Robert M. McBride, 1916), 26. The beanstalk quote is from Bertha Smith, "The Making of Los Angeles," *Sunset*, July 1907, 236. The article's subtitle is revealing: "A study of the astonishing growth of California's southland city—oranges, palms, and fast rising sky-scrapers . . ." Mike Davis, *Ecology of Fear: Los Angeles and the Imagination of Disaster* (New York: Metropolitan, 1998). One of Davis's chapters explores "How Eden Lost Its Garden," while this chapter seeks to explain how Los Angeles got its garden.

9. The wonderland phrase was used to describe the residence of A. H. Smiley of Redlands, though it is apt for the whole region. John Knight, "Redlands," *Land of Sunshine*, February 1899. For the linage between plant and economic growth, see Starr, *Material Dreams*.

10. Simon Schama, *Landscape and Memory* (New York: Knopf, 1995), 538.

11. Allan Bogue, *Frederick Jackson Turner: Strange Roads Going Down* (Norman: University of Oklahoma Press, 1998), 412–13. Patricia Limerick wryly points out that "The Fruit Frontier," along with "The Vegetable Frontier," "The Sewing Frontier," and "The Sexual Services Frontier," was missing from Turner's seminal essay; see Patricia Limerick, "The Adventures of the Frontier in the Twentieth Century," in *The Frontier in American Culture*, ed. James Grossman (Berkeley: University of California Press, 1994), 75. Frederick Jackson Turner, "The Significance of the Frontier in American History" (1893), reprinted in *Rereading Frederick Jackson Turner*, ed. John Mack Faragher (New York: Henry Holt, 1994).

12. Among the many insightful readings of Turner's thesis, see Richard White, "Frederick Jackson Turner and Buffalo Bill," in Grossman, *Frontier in American Culture*, 7–65.

13. See William Preston, "Serpent in the Garden: Environmental Change in Colonial California"; Kat Anderson, Michael Barbour, and Valerie Whitworth, "A World of Balance and Plenty: Land, Plants, Animals, and Humans in Pre-European California," in *Contested Eden: California Before the Gold Rush*, ed. Ramón Gutiérrez and Richard Orsi (Berkeley: University of California Press, 1997). For an important collection of essays arguing that California Indians created domesticated environments, see Thomas C. Blackburn and Kat Anderson, eds., *Before the Wilderness: Environmental Management by Native Californians* (Menlo Park, CA: Ballena, 1993).

14. I am using landscape and territory interchangeably here. The notion of landscape not as a picture of the earth but as a particular realm of earth—a space in which human involvement and control is manifest—is developed in J. B. Jackson, *Discovering the Vernacular Landscape* (New Haven, CT: Yale University Press, 1984), 1–8. Attention to the spatial dimension of conquest has been developed in a number of recent works in California history. See Lisbeth Haas, *Conquests and Historical Identities in California, 1769–1936* (Berkeley: University of California Press, 1995), esp. 1–12. Rosaura Sánchez explores California testimonials gathered by Herbert Hugh Bancroft as a response to spatial displacement and an attempt "to recover agency and to construct and recenter a precarious collective subjectivity [though] cognitive mapping," in *Telling Identities: The Californio Testimonios* (St. Paul: University of Minnesota Press, 1995), 2. Douglas Monroy also investigates spatial politics and the process of deterrito-

rialization in *Thrown Among Strangers* (Berkeley: University of California Press, 1990). The concept of deterritorialization was developed by Gilles Deleuze and Félix Guattari in *A Thousand Plateaus: Capitalism and Schizophrenia* (Minneapolis: University of Minnesota Press, 1993).

15. Tómas Almaguer, *Racial Fault Lines: The Historical Origins of White Supremacy in California* (Berkeley: University of California Press, 1994), 33. Almaguer's study is the best treatment of racial categories as sociohistorical constructs in the second half of the nineteenth century in California and the impact of these constructs on the material conditions of various cultural groups that had been subject to a process of racialization.

16. Frank Pixley, "Annual Address to the San Joaquin Valley Agricultural Association," *Transactions of the California State Agricultural Society, 1880* (Sacramento, CA: J. D. Young, 1880), 229.

17. Ezra Carr, "Art and Nature," *Southern California Horticulturist* 2, no. 1 (November 1878), 1.

18. E. J. Wickson, *The California Fruits and How to Grow Them* (San Francisco: Pacific Rural Press, 1914), 351, 355; California Fruit Growers Convention, *Hand in Hand Go Horticulture and Civilization: A Short Narrative of Fruit Raising in the United States and Particularly in California* (Sacramento, CA: Weinstock, Lubin, 1917); Ian Tyrell, *True Gardens of the Gods: Californian-Australian Environmental Reform, 1860–1930* (Berkeley: University of California Press, 1999), 9. See also Starr, *Inventing the Dream*, 137–39.

19. Llewellyn, "Pomona," 400. For an illuminating exploration of how "the idea of recovery functioned as ideology and legitimation for settlement of the New World," see Carolyn Merchant, "Reinventing Eden: Western Culture as a Recovery Narrative," in William Cronon, ed., *Uncommon Ground: Toward Reinventing Nature* (New York: Norton, 1995): 132–59. For the larger story of how this idea of human ingenuity and technology could be melded with Christian eschatology, see David Noble, *The Religion of Technology: The Divinity of Man and the Spirit of Invention* (New York: Knopf, 1998). The classic account of America's garden mythology, curiously neglecting materials from California, is Henry Nash Smith, *Virgin Land: The American West as Symbol and Myth* (Cambridge, MA: Harvard University Press, 1950).

20. The Pasadena quote is in Los Angeles County Pomological Society, *Southern California Souvenir* (n.p., 1888?), 30, copy at the Huntington Library, San Marino, CA. The Riverside quotes are in Alla Clarke, "In Orange Land—Riverside," *Sunset*, January 1902, 113–18. Perkins's quote is in *Semi-Tropic California: Devoted to Agriculture, Horticulture, and the Development of Southern California*, October 1881, 168. The cover of this particular issue abounds with tropical plants and imagery.

21. T. J. Jackson Lears, *Fables of Abundance: A Cultural History of Advertising in America* (New York: Basic Books, 1994), 21.

22. Los Angeles Chamber of Commerce, *Exhibit and Work of the Los Angeles Chamber of Commerce* (Los Angeles: Los Angeles Chamber of Commerce, 1910), 4–5; Norman Stanley, *No Little Plans: The Story of the Los Angeles Chamber of Commerce* (Los Angeles: Los Angeles Chamber of Commerce, 1956), 9. For an examination of the promotional activities of the Los Angeles Chamber of Commerce, see Tom Zimmerman, "Paradise Promoted: Boosterism and the Los Angeles Chamber of Commerce," *California History* 64 (Winter 1985): 22–33. On the Chicago fair, see Orsi, "Selling the Golden State," 517–24. for Holt's remarks, see *Report of the Managers of the Chicago Citrus Fair* (n.p., n.d.), Huntington Library, San Marino, CA. For the *Chicago Times* quote, see *Riverside Press and Horticulturist*, April 27, 1886, copy in the Coit Scrapbook, Special Collections, University of California, Riverside.

23. *Final Report of the California World's Fair Commission, Including a Description of All Exhibits from the State of California* (Sacramento, CA: A. J. Johnson, Supt. State Printing, 1894), 49–50, 74.

24. Harry Brook, *The Land of Sunshine: Southern California. An Authentic Description of Its Natural Features, Resources and Prospects* (Los Angeles: World's Fair Association and Bureau of Information, 1893), 23. This pamphlet was a revision of the Southern California Bureau of Information's *Southern California* (Los Angeles: Bureau of Information, 1892). For more on Sunkist, see "Citriculture and Southern California," special issue, *California History* 74 (Spring 1995).

25. *Los Angeles Times*, April 8, 1886, quoted in Orsi, "Selling the Golden State," 524; Glenn Dumke, *The Boom of the Eighties in Southern California* (San Marino, CA: Huntington Library, 1963); Ronald Tobey and Charles Wetherell, "The Citrus Industry and the Revolution of Corporate Capitalism in Southern California, 1887–1944," *California History* 74 (Spring 1995): 6–21.

26. "Address by I.N. Hoag to the Farmer's Institute," *Rural Californian*, January 1895, 22.

27. On the spatial segregation of workers and invisibility, see Carey McWilliams, *North From Mexico: The Spanish-Speaking People of the United States* (1948; repr., New York: Praeger, 1990); Gilbert González, *Labor and Community: Mexican Citrus Worker Villages in a Southern California County, 1900–1950* (Chicago: University of Illinois Press, 1994); Haas, *Conquests*; Martha Menchaca, *The Mexican Outsiders: A Community History of Marginalization and Discrimination in California* (Austin: University of Texas Press, 1995); Dolores Hayden, *The Power of Place: Urban Landscapes as Public History* (Cambridge, MA: MIT Press, 1995); Don Mitchell, *The Lie of the Land: Migrant Workers and the California Landscape* (Minneapolis: University of Minnesota Press, 1996). The social hierarchy theme is developed in Anthea Hartig, "'In A World He Has Created': Class Collectivity and the Growers' Landscape of the Southern California Citrus Industry, 1890–1940" *California History* 74 (Spring 1995): 100–11.

28. Victoria Padilla, *Southern California Gardens* (Berkeley: University of California Press, 1961), 236; Thorstein Veblen, *Theory of the Leisure Class* (1899; repr., New York: Penguin, 1994), 132.

29. Walter Woehlke, "The Land of Sunny Homes," *Sunset*, March 1915, 470.

30. The story of the duchess is in Londa Schiebinger, *Nature's Body: Gender in the Making of Modern Science* (Boston: Beacon, 1993), 3. See also Michael Osborne, *Nature, the Exotic, and the Science of French Colonialism* (Bloomington: Indiana University Press, 1994). For discussion of the intertwining of the exotic and self, see Lears, *Fables*.

31. Padilla, *Gardens*, 13.

32. The Pasadena quote is from David Streatfield, *California Gardens: Creating a New Eden* (New York: Abbeville Press, 1994), 63. An illustration of the advertising function of the gardens is Los Angeles County Pomological Society, *Souvenir*.

33. Charles Francis Saunders, *Trees and Shrubs of California Gardens* (New York: Robert M. McBride, 1926), xii–xiii, 198. On the immigrant workers, see, for example, "The Chinese Question to Fruit Growers," *Rural Californian*, April 1887. See also Alexander Saxton, *The Indispensable Enemy: Labor and the Anti-Chinese Movement in California* (Berkeley: University of California Press, 1971); Sucheng Chan, *This Bitter-Sweet Soil: The Chinese in California Agriculture, 1860–1910* (Berkeley: University of California Press, 1986).

34. For a description of Bard's garden, see Padilla, *Gardens*, 106–7. The quotes about the Smiley garden are in Knight, "Redlands."

35. The imperialism quote is from Vera Norwood, *Made From This Earth: American Women and Nature* (Chapel Hill: University of North Carolina Press, 1993), 119. See also

Tyrell, *True Gardens*. For information on the global shuffling of plant and animal life with the zones of British colonialism (or postcolonialism), see Thomas Dunlap, *Nature and the English Diaspora: Environment and History in the United States, Canada, Australia, and New Zealand* (New York: Cambridge University Press, 1999).

36. Quoted in Peter Dreyer, *A Gardener Touched with Genius: The Life of Luther Burbank*. (Berkeley: University of California Press, 1985), 98.

37. Quoted in Dreyer, *Touched with Genius*, 13.

38. David Harvey, *Justice, Nature and the Geography of Difference* (New York: Blackwell, 1996), 185.

39. See Vera Norwood, *Made From This Earth*, esp. 98–142.

40. Theodosia Shepard, "Horticulture," *Rural Californian*, May 1893, 233–39. For more information on Shepard, see Padilla, *Gardens*. For historical development of horticulture and pioneer women in the West, see Annette Kolodny, *The Land Before Her: Fantasy and Experience of the American Frontiers, 1630–1860* (Chapel Hill: University of North Carolina Press, 1984), 35–54.

41. See González, *Labor and Community*, 66; Hayden, *Power of Place*, 112–22.

42. "Partial List of Ornamental Trees and Shrubs at Carmelita, 1883," Jeanne Carr Papers, box 2, Huntington Library, San Marino, CA (hereafter Carr Papers); Charles Francis Saunders, *The Story of Carmelita* (Pasadena, CA: A. C. Vroman, 1928), 29. Muir is quoted in Padilla, *Gardens*, 214.

43. Jeanne Carr, "Paper Relating to the Wild Flowers of California," Carr Papers, box 2. Albert Carr told the story about Jackson in "The Genesis and Development of Carmelita, 1886–1892," manuscript, box 9, Carr Papers. Jackson actually did the writing at the Berkeley Hotel in New York.

44. John Muir, "The Hetch-Hetchy Valley," *Sierra Club Bulletin*, January 1908, 212, 217, 219–20.

45. For the creation of the Spanish fantasy past, see Carey McWilliams, *Southern California: An Island on the Land* (1946; repr., Salt Lake City: Gibbs-Smith, 1994). A recent analysis is William Deverell, "Privileging the Mission over the Mexican: The Rise of Regional Identity in Southern California," in *Many Wests: Place, Culture, & Regional Identity*, ed. Michael Steiner and David Wrobel (Lawrence: University Press of Kansas, 1997), 235–58. Helen Hunt Jackson, *Ramona* (1884; repr., New York: Signet, 1988), 16.

46. Alessandro calls Ramona Majel, and the naming seems to call her Indian essence into being; Jackson, *Ramona*, 196. But Ramona has a hybrid identity, and later Felipe will call her back into the California world, and her California identity, by calling her Ramona; Jackson, *Ramona*, 239.

47. Frederick Hoxie refers to this period as "the holocaust of the gold rush and the first years of American settlement" in *Parading Through History: The Making of the Crow Nation in America, 1805–1935* (New York: Cambridge University Press, 1995), 350. For a historical analysis of how Native Californians survived the 1850s, when being Indian basically meant being on the run, see Albert Hurtado, *Indian Survival on the California Frontier* (New Haven, CT: Yale University Press, 1988). Richard Henry Dana, *Two Years Before the Mast* (1840; repr., New York: Modern Library, 1964), 163.

48. For analysis of the stereotypes of California Indians, see James J. Rawls, *Indians of California: The Changing Image* (Norman: University of Oklahoma Press, 1984). On Kinney, see Starr, *Inventing the Dream*, 78–80; Tyrell, *True Gardens*, 42–47. Helen Jackson and Abbott Kinney, *Report on the Conditions and Needs of the Mission Indians of California* (Washington DC: Government Printing Office, 1883), 6–7, as cited in Michael Dorris, "Introduction," in

Jackson, *Ramona*, x. On agrarian reform, see David Lewis Smith, *Neither Wolf Nor Dog: American Indians, Environment, and Agrarian Change* (New York: Oxford University Press, 1994).

49. Richard Henry Pratt to Horatio Rust, July 11, 1890, Rust Papers, box 9; Rust, "Notes on the Mission Indians," 1893, Rust Papers, box 10.

50. C. W. Barton, "Riverside's New Indian School," *Sunset*, October 1901, 153–56.

51. Clipping, Rust Papers, box 11; "Petition to the Mayor and Council of South Pasadena," June 15, 1906, Rust Papers, box 15. The story of the gun-rigging growers is in McWilliams, *Southern California*.

52. On icons of abundance, see Lears, *Fables*. See also William Cronon, "Landscapes of Abundance and Scarcity," in *The Oxford History of the American West*, ed. Clyde Milner II, Carol O'Connor, and Martha Sandweiss (New York: Oxford University Press, 1994): 602–37. William Leach uses "land of desire" in *Land of Desire: Merchants, Power, and the Rise of a New American Culture* (New York: Pantheon, 1993). For a provocative development of the idea of the failure of the democratic ideal, see Mike Davis, *City of Quartz: Excavating the Future in Los Angeles* (London: Verso, 1990).

Chapter 13: Changing Attitudes toward Animals among Chicanas and Latinas in Los Angeles

The authors deeply appreciate the contributions of our focus group participants. We are grateful to our translators of the Latina group transcripts, Ricardo Hernandez and Felipe Diaz; to Yadira Arévalo for helping us recruit both groups of women, as well as moderating the Latina group; and to Alec Brownlow for technical assistance and initial coding of the discussions. Laura Pulido, Michael Dear, Greg Hise, Lorena Muñoz, and anonymous referees gave us thoughtful critiques, and we thank them. Finally, we wish to thank the National Science Foundation, Program in Geography and Regional Science (SBR-9605043) for financial support.

1. Don Normark, *Chavez Ravine, 1949: A Los Angeles Story* (San Francisco: Chronicle, 1999).

2. We are grateful to M. C. Molidor of the Los Angeles City Attorney's Office; Jackie David, public information director for the City of Los Angeles Animal Services Department; and Tom Frazier, licensed real estate appraiser, for sharing their information and insights.

3. We chose to hold these conversations with low-income inner-city women because little is known about their attitudes toward nature or animals, despite the fact that research has shown that gender and economic class bear significantly on people's attitudes toward animals. We use the term Chicanas to differentiate U.S.-born women of Mexican heritage from Latinas, who are Mexican-born women living in the United States, and not as a reflection of their own political stance on ethnic identity. One of the women is from Guatemala but played a significant and sometimes contrasting role in the discussions, and we thus decided to keep her contributions. We approximated their income status on the basis of their affiliation with an inner-city affordable-housing project through which they were contacted. Participants received twenty-five dollars for their contributions and time. All names have been changed.

4. Both discussions were analyzed using NU*DIST (nonnumerical unstructured data indexing searching and theorizing), a qualitative software package.

5. Ricardo Romo, *East Los Angeles: History of a Barrio* (Austin: University of Texas Press,1983), 9, 86.

6. Albert Camarillo, *Chicanos in a Changing Society* (Cambridge, MA: Harvard University Press, 1979, 1996); George J. Sánchez, *Becoming Mexican-American. Ethnicity, Culture, and Identity in Chicano Los Angeles, 1900–1945* (New York: Oxford University Press 1993), 7.

7. Romo, *East Los Angeles*, 10, 12; see also Sánchez, *Becoming Mexican-American*, 6. For

recent autobiographies, see See Jack Lopez, *Cholos and Surfers: A Latino Family Album* (Santa Barbara, CA: Capra, 1998); Dianne Walta Hart, *Undocumented in L.A.: An Immigrant's Story* (Wilmington, DE: Scholarly Resources Books, 1997); Mary Helen Ponce, *Hoyt Street: An Autobiography* (Albuquerque: University of New Mexico Press, 1993).

8. Ponce, *Hoyt Street*, 121.

9. Candace Nelson and Mata Tienda, "The Structuring of Hispanic Identity: Historical and Contemporary Perspectives," *Ethnic and Racial Studies* 8 (1985), 49–50.

10. Sánchez, *Becoming Mexican-American*, 5, 8.

11. David R. Diaz, "La Vide Libra: Cultura de la Calle en Los Angeles Este," *Places* 8 (1993): 30–37; Terezia Nemeth, "Downtown on Parade," *Places* 8 (1993): 38–41; Curtis C. Roseman and J. Diego Vigil, "From Broadway to Latinoway," *Places* 8 (1993): 20–29; James T. Rojas, "The Enacted Environment of East Los Angeles," *Places* 8 (1993): 42–53; James T. Rojas, "The Latino Landscape of East Los Angeles," *NACLA Report on the Americas* 28 (1995): 32–34.

12. John M.Baas, Alan W. Ewert, and Deborah J. Chavez, "Influence of Ethnicity on Recreation and Natural Environment Use Patterns: Managing Recreation Sites for Ethnic and Racial Diversity," *Environmental Management* 17 (1993): 523–29; James H. Gramann, Myron E. Floyd, and Rogelio Saenz, "Outdoor Recreation and Mexican Ethnicity: A Benefits Perspective," in *Culture, Conflict, and Communication in the Wildland-Urban Interface*, ed. Alan W. Ewert, Deborah J. Chavez, and A. W. Magill (Boulder, CO: Westview, 1993), 69–84; Sandra L. Shaull and James H. Gramann, "The Effects of Cultural Assimilation on the Importance of Family-Related and Nature-Related Recreation among Hispanic Americans," *Journal of Leisure Research* 30 (1998): 52; Myron F. Floyd and Francis P. Noe, "The New Environmental Paradigm and Hispanic Cultural Influence," in *Culture, Conflict, and Communication*, 85–98. The new environmental paradigm scale was devised in 1978 by Riley Dunlap and Kent D. Van Liere and remains one of the most extensively used scales to evaluate people's adherence to various environmental beliefs. Barbara Deutsch Lynch, "The Garden and the Sea: U.S. Latino Environmental Discourses and Mainstream Environmentalism," *Social Problems* 40 (1993): 115, 108; Victor Corral-Verdugo and Luz Irene Armendariz, "The 'New Environmental Paradigm' in a Mexican Community," *Journal of Environmental Education* 31 (2000): 25–40.

13. Stephen R. Kellert, "The Biological Basis for Human Values of Nature," in *The Biophilia Hypothesis*, ed. Edward O. Wilson and Stephen R. Kellert (Washington DC: Island, 1993), 44–45, 56.

14. Kimberly Sanchez, "Encyclopedic Botanicas; Need Some 'Evil Go Away' Oil? It's Probably at a Santeria Near You," *Los Angeles Times*, April 4, 1997; Sharon Bernstein, "Storefront Drug Sales Targeted; Crackdown: Task Force Is Arresting Retailers Who Sell Medications Illegally. But Some Latinos Protest That They Rely on Such Health Care Providers," *Los Angeles Times*, July 29, 1998; Daniel Yi, "Three in Family Charged with Sale of Illegal Medicines," *Los Angeles Times*, September 16, 1999.

15. Lorena Muñoz (2001, personal communication) suggests that there are strong regional differences in how the Mexican stories about animals are interpreted and how much meaning attaches to them. Gloria Anzaldúa, *Borderlands/La Frontera: The New Mestiza* (San Francisco: Aunt Lute Books, 1987), 65.

16. Sue Fox, "Teen 'Escaramuzas' Synchronize Their Horses in a Perilous Ballet." *Los Angeles Times*, June 10, 2000; J. A. Orihuela and J. Solano, "Some Characteristics of the People Who Attend Mexican Rooster (Cock) Fighting Events." *Anthrozoös* 4 (1995): 229–34.

17. In her introduction to *Spectacular Nature: Corporate Culture and the Sea World Experience* (Berkeley: University of California Press, 1997), 10, Susan Davis engages in a compelling

discussion of the media's appropriation of nature to produce "wholesome, inoffensive, and cross-generational" programs.

18. Adrian Franklin, *Animals and Modern Cultures: A Sociology of Human-Animal Relations in Modernity* (Thousand Oaks, CA: Sage, 1999), 56.

19. Ron Martin, "Chicks in the City. Feathered Pets Give Wing to Comforting Memories of Home," *Los Angeles Times*, August 26, 2000. See also Andrea Gaynor, "Regulation, Resistance and the Residential Area: The Keeping of Productive Animals in Twentieth Century Perth, Western Australia," *Urban Policy and Research* 17 (1999): 7–16.

20. Suzanne Michel, "Golden Eagles and the Environmental Politics of Care," in *Animal Geographies: Place, Politics, and Identity in the Nature-Culture Borderlands*, ed. Jennifer Wolch and Jody Emel (New York: Verso, 1998), 178.

21. Corral-Verdugo and Armendariz, "'New Environmental Paradigm,'" 22.

22. Glen Elder, Jennifer Wolch, and Jody Emel, "La Pratique Sauvage: Race, Place, and the Human-Animal Divide," in *Animal Geographies: Place, Politics, and Identity in the Nature-Culture Borderlands*, ed. Jennifer Wolch and Jody Emel (New York: Verso, 1998); Hart, *Undocumented in L.A.*, 115; Marcie Griffith, Unna Lassiter, and Jennifer Wolch, "Filipina Attitudes toward Animals" (unpublished working paper, Department of Geography, University of Southern California, 2000).

23. Santeria is a religious practice based on African animism and typically involves the sacrifice of animals.

24. Al Martinez, "Made in California," *Los Angeles Times*, October 25, 2000.

25. Anzaldúa, *Borderlands/La Frontera*, 80–81.

26. Rojas, "Enacted Environment"; Rojas, "Latino Lanscape"; Margaret Crawford, "Mi Casa es Su Casa," in *La Vida Latina en L.A.*, Urban Latino Cultures, ed. Gustavo Leclerc, Raul Villa, and Michael J. Dear (Thousand Oaks, CA: Sage, 1999), 120.

27. "Tortura No es Cultura," conference sponsored by the World Society for the Protection of Animals, 1995, www.wspa.org.uk; *Amores Perros*, directed by Alejandro Gonzales Inarritu (2000).

28. Rodolfo F. Acuña, *Anything but Mexican: Chicanos in Contemporary Los Angeles* (New York: Verso, 1996), 12.

29. Romo, *East Los Angeles*, 12.

Epilogue: The Present as History

1. See Robert Gottlieb, *Environmentalism Unbound: Exploring New Patterns for Change* (Cambridge, MA: MIT Press, 2001), 357–40.

2. Harriet Friedmann, "Distance and Durability: Shaky Foundations of the World Food Economy," *Third World Quarterly* 13, no. 2 (1992): 371–83.

3. John C. Everett, "Community and Propinquity in the City," *Annals of the Association of American Geographers* 66 (March 1976): 104–16.

Contributors

Christopher G. Boone is associate professor of geography at Ohio University. He is an urban geographer with research interests in environmental justice, public health, and urban infrastructure. His most recent work compares sewer provision in Baltimore and Paris as part of a collaborative research agreement between the Baltimore Ecosystem Study and the PIREN-Seine zone atelier. Dr. Boone is also a co-principal investigator for the Baltimore Ecosystem Study, an Urban Long Term Ecological Research site.

Karen Clay is assistant professor of economics and public policy in the Heinz School at Carnegie Mellon University. She received her PhD in economics from Stanford University in 1994 and from 1994 to 1999 was an assistant professor of economics at the University of Toronto. Her areas of research include economic history, industrial organization, and the economics of new technology.

Michael Dawson is a third-generation book dealer and owner of Dawson's Book Shop in Los Angeles. Founded in 1905, Dawson's is the oldest antiquarian book business in Southern California. Mr. Dawson is an expert in photographic literature as well as nineteenth- and twentieth-century photographs of Southern California and the Southwest. He has published in the journal *Archive* of the Center for Creative Photography and contributed to *LA's Early Moderns: Art/Architecture/Photography*.

William Deverell is professor of history at the University of Southern California and director of the Huntington-USC Institute on California and the West. He is the author of *Whitewashed Adobe: The Rise of Los Angeles and the Remaking of Its Mexican Past* and editor of *The Blackwell Companion to the American West*. With Greg Hise, he is coauthor of *Eden by Design: The 1930 Olmsted-Bartholomew Plan for the Los Angeles Region*. With Tom Sitton, he edited *California Progressivism Revisited* and *Metropolis in the Making: Los Angeles in the 1920s*.

Robert Gottlieb is the Henry R. Luce Professor of Urban and Environmental Policy at Occidental College. He has written extensively on resource, environmental, and urban issues. He is the author or coauthor of ten books, including *Environmentalism Unbound: Exploring New Pathways for Change* and *The Next*

Los Angeles: The Struggle for a Livable City. As director of the Urban and Environmental Policy Institute he has engaged in research and policy analysis on urban, environmental, food, and regional development issues.

Blake Gumprecht is an assistant professor of geography at the University of New Hampshire specializing in the cultural and historical geography of North America. He is the author of *The Los Angeles River: Its Life, Death, and Possible Rebirth*, winner of the Association of American Geographers' J. B. Jackson Prize. He has also published studies about urban tree planting on the Great Plains, the development of an Oklahoma town as an international grain center, and the role of place in popular music. His current project is a book about the American college town.

Terry Harkness is professor of landscape architecture at the University of Illinois at Urbana-Champaign, where he serves as project design faculty. His design work explores and interprets cultural and natural landscapes, especially the ordering and creation of new places that are rooted in and reflect the common American landscape.

Greg Hise is associate professor of urban history at the University of Southern California's School of Policy, Planning and Development. He is a coauthor, with William Deverell, of *Eden by Design: The 1930 Olmsted-Bartholomew Plan for the Los Angeles Region* and author of *Magnetic Los Angeles: Planning the Twentieth Century Metropolis*, winner of the Spiro Kostof Book Prize from the Society of Architectural Historians and the Donald Pflueger Prize from the Historical Society of Southern California. He is at work on a book exploring land use, architecture, and identity in nineteenth-century Los Angeles.

Daniel J. Johnson is an adjunct professor of history at California State University, Long Beach. He received his PhD from the University of California at Los Angeles in 1997. His areas of expertise include the United States in the Progressive era, urban development, and the histories of Los Angeles, California, and the West. He has written articles on the politics of early-twentieth-century Los Angeles, including a study of the 1911 Socialist campaign that appeared in *Labor History*.

Unna Lassiter is an assistant professor at Stephen F. Austin State University. Her research is at the intersection of cultural and political geography and the representation of animals. She has published on this topic in *Espaces et Societes*, *Society and Animals*, and the *California Geographer*.

William McClung is the author of *Landscapes of Desire: Anglo Mythologies of Los Angeles* and other books and articles on architecture in Los Angeles and its representation in literature. He is professor emeritus of English at Mississippi State University and now lives in Boston.

John McPhee's writing career began at *Time* magazine and led to his long association with *The New Yorker*, where he has been a staff writer since 1965. Among his many books are *Coming into the Country* (1977), *Basin and Range* (1981), *In Suspect Terrain* (1983), *La Place de la Concorde Suisse* (1984), *Rising from the Plains* (1986), *The Control of Nature* (1989), *Looking for a Ship* (1990), *Assembling California* (1993), *The Ransom of Russian Art* (1994), *Irons in the Fire* (1997), and his most recent title, *The Founding Fish* (2002). For his twenty-year undertaking to tell the geological story of North America, *Annals of the Former World* (1998), McPhee won the Pulitzer Prize for General Non-fiction.

Jared Orsi is assistant professor of history at Colorado State University, where he teaches courses on the history of the United States–Mexico borderlands. He is the author of *Hazardous Metropolis: Flooding and Urban Ecology in Los Angeles* and guest editor of a recent volume of the *Journal of the West* that examines the history of water in the urban North American West.

Jennifer Price is a freelance writer and environmental historian and author of *Flight Maps: Adventures with Nature in Modern America*. She has published in the anthology *Uncommon Ground: Rethinking the Human Place in Nature* and in the *L.A. Weekly*, *Los Angeles Times*, *American Scholar*, and *New York Times*. She has a PhD in history from Yale University and is living in Venice Beach while writing a book about nature in Los Angeles.

Mark Raab received his PhD in anthropology from Arizona State University in 1976, with a specialization in archaeology. A faculty member at California State University, Northridge since 1984, his research has focused during this time on coastal Southern California and Mexico. Current work includes the California Channel Islands, the cape region of the Baja California peninsula, and the Olmec region of the Mexican Gulf Coast. Recent California research focuses on prehistoric seafaring, including evidence of boat construction and voyages to the California Channel Islands between eight and ten thousand years ago.

Paul Sabin teaches energy politics and environmental history at Yale University and is the author of *Crude Politics: The California Oil Market, 1900–1940*. He has published articles on United States economic expansion overseas, oil development and native politics in Ecuador and Canada, and the California Supreme Court's 1970s equal protection decisions. He also serves as executive director of the Environmental Leadership Program, a national nonprofit organization that provides leadership training and support to relatively new professionals and civic leaders in the environmental field.

Douglas Sackman is an assistant professor of history at the University of Puget Sound. He wrote the foreword for the reissue of the Carey McWilliams classic,

Factories in the Field: The Story of Migratory Farm Labor in California, and is the author of *Orange Empire: California and the Fruits of Eden*.

Paula M. Schiffman is a professor of biology at California State University, Northridge, where she teaches ecology, evolution, and conservation biology. Her research specialty is plant ecology, and she is particularly interested in how disturbance and invasion affect natural plant communities. Most of her field activities are focused on the prairie vegetation of Carrizo Plain National Monument. The study of environmental history is a sideline that has proved to be central to her understanding of California ecology.

Tom Sitton is a curator and head of the History Department at the Natural History Museum of Los Angeles County and specializes in urban and political history. He is the author of *John Randolph Haynes: California Progressive* and *The Haynes Foundation and Urban Reform Philanthropy in Los Angeles* and coeditor with William Deverell of *California Progressivism Revisited* and *Metropolis in the Making: Los Angeles in the 1920s*. He has recently completed a political history of Los Angeles during the reform administration of Mayor Fletcher Bowron and is embarking on a study of Los Angeles County and its government from 1850 to 1920.

Werner Troesken is professor of economics and history at the University of Pittsburgh and a faculty research associate at the National Bureau of Economic Research. His first book, *Why Regulate Utilities?* explored the origins and effects of public utility regulation, and his second book, *Water, Race, and Disease*, explores the relationship between long-term trends in racial disease disparities and access to public water and sewer systems.

Jennifer Wolch is professor of geography and director of the Center for Sustainable Cities at the University of Southern California, where she teaches courses on Los Angeles, urban social problems, and sustainable cities. She is author or coauthor of *Landscapes of Despair: From Deinstitutionalization to Homelessness*, *The Shadow State: Government and Voluntary Sector in Transition*, and *Malign Neglect: Homelessness in an American City*. She recently coedited *Up Against the Sprawl: Public Policy and the Making of Southern California*.

Index

Note: Page numbers in *italic* type indicate figures or tables.